Papal Diplomacy

Other Titles of Interest from St. Augustine's Press

George J. Marlin, *The American Catholic Voter: Two Hundred Years of Political Impact*. Introduction by Michael Barone

Kenneth D. Whitehead, ed., *Voices of the New Springtim: The Life and Work of the Church in the 21st Century*

Kenneth D. Whitehead, ed., *The Catholic Citizen: Debating the Issues of Jutice*

Kenneth D. Whitehead, ed., *The Catholic Imagination*

Kenneth D. Whitehead, ed., *John Paul II – Witness to Truth*

Kenneth D. Whitehead, ed., *Marriage and the Common Good*

Gerard V. Bradley, J.D., and Don De Marco, eds., *Science and Faith*

Anthony J. Matroeni, S.T.D., J.D., ed., *Is a Culture of Life Still Possible in the U.S.?*

William E. May and Kenneth D. Whitehead, eds., *The Battle for the Catholic Mind: Catholic Faith and Catholic Intellect in the Work of the Fellowship of Catholic Scholars, 1978–1995*

George A. Kelly, *The Second Spring of the Church in America*

Teresa R. Wagner, ed., *Back to the Drawing Board: The Future of the Pro-Life Movement*

John Harvey, OSFS, and Gerard V. Bradley, eds., *Same -Sex Attraction: A Parents' Guide*

Servais Pinckaers, O.P., *Morality: The Catholic View*. Introduction by Alasdair MacIntyre

Richard Peddicord, O.P., *The Sacred Monter of Thomism An Introduction to the Life and Legacy of Reginald Garrigou-Lagrange, O.P.*

Ralph McInerny, *The Defamation of Pius XII*

John of St. Thomas, *Introduction to the Summa Theologiae of Thomas Aquinas*. Translation by Ralph McInerny

Joseph Bobik, *Veritas Divine: Aquinas on Divine Truth*

Thomas Aquinas, *Disputed Questions on Virtue*. Translated by Ralph McInerny

Fulvio di Blasi, *God and the Natural Law: A Rereading of Thomas Aquinas*

Josef Pieper, *Leisure, the Basis of Culture*

Josef Pieper, *Scholasticism: Personalities and Problems*

Josef Pieper, *The Silence of St. Thomas*

C.S. Lewis, and Don Giovanni Calabria, *The Latin Letters of C.S. Lewis*

Florent Gaboriau, *The Conversion of Edith Stein*. Translated by Ralph McInerny

Otto Bird and Katharine Bird, *From Witchery to Sanctity: The Religious Vicissitudes of the Hawthornes*

Jacques Maritain, *Natural Law: Reflections on Theory and Practice*

Gabriel Marcel, *The Mystery of Being* (in two volumes)

Yves R. Simon, *The Great Dialogue of Nature and Space*

Karl Rahner, *Encounters with Silence*

Timothy L. Smith, ed., *Faith and Reason*

Jerome J. Langford, *Galileo, Science and the Church*

PAPAL DIPLOMACY

John Paul II and the Culture of Peace

Bernard J. O'Connor

ST. AUGUSTINE'S PRESS
South Bend, Indiana
2005

Manufactured in the United States of America.

1 2 3 4 5 6   11 10 09 08 07 06 05

Library of Congress Cataloging in Publication Data
O'Connor, Bernard J., 1951–
    Papal diplomacy : John Paul II and the culture of peace / Bernard J. O'Connor.
      p. cm.
    Includes index.
    ISBN 1-58731-630-7 (hardbound : alk. paper)
    1. John Paul II, Pope, 1920 – Contributions in diplomacy. 2. Peace –
    Religious aspects – Catholic Church. 3. Catholic Church – Foreign rela-
    tions. I. John Paul II, Pope, 1920– Speeches. English. Selections. II. Title.
BX1378.5.O27 2004
327.456'34'0092 – dc22   2004014075

∞ *The paper used in this publication meets the minimum requirements of the American National Standard for Information Sciences – Permanence of Paper for Printed Materials, ANSI Z39.48-1984. Requirements for permanence – ISO 9706: 1994.*

ST. AUGUSTINE'S PRESS
www.staugustine.net

Dedicated to:

Most Rev. Raymond J. Lahey, Bishop of the Diocese of Antigonish, Nova Scotia, in appreciation for his sincere encouragement, and for a leadership model which balances strength and integrity with creativity and compassion;

Most Rev. Colin Campbell, Bishop (Emeritus) of the Diocese of Antigonish, Nova Scotia, in appreciation for the generosity of his counsel, and for his courageous efforts to promote fidelity to Catholic teaching;

Most Rev. William E. Power (dec. 2003), Bishop (Emeritus) of the Diocese of Antigonish, Nova Scotia, in appreciation for his sponsorship of my doctoral studies at the Gregorian University, Rome, and for his example of dedication to duty,

and

Most Rev. Carl F. Mengeling, Bishop of the Diocese of Lansing, Michigan, in appreciation for a decade of fraternal welcome during my service to Eastern Michigan University, and in admiration of his many pastoral and homiletic charisms.

Table of Contents

Introduction

Culture of Peace. Since the beginning of Pope John Paul II's papacy in 1978, this phrase echoes throughout the hundreds of messages which he has delivered on the theme of international relations. It is a phrase which reflects the Pope's conviction that the diplomatic process is inherently capable of reinforcing the deepest aspirations of mankind, among them: a hope for life without violence; a desire for fairness in the distribution of the world's resources; the freedom to exercise conscience, including the legitimacy of religious practice; and progress in the expansion of human rights awareness. "Culture of peace" refers to the sum of those fundamental conditions which constitute the foundation upon which peace is both constructed and sustained. Moreover, the Pope's concept of the culture of peace suggests his certainty that peace is not an obscure, aloof, or abstract ideal. Rather, peace is the natural consequence of humanity's ongoing efforts to promote global community and solidarity. According to Pope John Paul, the pillars of that community consist of cooperation, dialogue, reciprocity, and commitment to the irreplaceable dignity of all persons.

Within the following pages are found select examples of Pope John Paul's addresses to international diplomats during the initial twenty-five years of his pontificate. They are arranged in four chapters, each representing a context in which the Pope and diplomats interact. Each document proposes content by which the reader may deduce how the Pope considers "culture of peace" to translate from theory into practical action.

Chapter I contains the series of New Year speeches which the Pope offers annually to members of the Diplomatic Corps accredited to the Holy See. Chapter II derives from the exchange of formal statements made on the occasion when an ambassador presents his Letter of Credence. By the Pope's receiving these credentials, the ambassador's representation to the Holy See on behalf of his country commences. The Pope's support for the United Nations is indicated by Chapter III. In addition to his 1979 and 1995 remarks to the UN General Assembly, there are examples from his extensive discourse with such UN entities as UNESCO (United Nations Educational, Scientific and Cultural Organization) and the FAO (Food and Agricultural Organization). Chapter IV attests to the importance which the Pope assigns to meeting with diplomats during his visits to those countries in which they serve. Chapter IV also features a homily from one of the numerous papal liturgies to which diplomats resident in Rome are invited. What it conveys is the Pope's belief that diplomacy must be constantly mindful of humanity's inherent dimension of spiritual transcendence.

The edited collection concludes with an Appendix, consisting of an essay published by this author in *Foundation Theology 2002* (Bristol, Ind.: Cloverdale,

2003). The purpose of this essay's inclusion is to demonstrate how a reader's own response to this survey of Pope John Paul's contribution to diplomacy may encourage his or her further inquiry into the full complement of this remarkable documentary resource. Besides implying publication opportunities for the research analyst and scholar, the Pope's views on diplomacy embody insights which may prove invaluable for religious education programs, RCIA (Rite of Christian Initiation of Adults) formation, social justice organizations, ecumenical discussion groups, conflict management curricula, inter-cultural associations, etc. The range of possibilities challenges the imagination. But suffice it to say that the impact of this extraordinary pontificate upon world events and attitudes must not be overlooked. Nor should that impact be thought of as restricted to religious adherents, Catholic or otherwise. For the culture of peace, like the cause of peace, knows no boundaries.

A Note on Format

Each chapter is briefly introduced by an identification of possible characteristics of the culture of peace. The list, however, is neither exhaustive nor definitive. Readers may consider it to be somewhat symbolic, a sort of model which they may revise at their discretion. In fact, where this volume is adopted by groups, it is recommended that participants begin by examining a few of those instances in which the phrase "culture of peace" is expressly used by the Pope. (See Chapter I and the SMALL-CAP PRINT references in the addresses for 1986, 1994, 1997, and 1999.) The approach might be to explore whether the interpretation of the phrase varies according to its specific textual framework. Participants may then proceed to comment upon this author's enumerated characteristics, together with how these could be augmented or altered.

Bibliography

The addresses chosen for this project are available through primary, "user friendly" collections. The first is the English edition of the Vatican's *L'Osservatore Romano*. Besides its publication in CD-ROM, this weekly publication is regularly located in the libraries of Catholic seminaries and other institutions of higher education. For the sake of simplicity, *L'Osservatore Romano* is hereafter abbreviated as *"OR,"* and is cited with pertinent date and page references. If readers prefer to consult the original language in which speeches were presented, they may refer to an annual series published by the Vatican and entitled, *Insegnamenti*. For many of the Pope's addresses during 1997–2003, consult the Vatican website at www.vatican.va. After the choice of language, click "Holy Father." Next, select the name of Pope John Paul II. Then refer to the category of "speeches." The speeches for each year are provided according to month. The author's essay, included in the Appendix, employs the website option.

Acknowledgment

During 2003 the author was invited to teach a course, "The Diplomacy of Pope John Paul II," for the newly inaugurated Ave Maria College, Ypsilanti, Michigan.

The content for Chapter II of this book coincides with the syllabus requirements for that seminar. Each student became responsible for assessing the Pope's diplomatic messages for a particular time frame. Speeches which students deduced to be the most significant were recommended for this volume. Therefore, it is with sincere gratitude for their inspiration and editorial assistance that these students are recognized: Jessica N. Bouck, Sean F. Devine Meyer, Sean M. Hunter, Roman V. Lokhmotov, and Peter R. Reynolds. Thanks also to Sarah L. Reischl for volunteering her computer skills, to Eastern Michigan University (EMU) student, Rory Garnice, for proofreading the manuscript, to Maj. Timothy Cummins (Ret.) for his word-processing expertise, and to Thomas E. Malewitz for his arranging liaison with the library of Sacred Heart Seminary, Detroit. The fruition of this project has likewise been due in no small measure to the supportiveness of Dr. Rhonda Kinney Longworth, Head of EMU's Department of Political Science, of Dr. Michael Harris, Vice President for Academic Affairs, Ferris State University, and of Rev. Richard E. Donohoe, Rector of the Cathedral of St. Paul, Birmingham, Alabama.

Chapter I
Addresses to the Diplomatic Corps Accredited to the Holy See
The Culture of Peace as Born of Awareness

Karol Wojtyla, Archbishop of Cracow, was elected to the papacy on October 16, 1978. Just four days later, the Ambassador of Guatemala, Luis Valladores y Ayeinnen, in his role as Dean, expressed the greetings and best wishes of the Diplomatic Corps accredited to the Holy See. Pope John Paul II's response alluded to his own origins. His experience of life and ministry in Poland enabled him to affirm an intent "to respect the . . . values of each nation . . . its tradition and its rights among other peoples." The condition of "those who have suffered" was uppermost in his thinking. The actualization of the culture of peace, according to the Pope, should therefore mean convergence between that "respect" and that compassion. These first remarks to representatives of the world's nations set a tone which has been magnified during each of the Pope's subsequent New Year messages to diplomats, messages which comprise the basis of this chapter.

What traits of the culture of peace emerge from the twenty-six papal addresses contained in Chapter I? Ten come readily to mind. The culture of peace:

(1) . . . *exhibits a natural courtesy.*
This amounts to a recognition that inter-personal encounter will elicit "discretion and loyalty" when it is correspondingly vested "under the sign of politeness" (1978, para. 5).

Readers will note that each of the Pope's speeches in this section begins with his explicit welcome to diplomatic personnel, their families and guests. And there is always mention of his grateful acceptance of the current Dean's tribute to the Pope's initiatives toward the cultivation of peace (1987, no. 1). Courtesy means nothing other than reverence speaking the language of humility.

(2) . . . *embraces a disciplined challenge.*
In 1983, the Pope cautioned diplomats that their essential "dialogue for peace is not easy; it is demanding; it is strewn with snares" (no. 2, para. 3). The culture of peace is analogous to the biblical merchant's search for fine pearls (Mt. 13:45–46). They will never be attained by those who resent the relentless return to the marketplace or who constantly quibble about the price.

(3) . . . *necessitates the transformation of the will.*
When recalling the doctrine of nuclear deterrence with its concomitant "fear of mutually assured destruction," the Pope advocated changing international reason by a reordering of international volition. States are able to understand that their security "is always furthered by an interpenetration of interests" (1988, no. 5 and

no. 3, line 1). But what of the choices born of their will? The culture of peace bids that the will must surrender to the rationality which strives to inform it.

(4) . . . *involves "an irrepressible thirst for freedom"* (1990, no. 5, para. 2).
Freedom is said to accelerate "the process of evolution." That evolution, however, is not the product of an arbitrary excursion through history. Evolution inclines to purposeful direction, and it is perpetually guided by freedom. The thirst for freedom in the culture of peace will fail to be quenched without humanity's acceptance of its vocation to link that freedom to truth and justice (no. 13, para. 5).

(5) . . . *resists the temptation to abandon hope.*
Despite the many conflicts and atrocities conspicuous during 1991–1992, it would be an exaggerated error to "despair of man" (1992, no. 9). Hope resides in man's underlying "good will [and] creativity." The culture of peace is witness to his ceaseless capacity to comfort sorrow and to relieve pain. Hope is the celebration of our agency as instruments of divine love.

(6) . . . *is attentive to objective moral responsibility.*
In his 1994 address, the Pope cited his prior encyclical, *Veritatis Splendor*, no. 101. Once more he summarized the moral obligations of the State which conforms to the culture of peace. It is a State marked by "openness in public administration, impartiality in the service of the body politic . . . which safeguard[s] the rights of the accused against summary trials and conviction, the just and honest use of public funds, the rejection of equivocal or illicit means in order to gain, preserve or increase power at any cost" (1994, no. 8). The culture of peace disdains any utilitarian philosophy which excuses means in the pursuit of ends, and which reduces persons to their net worth instead of esteeming them for their intrinsic worth.

(7) . . . *endorses the rule of law.*
Society requires, the Pope states, "a rule of law" which is "valid for all . . . without exception." Judicial systems universally point to the common good, the norms of the international community being no different. "This is what makes possible equitable solutions in which gain is not made at the expense of others, even when those who benefit are the majority: justice is for all, without injustice being inflicted on anyone. The function of law is to give each person his due, to give him what is owed to him in justice" (1997, no. 4b). The culture of peace seeks to enact law based upon principle. The result is law with principle.

(8) . . . *is receptive to the benefit afforded by religion.*
The Pope deplored, in his 1999 message, the situation in parts of Western Europe where, perhaps because of "a deep-seated agnosticism," there is a bid "to confine the Churches within the religious sphere alone." These are countries which also apparently "find it difficult to accept public statements" from these same Churches. Similarly, there are nations in Central and Eastern Europe which show

animosity for "the religious pluralism proper to democratic societies and [which] attempt to limit, by . . . restrictive and petty bureaucratic practice, the freedom of conscience and of religion which their Constitutions solemnly proclaim" (no. 4d). The agenda of the culture of peace is widely tolerant and not narrowly preoccupied with such denial of religion's record of indisputable gift to social development.

(9) . . . *structures priorities and strategies in accord with the needs which confront it.* Humanity's dilemmas are never a justification for passivity. Having trials does not condone withdrawal. Pope John Paul maintains that identifying affliction is a vital first step in its eradication. Progress declines when humanity becomes more comfortable with blindness than with vision. And so the Pope candidly reiterates what humanity must face, including the recognition of our having the resources to overcome every such obstacle. He points to the implications of genetic manipulation, to threats against the family, to a level of poverty which could be diminished by "the reduction of debt and the opening up of international trade." And he is as overtly optimistic as he is realistic in his belief that "arms sales to poor countries" can be thwarted, that medical care can be extended to the destitute, and that the natural environment can be protected. The culture of peace invites us to think of success in these problem areas as being less of an ideal and more as a contender for the energy and focus of our "daily endeavors" (2002, no. 6).

(10) . . . *insists upon mechanisms to ensure dialogue.*
Pope John Paul often refers to a "new Europe," the European Union. And he continually decries that any constitution for the European Union could ever consider dispensing with the mention of the Christian legacy which is woven into the fabric of Europe's "history and institutions." As an antidote to disavowal of its own past, European citizens should campaign for "the appropriateness of structures for dialogue and consultation between the Governing bodies . . . and communities of believers" (2003, no. 5b). Negotiation – the appeal to dialogue – together with the formal means to implement its process, are crucial to the Pope's perspective on peace. He describes, for example, how positive incremental changes have arisen in Angola, the Republic of the Congo, and Sudan. Each example verifies the validity of dialogue as a precursor to democracy. In the context of the culture of peace, as the channels of dialogue open, the prospect of enduring peace is conveyed.

October 20, 1978
(*L'Osservatore Romano*, November 2, 1978, p. 3)

I am very touched by the words and generous wishes that your spokesman has just addressed to me. I know of the relations full of mutual esteem and trust which had been established between Pope Paul VI and each of the diplomatic representations accredited to the Holy See. This climate was due to the understanding, respectful and benevolent, that this great Pope had responsibility for the common good of peoples, and above all to the superior ideals that animated him as regards peace and development. My immediate Predecessor, dear Pope John Paul I, receiving you less than two months ago, had initiated similar relations, and each of you still remembers his words full of humility, availability and pastoral judgment, which I make entirely mine. And now today I inherit the same office and you, you express the same trust, with the same enthusiasm. I thank you heartily for the sentiments which, through my person you thus testify faithfully to the Holy See.

In the very first place, may each of you feel that he is cordially welcomed here for his own sake, and for the country, the people that he represents. Yes, if there is a place where all peoples must come into contact in peace, and meet respect, sympathy and a sincere desire for their dignity, their happiness, and their progress, it is at the heart of the Church, around the Apostolic See, which was set up to bear witness to truth and to love of Christ.

My esteem and my wishes go, therefore, to one and all of you, in the diversity of your situations. At this meeting, in fact, not only Governments, but also peoples and nations are represented. And among them there are the old "nations," rich in a great past, a fruitful history, a tradition and culture of their own; there are also young nations which have arisen recently, with great possibilities to bring into use, or which are still awakening and being formed. The Church has always wished to participate in the life of peoples and nations and to contribute to their development. The Church has always recognized particular richness in the diversity and plurality of their cultures, their histories, their languages. In many cases the Church has made her specific contribution to the formation of these cultures. The Church has considered, and continues to be of the opinion, that in international relations it is obligatory to respect the rights of each nation.

As for me, called from one of these nations to succeed the Apostle Peter in the service of the universal Church, and of all nations, I will endeavor to manifest to each one the esteem which it has the right to expect. You must, therefore, echo my fervent wishes within your Governments and among all your fellow countrymen. And here, I must add that the history of my native country has taught me to respect the specific values of each nation, and of each people, its tradition and its rights among other peoples. As a Christian, and even more as Pope, I am, I shall be, a witness to this attitude and to universal love, reserving the same goodwill for everyone, especially those who have suffered.

Diplomatic relations mean stable, reciprocal relations, under the sign of politeness, discretion and loyalty. Without confusing competences, they do not necessarily manifest, on my side, approval of such and such a regime – that is not my business. Obviously, neither do they manifest approval of all its acts in the conduct of public affairs. But they show an appreciation of positive temporal values, a desire for dialogue with those who are legitimately charged with the common good of society; an understanding of their role which is often a difficult one; interest and aid for the human causes they have to promote, sometimes by direct interventions, above all by the formation of consciences, which is a specific contribution to justice and peace on the international plane. By doing so, the Holy See does not want to emerge from its pastoral role. Anxious to put into practice the solicitude of Christ, while preparing the eternal salvation of men which is its first duty, how could it fail to take an interest in the welfare and progress of peoples in this world?

On the other hand, the Church and the Holy See in particular ask your nations, your Governments, to take increasingly into consideration a certain number of needs. The Holy See does not seek this for itself. It does so, in union with the local episcopate, for the Christians or believers who inhabit your countries, in order that, without any special privilege but in all justice, they may nourish their faith, ensure religious worship and be admitted, as loyal citizens, to full participation in social life. The Holy See does so also in the interest of men whoever they may be, knowing that freedom, respect for the life and dignity of persons – who are never instruments – fairness in treatment, professional conscientiousness in work, and a united pursuit of the common good, the spirit of reconciliation, open[ness] to spiritual values, are fundamental requirements of harmonious life in society, and of the progress of citizens and their civilization. Certainly, the last-mentioned goals generally figure [i]n the program of those responsible. But the result, for all that, cannot be taken for granted, and all means are not equally valued. There are still too many physical and moral miseries which depend on negligence, selfishness, and the blindness or hardness of men. The Church wishes to contribute to diminish these miseries with her peaceful means, by education to the moral sense, by the loyal action of Christians and men of goodwill. Doing so, the Church may sometimes not be understood; but she is convinced that she is rendering a service which mankind cannot do without. She is faithful to her Teacher and Savior, Jesus Christ.

It is in this spirit that I hope to maintain and develop, with all the countries that you represent, cordial and truthful relationships. I encourage you in your high office and I encourage, above all, your Governments to seek justice and peace more and more, in understandable love for your fellow countrymen, and with your minds and hearts open to other peoples. On this way, may God enlighten you and strengthen yourselves and all of your leaders, and may he bless each of your countries.

January 12, 1979
(*OR*, January 22, 1979, pp. 6–7)

Just now, on the threshold of the new year, your Dean has interpreted your feelings and your good wishes in a way that moves me deeply. I thank him, and I thank you all, for this comforting testimony. Be assured, in return, of my fervent wishes for each of you, for all the members of your Embassies, for your families, and for the countries you represent. It is before God that I express these wishes, asking him to shed light on your way, as on that of the Magi in the Gospel, and to give you, from day to day, the courage and the joys that you need in order to face up to your duties. I pray to him to bless you, that is, to lavish his goods on you.

On this solemn occasion which gathers round the Pope all the diplomatic Missions accredited to the Holy See, it is usual to add to these cordial wishes some considerations on your noble function and on the framework in which it takes its place: the Church and the world.

A look at past events
1. I will begin by looking with you toward the very recent past, renewing the gratitude of the Apostolic See to the many Delegations which honored the funeral ceremonies of Pope Paul VI and of Pope John Paul I, of holy memory, as well as the inaugural ceremonies of my predecessor's pontificate and those of my own.

Let us try to grasp the significance of this. Is not this participation in the most important events of the life of the Church, by the representatives of those who wield political responsibilities, a way of emphasizing the presence of the Church within the modern world, and in particular of recognizing the importance of her mission – especially the mission of the Apostolic See? This mission, while being strictly religious, also fits into the general pattern of the principles of morality, which are indissolubly bound up with it. This brings us back to the order to which the modern world aspires, an order based on justice and peace. The Church, following the inspiration of the Second Vatican Council and conforming to the constant tradition of Christian doctrine, is eager to contribute to it with the means that are within her reach.

Primacy of the spiritual
2. Of course, these means are "poor means" which Christ himself taught us to use and which are characteristic of the Church's evangelical mission. However, in this age of enormous progress of the "rich means" at the disposal of the present-day political, economic and civic structures, these specific means of the Church retain all their meaning, keep their finality, and even acquire a new splendor. The "poor means" are strictly bound up with the primacy of the spiritual. They are certain signs of the presence of the Spirit in the history of mankind. Many contemporaries seem to manifest particular comprehension for this scale of values: let [it] suffice to recall, to speak only of non-Catholics, Mahatma Gandhi, Mr. Dag Hammarskjold, Pastor Martin Luther King. Christ remains forever the highest expression of this paucity of means in which the primacy of the Spirit is revealed: the plenitude of the spirituality of which man is capable, with the grace of God, and to which he is called.

Presence of "all nations"

3. Allow me to appreciate, in this perspective, all the acts of good will manifested at the beginning of my pontificate, as also this meeting today. Yes, let us consider this fact of the presence, at the Apostolic See, of the representatives of so many States, so different in their history, their way of organization, and their confessional character; those who represent European or Asian peoples known from antiquity, or younger states, such as most of those of America whose history goes back a few centuries, and finally the most recent States, born in the course of this century. This presence corresponds in depth to the vision that the Lord Jesus revealed to us one day, speaking of "all nations" of the world, at the moment when he entrusted to the Apostles the mandate of taking the Good News all over the world (cf. Mt 28.19 and Mk 16.15). It also corresponds to the splendid analyses made by the Second Vatican Council (cf. Dogmatic Constitution *Lumen Gentium*, chapter 11, pp. 13–17) and the Pastoral Constitution *Gaudium et Spes*, pp. 2, 41, 89, etc.)

Esteem for all peoples
4. Maintaining contacts – among others by means of diplomatic representations – with so many and such different States, the Apostolic See wishes above all to express its deep esteem for each nation and each people, for its tradition, its culture, its progress in every field, as I said already in the letters addressed to the Heads of State on the occasion of my election to Peter's See. The State, as the expression of the sovereign self-determination of peoples and nations, is a normal realization of social order. Its moral authority consists in that. The son of a people with a millenary culture which was deprived for a considerable time of its independence as a State, I know, from experience, the high significance of this principle.

The Apostolic See welcomes joyfully all diplomatic representatives, not only as spokesmen of their own governments, regimes and political structures, but also and above all as representatives of peoples and nations which, through these political structures, manifest their sovereignty, their political independence, and the possibility of deciding their destiny autonomously. And it does so without any prejudice as regards the numerical importance of the population: here, it is not the numerical factor that is decisive.

Development of ecumenism
5. The Apostolic See rejoices at the presence of so many representatives; it would likewise be happy to see many others, especially of nations and peoples which at times had a centuries-old tradition in this connection. I am thinking here particularly of the nations that can be considered Catholic; but also of others. For, at present, just as ecumenism between the Catholic Church and other Christian Churches is developing, just as there is a tendency to establish contacts with all men by appealing to good will, so this circle is widening, as the presence here of many representatives of non-Catholic Countries shows. And it continually finds a reason for extension in the Church's awareness of her mission, as my venerated predecessor Paul VI expressed so well in his Encyclical *Ecclesiam Suam*. Wishes have arrived from everywhere. I noted it particularly in the Messages coming from the countries of the "East" that the new pontificate may serve peace and the rapprochement of nations. The Apostolic See, in conformity with the mission of the Church, wishes to be at the center of this brotherly rapprochement. It wishes to serve the cause of peace, not through political activity, but

by serving the values and principles which condition peace and rapprochement, and which are at the basis of [the] international common good.

Need of concerted action
6. There is, in fact, a common good of mankind, with very serious interests at stake which require the concerted action of governments and all men of good will: human rights to be guaranteed, the problems of food, health, culture, international economic cooperation, the reduction of armaments, the elimination of racialism. The common good of humanity! A "utopia" which Christian thought pursues tirelessly and which consists in the unceasing quest for just and humane solutions, taking into account at once the good of persons and the good of States, the rights of each one and the rights of others, particular interests and general necessities.

Lebanon, the Middle East, Northern Ireland
It is the common good that inspires not only the social teaching of the Apostolic See but also the initiatives which are possible for it in the framework of its own specific field. This is the case, a very topical one, of Lebanon. In a country upset by hatred and destruction, with innumerable victims, what possibility remains of re-establishing relations of common life between Christians of various tendencies and Moslems, between Lebanese and Palestinians, if not in a loyal and generous effort which respects the identity and vital requirements of all, without the vexation of any? And of considering the Middle East as a whole, while certain statesmen are tenaciously trying to arrive at an agreement and others are hesitating to commit themselves to it, who does not see that, just as much as military or territorial security, the fundamental problem is real mutual trust? Only the latter can help to harmonize the rights of all, distributing advantages and sacrifices in a realistic way. It is the same for Northern Ireland: the Bishops and leaders of non-Catholic Confessions have for years been exhorting their followers to overcome the virus of violence in its form of terrorism or of reprisals. They call upon them to reject hatred, to respect human rights completely, to pledge themselves to an effort to understand and to meet each other. Is that not a common good in which justice and realism meet?

Mediation between Argentina and Chile
Diplomacy and negotiations are also for the Holy See a specialized means of trusting in the moral resources of peoples. It was in this spirit that, accepting the appeal of Argentina and Chile, I made a point of sending Cardinal Samore to these two countries, in order that, as a diplomat of great experience, he might advocate solutions acceptable to the two peoples who are Christians and neighbors. I am happy to see that this patient work has already led to a first positive and precious result.

Drama of Iran
My thought and my prayer also turn to so many other problems that, these days in particular, are seriously troubling the life of the world, and which are again causing so many deaths, so much destruction and rancor in countries which contain few Catholics but which are equally dear to the Apostolic See. We are following the dramatic events in Iran and are very attentive to the news reaching us with regard to the Khmer country and all the peoples of this, already so sorely tried, South East Asia.

Human Rights

7. We see clearly that humanity is divided in a great many ways. It is a question also, and perhaps above all, of ideological divisions bound up with the different state systems. The search for solutions that will permit human societies to carry out their own tasks and to live in justice, is perhaps the main sign of our time. Everything that can serve this great cause must be respected, in whatever regime it may be. Advantage must be taken of mutual experiences. On the other hand, this multiform search for solutions cannot be transformed into a program of struggle to secure power over the world, whatever may be the imperialism on which this struggle is based. It is only along this line that we can avoid the threat of modern arms, particularly nuclear armaments, which remains such a matter of concern for the modern world.

The Apostolic See, which has already given proof of this, is always ready to manifest its openness with regard to countries or regimes, seeking the essential good which is man's real good. A good number of exigencies connected with this good have been expressed in the "Declaration on Human Rights" and in the international Pacts which permit its concrete application. In this matter, great praise goes to the United Nations Organization as the political platform on which the pursuit of peace and détente, rapprochement and mutual understanding find a foundation, a support, a guarantee.

Religious freedom and freedom of conscience

8. The Church's mission is, by its very nature, religious, and consequently the meeting point of the Church or the Apostolic See with the multiform and differential life of the political communities of the modern world, is characterized particularly by the universally recognized principle of religious freedom and freedom of conscience. This principle is not only contained in the list of human rights admitted by everyone, but it has a key position on it. It is a question, in fact, of respect for a fundamental right of the human spirit, in which man expresses himself most deeply, perhaps, as man.

The Second Vatican Council drew up the declaration on religious freedom. It comprises both the motivation of this right and its principal practical applications: in other words, all the data that confirm the real operation of the principle of religious freedom in social and public life.

Respecting the similar rights of all other religious communities in the world, the Apostolic See feels urged to undertake, in this field, steps in favor of all the Churches attached to it in full communion. It seeks to do so always in union with the respective Episcopates, and with the clergy and communities of faithful.

These initiatives yield, for the most part, satisfactory results. But it is difficult not to mention certain local Churches, certain rites, the situation of which, as regards religious freedom, leaves so much to be desired, when it is not quite deplorable.

There are even heart-rending cries for help or assistance, which the Apostolic See cannot but hear. And consequently it must present them, in all clarity, to the conscience of states, regimes, and the whole of mankind. It is a question here of a simple duty which coincides with the aspirations to peace and justice in the world.

It was in accordance with this way of thinking that the Holy See delegation was induced to raise its voice at the Belgrade meeting in October 1977 (cf. *L'Osservatore Romano*, October 8, 1977, p. 21), referring to the declarations approved at the

Helsinki Conference on security and cooperation in Europe, in particular on the matter of religious freedom.

On the other hand, the Apostolic See is always ready to take into account changes in realities and social mentalities that occur in the different States; and it is ready, for example, to agree to revise solemn Pacts which had been concluded in other times, under other circumstances.

Journey to Mexico

9. Very soon, I am going to go to Puebla to meet the representatives of all the Latin American Episcopates, and to inaugurate a very important meeting with them. That is part of my mission as Bishop of Rome, and Head of the College of Bishops. I wish to express publicly my joy at the comprehension and benevolent attitude of the Mexican authorities as regards this journey. The Pope hopes to be able to carry out this mission in other nations too, all the more so as many similar invitations have already been presented to him.

Once more I renew my cordial wishes for peace and progress for the whole world, this progress which fully corresponds to the Creator's will [to] "fill the earth and subdue it" (Gen 1:28). This order must be understood as applying to moral mastery, and not just economic domination. Yes, I wish mankind every kind of good, in order that all may live in real freedom, in truth, justice, and love.

January 14, 1980
(*OR*, January 28, 1980, pp. 6–8)

1. The warm feelings and fervent wishes that your Dean has just expressed, interpreting your thoughts, constitute a moving testimony, for which I thank you deeply. The perspective he developed certainly goes beyond my personal merits, but I rejoice with you at what can show, through my activity, the vitality of the Church and the special role of the Holy See.

My greeting and my own good wishes go to one and all of the diplomats present, and their families. In you I greet also the peoples and nations to which you belong, the countries you represent, the Governments in whose name you are carrying out your functions to the Apostolic See. Today I extend my greetings to all counties and all peoples, even if they are not represented here. Some of your countries, in fact, have ties of centuries-old traditions with the Catholic Church, because the sons and daughters of these nations, in the vast majority, have long professed the Catholic Faith. In others, the Catholic Church is present only with a small group of faithful, sometimes a very small one, but those who exercise power there consider it opportune, however, to maintain diplomatic relations with the Holy See. I am particularly glad to greet the countries that have established such relations in the course of the past year, even if their Ambassadors are not yet among you. Without forgetting any of these nations which are equally dear to us, I would like to mention Greece in particular, with all that the evocation of this name represents for civilization and Christianity. Finally, I cannot help thinking of other countries whose deeply Catholic populations would aspire to aspire to establishing closer relations with the Holy See.

In short, the composition of the Diplomatic Corps makes it possible to understand better, in a proper way, the important problem of the presence of the Church in the modern world. This form does not, of course, take away anything from the urgency of the apostolate of members of the Church, thanks to their daily witness and their action in all the temporal fields in which their life and their profession give them a place. But diplomatic relations permit, at another level, a direct and at the same time discreet presence of the Catholic Church, as such and in her head, among the most different peoples, their Governments or their representatives. The Church respects their political systems and their temporal responsibilities, while bringing them the assistance of the spiritual and moral exigencies to which she bears witness and which her sons endeavor to put into practice. In this sense, she intends to contribute to the good of the populations of every country. And in exchange, the activity of each of the diplomatic representatives encourages the accomplishment of the mission that the Church considers it her duty to carry out in the modern world. For this mission concerns the various dimensions of human existence and the various communities, and so also the political dimension and political communities.

The apostolic pilgrimages
2. Our meeting takes place at the beginning of the new year. It is good, however, to cast a glance at the past, coming back to some events which, for the Holy See, and particularly for him who is speaking to you, were deeply significant and remain of vital importance for a long time. Your Dean, moreover, was kind enough to recall them. It is a question of my journeys – they were so many opportunities for deep contacts with

the peoples and their rulers, not to mention the strengthened communion with local Churches, which was always the first apostolic aim.

And in the very first place, my visit to Mexico, in relation with the Puebla Conference, and to meet the desire of the Latin-American Episcopal Conference and particularly the Mexican bishops. If I was able to carry out my pastoral service there, it was thanks also to the President of Mexico, who invited me in spite of the absence of diplomatic relations, and to the administrative organisms which kindly facilitated the program. It was the first time that the Successor of Peter had set foot on Mexican soil and become a pilgrim to Our Lady of Guadalupe. It was right to pay tribute to the Catholic people of Mexico, which has won such great merits. Nor do I forget the pleasant meeting with the people of Santo Domingo, which has since then suffered so much as a result of the typhoon, and finally the stop in the Bahamas.

I had also a special debt to pay to the Polish people, and that was the reason for my pilgrimage in June last. It was the first visit of a Pope to this land and to this people of Poland, and, what is more, of the first Pope precisely of Polish stock, the first Slav Pope. How can I express the strength of the feelings that marked this pilgrimage, echoing the whole content of history and of the present moment! Beyond the more personal aspect, this pilgrimage was to be set in the whole texture of history, based on faith and the Christian tradition, and bear witness to the union, which, after so many historical trials, continues in the present situation – between the nation and the Church. I must also note the courteous and hospitable attitude of the civil Authorities, on this occasion.

To the United Nations
In the autumn, on my way to the UN, I felt equally called to visit Ireland for two reasons. The Church and Christendom owe so much to the Irish people for its historic contribution and its present vigor, and I had to strengthen these brothers and these sons in their faith and encourage them in their Christian identity. Moreover, the present situation was at once a challenge and a cry that drew me to the spot in order to utter forceful exhortations to peace, forgiveness and brotherly collaboration in justice. I continue to hope that they will be heard one day by these divided and tormented brothers, and in the first place by the political leaders.

Then, I did not want to go to the headquarters of the United Nations, in New York, without trying to carry out my pastoral task by contacting the Church and society of the United States of America with visits, at least for the moment, to the populations of some prestigious cities or lands. I greatly appreciated the welcome that these crowds gave me. Catholics, of course, but also members of other confessions or religions, and I esteemed at its rightful value the unprecedented act of President Carter and his Government who invited me to the White House. I pay tribute to political leaders who contrive to find space for exchanges with spiritual leaders for the benefit of peace.

Finally, in my recent journey to Turkey, I also met with comprehension from the Turkish Authorities, whereas the citizens are nearly all Moslems and the State has chosen to adopt a policy of neutrality with regard to religions, clearly separating religious matters and political action. Although my visit was motivated above all by the desire to meet the Patriarch of Constantinople, His Holiness Dimitrios I, with an ecumenical purpose, and the other Christian communities, particularly the Armenians, I was also concerned to promote ties of friendship with the Turkish country and populations, especially in the person of their rulers. It was also an opportunity to reaffirm the great principles of the Second Vatican Council with regard to relations with non-Christian religions and particularly with Islam.

All these visits, Your Excellencies, were intended to serve the cause of peace, and that is the reason why I have taken the liberty of recalling them before you. Certainly, they remain entirely in the service of religious, pastoral and ecumenical aims, but, at the same time, by taking the Pope to various points of the globe, they create the opportunity for meetings with societies, situations and even political systems that are very different. How can one fail to see that they stimulate rapprochement? For that, too, is a role of the Church, which wishes to unite, which wishes to serve the brotherhood of men and peoples, going beyond what separates them and sometimes sets them against one another.

The commitment of the Church for peace
3. My visit to the Organization of the United Nations was dedicated quite particularly to this mission of peace. The continual efforts of the Holy See to ensure and strengthen peace in the world found an additional expression there. It was not just a question of making a declaration, of giving a message, but of studying more deeply the very foundations of peace among nations, among countries, among systems, in the line of the encyclicals *Pacem in Terris* and *Populorum Progressio*, prolonging the activity of John XXIII and Paul VI.

The Church, in fact, has her own method to approach the problem of peace, a method that corresponds to her doctrinal and pastoral mission, and that wished to find its synthetic expression in the address to the UN, as well as in the annual message for January 1, centered this year on the subject "Truth, the power of peace," and in general in the attitude and activities of the Apostolic See.

In New York, for me as for my predecessor Paul VI, the meeting of the Pope, the leader of a universal spiritual community with the representatives of nearly every country in the world, was a unique occasion of its kind, taking on exceptional significance. It shows, as I said, that "the United Nations Organization accepts and respects the religious and moral dimension of those human problems that the Church attends to, in view of the message of truth and love that it is her duty to bring to the world" (p. 5). On her part, the Church is deeply interested in the ideals pursued by this Organization, which, guaranteeing all men and all women, as well as all nations, large and small, equal rights, wishes to help them to respect one another and collaborate. Yes, the Church highly appreciates the effort of the UN to establish peaceful cooperation among these nations. Seeing in this organization, even with its imperfections or its weaknesses, the "obligatory way of modern civilization and world peace," as Paul VI had said, she hopes that it will find more and more the ways and means adequate for such an important purpose, and that the authority which it needs to carry out its task in the service of all, will be recognized and respected everywhere. The common good which it has the duty of promoting, necessarily goes beyond the particular interest of each nation.

Concern for the present situation
The problems that arise, in fact, at the present time do not fail to arouse concern

whether it is that of the ruinous and dangerous proliferation of armaments, everywhere in the world; or that of armed struggles at certain critical points in Asia, among others the situation in Afghanistan, in the immediate neighborhood of Iran.

Yes, in the light of the dramatic events that are taking place in Afghanistan and that are keeping in suspense the public opinion of the whole world or almost, one cannot help wondering about the motives that can trigger off events so serious and so threatening for international détente. In any case, is it really possible to claim to circumscribe the problem of a region by detaching it from the context of a whole set of factors with which it is connected? Are not the greatest responsibilities incumbent on everyone, of course, but in a particularly serious way on those who have the greatest powers? I say this in the framework of my spiritual mission, to strengthen, in all parties, awareness of the fundamental requirements for peaceful international life, in the first place respect of the independence of each country, the rights of peoples to guide their own destiny, according to their patriotic and religious sentiments. I say so to defend the populations, for the hardening of conflicts is always at their expense. I say so to appeal, as I did in the Message for the first of January, for a supplement of truth and justice. All that applies moreover to other critical points of Asia. My solicitude and my sympathy go in particular to the people of Iran, whose glorious history and humanitarian traditions are universally known. We all wish it success in overcoming the present difficulties, and I form the best wishes for its life, tranquility and progress.

The other continents are not forgotten for all that. I am thinking also of the peaceful relations of the American States, the Organization of which I had the honor of addressing, on the occasion of my visit to the UN. Nor should I like the vast African continent to be absent from the solicitude of the human family, on the pretext that today the great economic stakes lie elsewhere. Africa has experienced and still experiences redoubtable fratricidal oppositions, from which certain powers sometimes wish to benefit; but she can also overcome them and reach positive agreements such as the one in the process of being established in Zimbabwe-Rhodesia. Africa is patiently carrying out its development efforts often with limited means. It must continue its way in peace, with disinterested mutual aid which respects its specific genius and the human and spiritual qualities of its civilizations. In the course of the past year I was happy to receive here myself several heads of State from this continent.

Dignity of the human person
4. What, therefore, is the principle that inspires the Apostolic See when it addresses politicians or occupies itself with political matters? A sentence of the Second Vatican Council would sum it up well. "The Church, by reason of her role and competence, is not identified with any political community nor bound by ties to any political system. It is at once the sign and the safeguard of the transcendental dimension of the human person" (Constitution *Gaudium et Spes*. no. 76. par 2). It is one of the principles on which my first encyclical *Redemptor Hominis* is also based (cf. no. m13).

It is true that the common good of society, a nation, must be promoted in many ways, like the set of social conditions permitting the development of groups and persons, and this common good takes on a more and more universal extension. "At the same time, however, there is a growing awareness of the sublime dignity of the human person, who stands above all things and whose rights and duties are universal and inviolable" (Constitution *Gaudium et Spes*, no. 26). The prologue of the United Nations Charter itself reaffirms "the faith [of the signatory peoples] in the fundamental rights of man, in the dignity and the value of the human person."

What the wisdom of nations recognizes, the Church has special and very deep reasons for bearing witness to and safeguarding, because Christ united himself with each man, and his solicitude for each man he redeemed has become that of the Church. "The Church cannot remain insensible to whatever serves man's true welfare, any more than she can remain indifferent to what threatens it" (Encyclical *Redemptor Hominis*, p. 13). That is why, in this encyclical, as in the address to the United Nations, I was able to stress human rights and I enumerated a certain number of them (cf. address to UN, no. 13). The set of human rights corresponds, in fact, to the substance of the dignity of the human being, understood in his integrality, and not reduced to a single dimension. And I have very often had the opportunity to come back to this essential subject.

These rights, however, must be conceived in their correct meaning. The right to freedom, for example, does not, of course, include the right to moral evil, as if it were possible to claim, among other things, the right to suppress human life, as in abortion, or the freedom to use things harmful to oneself or to others. Likewise one should not deal with the rights of man without envisaging also his correlative duties, which express precisely his own responsibility and his respect of the rights of others and of the community.

Freedom of conscience and religion
Allow me further to return to one of the fundamental human rights which is, of course very dear to the Church, that of freedom of conscience and religion. How often already has the Holy See made appeals, sometimes dramatic ones in favor of persons, groups and Churches deprived of the fundamental right of professing their faith, personally and as a community! I recalled it solemnly before the United Nations Organization (cf. no. 20). The Holy See deems it as duty to address the Authorities of all States, as well as international Organizations, on this subject again. Today there are still, in fact, many cases of real violation of religious freedom, whatever may be the explanations put forward, and I myself often receive testimony of this. The Holy See also thinks that religious communities have a particular claim to make their voice heard when it is a question of formulating the concrete applications of the principle of religious freedom, or of watching over their practical implementation.

Conditions of peace
5. But let us come back now to the object of this meeting, which is to mark the beginning of a new year, and even a new decade. So I come finally to the heartfelt good wishes I am anxious to offer you. In view of the universal character of the Holy See and the universality also of Christ's love, to which it is my mission in the first place to bear witness, in spite of my unworthiness, I venture to say that my wishes are addressed to the whole human family, to all peoples, all political communities, national and international, especially to the nations and their Governments represented here. May God grant them all the possibility of advancing, in peace and in the truth that is the condition of peace, toward happier and more just situations, thanks to constant material, social and moral progress!

The thoughts of us all turn especially to each of the countries subjected even today, to the ordeal of armed conflicts, or which are still under the shock of unspeakable prostration, such as Cambodia.

My wishes also go to categories of persons who are the object of special attention at the international level. May the children of the different countries continue to benefit, in particular, from the solicitude that the Year of the Child brought them!

Year of the Child

In too many countries, these children are already suffering tragically from hunger, and with them a large number of adults. How will the generations of tomorrow fare? At present the world food situation is seen to be very serious. I made a point, last year, of going to the headquarters of FAO, on the kind invitation of the Director General, to share, with the persons responsible for this international Organization, concern about the urgent necessity of increasing food products and distributing them more fairly. But the general plans which should reduce want now and in the future are compromised by so many obstacles which depend less on the possibilities of nature than on the faults of men themselves, their indifference to this problem, their lack of solidarity, and bad use of their resources. Yet this is a matter that should mobilize men and make the efforts of all converge. Instead of that, how much money is spent in multiplying armaments and engines of death! How many inconsistencies in the terms of trade! How many energies wasted in ideological struggles, policies of prestige and power! But power for whom? For what? For what common good? The generations to come will call us to account. God calls us to account. May we, Your Excellencies, we who are gathered today in this place which is a symbol of peace and charity, help in every way we can to give the distressing reality of the hunger of our brothers a very special place in the policies of our countries.

Ladies and Gentlemen, my last wishes be for yourselves, for your persons and your families. I hope you will find a great many satisfactions in your functions as Ambassadors to the Holy See, which are *sui generis*. May God heap joy and peace upon you!

January 12, 1981
(*OR*, January 26, 1981, pp. 3–5)

1. The very worthy Dean of Ambassadors has just expressed the sentiments that fill the hearts of all of you members of the Diplomatic Corps accredited to the Holy See, at this meeting always so solemn and significant, at the beginning of the new year. I heartily thank him for his noble words and, with him, I thank you all for your presence for this exchange of good wishes. I greet with you your wives, who have accompanied you for this kind step which I greatly appreciate. I wish to greet all your families too from afar. I greet your collaborators, who form the effective and organized team of each of your Embassies. *And I greet above all the populations of your countries, whom you represent so worthily in your delicate office.* Yes, they are here, spiritually close to us, and I like to feel that they are – all the peoples of the world, even those who, unfortunately, have no official representative to the humble successor of Peter. I feel they are very close, and I relive in thought the meetings I had the joy of having with some of them in the course of my journeys, especially in the year that has just ended. All the peoples should be here, because this is the house of all. *The universal vocation of the Church concerns, in fact, each of the peoples.* So I address my greeting and my good wishes to everyone for a serene and active new year, rich in the blessings of Almighty God.

2. I am happy to see again on this occasion, with the well-known faces of the Ambassadors who have been accredited for some years, the new Heads of Mission who officially began their diplomatic mission to the Holy See during the past year, and even in the last few days. They are twenty three in number and represent the Dominican Republic, Gabon, Jamaica, Uganda, Indonesia, Nicaragua, San Marino, the People's Republic of the Congo, Great Britain, Greece, Ireland, Australia, the Central African Republic, Venezuela, Egypt, Belgium, Spain, Colombia, Madagascar, Iraq, Mali, Japan and Austria. Among them, as I already had occasion to stress in the presence of the Sacred College before Christmas, there are Ambassadors of countries which, for the first time in their history, have established diplomatic relations with the Holy See. They come to join your large family for, as I well know, the Diplomatic Corps to the Holy See is a real family and in this way they take their place in the line of continuity which gives a quite particular significance to the official presence, in the Pope's house, of representatives of the peoples of the whole world to him and his direct collaborators. *It is a continuity which persists and becomes deeper, a continuity which stimulates mutual understanding between Peter's See and each of your governments and peoples*, a continuity which encourages mutual support, in the cause of peace, the defense of man and the development of the life of nations. This continuity expresses very well the relations of friendship, esteem, and collaboration with all the nations of the world that the Holy See wishes to maintain, in a peaceful and respectful spirit, with those responsible for public life.

Heads of State
3. The coming of some Heads of State to the Vatican highlights this reality. I recall with great pleasure the visits paid last year by the President of the Republic of Senegal, the Grand Duke and Duchess of Luxembourg, the President of the Republic

of Cyprus, the President of the Republic of Tanzania, King Hassan of Morocco, the President of the Republic of Portugal, the President of the United States of America, the Grand Master of the Sovereign Military Order of Malta, King Hussein of Jordan, the Captains Regent of San Marino, the President of the Republic of Zaire, the President of the Republic of Mali, Queen Elizabeth of the United Kingdom, the Reigning Prince of Liechtenstein, the Prince and Princess of Sweden, the President of the Republic of Sierra Leone, the President of the Republic of Yugoslavia.

I also remember the visits of the other personalities of the governments of various States and of international Organizations.

In the variety of historical situations, these presences of high authorities beside the humble Successor of St. Peter emphasize the mutual desire to deepen the ties of an understanding from which the peoples benefit in whose midst the Church lives and wishes to serve man.

4. So I think that this annual meeting with you, illustrious members of the Diplomatic Corps, represents a particularly significant moment of my pastoral ministry. Through your presence, I have, in fact, before my eyes the whole international community, so varied in appearance and in composition. You are a real "forum" which reminds me of my meetings with the representatives of the peoples at the UN, FAO, and UNESCO; *it is, indeed, your own communities, and also the entire community of the various nations in the world, that I have before my eyes.*

On the occasion of the pastoral journeys that I carry out in the different regions of the world, I feel the experience of a double reality; on the one hand, the populations that are met, bringing their weight of history and life which is expressed in religious faith, culture, convictions, hopes and even sufferings, all things in which the Church, a community of believers, is deeply integrated as a part, more or less extensive, of this human reality; on the other hand, the representatives and those responsible for the institutional life of each country, the government Authorities, with whom I was able, every time, to have useful meetings and conversations.

This double reality corresponds to the *double dialogue* which, in my mission as universal Pastor, I feel the duty of maintaining constantly; one is carried on with *the man of concrete life*, to revive in him the animating power of the Gospel word, or at least to proclaim it to him so that he may get to know it and determine his attitude with regard to it; the other dialogue is addressed to *those responsible for political and social life*, to offer a simple, disinterested cooperation in the great causes that concern the life of humanity: peace, justice, the rights of the person, [the] common good.

The universal mission of the Church
5. I am convinced that, acting in this way, the Holy See, far from interfering in fields that are not hers, merely gives concrete expression to the universal mission of the Church, which is addressed to all men, which is spread throughout every region on earth, and which is, by her very nature, united in solidarity with all human beings, men and women, especially the poor and the suffering. Her historical vicissitudes for nearly two millennia, through so many generations, and her experience among the most varied human groups, of such different origin and civilizations, give the Church great facility of approach and dialogue on many problems.

It is true that civil society does not coincide with religious society, and that the two missions, that of the Church and that of the State, must remain clearly distinct. But it is also true that the Church and the State are ordained to the good – spiritual on the one hand, temporal on the other – of human persons, and that their mutual dialogue, respectful and loyal, far from disturbing society, on the contrary enriches it.

What does the Church come to offer? In *bilateral dialogue*, with governments, she puts at their disposal the contribution of an institution which holds in honor the highest values of man and which can never feel alien to any of the problems discussed in any social context whatever. Even when she finds obstacles in front of her, when she undergoes coercion or when she is persecuted, the Church does not cease to be *"internal," deep-rooted in the overall reality of the country in which she lives, and in solidarity with it*. And that is the reason why the Holy See, as I said, feels united with every people, with every nation. That is also the reason why the diplomatic representative accredited to the Holy See cannot – even if they are not Catholics or Christians – feel "foreign" in the house of the universal Pastor; just as the Pope, when he visits the various countries, feels "at home" in every nation that receives him.

6. This global reality which the Church always has before her eyes and which constitutes the common denominator of the life of each of the peoples of the world, is their culture, their spiritual life, in whatever forum it may be manifested. Speaking of global reality, of spiritual life, I would like to dwell this year, in this talk with you, on the duty that is incumbent on all leaders to defend culture in this broadest sense and guarantee it at all costs.

Culture is the life of the spirit: It is the key that gives access to the deepest and most jealously guarded secrets of the life of peoples; it is the fundamental and unifying expression of their existence, because, in culture are found the riches, almost inexpressible, I would say, of religious convictions, history, the literary and artistic heritage, the ethnological substratum, the attitudes and *"forma mentis"* of peoples. In short, to say "culture" is to express in one word the national identity which constitutes the soul of these peoples and which survives in spite of adverse conditions, trials of all kinds, historical or natural cataclysms, remaining one and compact throughout the centuries. According to its culture, its spiritual life, every people is distinguished from the other, which it is called, moreover, to complete by supplying it with the specific contribution that the other needs.

Culture and growth of peoples

7. In my address to UNESCO on June 2, in Paris, I highlighted this reality; if culture is the expression par excellence of the spiritual life of peoples, it must never be separated from all the other problems of human existence, whether it is a question of peace, freedom, defense, hunger, employment, etc. The solution of these problems depends on the correct way of understanding and approaching the problems of spiritual life, which thus conditions all others and is conditioned by them.

It is culture, understood in this wide sense, which guarantees the growth of peoples and preserves their integrity. If it is forgotten, the barriers that safeguard the identity and the real riches of peoples are seen to fall. As I said on this occasion, "the Nation is, in fact, the great community of men who are united by various ties, but above all, precisely by culture. The Nation exists *"through" culture and "for" culture*, and it is therefore the great educator of men in order that they may "be more" in the community. It is this community which possesses a history that goes beyond the history of the individual and the family. It is also in this community, with respect to which every family educates, that the family begins its work of education with what is the most simple thing, language, thus enabling man who is at the very beginning to learn to speak in order to become a member of the community of his family and of his Nation . . . " My words express a particular experience, *a particular testimony* in its kind. I am the son of a Nation which has lived the greatest experiences of history, which its neighbors have condemned to death several times, but which has survived and remained itself. It has kept its identity, and it has kept, in spite of partitions and foreign occupations, its national sovereignty, not by relying on the resources of physical power, but solely *by relying on its culture*. This culture turned out in the circumstances to be more powerful than all other forces.

What I say here concerning the right of the Nation to the foundation of its culture and its future is not, therefore, the echo of any "nationalism," but it is always a question of a stable element of human experience and of the *humanistic perspective of man's development*. There exists a fundamental sovereignty of society which is manifested in the culture of the Nation. It is a question of the sovereignty through which, at the same time, man is supremely sovereign. When I express myself in this way, I am also thinking, with deep interior emotion, of *the cultures of so many ancient peoples* which did not give way when confronted with the civilizations of the invaders: and they still remain for man the source of his "being" as a man in the interior truth of his humanity. I am also thinking with admiration of the *cultures of new societies*, those that are awakening to life in the community of their own Nation – just as my Nation awakened to life ten centuries ago – and that are struggling to maintain their own identity and their own values against the influences and pressure of models proposed from outside (*L'Osservatore Romano*, English Edition, June 23, 1980, p. 14). It can be said, in this sense, that culture is the foundation of the life of peoples, the root of their deep identity, the support of their survival and their independence.

8. But that holds good all the more [for] peoples insofar as culture is the highest expression of the life of each man. Man, I said further at UNESCO, "is the prime and *fundamental fact of culture*" (ibid., p. 8). It is culture that unifies the elements of which man is composed and which complete each other though sometimes being in deep mutual tension: spirit and body. One cannot go beyond its limits to the detriment of the other; and what guarantees this difficult balance – with the Grace of God – is precisely man's global life, culture, which I defined in Paris as "a truly human system, a splendid synthesis of spirit and body" (ibid., p. 8).

The bimillenary history of the Church, as we know, is intermingled with the highest expressions of the spiritual and cultural life of the various nations of the old and new world, and today the Church is following with particular attention, as I stressed in my journey to Africa, the delicate process of enhancing the value of autochthonous cultures. That is why she takes to heart the widest range of values that the word, "culture" contains and signifies. In the address I delivered to your colleagues of the Diplomatic Corps in Kenya, I was anxious to point out that "the path that every human community must walk in its quest to ascertain the deeper meaning of its existence in the path of truth about man in his totality" (Nairobi, May 6, 1980: *L'Oss. Rom.*, English edition, May 26, 1980, p. 3).

Well, Gentlemen, as for you and your governments, it is the whole man, formed of spirit and body, that is close to the heart of the Church, in accordance with the mission received from her Founder, that encompasses his problems and his interests, on the spiritual plane as well on the material plane, for without the material, the spiritual cannot adequately develop.

The Holy See and great initiatives

9. In this grandiose unitary vision, the Holy See feels in solidarity with all the great initiatives which are trying to solve the problems of mankind: in the first place, *as regards the material plane*, the generous and effective aid brought to the peoples of regions that are suffering from hunger, thirst, or other calamities and I express here once more all my solidarity with the badly hit region of Sahel, to which I do not cease to look with particular attention; the impetus given to the increase of agriculture to ensure sufficient food; medical action against diseases, especially in favor of children and of the poorest people; a fairer distribution of resources, not only material ones, but also technological and scientific ones, to offer populations more and more concrete possibilities of being the architects of their own life and development.'

Materially, the Holy See has very limited means to contribute to these initiatives; the Catholic organizations of the various countries, or those which have an international character, are able to make a larger contribution. But I think that what the peoples as a whole expect constantly and above all from the Holy See is *the contribution of a spiritual power* aiming at encouraging and bringing forth in a more effective way the international cooperation which is already at work in the appropriate authorities, such as FAO, UNESCO AND WHO.

10. Precisely, it is *on the spiritual plane* that the solicitude of the Church is exercised especially, because what is at stake there is the eternal destiny of men and the orderly life of peoples.

Mention must be made first and foremost of the fundamental problems of peace; it polarizes all the efforts of men of good will and the Church brings it her encouragement by all the means at her disposal, above all by driving home to consciences on the world plane the duty of defending this frail and threatened good, which is, however, the priority one at all levels. In the address to Cardinals last December, I spoke at length of the action carried out by the Church in this field. Allow me to recall here once more the annual observance of the Day of Peace; it offers me, furthermore, the opportunity to thank you publicly for the way in which you have collaborated with your Governments and for the presence of practically all of you every year to celebrate this Day with me in St. Peter's Basilica.

As regards the defense of peace, *the role of the Holy See is exercised in tensions and in crises of international life.* There again, it wishes to be inspired always by an overall view of the common good. That is not done without difficulties, due to the contrary positions held by the parties. On the one hand, the Holy See wishes to be full of attention and respect for the subjective reasons claimed or put forward by each of the parties; then, too, there is also the complexity of highly technical aspects, or the lack of real data. As a result of all that, the Holy See has quite often to abstain from expressing a concrete judgment on the conflicting theses. This is the case, among other things, of *disarmament.*

The Holy See is deeply convinced and it has been able to repeat it on many occasions that the arms race is ruinous for mankind and that far from reducing the threat that weighs on security and world peace, it increases it. It emphasizes the fundamental elements that make possible and realistic an agreement that would put an end to the race forever new and more powerful means of destruction. These elements are particularly a *climate of greater trustfulness*, which can spring from real and global détente in international relations; respect for the *prerogatives of all peoples*, even if they are small and disarmed, prerogatives based on their cultural identity; sincere collaboration to improve "the human component of peace," represented above all by respect for human rights.

In this context, it is perfectly logical to wonder if peace should be measured only by the absence of direct confrontation between the great Powers. Can the international community resign itself to the prolongation of *a war as fierce as the one that has been going on for some months between Iraq and Iran*? The victims who lose their lives, the peoples subjected to sufferings and hardships, the impoverishment of resources in both countries, is not all that sufficient to appeal to the conscience of the rulers and peoples who witness the tragedy without reacting?

The soul of peace

11. The Holy See is, therefore, convinced that it is above all "the soul of peace" that must be strengthened, that is, a better relationship between the States, achieved by improving the human condition of persons and peoples in enjoyment of their freedoms and their fundamental rights, such as they are presented by the various civilizations. For this reason, just as it had been led to take part in the *Helsinki Conference* on security and cooperation in Europe, the Holy See is participating in the same way in the meeting that is now being held in *Madrid*. It is logical that, in this context, in Madrid as previously in Helsinki and Belgrade, the voice of the Holy See is raised in favor of respect of *religious freedom, a fundamental element for the peace of souls*. I dedicated to this subject a particular reflection in a Document sent to the Heads of State of the countries that signed the Final Helsinki Document, a reflection which I consider applicable also in a wider international field, for other countries and other continents.

It is not possible to speak of religious freedom, the highest form of spiritual freedom that can germinate from the humus of civilization and culture, if the principle that I have recalled several times is disregarded, namely that the complete man is the first subject of culture, as he is its only object and purpose (cf. Address to UNESCO, no.7). To violate religious freedom, oppress it, limit it, and stifle it, is the greatest affront to man, for the spiritual and religious dimension is the one on the basis of which every other human greatness is measured. Actually, a fundamental bond unites religion in general, and particularly Christianity, with the highest forms of culture (cf. ibid., no. 9).

This is attested by innumerable testimonies among which it is enough to recall, for Europe, the determinant influence that the figures and work of the Patron Saints of our continent had on the spiritual and material development of such different peoples, deeply united, nevertheless, by common spiritual interests, to which these extraordinary men that St. Benedict was in the West and St. Cyril and St. Methodius were in the East, dedicated their lives. And I am happy to recall them here, in the course of the meeting today, in view of the fact the St. Benedict has been celebrated

on various solemn occasions during the past year, on the occasion of the fifteenth centenary of his birth, and that SS Cyril and Methodius have recently been proclaimed
Patron Saints of Europe too, an event which has met with favor in this continent and
in the world.

Moreover, it must be stressed, the heritage which characterizes the other continents with, however, differentiated cultural and historical models also finds its origin
and explanation in the religious, humanistic and ethical inspiration of the various religions, as I emphasized further at UNESCO (cf. ibid., no. 9).

12. I would like to add another reflection with regard to the spiritual plane, which
interests man's development in his integrality as well as the progress of peoples. In my
recent encyclical *Dives in Misericordia*, I pointed out that, among the causes of
uneasiness that beset modern man, there is a "kind of *abuse of the idea of justice*" and
even "a *practical distortion*" due to the fact that "often programs which start from the
idea of justice and which ought to assist its fulfillment among individuals, groups, and
human societies, in practice suffer from distortions. Although they continue to appeal
to the idea of justice, nevertheless experience shows that other negative forces have
gained the upper hand over justice, such as spite, hatred, and even cruelty. In such
cases, the desire to annihilate the enemy, limit his freedom, or even force him into total
dependence, becomes the fundamental motive for action; and this contrasts with the
essence of justice, which by its nature tends to establish equality and harmony
between the parties in conflict" (*Dives in Misericordia*, p. 12).

Such a "distortion" of justice is an experience that humanity still undergoes today
through wars, revolutions, or international crises, and that makes it difficult, if not
impossible, to bring about the progress of adequate peaceful solutions, stable and in
conformity with the natural dignity of peoples. This criterion could be applied to nearly all crises, and in particular to those which seem insoluble or chronic. Among the
latter, the *problem of the Middle East* must be mentioned as typical. How is it possible, in fact, to think of establishing a stable peace without taking into account, to an
equal extent, the requirements of *all* the peoples concerned, of their existence and their
security, as well as the possibility of laying the foundations for future collaboration.

Here it is clear that to demand one's own right, with absolute claims, will never
lead to peace, because this demand presupposes the denial, or the excessive diminution, of the right of others; whereas only *equity*, that is, the capacity of balancing
advantages and renunciations on the part of all the parties concerned, can open the
way to a global agreement in order to live in common. That means that, as I said in the
encyclical, there is no justice if it is not completed by love. Such an attitude of mind
is facilitated if we realize that peoples like persons have goods *of their own* and *common* goods, and that the latter are not divisible, but can only *be enjoyed together*, by
putting into practice a loyal and trusting collaboration.

To promote justice by safeguarding faith and freedom

13. A distortion of justice can be noted also *in the process of certain revolutions* when,
to change a social situation considered unjust, and which often really is, people claim
to impose an ideological regime which often really is in contradiction with ancient and
deep religious and ethical convictions of the peoples concerned. But apart from the
fact that it is not possible to exchange spiritual goods for material ones, the dilemma

in question is a false one, because it is a duty of conscience, for anyone inspired by a Christian concept, to promote justice effectively by safeguarding faith and freedom, as well as the other spiritual goods of a people. It is not possible to betray the identity and sovereignty of peoples, for they spring from the spiritual heritage peculiar to each of them, on which their dignity and nobility, superior to all party interests, are based. I hope and trust that certain tormented regions of the world, such as Latin America, may find in their spiritual and human roots the wisdom and the strength to advance toward a wholesome progress, which will not deny the past and which will guarantee a real civilization.

Speaking of Latin America, I cannot but draw the attention of all to the negotiations going on between Argentina and Chile, two nations which desired the mediation of the Apostolic See for the solution of a delicate problem regarding mutual concord between these two great and noble countries. The request for mediation was a sign of great good will. That is why I hope, and I ask for prayers, that a happy solution may come to crown definitively so many negotiations which led, in the course of the audience last December 12, to the solemn presentation of precise proposals to the two Ministers of Foreign Affairs accompanied by their respective delegations

14. Your Excellencies, Ladies and Gentlemen, the problems that I have just reviewed with you, considering them in the superior light of the culture, soul, and life of peoples, call for universal solidarity, transcending all preconceived hostility, misunderstanding or economic speculation, which make the life of the international community so difficult and full of anguish today. The Church is ready to carry out the part that belongs to her, as she endeavors to carry it out habitually, thanks to the best of her men and women. And I wish to mention here especially the missionaries who work in all latitudes, all over the world, and also the men and women engaged in international organizations and in various social organisms.

This immense work, which the Church and your leaders wish to carry out together, can be summed up in one word: *service of man*. That is what must be the inspiration of today, the fundamental reason for the promotion of peace, mutual respect and international concord which the Church wishes to encourage with all her strength under God's eyes, and which she calls people to accomplish for love of man.

This is the wish that I address to you, at the beginning of this year which is just starting, and which, I beg you to relay to your governments. May the new year see the international community commit itself more and more sincerely and effectively in the service of man and the public good, and not of private interests, in a brotherhood that is more and more real, the one founded for all peoples on the common bonds of mutual respect, and which has for Christians only one foundation: Christ, his incarnation, and the Redemption he carried out for his brothers and sisters.

My most cordial and affectionate wishes to all of you again, to your families, and to the nations you represent.

A Happy New Year!

January 16, 1982
(*OR*, January 25, 1982, pp. 1–4)

1. The pleasant custom of exchanging greetings at the threshold of the new year unites us once more today. I thank your worthy Dean for having expressed in elevated terms the sentiments which are in your hearts at this moment and for having thus interpreted your wishes and your thoughts.

I greet each of you and I thank you for having come in person to this significant meeting, which is one of the outstanding moments of your mission to Peter's See and to which the latter attaches particular importance. I thank and greet you, as [I] do every year, which touches me deeply; and my thought turns also to each of your families, to which I address all my good wishes. Finally, I thank and greet the collaborators who assist you competently and generously in your respective embassies, assuring you a service that is always efficient and attentive in your relations with the various departments of the Apostolic See. I express fervent good wishes for everyone, and particularly that the year which has just begun may see rising in the world – in each of your countries which you represent so worthily – the dawn of a more serene and peaceful future, marked by the goodwill and collaboration of all in view of the welfare of men, our brothers.

For peace and human advancement
2. To your countries I address an affectionate thought, full of good wishes. The relations which the Holy See maintains with each of them, and of which you are the visible and immediate intermediaries, are, for the Apostolic See, the pontifical representatives, to whom I send the assurance of my remembrance and my satisfaction with the pastoral and evangelical spirit with which they carry out their mission – the relations, I say, between the Holy See and your countries represent an element of mutual understanding, a factor of peace and human advancement, mutual help for the mission that the States and Church, each in its well-defined field, are called to fulfill for the spiritual and social good of men. The presence here, at the heart of Christendom, of the legitimate and qualified representatives of the various governments, bears witness, better than words, to the intention of your rulers to collaborate sincerely with the Church to ensure the constant elevation of peoples, to ensure the ways of an understanding that is always constructive and peaceful because it is directed to the common good, and to guarantee the world the march toward peace, which is difficult but so profitable.

You are men of peace! Your life and your mission aim at procuring for your fellow countrymen the instruments of peace. Your function is exercised at the Holy See, whose initiatives in favor of peace are well known to you. This See of Peter remains faithful to its mission, that of promoting rightful understanding among peoples and of safeguarding the good of peace, which is the most precious heritage, the indispensable heritage for man's complete development, even in the framework of the earthly city. The Church carries out this task for the good of man, taking up its position above parties, as is testified particularly by the recent initiative carried out, according to my express desire, under the sponsorship of the Pontifical Academy of Sciences. To the Heads of State of nuclear powers and to the President of the General Assembly of the United Nations, a study was presented on the terrible and irreversible consequences of a nuclear conflict. In the perspective of the Holy See, the initiative does not intend to deal with technical details of the negotiations in course or of other possible negotiations; it wants to show clearly from the human and moral point of view, and appealing to men of science to make their contribution to the great cause of peace, that the only solution possible, in face of the hypothesis of nuclear war, is to reduce at once, and subsequently to eliminate completely, nuclear armaments, by means of specific agreements and effective controls.

For all these reasons, I appreciate your presence greatly. I hope with all my heart that you will always and truly be men of peace. The world needs such men today!

No alien people
3. But, as I already confided to you last year, I am thinking of the gaps that should still be filled within the well-deserving Diplomatic Corps accredited to the Holy See. I am thinking of the peoples who could also be represented here, in this house which is the house of all because the Church is by definition "catholic," open to the dimensions of the whole world. She is not alien to any culture, to any civilization, to any ethnic and social tradition. Likewise, she does not consider any people alien – all are dear and close to her because she knows that she is sent to all by divine mission. And likewise that all peoples on earth are close and dear to her, just as she would not like to be considered by any as alien, distant or suspect.

The work of the Church is turned solely toward good, she seeks constantly to dedicate herself to others, to take an interest in their concerns and their needs, to share their fate.

Express gratitude
4. I would like to greet in a particularly cordial way the diplomatic representatives who began a new stage of their noble service this year at the Holy See. They are the ambassadors of Japan, Austria, Ghana, Portugal, Korea, Iran, Brazil, Italy, Argentina, Bolivia, Yugoslavia, Honduras, Ecuador, the Dominican Republic, Finland, India, Tunisia and Luxembourg. I have also the pleasure of announcing to you that, from today, as the result of an agreement with [the] Government of the United Kingdom, sanctioning the excellent relations that exist with the Apostolic See and for the purpose of developing them, the Legation of Great Britain to the Holy See has been raised to the rank of Embassy, while an Apostolic Nunciature has been erected in London, with a Pro Nuncio as Head of Mission.

The particular circumstances of this year, when the Lord permitted his Vicar on earth to be sorely tried, caused most of the new ambassadors to begin their official mission by presenting a copy of their Letters of Credence to my Secretary of State, as the Vienna Convention lays down. Providence then gave me the possibility of receiving them one after the other for the usual solemn audience granted to my new ambassadors.

Recalling what happened, I am anxious once more to repeat to you my sincere and deeply felt thanks for the part you took on the occasion of the tragic event in May last, whether personally, through the eager and assiduous interest you showed, or on behalf of your governments and the various authorities. May the Lord reward you for all the delicacy of which you gave proof on this occasion through your testimonies of human solidarity and sympathy, which I will never be able to forget!

The Church and human rights

5. You are called to follow more closely, by virtue of your mission, really unique in the world, the life of the Apostolic See and of the humble Successor of Peter who is speaking to you and as attentive observers of what happens here, you certainly do not miss any aspect of this activity. Your task is to have not only exact information about the events and facts that concern the life of the Church, but also and above all to give them an interpretation which grasps their authentic and deep meaning, and which enables yourselves and your governments to go to the heart of ecclesial problems and perceive them exactly.

The Church turns in fact to all men – whatever may be their belief or their ideology – who are seeking the common good with uprightness and sincerity. She wishes to safeguard the inviolable rights of the dignity of man, to whatever civilization or mentality he may belong, and she is open to the expectations, affirmations and concerns characteristic of man, in relation to truth, beauty and goodness.

Man's fundamental rights

6. In this wide perspective, you understand that the Holy See, with the episcopates of the various continents and with the whole Church, rightly attributes essential importance to man's fundamental rights, whether they are of a personal or social nature. That is an indispensable duty of the Church, and it is consoling to see our brothers of other Christian denominations working at it with all their might. Actually, as I wrote in my first encyclical *Redemptor Hominis*, "Man in the full truth of his existence, of his personal being and also of his continuity and social being – in the sphere of his own family. In the sphere of society and very diverse contexts. In the sphere of his own nations or people (perhaps still only that of his clan or tribe) and in the sphere of the whole of mankind – this man is the primary route that the Church must travel in fulfilling her mission: *he is the primary and fundamental way for the Church*, the way traced out by Christ himself" (no. 14). We find here the reason for the indefatigable action that the Church carries out with regard to man, seen as an individual person or through his integration in the public context of his existence.

It is precisely on considering this second dimension – that of man's community and social being – that the meaning of the rights of each people appears, for the nation is the "natural" society in which man, through the family, comes into the world and forms his own social identity; that is, he lives in a given culture which moulds the genius of his people and imprints on men, making them different from on another, the characteristics of their personality and their formation. As I said at the impressive seat of UNESCO in Paris on June 2 1980; "Culture is a specific way of man's "existing" and "being." Man always lives according to a culture which is specifically his, and which in its turn creates among men a tie which is also specifically theirs, determining the inner-human and social character of human existence. In the unity of culture as the specific way of human existence, there is rooted at the same time the plurality of cultures in the midst of which man lives. In this plurality, man develops, without losing, however, the essential contact with the unity of culture as the fundamental and essential dimension of his existence and his being" (no. 6). In my address last year, you remember, I drew your attention to the unifying character of culture, and I come back to it today to propose views of the Holy See on the international situation today.

Participation in the events of the life of peoples

7. Taking her stand precisely on these premises, the Church takes part attentively, even with deep emotion, in the events of the life of peoples, in particular, in certain parts of the world.

In the first place, I recall the seriously tense situations in several Central American countries, in which the number of victims caused by actions of repression or guerrilla warfare countries to grow, with a macabre monthly balance sheet, as if it were a question of an uncontrollable epidemic of violence.

I return to the situation in the Middle East in which an already fragile truce is continually threatened by constantly renewed acts of violence and by the rigidity of intransigent positions.

I mention a wound, still open, of internal terrorism and of international terrorism, which touches particularly, albeit in different contexts and for different reasons, regions which are so dear to us and which we love so much. I am thinking here of Northern Ireland: I am thinking also of what is happening in Italy.

Furthermore, during the last few weeks, my beloved country has found itself at the center of the world attention, of the Western world in particular, owing to the proclamation of "martial law," still in force today, the imprisonment of thousands of citizens, especially intellectuals and leaders of the workers' free organization, and the moral constraint imposed on citizens in order to survive and work. The aggravation of this situation is felt all the more in the conscience of peoples, especially those of Europe, in that they know very well the remarkable contribution, of sacrifice and of blood, that the Poles have made, particularly since the end of the eighteenth century, and with the holocaust of six million citizens during the last war, in order that the independent and sovereign existence of the nation, recovered only after the First World War, might be assured.

Particular problems in Poland

Belonging to this proud and hardworking people, I have felt particularly deeply in my heart the repercussions of the recent vicissitudes. But those of other countries make me suffer equally. For it is not only the son of Poland who is suffering, but also the visible Head of the Catholic Church, the leader of the Holy See, to whom all peoples, as I said at the beginning, are equally dear and close. It is impossible to be silent when the inviolable rights of man and the no less sacred ones of the different nations are endangered. The Holy See gives its attention to such problems in such a sad hour, for it considers that they involve not only political interests, but also and above all inestimable moral values, on which a human society worthy of the name rests.

It is consoling to see how the sufferings of these peoples – and without forgetting the situations recalled, I refer again in particular to Poland, which receives the aid of so many States and Organizations which I thank again – and how the tensions of this country are taken concretely into consideration and bring forth the common cooperation of governments. Such an action on the part of all peoples to which moral values are precious, is supported by the Holy See in the sphere of its own competence and in a way that corresponds to its mission, which does not have any political character.

The conviction is gaining ground daily in public opinion that the peoples must be able to choose freely the social organization to which they aspire for their own coun-

try, and that this organization should be in conformity with justice, in respect of freedom, religious faith, and human rights is general. It is a commonly shared conviction
that no people should be treated by other peoples as subordinate or as an instrument,
in defiance of equality which is inscribed in human conscience and recognized by the
norms of international law. Just as, in interpersonal relations, one party cannot do as
he likes with another as if he were an object, in the same way, in international life,
everything that attacks the free expression of the will of nations should be denounced.
The fact of divisions into spheres of hegemony, which may have had their origin in
particular and contingent situations should not justify their continuance, all the more
so if they tend to limit the sovereignty of others. Every people must be able to act
freely in what regards the free determination of its own destiny. The Church cannot
fail to give her support to such a conviction.

The interior peace of nations, too can be threatened in different ways: either
through an authoritarian form, already existing, which a people tries to overthrow in
order to arrive at a fresh form, more in conformity with its genius, or else through the
threat of totalitarian forms repugnant to the humanistic and religious culture of such
and such a people, which one would attempt to impose, with the support of ideologies
which, under pretext of a new social organization, do not respect man's free expression.

Confronted with these different situations, painful and sometimes dramatic,
always important and decisive for the life of nations, the Church, like a mother concerned about the good of persons and peoples, can never remain indifferent. The
action she exercises has a human and moral character, not concerned with political
calculations.

It is in this context, furthermore, that one must understand the active part I have
taken through my work of mediation in the controversy about the southern zone, in
order that the populations, so generous and worthy of esteem, of the two countries of
old and authentic Christian tradition – Chile and Argentina – may definitively advance
on the way of prosperity and progress, while respecting the inestimable treasure of
true peace.

The tragedy of the exiled
8. Always in this perspective of safeguarding and promoting human values, over and
above all evaluation of a political character, there should be considered the solicitude
of the Holy See for those who are "exiled" outside the frontiers of their country for
political reasons. This is a problem about which I wish to draw the attention of your
governments, as well as of the different international organizations.

This measure, a fundamentally violent one, is an attempt to get rid of citizens who
are disliked, or who disturb, by uprooting them from their native country and condemning them to a precarious and difficult life, in which they will often be victims of
discouragement and hardships as a result of the difficulties inherent in the search for
a job and in acclimatization to a new environment, even on the part of their respective
families.

It cannot escape the attention of anyone that exile is a serious violation of the
norms of life in society, clearly contrary to the universal Declaration of Human Rights
and to international law itself; and the consequences of such a punishment prove to be
dramatic on the individual, social and moral plane. Man must not be deprived of the

fundamental right of living and breathing in the country in which he was born, where there are the dearest memories of his family, the tombs of his ancestors, the culture which confers on him his spiritual identity and which nourishes it, the traditions which give him vitality and happiness, and all the human relationships which sustain and defend him.

In the Encyclical *Laborem Exercens* speaking of the phenomenon of a migration due to lack of work, I maintained that man, if he has the right to leave his country of origin, has also the right to return to it (cf. no. 23). I stressed the impoverishment that results for the country abandoned, as well as the duty of the host nation to see to it that the worker should not be "placed at a disadvantage" and that his "situation of constraint" should not be exploited (ibid.). But for the exiled, it is not a question of an emergency situation, a provisional matter, but of a real enforced exclusion, which strikes them in their deepest affections and may quite often correspond to what is called "civil death."

I hope that, thanks to the joint action of the authorities and of the responsible organizations, an adequate plan of action may be drawn up – in the frame of relevance of international law – in order to end in every country the tragedy of exile which is in conflict with the fundamental conquests of the human spirit.

At the same time, I cannot forget the situation in which several hundreds of thousands of refugees from South-East Asia find themselves, a situation which is being prolonged dramatically. They are received in holding centers, especially in Thailand, but they are waiting, as regards residence and work, for a definitive solution worthy of the respect due to man. Some nations, advanced on the economic plane, have already opened their frontiers to them; others again could and should engage in this noble competition, thus proving their real sensitiveness to these human masses, to these families deprived of elementary rights regarding their life, and forced to accept inaction and want.

Thinking of the responsibility, which weighs on all peoples of taking an interest in the situation of refugees, I launch a warm appeal to the heads of States of the world, and particularly to those who have received more abundant goods from Providence, in order that they may do everything in their power to meet the human aspirations of all those who are our brothers, either by welcoming them, or by extending the hospitality which has already been granted to them.

Thus, I cannot help thinking of the millions of men, women and children, including many sick and old persons, who have left Afghanistan and I am anxious also to mention the refugees from various African countries. They are nations which see a large part of their populations flee from their territory, obliged to seek elsewhere conditions of subsistence and necessary spaces of freedom. Their sufferings are also ours, and they want the generous, concrete and effective response of international solidarity.

Carrying out this duty, the Church, I repeat, is impelled solely by her love for the human person and by respect of his dignity, which has its source in God himself.

Work and the family
9. I recalled in the first place the guiding principle of the action of the Holy See in its relations with international life, namely that man "is the first way and the fundamental way of the Church." It is in this context that the two crucial problems concerning modern man, to which I devoted my ordinary *magisterium* this year, work and the

need by other men who play with interests contrary to the good of the person, and manipulate the latter at their pleasure.

That is why I wished to recall in the first place that man remains the subject of work, precisely as a person. I emphasized the fact that, when a one-sidedly materialistic civilization prevails, in which the subjective dimension of work is relegated to a secondary plane, man is treated as an instrument of production. Now, in actual fact, independently of the work that he carries out, he should be considered its efficient subject and it real creator and artisan. In this light, stress must be laid on the trade union rights of the world of work in view of the defense of a just wage and of the security of the person of the worker and of his family. They are rights which are opposed to the totalitarian tendencies of every system or organization which aims at suffocating them, of devouring them to its own advantage.

The real responsibility for the humanization of working conditions in every country is incumbent in the first place on the public authorities. And there is formed, furthermore, a network of exchanges and dependences which influence international life and are capable of creating various forms of legalized exploitation, so to speak. It is well known, in fact, that highly industrialized countries establish prices as high as possible for their products, seeking at the same time to keep the prices of raw materials and semi-manufactured products as low as possible. It is for this reason, among others, that there is an ever increasing disproportion between the national income of rich countries and those of the poorest countries.

In this field the international Organizations – mainly UNO, ILO, FAO – have a primary role to play. I address to them all my encouragements to pursue with ardor and wisdom the purposes for which they have been established, for they must aim at promoting the dignity and rights of the human person in the framework of each State, under conditions of equality and parity.

11. You see what a horizon opens to the long-term action of the nations which you represent, and your understand also why the Church intervenes with frankness and humility in problems of work, indicating the best directions to follow. She intends to encourage good will, dictate principles and, if necessary, denounce dangers and imbalances. If the progressive solution of the social question must be sought in the direction of a more human life, if work is for man and not man for work, if the social degradation of the subject of work, the exploitation of workers and the growing areas of poverty and even of hunger are being discovered with more fear every day, then it cannot escape the attention of anyone to what extent the Church feels committed to this cause, which she considers her mission and her service.

The Church, through her divine mandate, is on the side of man. Safeguarding the dignity of work, she is aware of contributing, thanks to the peaceful and liberating power of truth, to the defense of the dignity of man and of society. I am certain that you will do your utmost to collaborate in this great plan, in this admirable plan. Likewise, your countries will want to authorize the necessary efforts to continue, along the same line, the work of the advancement of man, particularly in the difficult and complex field of the problems regarding human work.

The help of the Church for the affirmation of [a] new humanism
12. The problem of the family, closely linked with that of work, is certainly an even

more crucial one for the life of present-day society. Serving the natural development of man which consists, normally and universally, in forming a family, the Church carries out one of her primary and indispensable duties. That explains the solicitude that, on the occasion of the last Synod, the episcopates of the whole world, with me, manifested for the family, in all the socio-cultural and political situations of the various continents, and I know very well that you have devoted particular attention to it. The apostolic exhortation quoted above adopted its indications and suggestions.

Taking into account the reality which appears in the context of the rapid change in the mentalities and morals, and also the perils for man's real dignity, the Church, ready to accept sound contributions of all cultures, feels that she must help a "new humanism" to assert itself. It will be clear to everyone that the seeds of disintegration which are at work within so many families have as their unavoidable consequence the decay of society. It is necessary to make the family again a community of persons that lives the indivisible unity of conjugal love and accepts the indissolubility of the conjugal pact, in spite of the contrary opinion of all those who nowadays are of the opinion that it is difficult, or even impossible, to bind oneself to a person for the whole of one's life, or who are swept along by a culture which rejects the indissolubility of marriage and which openly mocks the commitment of spouses to faithfulness.

Mention must then be made, still in the context of the service of man, of the very serious responsibility of the *transmission of human life*. The Church is aware of the difficulties that the present social and cultural situation raises for this mission of man, while knowing to what extent the latter is urgent and irreplaceable. But, I repeat again, "she takes the side of life." Unfortunately, this project is threatened by the dangers inherent in scientific progress, by the spread of a mentality really contrary to life, and by governmental interventions which aim at limiting the freedom of spouses in their decisions with regard to their children, as well as by the discriminations made in international subsidies, which are sometimes granted for the purpose of facilitating contraception programs.

In the same way, it is necessary to recall forcefully the right and the duty of spouses to take charge of the education of their children, especially by choosing an education in conformity with their religious faith. The State and the Church have the obligation to give families all the help possible, in order that they may carry out their educational tasks properly. All those in society who are responsible for schools must never forget that the parents were constituted by God himself as the first and principal educators of their children, and that their right is absolutely inalienable.

For a charter of family rights
13. Since, moreover, the family is "the first vital cell of society," as the Second Vatican Council said (Decree *Apostolicam Actuositatem*, no. 11), far from withdrawing into itself, it must open to the social environment that surrounds it. In this way the role that the family has in relation to society is clearly shown. In fact, the family is the first school of social life for its young members, and it is irreplaceable. Acting in this way, the family becomes the most effective instrument of humanization and personalization of a society, which runs the risk of becoming more and more depersonalized and 'massified,' and therefore inhuman and dehumanizing, with the negative consequences of so many forms of escapism, such as, for example, alcoholism, drugs, and even terrorism.

Moreover, families, alone or in a group, can and must dedicate themselves to multiple works of social service, especially for the sake of the poor, and their social task is also called to find its expression in the form of political intervention. In other words, families must be the first to work in order to ensure that the laws and institutions of the State will abstain from doing harm, but above all, that they will support and defend positively the rights and duties of the family. In this sense families must be more and more aware of being the "protagonists" of "family policy" and assume responsibility for changing society. They are also called to cooperate in a new international order.

Then, too, society must realize that it is in the service of the family. The family and society have a complementary function in the defense and promotion of the good of all men and of the whole man.

I am sure that your have directed particular attention to all the rights of the family which the Synod Fathers enumerated and which the Holy See proposes to study more deeply, by drawing up a "charter of the rights of the family" to propose to the circles concerned and to the authorities of the various States as well as those of the competent international organizations.

The Lord must build

14. As you see, in devoting her attention to the family, safeguarding its rights, and seeking to promote the dignity of its members, the Church intends to propose a positive contribution not only to the human person – the main object of her solicitude – but also to the orderly progress, prosperity and peace of the various nations. It cannot be thought, in fact, that a people will grow in a worthy way, far less that God will continue to pour his blessings upon it – for "unless the Lord builds the house, those who build it labor in vain; unless the Lord watches over the city, the watchman stays awake in vain" (Ps 126 [127]: 1) – where the fundamental rights of man and woman are trampled upon, where life is stifled in the mother's womb, where blind and irresponsible permissiveness allows spiritual and moral values, without which not only families but also nations collapse, to be undermined at their foundation.

On this really important point I appeal to your feelings and I hope that in all your countries priority will be given, thanks to provisions of the judicial, social and social insurance order, to the major concerns for the good of the *familiaris consortio*, that is, the "family community" which constitutes man's most precious good.

Good prevails

15. Your Excellencies, Ladies and Gentlemen!

In the promising field which opens to the joint action of the Church and States, each one working autonomously in its own sphere of responsibility for the defense of peace in the world, for the cultural, spiritual and moral elevation of man and of society and, particularly, for the promotion of the rights concerning work and the family, our optimism must not fail, nor our hope. Certainly the times are difficult, and dark clouds are rising on the horizon. But let us not be afraid. The forces of good are greater! They work in silence for the construction, begun again constantly, of a healthier and more just world. Millions and millions of men want peace in their country and the possibility of being really free men, with a constructive spirit, in their families and at work. Let us help them!

The Church will never fail to play her role, even at the cost of paying dearly in the best of her sons.

I wish each of the Heads of State whom you represent, each of your governments, and your fellow countrymen, that brotherhood, mutual understanding and sincere and voluntary collaboration may grow among the peoples. That peace, the fruit of justice, understanding and love, may be established, this peace which, for Christians, is "God's gift," and which has one foundation: the image and likeness of men with God the Father, because they were created by him, and redeemed by his Son, Jesus Christ.

To you all, to your families, I repeat the traditional greeting of "a happy new year": a really happy year, the source and token of good, and I do so with the words of the solemn blessing, inspired by the Bible, formulated by St. Francis, the universal saint, the eighth centenary of whose birth we are celebrating this year. "May the Lord bless you and keep you! – May he show you his face and have pity on you! – May he turn his eyes upon you and give you peace!"

January 15, 1983
(*OR*, February 21, 1983, pp. 6–8)

1. It is always a great joy to welcome you all as a group in this house at the threshold of a new year. I am thus able to meet again each of the Ambassadors with whom I have had a meeting, both personal and official, on the occasion of the presentation of their Letters of Credence. I establish contact with the other members of the Embassies. And, beyond your persons, I have as it were the impression of dialoguing with the peoples and the nations, with the Heads of State and the Governments you represent, that is to say, with a hundred and five countries, very diverse in terms of demographic importance, culture, economic power, but all welcome here with the same respect and the same good will. Yes, it is always a moving moment of my pontificate; and I greet especially the new members of the Diplomatic Corps accredited to the Holy See during the course of the last year. For several countries, their missions have been elevated to the rank of Embassy: those of Great Britain, the Principality of Monaco, the Sovereign and Military Order of Malta; others have decided to establish diplomatic relationships with the Holy See: Denmark, Norway, Sweden.

With his customary delicacy, and in serving as your spokesman, your beloved Dean has undertaken to enumerate a certain number of initiatives of my pontificate that have a spiritual or peaceful impact. I heartily thank him for his generous remarks. May his wishes be fulfilled, with the grace of God, that the Apostolic See may become, at its own level, an ever more adequate and effective instrument of dialogue among men, in order to serve them better!

This collective encounter takes on a relief all the more marked in that it allows us, while exchanging greetings, to recall some problems vital to international relations.

Importance of dialogue for peace

2. It was precisely *dialogue for peace* that was the theme chosen for the recent World Day of Peace, and you understand that I return to this theme here, not so much to demonstrate its necessity, its possibility, its qualities or its difficulties, as I have done in my Message, but rather to evoke its application to concrete situations.

In this Message, I addressed a particular appeal to *you diplomats*, saying, "whose noble profession it is, among other things, to deal with disputed points and to seek to resolve them through dialogue and negotiation, in order to avoid recourse to arms, or to take the place of the belligerents" (no. 11). And I paid tribute to this work of patience and perseverance. This insistence is not new for the Holy See. Already my venerable predecessor Paul VI said to the Diplomatic Corps in 1965: "The more the right is forgotten, neglected . . . the more apparent it becomes . . . that it is reason, human understanding, negotiation, calm and free of passion – and therefore in the last analysis, gentlemen, diplomacy – that must regulate human relationships and that these things alone can construct the edifice of peace" (*AAS* 57, 1965, pp. 231–232). Yes, if the dialogue is the concern of everyone to break down the barriers of selfishness, lack of understanding and aggression (cf. Message 1983, no. 11) after the Heads of State and Government, the diplomats are surely the first concerned. They are, they ought to be, masters in the art of this dialogue that supposes and requires (ibid., no. 6) openness to the real problems of the other, consideration of what makes the difference and the specific nature of the other party, who can never be reduced to an object, the acceptance of the fact that each one is a responsible partner and thus has elements to offer to the solution, the adherence to solely peaceful means, and above all, beyond the various viewpoints often difficult to reconcile, the search for what is finally common to the two parties, vital to their existence and required by the common concern, because it has to do with what is true, right and just. Without this positive finality, there is no true dialogue. And there is reason to fear today a fresh outbreak of mutual distrust, which utilizes even certain proposals of dialogue as means of propaganda.

Dialogue demands reciprocity

I underline an important point: dialogue demands *reciprocity*. I insisted on this in my homily for this January 1st with regard to the progressive reduction of nuclear or conventional weapons: the parties in question must be committed in equal measure and must travel together the various stages of disarmament, striving to reach, without delay, the maximum reduction. I would hope that this final objective never be lost sight of in all the negotiations on disarmament at Geneva or elsewhere. This reciprocal effort applies to the other types of negotiations: peace can never be constructed by some without the others, in a unilateral way. When, then, will men ever be convinced that in the last analysis the welfare of a people can never be accomplished in opposition to the welfare of another people, that one people will never be able to destroy another, and that in any case there are rights of persons and communities to respect, destructive procedures – and perilous for all – to avoid, to discard?

No, dialogue for peace is not easy; it is demanding, it is strewn with snares; and there are some who, annoyed at having to recognize or concede some reasonable proposition, prefer to reject it, or furnish it with conditions that render it impossible, or delay it indefinitely. Certainly it requires clear-headedness to reveal the possible snares; it demands firmness and perseverance. But the difficulties do not prevent there always being something to be gained by endeavoring to resume dialogue on solid bases and by helping the other party to resume it without humiliation; indeed this is a necessity. Otherwise, where would this refusal to dialogue lead? Would it not lead to maintaining a status quo of injustice or oppression, to cold war or even to war?

It is in this sense that the Holy See appreciates the commitment of diplomats and pays its respect. And for your part, I dare to hope that you will find a source of inspiration and encouragement in the way the Holy See, in addition to its exhortations, becomes itself involved in bilateral diplomatic relations and in participating in international conferences and institutions: it makes of dialogue, founded on truth and respect for the other party, the privileged method and instrument of its action and its relationships, striving to recommend it to others and urging them to adopt it as the most suitable means for resolving their difficulties and differences. The fact that so many countries have been anxious to establish diplomatic relationships with the Holy See attests to this reciprocal trust.

Regarding Lebanon and the Near East

3. What is one to make of these principles when one looks hard in the face the various hot-beds of war, the states of war, the guerrilla activity or the grave tensions that exist today throughout the world?

Regarding *Lebanon*, for example, it is evident that the Holy See, while offering relief after each episode of the drama, as everyone knows, has never ceased to encourage the resumption of negotiations and the search for a global settlement for the whole region of the Near East, "convinced above all that there can be no true peace without justice, and that there will be no justice if there are not recognized and accepted in a stable, adequate and equitable way, the rights of all peoples concerned" (cf. my discourse of September 15, *L'Osservatore Romano* in English, September 20, 1982, p. 7). Let us hope that this cause is progressing in the talks that have begun. The parties must cease to live in fear or to resort to violence, to terrorism or to reprisals; they must conduct an honest search, accept and apply the conditions of existence and security for all, in peace, dignity, liberty, tolerance and reconciliation.

If the case of the Near East is typical in the extent of its disasters, in the harshness of the problems to be resolved and the multiplicity of the communities involved, we must not forget all the other areas of combat, tensions, sufferings.

The mission of the Holy See is always to contribute to making everyone reach a better understanding and renounce what is unbefitting, to entertain the hope for a solution, to point out the ethical conditions for a true peace. It strives to do this even when its appeals are difficult to hear in the midst of the conflicts.

Holy See's distress over tragic events

Suffice it to recall the prolonged war between *Iran and Iraq*, with its wake of destructions, deaths, rekindled hatred: the Holy See is distressed over this human tragedy; it encourages the neighboring countries and the international community to facilitate true dialogue, begging them not to resign themselves to this destructive undertaking, and above all not to take advantage of these local rivalries to further short-sighted governmental interests of one or another country or to engage in the traffic of arms.

How can we close our eyes to the tragic situation of the *Afghan* people, legitimately proud of its independence, who find themselves involved in a fate that is resolving itself by so many victims, so much misery, and such an exodus of refugees? Is it impossible then to strive toward attitudes that would inspire the trust necessary to stop all this?

I think too of the countries of *Central America*: can we not hope that true internal dialogue will permit the resolution of the serious problems of social miseries and internal tensions, and that the parties involved not become victims of materialistic options nor be subjected to interferences from outside that are trying to radicalize the oppositions?

One could mention a good many other places where tensions remains alive and dangerous, easily degenerating into acts of violence as in Northern Ireland; and even situations that are apparently calm, but that hide a false peace, without progress, because legitimate rights remain unrecognized, with no possibility of a true dialogue between the social and political partners.

The Holy See does not wish to believe in the inevitability of the state of war nor of guerilla conflict for achieving justice. Justice and peace are ultimately on the road of a true dialogue, free and without deceit, when one has the courage to undertake it, when one prides himself on taking the risk and when the other countries respect it. Of these principles, which ought to be evident to all, the Holy See will make itself, with you, with your consent, the herald.

Humanitarian aspect of the Church's commitment

4. I come now to an aspect that characterizes the *diplomacy and international activity of the Holy See: humanitarian concern*, the shunning of everything gravely injurious to the life, to the dignity, of individuals and communities, whatever be their party or minority situation. This preoccupation certainly should inhabit and inspire all the diplomats of the various countries.

I know that the object of negotiations is far larger than this, as I remarked in my Message of Peace (no. 10). The Holy See does not ignore the importance of territorial questions, nor of commercial and economic questions like those, for example, that will be treated this year at Belgrade, at the meeting of the [UNCTAD], and it willingly offers its contribution to the resolution of these, within the limits of its competence and means.

But the Church feels particularly called on to make itself, as much as possible, the *Good Samaritan of those who are left abandoned along the path of history*. And when I say "the Church," I am thinking not only of diplomacy, but of the various organisms of the Holy See, like the Pontifical Council *Cor Unum*, the many ecclesial institutions, and all those who act, on the field of conflicts and tensions, according to their Christian conscience. Yes, the Church would like to make itself above all the voice of those without a voice, the poor, the victims of every kind, to draw attention to fundamental human rights that have been forgotten or despised, to the problems of minorities, to the threats that from time to time weigh on populations. This charity is intended to be open in all directions, for all the forms of threats, for the citizens of all the nations. The Holy See, which in the name of the Church has the opportunity of entering into relationships with the leaders of countries, hopes that its intervention will at least be accepted, that it will afford a chance for relief for the victims. It requires nothing; it demands nothing for itself; it lends its voice and offers a humanitarian gesture. It has no intention of annoying, of condemning; it wishes only to save. A State that might be tempted to harden itself today before an intervention, courteous and discreet, of the Holy See will perhaps be happy tomorrow to benefit by it for one of its appeals to a foreign power. The universal vocation of the Church must be to the eyes of everyone a proof of its disinterestedness and impartiality. It is man, as man, that concerns it, and all the more so in that it sees in him the image of the Creator, the brother of Christ.

Eliminating various types of oppression

5. To take a few typical examples now, ladies and gentlemen, you can understand then why, in its humanitarian concern, the Holy See strives to recommend clemency, even pardon, for those *condemned to death*, above all when these have been condemned for political reasons, which can moreover be very changeable, tied to the personality of those in power at the moment.

Likewise, the Church takes to heart the fate of those who are subjected to *torture*, whatever be the political regime, for nothing in its eyes can justify this degradation which unfortunately is often accompanied by barbaric and repulsive savagery.

Likewise, it cannot remain silent over the criminal action that consists in *making* a certain number of persons *disappear* without trial, leaving their families in cruel uncertainty besides.

The Apostolic See is intent on assisting peoples to rediscover the path of honor, begging them to see that such practices be eliminated, as also all other forms of arbitrary arrests and detentions, concentration camps and various types of oppression. Today, I am anxious besides to acknowledge the efforts that have led to a certain progress in this area, and I give these my full support.

Surely we are not unaware that in other countries internments are practiced without guarantee of justice, and even numerous summary executions continue to take place, under the pretext of political opposition. The Holy See regrets, for its part, not being able to persuade those responsible for such injustice. We have only to hope that international appeals, whether political or humanitarian, may continue to intervene in behalf of the victims, on points where international law and the declarations of the United Nations so explicitly aim at protecting people against such exactions.

Finally, even within the limits of open conflict, there are practices that reach a particularly inhuman level, for example when entire populations are victims of chemical and biological weapons, which the international conscience condemns and even, since long ago, international law condemns (cf. *Protocole de Geneve* of 1925).

Displaced peoples

6. The humanitarian concern of the Holy See embraces also the *displacements of peoples*, which today have become more and more frequent and intense. There are, of course, phenomena of migration that take place within a context of dialogue, respecting the dignity of the displaced persons, for example when immigrant workers are welcomed with their families, and when they are honestly paid and included in systems of social security, or again when contracts are entered into with foreign business to place at their disposal a labor force that remains free and well treated. But there are people who come or are sent to a foreign land for motives and under conditions that do a disservice to the host country. And above all there exist hordes of workers who have been forced to expatriate and move to a foreign country for a work that resembles forced labor, under wretched conditions of climate, salary and housing. Also worthy of mention are those who have been forced into exile on account of their political or religious opinions, and those who have been refused the possibility of rejoining their fatherland and their family. On this point, efforts would be possible that would not endanger the security of nations, and a number of countries have recently distinguished themselves by taking steps forward in this humanitarian direction.

Refugee situation

But I am thinking here especially of the more and more numerous crowds of *refugees*: those of South-East Asia, of whom I have spoken on several occasions and whose fate remains so precarious; those of Afghanistan, the Middle East; those that are found in Europe, those of Central America; those of a number of African countries which are in great distress. Has not the number of refugees in the world been estimated at ten million? The causes are varied, sometimes frontier situations inherited from a colonial past, natural catastrophes, hunger, but also the violation of the most elementary rights, committed by despotic powers, racial, religious, political persecutions, insecurity due to conflicts or guerilla activity. The persons who are obliged to emigrate often belong to the most humble social groups, with a high percentage of orphans, widows, elderly. These uprooted populations desperately nourish the desire to return to their land, their culture, their society; and their survival is often poor, for most are guests of countries already extremely poor, in several regions of Africa, in Thailand, in Pakistan. It seems necessary then that the international community aid these countries, with purely humanitarian and peaceful motives, and that an effort be made moreover, thanks to a politic of justice and peace, to do away with the causes of a situation that is so lamentable, but not inevitable. May our generation rise to this challenge!

Problem of hunger

7. I made allusion to *hunger*, and I would like to draw more explicit attention to this distress. A certain number of countries – in Asia, in Central America, in Africa, above all in the sub-Saharan zones – are suffering a food shortage of catastrophic human consequences. For the last few years, the per capita food production has been steadily diminishing, though the population continues to increase, and though there would after all be enough resources in the entire world to face this situation. Certainly, natural elements are a factor here – prolonged drought, for example, increases the difficulties of the fight against hunger – but these things do not justify resignation and fatalism. Agricultural politics better suited to the alimentary needs of the population must be applied. Economic and commercial cooperation between rich countries and poor countries ought to find more advantageous forms for the farms in desperation. International governmental and non-governmental organizations should redouble their courage and inventive spirit in an effort to reverse the trend of famine that is so severe in some places. In short, action is urgent, for even today populations are being decimated by hunger and if efforts are not intensified, the catastrophe will assume unprecedented proportions and will attest to a culpable lack of solidarity on the part of the peoples that have an abundant food supply.

The forgotten poor

8. I am well aware that these things are known by Governments and international institutions, and that sound initiatives have been undertaken. But, in its desire to lend its voice to the poor, the Holy See is anxious to remind diplomats and public opinion of the urgency of these needs. Indeed, if certain countries are always of interest to the great powers for strategic or economic reasons, even to the point of attracting upon themselves greed and war, it is others that are in danger of being completely *forgotten!* Sometimes it is because they have less material wealth to exchange, although their populations are just as deserving and just as needy. Sometimes they even appear doomed to extinction and to the loss of their independence, especially the small countries, because they are unable to meet their debts. In other cases, the liberties of a people, its faculty of self-determination, have been smothered in an effort to suppress national identity and absorb the country into a foreign whole. Finally, within nations themselves, *ethnic and religious minorities* have sometimes experienced a somewhat similar fate: they are not respected in their identity even though they do not refuse to collaborate loyally in the common good. The Church experiences anxiety over the lot of all those who are not sufficiently taken into account.

Terrorism, drugs

9. In its care for humanity, the Holy See cannot remain aloof with regard to the plagues that your countries continue to dread and to combat: *terrorism, abductions, drug traffic* that is so harmful to the youth, etc. Here too the Church, which well knows how

seriously peace is threatened by such practices, is above all concerned to plead for the innocent victims. Certain of these practices are performed with the sordid objective of fraudulent traffic and gain; others assume the pretext of political combat. But the Church reaffirms the position that no motive is sufficient to justify these things. Today, as is well known, they have a tendency to rely more and more on international networks. A unanimous denunciation should continue to discourage all these terrorist activities; they would not be successful if they were not accompanied by real international collaboration. No country should refuse its participation when such grave problems, which go beyond any frontiers, are at issue. By this means, progress is possible, which I am pleased to underline: has not a considerable decrease been noticed in the case of airplane hijacking since international solidarity has shown its firmness?

Religious convictions

10. Finally, among the grave blows to the dignity of man, I cannot fail to mention once again those leveled against his intimate convictions, especially his *religious convictions*, against the free expression of his faith, his vital connections with the religious community to which he belongs. Last November 16 the Holy See's representative at the Conference on security and cooperation in Europe, at Madrid, expressed in this regard certain precisions and aspirations which are slow in being taken into account (cf. *L'Osservatore Romano*, November 17, 1982). The Holy See – and one can easily understand why – will never cease drawing the world's attention to the violations of religious liberty, which assume a variety of forms, brutal or subtle, always dangerous and unjust, in so many countries.

Independence of the Holy See's activity

11. Lastly, Your Excellencies, ladies and gentlemen, I would like to draw your attention to a practice to which the Holy See is attached, in its humanitarian concern and in its contribution to the cause of peace. To serve the common good, the cause of the poor and the oppressed, the Apostolic See is firmly convinced that it must act in all independence. It is then prepared to listen to all human, religious and political expressions, *to open its door* to all who, in fact, have some responsibility, some influence, in the matter. This evidently does not mean to say that the Holy See recognizes the legitimacy of political representation of such persons, nor that it approves the ideology they may profess. The role of a priest, of a bishop, the duty of a Pope is to receive the persons, if this can be of service to a progress in justice and in peace; and precisely to encourage them, with all clarity, in this direction, to exhort them, without any compromise whatever, to renounce the means of violence and terrorism in support of the cause of the poor which they claim to be defending – and this cause is real and important. The Holy See is not exclusive, and it is ready to deal with everyone, if it judges it salutary and prudent to do so.

Clear and welcoming

12. In short, the Church wishes to be *clear*, but it also wishes to be *welcoming*, like Christ. She knows that the power of evil is great; the hardening can endure; she is without illusions. But she *can never despair of a change in people* even when they continue to offend, even to persecute her. She sends out an appeal to dialogue. She strives to arouse the sense of truth, of justice, of fraternity, at least of prudence, which

may lie dormant in the human conscience, which is never totally perverted, despite certain contrary ideologies. She has in view the welfare of people who are suffering, in great numbers, behind these situations of distress. She wishes to entreat the world to offer these relief. In her opinion, the major obstacles erected by certain persons in positions of responsibility will inevitably collapse in the long run, for the generations renew themselves. Nevertheless, she will not yield to the present trials. In short, her attitude is built on confidence in the progress of persons and in the future. Who can reproach her for this?

I dare to add that, on the part of the Church, this is not a facile attitude. Hers is not a demagogic language. Well aware is she of her own inadequacies; her members are far from being exempt from weakness, from cowardice, today as in the past; in any case, her means do not permit her to follow up on all the humanitarian causes. The Holy See knows its limits, and it is delighted with the convergent contribution of so many persons and institutions in this domain. Its role is then to acknowledge their worthy efforts and to encourage them, whether they be Catholic or non-confessional. Thus, last year, I was happy to go to Geneva and encourage the International Labor Organization for social justice, and the International Red Cross for humanitarian aid. But I can say that the Church also has had to pay the price of its involvement. Its members are exposed, often those of the highest rank. How many priests, religious and lay missionaries, bishops, have paid for their charity with their liberty, with their health or even with their life? And these institutions continue to care for the wounds of those who are smitten, right and left. It is often with bare hands that she must defend the objective and inalienable rights of man. In you, Your Excellencies, ladies and gentlemen, she has come to find allies, not of herself, but of the cause of man.

Blessings to all

13. We have just ended, in the Catholic liturgy, the Christmas and Epiphany season, which gives meaning to all of your New Year's wishes. This mystery has revealed the Son of God present in the humanity of Jesus, in solidarity with our human journey so that we might be sharers in his love and in his life.

In these sentiments of faith, I pray the Lord to fill you with his blessings; to bless you yourselves and your families; to bless each of your countries. Do we not all express ardent hopes for the well-being, the peace, the liberty, the social and spiritual progress of our own country, as I myself do for my native land? May we all respond, each in our way, to our sublime vocation as shepherds of the peace that God has entrusted to man!

January 14, 1984
(*OR*, January 30, 1984, pp. 6–8)

1. Your spokesman, the Dean of the Diplomatic Corps and for the first time a representative of an African country, has interpreted your sentiments and good wishes in a manner that has moved all of us and has deeply touched my heart. With a delicacy and clarity for which I deeply thank him, he placed before us a certain number of important problems of justice and peace, which interest Governments and the entire international community, and which are the subject of the constant concern of the Holy See. I am grateful to all of you who are here today and who thus associate yourselves with the remarks made by his Excellency Mr. Joseph Amichia.

In a few moments, I hope to be able to greet each one of you individually. For now, I express to you my cordial wishes for the New Year, to each one of you of whom only God knows the needs, the deep aspirations and eventually the secret trials, to each of your families, to the entire personnel who staff your embassies and devote themselves together with you to the worthy representation of your countries, and to each of your countries. In asking God for a year of happiness and peace upon the whole world, I pray also that he may bequeath his light and his peace upon your hearts as a source of courage and hope in your lives.

In this traditional meeting, we are invited each year to look together at the international scene, to discern therein the comforting or the disturbing aspects which command the involvement of all people of good will, and especially the commitment of those who, like you, have the mission to weave a network of peacemaking relations by means of the diplomatic process.

2. As of this date, there are 108 countries which have established diplomatic relations with the Holy See. Since the exchange of greetings last year, Belize and Nepal were accredited, and this week, it was announced that the United States of America and the Holy See are to establish diplomatic relations – an event whose significance can easily be appreciated. As I stated when I first met with the Diplomatic Corps on January 12, 1979, the Holy See would be pleased to see here other Ambassadors, especially from countries which have in this regard a time-honored tradition, especially from those which can be regarded as Catholic.

Besides the Sovereign Military Order of Malta, whose mission has been raised to the rank of embassy, we are very happy to welcome the Ambassadors of Sweden, Belize, Fiji and Cape Verde, whose governments are for the first time represented in this solemn assembly of the Diplomatic Corps. We also welcome the twenty-four new Ambassadors who have presented their credentials during the course of the past year. Among your countries, there is a great variety and diversity of geographical dimension, culture, history and religious belief. There are countries in which the Catholic community is practically the entire population. There are others in which Catholics form a large proportion, and some also in which they are only a tiny minority. But with all, the Apostolic See tries to consider the human problems of justice, peace and development, and all the questions relating to the international moral order, which confront these countries, their neighbors, and the entire human community. On the part of the Holy See, there is the same welcome, the same esteem for each of the nations represented, and the same regard for the sovereign States that govern them.

In 1950, only twenty-five countries were represented at the Holy See by an Ambassador Extraordinary and Plenipotentiary, and twenty-one by a Minister. The great increase in number is worth some reflection. It seems to indicate that the Holy See, in its unique position of spiritual and moral authority in the service of peace for all, according to the spirit of the Gospel of Christ, and without material interests to defend, has been able to inspire the trust of an increasing number of nations. This includes the countries whose populations are Christian, but of an Orthodox or Protestant confession, and also countries whose populations profess other religions and beliefs. The Holy See sees in this especially a major responsibility, which it wishes to fulfill as well as possible.

But this situation derives also and above all from the fact that the number of sovereign States has multiplied during the past thirty years. The United Nations knows this well, since it receives them solemnly into membership. It is largely the effect of a process of decolonization, which has permitted numerous peoples to come to full sovereignty and the free management of their own public affairs by citizens who have emerged from their own ranks. In itself, whether the past has been more or less happy, more or less marked by progress at different levels – and these are not matters for us to judge here – it is a situation which corresponds to a historical evolution, and which expresses the dignity, the responsibility and maturity of a variety of peoples, equal to each other in rights and duties, and in fidelity to their traditions, cultures and needs. The Church gladly welcomes such an evolution; she herself has been in the vanguard in what pertains to her. She regards this situation with great hope, and these diplomatic relations are a sign of relief.

Limits to the attainment of independence

3. Does this process of the birth and recognition of sovereign States have limits? Certainly it is a process that has not yet run its course. But it is a delicate question to determine, because it is a complex matter of judicial, political, and historical elements, which must be carefully weighed and always considered in the light of the common good of the populations concerned and of their will, unequivocally expressed. It is always to be hoped that the transition will be accomplished without violence, and with respect for the rights of all.

Some peoples are impatiently waiting to become independent and to be recognized as such within the UN. We share their hope. Among these we could at least mention Namibia, whose slow and laborious progress in this regard has not yet come to fruition.

It is also desirable that other populations, such as the Palestinian people, have their own homeland. This has always seemed to us a condition for justice and peace in the troubled Middle East, provided that the security of all the peoples of the region, including Israel, is guaranteed.

Finally, there exist in our day new and subtle forms of dependence for which the term "colonialism" is carefully avoided, but which have their most negative and questionable characteristics, with limitation of independence and political liberties, with economic subjugation – and all this, even though the peoples concerned seem to enjoy their own government institutions, but one does not know to what extent they are in accord with the wishes of the citizens.

On the other hand some sovereign countries, whose independence is long standing or recent, see themselves at times threatened in their integrity by the internal contestation of a minority which goes so far as to aim at or demand secession. The cases are complex and different, each one requiring a different judgment, according to an ethic which takes into account both the rights of nations based on the homogeneous culture of peoples (see my address to UNESCO, June 2, 1980, paragraph 15), and on the right of States to their integrity and sovereignty. We desire that beyond all passion – and always avoiding violence – one may arrive at well-articulated and balanced political forms which will know how to respect cultural, ethnic and religious peculiarities, and in the general the rights of minorities.

In any case, the well-founded good of the sovereignty of States and the progress which it represents do not preclude but rather impel them to establish agreements, alliances, "communities" and regional or continental organizations, which will better enable them to confront together the enormous problems which spare practically no country at a time of economic crisis, of technological change, and their repercussions on daily life, especially the conditions of employment. To the extent that they do not compromise the prerogatives of sovereignty, and to the extent that they are freely agreed [upon], such new forms of solidarity are indeed progress.

Rights and duties of a sovereign people

4. What are, finally, the rights and duties of a sovereign people? They would naturally include the right to choose, without foreign interference, its political regime and those charged with the exercise of the authority of the State to determine and apply the measures judged necessary for the common good of the nation, as a means of furthering its destiny in accordance with the characteristics of its culture.

But just as the human person has inviolable rights and corresponding duties, so do peoples have duties with respect to one another, and States vis-à-vis the peoples. Peoples must prove themselves worthy of them by an increased sense of responsibility. States must be at the service of the authentic culture proper to each (see UNESCO address referred to above), at the service of the common good, of every person under their jurisdiction, and of associations. They must seek to establish for everyone favorable living conditions according to the essential needs and possibilities of the country, and in an equitable relationship between the living standards of different citizens and social environments. They are no less bound to respect more and more the fundamental rights and liberties of persons, of families and intermediate bodies of society, including freedom of conscience and of religion. States must offer to all, by law, a guarantee of justice. They must take into account the reasonable aspirations of the citizenry, including the desire for political participation. Whenever there is conflict within the society, they must absolutely shun the use of arbitrary procedures, torture, abductions, banishment, forced emigration of families or execution after summary trial. Such activities are unworthy of self-respecting sovereign States. One might ask if the international community – to whose principles and charters such countries moreover subscribe – could not denounce more clearly such an illogical situation and provide a remedy for it. For our part, we make a solemn appeal to the conscience of these Governments, before God and their peoples.

In some sovereign countries which have achieved national unity and taken their place in history as nations, internal peace remains unfortunately precarious for other reasons: because [these countries] must confront armed rebellions that tear the people family, take on their full meaning. They are two fundamental problems not only for man's personal life, but also and above all for the whole of society. As such, they concern the life of each of your nations, because they form, as it were, its essential supports, the tissue that binds them together.

You know that the document on work was desired as a contribution of the thought of the Church today on the social question, for the ninetieth anniversary of the Encyclical *Rerum Novarum* of my predecessor Leo XIII, and in the wake of the pontifical teaching which developed during these ninety years on the subject of work. It was a matter of reflection on the considerable evolution that work has experienced in the modern world, up to the universal dimensions it has reached at present. You know, too, that the exhortation on the family gathered together and summed up the contributions of the Synod of Bishops, which met here in Rome in the month of October 1980. In this way there was drawn up, in line with the "Proposals" that resulted from the bishops' discussion, a complete treatise on the present problems of family life, comparing it with the traditional positions on the immutable doctrine of the Church, which have their source in Revelation.

Work and the family are the two poles around which man's life has been unfolded from the dawn of humanity. Work exists in terms of the family and the family can develop only through the contribution of work. The latter is the foundation on which the family life, which is a natural right and human vocation, is built. These two spheres of values – one concerning work, and the other springing from the family character of human life – must be united correctly with each other and be imbued correctly with each other. Interaction between work and the family enables me this year to recall to your benevolent attention [to] the fundamental values of these two realities which the Church wishes to proclaim and support at all costs, for they concern closely and even intimately the life and the condition of man, apart from considerations of a theological character, characteristic of Christian civilization. Work and the family are a human good, a social good.

Man remains the subject of work
10. Today, the problem of work has taken on world proportions. "While in the past," as I wrote at the beginning of the encyclical, "the class question was specially highlighted as the center of this issue, in more recent time it is the "world" question that is emphasized. Thus, not only the sphere of class is taken into consideration, but also the world sphere of inequality and injustice and as a consequence, not only the class dimension, but also the world dimension of the tasks involved in the path toward the achievements of justice in the modern world" (no. 2). In this perspective, which cannot be compared with any other period of history, you understand very well, Your Excellencies, ladies and gentlemen, that the great danger that weighs upon the evolution of social life today is constituted above all by the fact that such enormous and complex mechanisms, now of international dimensions, threaten man actually and seriously. Man, who must be at the center of common interest, this man who, according to God's original plan, is called to become the master of the earth, to "subdue" it (Gen 1:28) through the superiority of his intelligence and the strength of his physical labor, runs the risk of being reduced to the state of an instrument, of becoming an anonymous and faceless piece of machinery, until he is crushed by forces greater than himself, which can be used to his detriment, to dominate the masses pressed down by

apart. What an enormous cost in the squandering of goods of vital necessity, in ruin of every kind, in violence and loss of human life, not to mention the legacies of hatred which are the result! In this matter, there must be courageous and clear questions asked about such phenomena. Does the rebellion come from a foreign power seeking to destabilize a region, intervening by a process of ideological manipulation, by stirring up hatred, even taking part in armed combat, by supporting or maintaining it, to topple a legitimate political regime? Such cases are deplorable, and should be revealed in their true aspect. Or perhaps the conflict within a country arises out of conditions in the nation itself; flagrant injustice, or unbearable totalitarianism on the part of Governments? In such cases, those Governments must hasten to institute just and necessary reforms. In any case, one could not be a party to prolonging such a state of war, sacrificing innocent lives and slowing the advance towardss the solution of the real problems in so many countries, where life is already precarious.

It seems to me that one can easily find some helpful directions toward the solution of current conflicts in these reflections which are in accord with the social doctrine of the Church. Please be aware that the Holy See, like many of your countries, without doubt, is very concerned about the current situation in Central America, in Lebanon, in Afghanistan, in several areas of Africa, in Cambodia. Should not the foreign troops who occupy such places be withdrawn? At the same time, could not political accord be freely established within such countries through a genuine search for the common good of all citizens and with respect for the duties of a sovereign State, as I enumerated above? In other places of the world – for whatever reasons they have begun – we equally deplore the prolongation of war, as in the case of Iran and Iraq. We also desire international consensus to discourage terrorism, especially where it is still rampant. We all remember some particularly loathsome massacres perpetrated during the past year.

5. Nowadays, if one considers the tensions existing between sovereign countries, one often speaks of a dual polarization. The serious *East-West tension* more frequently engages our attention, since it is in these countries that one finds the greatest concentration of technological expertise, economic power, major industries, production capacity, mass communication networks and also, unfortunately, nuclear or conventional armaments. The tension is indeed real and full of menace. It is based on ideological differences. It is a fact that the peoples concerned are disturbed and even anguished. We are constantly receiving evidence of this, particularly from the different episcopates, and the Holy See deems it its duty to express it, not to heighten fears, but as a better guarantee of peace. This is why I myself intervened recently, asking for a resumption of the negotiations on the reduction of nuclear armaments. There is not a day to lose. We are convinced that this is a serious duty for all the parties concerned, and anyone who would withdraw from such all-important negotiations would incur a grave responsibility before humanity and before history.

A complete view of the world requires that one also focus attention on the *North-South contrast*, as I mentioned in my message for the World Day of Peace and in my homily of January 1. This problem touches the lives of a great part of the human race, and at stake is the life, the survival of those people who are in the grip of underdevelopment, and who are classified by the term "South" no matter to what continent they belong. They look at certain rich countries spending fabulous sums on armaments, often out of fear. And they themselves are tempted to commit too much of their resources in acquiring such arms, while elementary conditions of food, hygiene and literacy are cruelly lacking. This is the cause of an enormous amount of suffering, of anxiety, of bitterness, and even of revolt. The situation, by its very nature, brings in its train an endemic state of violence, all the more so if exploited by other powers. The enlargement of poverty zones is, in the long term, the most serious threat to peace.

To the human causes which have their source among others in the inequality of the terms of exchange and in certain injustices, are to be added natural catastrophes, such as the terrible drought in the Sahel region. In the face of such huge and certainly very complex problems, the international community is called to show itself resolutely committed to effective and disinterested assistance. In doing so, it must show great respect for the cultures and for whatever is sound in local traditions, with a concern for developing responsibility, free participation, and the unity of the poor countries. For sooner or later, these poor countries will come to recognize who really loves them, who assists them effectively, according to their real needs, beginning with food supplies.

For its part – and I insist on this point – *the Church wishes to continue its resolute commitment to the development of the countries of the so-called South*. Furthermore, the Church encourages other countries to commit themselves more intensely to this cause, because such efforts in the work of justice and fraternal solidarity are the best way to open pathways to peace.

6. Excellencies, I have just placed before you a certain number of questions which indeed touch upon political considerations. They are questions which are familiar to you as diplomats, as your Dean indicated. You are well aware, however, that I refer to these matters, not in the name of a State, but in the name of the Holy See, in the name of the Catholic Church and in the name of Christian conscience. It is a matter of seeking the conditions for a more human world. As I said to you last year, the Holy See feels itself free to take the initiatives which this requires, without pretensions, but with the assurance that comes from making its own the cause of those who suffer, and who cannot make themselves heard. We are sure that this vision is shared by many people of good will, including Heads of State, and those responsible for international life. But faith gives us a renewed concept of man and society, with the particular motivations that can deepen his impact.

Within the framework of international diplomatic circles, the Holy See desires first of all to promote *trust*, it does not cease to extol fairly negotiated settlements, and it does not hesitate to demand a return to genuine and sincere *dialogue*, beyond blinding passions and prejudices. It is precisely this that is lacking to those nations and blocs which fail to establish their relations on trust.

Such dialogue and trust may not be dismissed out of hand as unrealistic. On the contrary, rather than waiting for decisive results arising from changes which some philosophical-political theories promise for an indefinite future, the Holy See would prefer to assist in resolving today's impasse by encouraging persons and groups to take concrete steps and timely measures to resolve the most basic problems of justice in our world.

Inspiration from the Gospel
7. I have spoken of the consistency of this discourse with the Gospel. In fact, when the

Church issues the invitation to face up to the dramatic situation of *starving peoples*, it is simply remembering that Christ identified himself with the hungry.

She is on the side of *life*, so that it be welcomed, respected, defended and promoted. She well knows, too, that the world can appreciate this battle, because the life of even one innocent person – when one is kidnapped, for example – rightly generates so much compassion and solidarity. She would like one to have the same sensitivity in regard to the thousands of human beings who are being wiped out by abortion, famine and war.

The Church is on the side of all that is deep and inviolable in man; his conscience and his relationship with God. She knows that a regime which attempts to eliminate faith in God cannot safeguard respect for man and for the brotherhood of men. She does not cease to speak out for *religious liberty* as a fundamental right.

As far as she herself is concerned, especially during this Holy Year of Redemption, the Church extols *reconciliation*, pardon. In asking pardon of God, she invites men to practice it among themselves. People themselves have a need to be reconciled, to look upon others with new eyes, to overcome old grievances, to open their doors to their "enemies" without humbling them, and to seek to build unity again.

The Church issues a call for *love*, for a spirit of brotherhood and service, as she has learned it from Christ. She is sure that without such dispositions, the great words of peace, justice and solidarity risk being mere cymbals clanging without effect.

Furthermore, as I stated on New Year's Day, the deepest justification for such fraternity lies in the fact that we are *all children of the same Father*. How can one think of war, of whatever kind, between the children of the same father?

8. For this reason, the Church dares to speak of hope. Christmas reminded us that the birth of a child is the beginning of something new; all the more so, when the Child is the Son of God who entered human history, not to condemn, but to save. To the eyes of the believer, Jesus brings the first fruits of a new humanity. He is the dividing point of history. Every man is loved and esteemed by God, whatever his personal or collective past. No longer are there stalemated and impossible situations. Our fears and self-centeredness can be passed [over] to him, the Redeemer. A Christian does not believe that history is dictated by fate. By the grace of God, man can change the trajectory of the world's history. In this conviction is rooted the service which the Holy See humbly offers, within the limits of its own sphere, to the international society.

In truth, the Church is very conscious that this patient transformation of international relations surpasses human powers, due to the limited and sinful character of man. That is why, in the midst of her activity, including also her diplomatic activity, *the Church prays*. She entreats God, and invites others to pray. For prayer is not simply aimed at making up for something lacking. To her eyes, prayer is essentially a bringing of oneself more closely into line with the will of God, who alone is absolutely just. For us, it is precisely to make us disciples of Christ in the truth of our being. If Christians dare to speak and put into words before the whole human race the requirements which I have recalled, it is because they are trying to be faithful to the interior light they receive from God, by the gift of Christ's love, present in history. In this spirit, they can work for a change of heart at the deepest level. Then shall peace be born and affirmed in conformity with the Message which I addressed to all political leaders.

This is the ideal which the Holy See, in the name of the Church, freely proposes and desires to share with you and with the Governments of the whole world which you represent. And you, diplomats accredited to the Holy See, I take the liberty to invite you especially to be witnesses to this ideal, both personally and as a diplomatic corps that is called to a representation unique in its kind.

Your Excellencies, Ladies and Gentlemen, it is on such words of hope that I again express to you my good wishes. May the Lord, the source of all good, liberally bestow his blessings upon you and upon all who are dear to you.

January 12, 1985
(*OR*, January 28, 1985, pp. 6–8)

1. The noble words just spoken by His Excellency, Mr. Joseph Amichia, interpreting the sentiments and the best wishes of the entire Diplomatic Corps accredited to the Holy See, would receive, I am sure, the approval of all the participants. Who would not share those aspirations to peace in the face of current conflicts, threats, starvation, racial discrimination, national debts, and unemployment? I am particularly grateful to your Dean for the generous and confident regard with which he reviewed the action of the Holy See, and brought out several aspects of my spiritual mission. May God grant that these best wishes, so beautifully expressed, be more effectively realized in 1985, despite our human limitations, for the community of nations and for the Church!

In a few moments, I will have the joy of greeting each of you individually. A number of you are participating for the first time in a meeting of this kind, having but recently presented [your] Letters of Credence and, in some cases, as first Ambassadors of [your] countries to the Holy See. Several others have had to wait, since it was some time last year that their Governments established diplomatic relations with the Holy See. In the name of all, I wish all the newcomers a hearty welcome in this gathering of distinguished diplomats, which would like to be a family as well. The great variety of your faces, of languages, of the countries and cultures you represent – can all these not symbolize, in a climate of respect, mutual esteem and peace, the harmony of nations in search of mutual understanding and brotherhood?

My cordial best wishes go to each of you, Heads of Missions and collaborators to your families, to the peoples and the institutions, that is to say, the Governments, you serve, and even more to the nations whose physiognomy and energy remain beyond the vicissitudes of history and the lot of statesmen.

I could likewise send greetings through you to the various continents. A part of *Europe* is always very much present at the Holy See.

But *Africa* is no less so, as is attested by the intervention of your Dean, the Ambassador of the Ivory Coast. Through you, the Holy See makes its own the hopes and the concerns of the various African countries. The Holy See is aware of their youth and vitality, the aspirations and the drives in the areas of development, the needs to articulate authority, liberty and peace, the efforts to promote the unity of the continent, to ensure human dignity and notably to overcome intolerable racial discriminations. It expresses the fervent desire that they may chart their course, still rather new, in a way that is satisfying and just for all.

Latin America, where there is such a concentration of peoples of great Catholic majority, likewise assumes considerable importance in our eyes. I have underlined this by going to Santo Domingo in preparation for the fifth centenary of Latin America's evangelization. In the near future I will be visiting four of these countries. Their preoccupations – the struggle against all forms of poverty, the better distribution of wealth, the concern to ensure the formation and the employment of the very numerous youth, to guarantee human rights to ensure internal and external peace – all these are so many questions that hold the interest of the whole community of nations, and the Holy See expresses to these countries its warm encouragement and support.

Asia is likewise well represented among us, from the Near East to the Far East, and, beyond the permanent Missions, we cannot forget the other nations, in particular the *great Chinese nation*, whose aspirations and dynamism the Church always follows with respect and interest. My visits to Korea and Thailand demonstrated the Church's solicitude for the Asiatic peoples and their remarkable cultures, represented moreover in the Catholic Church; the personal experience I had remains engraved in my heart's memory.

It is not necessary for me to dwell at any length here on *North America*. As far as the United States is concerned, everyone is aware of the possibilities of this great country, its world influence, its people's attachment to liberty. And I have a grateful memory of what I observed on the spot, still recently, in Canada.

Finally, I would like the many islands of *Oceania* to feel, in spite of their great geographical distance, the concern of the Holy See, which was demonstrated, among other ways, by the papal visit to Papua New Guinea and Solomon Islands, and by a message to Tahiti.

This moment of best wishes to the Pope has a certain simplicity about it, for it discards all pointless artificiality. But it is also a solemn moment, for in it we are invited, you and I, to cast a lucid glance, as far and as deep as possible, on the year that is beginning, on the whole world scene, disclosing the threats and the signs of hope, before God who probes minds and hearts and who, on Christmas night, calls all men and women of good will to peace.

Things that are still far from perfect
2. Lucidity may lead us to see first *the things that are still far from perfect* as the media relentlessly point out every day. Christmas Day, when our glance was focused on the poor crib of the Infant-God at Bethlehem, I myself mentioned several types of suffering, of evils, of "poverties" in every sense of the word (like those of the refugees I met in Thailand), of violences, of dangers, so as to make all victims conscious of our solidarity and of the Church's preferential option for the poor, but also so that hope might be born in their hearts in light of him who came to enrich us with his divinity and to scatter the darkness of error, egoism and hatred.

For this very reason, we also, and perhaps first, must consider the undeniable *positive accomplishments*, so as better to estimate what is possible, to strengthen the hope and the desire to undertake such gestures of peace.

By way of significant example, you will understand my citing the signing of the *Treaty of Peace and Friendship between Argentina and Chile*, which ended the dispute over the southern zone. This was an affair which, six years ago, could have degenerated into a fratricidal war and consumed the energies of these dynamic peoples in destructive enterprises. But the two parties were determined to continue along the course of dialogues, which had reached an impasse, and they requested the mediation of the Holy See. The work was laborious, for the question involved was extremely complex. An iron will was required on both sides. Each of the countries emerged with honor and without detriment to its national interests, with simply a few reasonable concessions on both sides. This procedure at the same time opens up promising prospects for the different sectors of fruitful collaboration about which we are going to speak. The example shows that the way of negotiation, prudent and patient, directly between parties or with the help of an intermediary, can lead to the solution of apparently insoluble controversies. The Holy See continues to give thanks for this event to Providence, who granted it this opportunity to offer its services, to be his humble instrument, and who disposed the persons and the circumstances in a favorable direction.

One could even mention as positive signs the advances attained in the *direction of democracy* in several countries which had known a kind of totalitarianism. Not that the new situation simplifies the problems of economy or social equilibrium; but it constitutes, in our view, while ensuring a sufficiently strong public authority which is necessary and the unity of the nation, a way more normal, more sure, more respectful of liberties, in a word, more just; it puts an end to unjust oppressions and opens the field to the responsible participation of all (cf. Encyclical *Redemptor Hominis*, no. 17, para. 6,7).

I would like also to cite as another positive sign the recent opening of *discussions in Geneva between the United States of America and the Soviet Union on the limitation of nuclear arms*. It was indeed very necessary that the dialogue, too long frozen, be resumed on a question as vital as this. After this first meeting, it seems that one can feel a prudent optimism. God grant that the actual negotiations, which will without doubt be laborious, will confirm the favorable forecasts! The eyes of the whole world are fixed on the relations between these two great powers, because of the potential economic and military supremacy, and thus of their enormous responsibilities, in the area of nuclear power which affects the lot of humanity, but also in many other political and moral domains.

This situation of *bipolarization* cannot, however, condition the free expression, the latitude for action and the possibilities of initiative of the other countries; rather, this responsibility of two powers – like that of the permanent members of the Security Council within the United Nations Organization – finds its justification only to the extent that it allows the other nations to assume their place, to undertake their initiatives, to exercise their influence and their expansion within just conditions and for the good of the world community.

Three key words

3. So that international relationships might favor and strengthen a just peace, there must be at the same time *reciprocity, solidarity*, and the effective *collaboration* which is the fruit of the other two. These three key words will serve this year as the *leitmotif* for our discourse.

These orientations could moreover be compared with the great project of the *Conference on Security and Cooperation in Europe*, which was concluded at *Helsinki* in 1975. It opened a hope in what concerns, among other things, the development of mutual relations, in consideration of the realities of the technical, cultural, social and humanitarian orders proper to each, the respect for human rights and fundamental liberties. This year will mark, in the month of August, the tenth anniversary of the signing of the Final Act. The difficulties of cooperation are many and one must often await its fruits from one session to the next. A long way still lies ahead, a way of patience, much good will and sincerity. But who will deny that a direction has now been charted to help all the countries concerned, those of Europe and those beyond the Atlantic, to realize a real advance in exchanges, to the benefit of the quality of life of their respective peoples? The Holy See, which is a member of the Conference, continue to hope for this.

Regarding *reciprocity* in relations, it is not opposed to sovereignty, but rather is a condition for its worthy exercise. Each of the countries here represented is indeed sovereign in the eyes of the community of peoples, equal in dignity, proud of its independence and in search of its own legitimate interests. You yourselves, Ladies and Gentlemen, members of the Diplomatic Corps, are appointed to serve the good of your respective countries. Last year, on this occasion, I spoke to you regarding the benefits, conditions and exigencies of such a sovereignty.

But when a country claims its rights, the right to be treated – at times to be assisted – with justice and in honor, with account taken of its interests, it then can hardly ignore the *similar rights of the others*. True political dialogue – which constituted the object of my message for the 1983 Day of Peace and of the allocation to the diplomats that same year – requires openness, receptivity and *reciprocity*; it accepts the difference and the distinctiveness of the other, for an honest conciliation. It is at the same time a search for what is and remains common to humanity, even within tensions, oppositions and conflicts, because it has to do with what is true, good and just for every man, every group and every society. There is no dialogue of peace without this acceptance of the justice that is above parties, that judges all, and that implies, in practice, reciprocity. How can one claim at the international level or in bilateral relations what one has refused to concede to others in conformity with their rights? It is a question of integrity, of justice: the only things that can be obstacles here are, on the one hand, fear of the unjust violence of the others, and on the other hand, fear of the truth, the blind egoism of a people or of a fraction of a people, the will for power on the part of its leader, and even more their ideological inflexibility.

Christians receive *in the Gospel* a word of Christ himself which brings at the same time light, strength and urgency to the course of reciprocity; "Treat others the way you would have them treat you" (Mt 7:12). These words express the commandment: "Love your neighbor as yourself."

This would have many applications in international life.

How can one invoke respect for the *fundamental rights of man*, about which more has never been spoken, if one does not respect them at home?

How can one speak of the right to *independence*, as the ABC's of the principles governing international relations, if one is intervening from outside to arouse and support subversive forces in another country, whether indirectly or even directly, by force, and this against the wish of the majority of the population? And one could say as much when a country has practically imposed a regime and its ruling apparatus on another. How, *within a country*, can one invoke the rights of a part of the population while excluding the rights of the others to live peacefully on the same land?

Or how can one impose on a whole country a particular law that suppresses the civil and religious rights of a *minority*?

A glance at the activity of *international organizations* likewise arouses some perplexity. These organizations have their value to the extent that they are receiving the cooperation of all the members and are pursuing the common good of all, while seeking to communicate to them the fruits that come from concerted action. It is to be desired that they benefit from the most universal participation possible.

As for the domain of religious liberty, it must also include a reciprocity, that is to say an equality of treatment. Certainly, those who believe in the true God, through respect for the truth to which they adhere with their whole faith, cannot admit the equivalence of all religious faiths, and still less can they fall into religious indifference; they even desire, quite naturally, that all come to the truth that they know, and they engage themselves to this end by a witness that respects the liberty of compliance, for at issue here is the dignity of man in opening himself to religious faith by a free homage of mind and of heart, with grace, according to what his well-formed conscience discovers and prescribes. They can then at the same time – and indeed they must – respect the dignity of other persons, who cannot be prevented from acting according to their consciences, above all in religious matters. The Second Vatican Council made this distinction well in the Declaration *Dignitatis Humanae* (no. 2), thus resolving a problem that may have left something to be desired in the past history of Christian communities. Also – you will allow me to express this to you here in all confidence – one can understand the astonishment and the feeling of frustration of Christians who welcome, for example in Europe, believers of other religions, giving them the possibility of exercising their worship, and who see themselves forbidden all exercise of Christian worship in the countries where these believers are in the majority and have made their faith the State religion.

Moreover, serious difficulties arise in cases where the State adopts an *atheistic ideology*. There is, to be sure, a great variety of situations according to which the State does or does not find itself confronted with strong confessional communities of staunch faith. But, in general, there exists a contradiction between the official declarations on religious liberty, supposedly allowed to private individuals, and anti-religious propaganda, to which are added, here and there, measures of coercion preventing the free exercise of religion, the free choice of ministers of worship, free access to seminaries, the possibility of catechizing the youth, not to mention discrimination against the civil rights of believers, as if the assent of faith were a threat to the common good!

Moreover, there exists at least one situation in Europe where atheistic ideology is so bound up with the State that atheism is imposed on consciences and *every religious act*, of whatever confession, is *absolutely forbidden* and severely punished.

In these different situations, what is at stake is the *spirit of tolerance* properly understood, which is not religious indifference but respect for consciences, that is to say respect for one of the most basic liberties, and respect for the distinction between the political and the religious domains as Christ so well expressed it: "Give to Caesar what is Caesar's, but give to God what is God's" (Mt 22:21).

To arrive at a common solidarity

4. Beyond the reciprocity of rights and strict justice in equality of treatment, we must arrive at a *common solidarity in the face of great stakes of humanity*. All peoples are in a situation of mutual interdependence, on the economical, political, cultural levels. Each country needs or will need the others. God has entrusted the earth to mankind as a whole, making solidarity a law that holds for the good as well as for the evil. To be sure, there have been various degrees of good fortune in such matters as the natural richness of lands or of sub-soils, favorable climates, talents connected with this or that civilization, and there also has been the effort expended by individuals, according to their more or less developed spirit of enterprise. Economic and social progress can be delayed by the difficulties experienced above all by the young nations in mastering the new processes of production and marketing, and sometimes also by negligence, or corruption, by individuals, to whom remedial measures should be courageously

applied. But, in any case, these situations of inequality invite the rational beings that men are, to join in overcoming these handicaps, and, confronted with hardships of the kind that touches entire segments of humanity, there are no valid pretexts for refusing to contribute to their survival and their development. United assistance is the only fully human response, and is even in the interest, rightly understood, of everyone in the long run. It is one and the same adventure that we are involved in. At Edmonton, in Canada, I pleaded once again for the countries of the South, and I am happy to see Heads of State sensitizing the opinion of their people to this capital emergency.

The urgent need to progress in this spirit of solidarity is so evident that I will content myself with citing but two examples.

Many developing countries have contracted *enormous debts*, which are getting worse. I know that the problem is complex and that it ultimately involves the question of the prudence of the loans and of their actual utilization for investments in the countries. But the situation has become inextricable for many of the countries in debt: without a new system of solidarity, how will they ever be able to repay? How will they ever escape the impasse? The interest of all is at stake here, including the rich countries who risk finding themselves isolated. The human sense of solidarity is at stake here. For Christians, such a renewal of relations could hardly be achieved without the generous and disinterested love of which Christ himself is the model and the source.

The other example is that which, every day, the news brings out before our astonished eyes, at least if we do not turn away our eyes and our heart, as your Dean so well put it: *the starvation of the drought countries, notably in Africa*. We know only too well that the countries concerned cannot at the present time – and by themselves – emerge from this tragic situation, prevent millions of people from dying, or stop for tomorrow the expansion of the *desert*. But the situation can be rectified: not only must we continue to supply the emergency aid, levied, among other things, on surplus crops which some are tempted to destroy for the sake of balancing a too circumscribed economy, but we must place at everyone's disposal the techniques that God has allowed us to discover. I was speaking, at the beginning, about positive signs. I am anxious to underline this one: the fact that, in recent times, organizations of the international community, countries and private institutions have been willing to respond to the challenge, is very encouraging.

Effective collaboration
5. According to the principles of reciprocity and of solidarity which we brought out, it would be possible to implement a *more effective collaboration of the members of the world community* in other precise domains where violence is wreaking havoc and where grave menaces are weighing upon humanity.

It is a question of contributing to the *discouragement of solutions of violence* and *helping to overcome fear*, that climate of distrust which paralyses certain countries, causes them to turn in on themselves, but may also involve them in lying, inflexibility, provocation, violence. Of course, here too justice or self-defense are invoked, but another climate, a new philosophical perspective, as I put it on January 1 of this year, would allow them to find other solutions to achieve justice and security. I limit myself to mentioning four domains here. And in these there could be cooperation from not only the parties directly involved in this dispute or in that conflict, but also from a growing number of countries and especially the international organizations.

a) Without doing anything that could be described as meddling in the internal affairs of others, would it not be possible for them to use their influence to *discourage the conflicts in progress*, to assist the parties involved to resume the paths of dialogue, to search for negotiated solutions capable of being accepted by all, except perhaps by those whom a blind ideology or Machiavellian interest maintains in their designs? One could at least expect of other countries that they abstain from supporting the parties in conflict in the pursuit of operations that are causing so many deaths and so much destruction.

Here, one cannot fail to think of *Lebanon*. When will it finally be able to find the desired peace and the capacity to strengthen its own institutions in loyal collaboration between the various components of the nation? How can we prudently put an end to the external interventions and, when these are terminated, how can we guarantee peace, prevent the reprisals and the massacres that all the world still vividly recalls?

One could reason in a similar way for the wars and the acts of merciless violence that are taking place between *Iran* and *Iraq* – this conflict being fed by a continuous flow of arms furnished by the most diverse parties – and moreover in *Afghanistan*, in *Cambodia*, in *several countries of Central America*. If the Holy See speaks of them, even when its own faithful are not involved, it is because it cannot be resigned to seeing the destruction and massacre of innocent people, who have already paid so highly for the absurdity of war.

The Church is well aware that de-escalation is difficult; but we must have the courage to begin it. For her part, for example in Central America, she is prepared to offer herself as a place or a forum that would allow the parties to meet each other, to understand each other, to begin a sincere dialogue of peace.

b) We likewise need to discourage violence and fear at the level of *disarmament*, to lower as much as possible the level of armaments, to encourage a new philosophy of international relations, to renounce selfish and ideological interests which nourish tensions, hatred [and] subversive activities, and to devote the energies and the resources liberated through disarmament to the great causes of our time: the struggle against hunger; development; human advancement (cf. my statement after the Angelus on January 1, 1985).

c) It is also important to fight together against *international terrorism*, by not in any way encouraging the terrorists, and, on another plane, the drug traffic which has become a veritable plague. In these areas it seems, moreover, that, apart from the tragedy once again recently created by some air pirates, there has been progress here, which results above all from a greater international solidarity.

d) But we must also *discourage violence under all its aspects*, including that perpetrated against *political prisoners*, secretly and without restraint, as though it were a matter left to the arbitrary discretion of the powers, even under the pretext of security, in concentration camps, in prisons, in other places of confinement. There are cases where they are set upon in an ignoble way by those who are willing to go so far as the complete destruction of their personality. This is a disgrace of our humanity. There must be at least a denunciation of these deeds, a very clear condemnation on the part of international opinion, and visiting rights for humanitarian agencies legitimately recognized for this purpose.

This holds true for all violated human rights, as for religious liberty.

Count on youth

6. By way of conclusion, I would like to offer you three more reflections: on the contribution of youth, on the education to moral values, on the spiritual depth of reconciliation.

Yes, it is good, it is necessary, to count on *youth*. Most countries represented in the Diplomatic Corps have an enormous proportion of young people. In the interest of peace, it is important that these be able to make valid ethical choices. The United Nations Organization has invited us to enter into the International Youth Year, and I devoted to this subject the Message of the Day of Peace: "Peace and Youth Go Forward Together." It is not that the young people have the experience that you have: without doubt they do not see all the difficulties of political, national and international life. They have their weaknesses as well, their temptations, their moments of violence, and sometimes they shirk concrete responsibilities. It is not a question of using demagogy with them. But do we know how to take their legitimate aspirations into account, which often go, in a generous spirit, right to the essential? In any case, it is they who tomorrow will be the artisans of peace. How are they being prepared for this role? Are our ways of treating questions of justice and peace really able to satisfy them? How can we provide them with an example, a hope, an insertion into professional life which will lead them out of the trauma of unemployment, which will bring them to active participation? Above all, how are we to educate them to true values and respect for others?

Education to moral values

7. Without this *education* to *moral values*, in the people and with their leaders or future leaders, every construction of peace remains fragile; it is even doomed to failure, whatever [may] be the cleverness of diplomats on the forces displayed. It is the duty of politicians, educators, families, those in charge of the media to contribute to this formation. And the Church is always ready to make her contribution.

I do not need here to specify these moral values. One thinks of integrity, fidelity to commitments, honesty, justice, tolerance, respect for others – their life, their life conditions, their race-sharing, solidarity. Christians like to link all these social virtues to charity, to love, and to found them on every human person's transcendent dignity, of which God is the guarantor, and on the example of Christ.

But how far does one go in respect for man? Should one not begin with the human embryo? Today, genetic manipulations, daring experiments, are multiplying, and they pass rapidly from one country to another. These problems are becoming in some sense international. Who will dare say that this is merely a question of technical prowess? Who does not see the serious human problems that are at issue, and who will have to find solutions on the level of right, on the level of ethics? Respect for moral values at this level forms part of the respect for man which obviously begins with respect for human life. Every country, especially if it has powerful means of influence at its disposal, should weigh its responsibility as to the ethical value of the technical achievements, of the methods or of the more or less moral or sectarian ideas it exports or allows to be exported.

Your noble profession

8. Finally, the Church is well aware that it is difficult to cure man of the temptation to

war, to egoism, to hatred. She has sometimes been called utopian. She is not so naïve as to think that one will succeed on earth in exorcising all violence. In the post-synodal exhortation published last December, *Reconciliatio et Paenitentia*, I spoke of "a world shattered to its very foundation." And for us, the root of these shatterings is a wound in man's inmost self, an original sin. The drama of humanity – many philosophers assert this themselves – is a spiritual drama, a drama above all of atheistic humanism (cf. *Exhortation*, cited, no. 2). But while knowing that on this earth one cannot achieve the definitive reconciliation of people with God, with others, with themselves, with creation, the Church intends to work fervently at this, as a sign, sketch and witness of the world to come. She always believes that the liberation of man's sinful heart, through forgiveness and through love, is possible, that the progress of dialogue, of reconciliation, of brotherhood is possible, above all if people are reconciled with God. Her specific role is to labor at this level, in her catechesis and in her sacraments. But she is also engaged in the work of social reconciliation, above all through the activity of the Holy See and its various organisms. Its intention is to place its institutional structure and its moral authority at the service of harmony and peace (cf. ibid., no. 25).

It is to this, I hope, that you will continue to be witnesses here. My purpose has been not so much to point out to you the achievements of the Holy See – which are well below our desires and our ideal – as to encourage you, Excellencies, Ladies and Gentlemen, to contribute to creating a climate of reciprocity, of solidarity and of international collaboration about which we have spoken. This is the honor of your noble profession, especially when you exercise it before a spiritual authority. We will have contributed together to prepare a world more human, more worthy of man and of God. We entrust this project to the inspiration and to the grace of God. I invoke his Blessing upon each one of you. This is the essential part of the cordial best wishes that I am happy to extend to you.

January 11, 1986
(*OR*, January 20, 1986, 1–4)

1. Your Dean, His Excellency, Mr. Joseph Amichia, as your spokesman, has just conveyed your respectful sentiments and good wishes at the beginning of the New Year. He has done this with a warmth of expression, freedom of spirit, and a precision and depth that we know he possesses and which we appreciate. I thank him wholeheartedly for this address which is to the honor of the Diplomatic Corps accredited to the Holy See. Beyond being a noble tribute to the Church and a clear observation of world problems, it is a testimony of what you can perceive of the activity or intentions of the Holy See.

I am happy to greet each of the Ambassadors here present, before meeting them personally at the end of this audience. I would like to extend a special welcome to those who are for the first time in this assembly, since they have begun their mission here during the past year. Certain countries have begun or will soon begin their first diplomatic mission to the Holy See: Saint Lucia, Nepal, Zimbabwe, and Liechtenstein.

I extend a cordial greeting to the wives of the Heads of Mission, as well as to all the members of the Embassies and their families. And I express my best wishes to each of the countries which you represent.

2. Peace! The United Nations Organizations chose this theme for the current year, 1986. The Holy See rejoices in this and is ready to make its own contribution. We hope that theoretical discussions or slogans used here or there will not be the only results from the choice of this theme. But we hope that humanity will make true progress in its desire for peace, in concrete initiatives for peace, and more profoundly, in a CULTURE OF PEACE, and in education for peace – on the level of governments, on that of numerous responsible interventions, on the level of public opinion of peoples and, I would say, especially on the level of consciences.

Today, in the presence of qualified representatives from so many nations of the world, I would like to center my reflection on the need for expanding our horizons in our search for peace. I want to encourage peoples to be open to the problems of others, to become more aware of their interdependence, and to live with a concern for a solidarity without frontiers. I said that in my Message for the World Day of Peace on January 1, 1986: "All of the nations of the world can fully realize their closely linked destinies only if, together, they pursue peace as a universal value."

Yes, the promotion of a just and lasting peace makes universal demands at least under three headings which will be developed in this allocution. True men of peace realize that peace must be sought for each and every member of the one human family, and they do not want to have any part in local conflicts. Still further, peace demands an awareness of a shared responsibility, and of a more extensive joint collaboration on the level of a region, a continent, the whole world, and beyond blocs or collective self-interest groups. Finally, peace must be based especially on justice and respect for the rights of man which is something indispensable for all.

Peace concerns all mankind
3. The global character of peace does not mean that it is sought only to avoid wide-

spread conflicts. Since 1945, even though there has not been a world war, one can enumerate more than 130 local conflicts, which caused more than thirty million people to be killed or wounded, and which brought about enormous damage, ruined certain countries, and on all sides left serious after-effects in consciences, especially among the new generations. Who would dare to take part in this? Peace definitely concerns all countries and all groups of human beings living together: if war affects one or another part of the human family, it wounds the entire family, which cannot resign itself in indifference to the massacre of its brothers. The human family is unique. Certainly, today, with the media, all people are informed and can be sympathetic. But, over and above a distant sympathy, the whole drama of war must arouse, at the same time as prayer for peace, the desire to lend assistance, and to offer one's services to help bring an end to this passion, often blind, so that negotiated solutions may get under way, and while awaiting this, the desire to contribute to the aid of the victims may be aroused. This role belongs eminently to the United Nations, but the United Nations itself has authority only through the adherence and active support of its members. It is here where they must decide at what point all nations must take to heart the lack of peace from which certain peoples are suffering.

4. Allow me to pause here and recall several countries or regions presently involved in conflicts, or regrettable tensions, which your Dean has already mentioned.

We are always thinking of the dear *Lebanese people*. Some new signs and recent attempts underline their desire and will for peace. I am united with you in your wish that such a desire might be realized without further delay, with the help of all those who make up the Lebanese society – and at the same time guaranteeing the honor, the rights, and the specific traditions of all the different parties – and with the loyal support of the friends of Lebanon.

We also think with sadness of the continuing murderous and destructive combats between *Iran and Iraq*, always hoping that the parties involved will find a reasonable way for a just peace.

For the *people of Afghanistan*, each one of you knows in what conditions they have been living for the last six years, and moreover, the United Nations has underlined this on several occasions. We follow very attentively the present attempts which aim to resolve the problem in all its complexity. May we not be disappointed in this fragile hope!

The situation of *Cambodia*, which has been so dramatic, continues to be painful and difficult. The international community is anxious, and rightly so, about finding a solution which will permit the Cambodian people to enjoy a true independence, worthy of their cultural traditions.

South Africa continues to suffer from bloody racial conflicts and tribal opposition. Your Dean was right when he stressed this scourge. The solution to the problem of apartheid and the beginning of a concrete dialogue between government authorities and representatives of the legitimate aspirations of the people are indispensable means for re-establishing justice and concord, and banishing fear which today provokes so much inflexibility. As far as possible, it is necessary to avoid allowing internal conflicts to be exploited by others to the detriment of justice and peace. The international community can and must exercise its influence on different levels in a constructive sense, using the means guaranteed by law.

The situation in *Uganda*, despite the agreement signed by the government and representatives of the opposition, is still characterized by profound insecurity. With all my heart, I repeat my appeal of December 22 last, for peace among the people in Uganda.

Chad is still far from having found an acceptable solution to the crucial problem of unity and national independence. Despite attempts at mediation, the continuation of internal conflicts, with outside interference, is causing the population to live an unending, bloody tragedy, while insufficient economic and social development is keeping the people in misery.

Who could remain uninterested in the outcome of the situation of the *Ethiopian peoples* for whom internal war and displacement of the population have increased the drama, already too well known, of drought, hunger, and lack of the care needed by them?

Add to all these dramas the Christmas day episode of the conflict between the *Burkina Faso and Mali*, because of disputes over their borders. This was not without its victims and great damage. We would like to hope that the ceasefire which began will be prolonged and that these two countries will find ground for entente so that they can devote their energies and their meager resources to the well-being of their peoples.

In *Central America*, the outlook for bringing about peace remains very uncertain. The parties in conflict have not begun, or do not intend to be interested in opting effectively for dialogue as an appropriate means to determine the solution for their problems, either due to a poor understanding of what a true democracy involves, or because of the intervention of forces and powers that are foreign to the situation of these countries.

In certain countries of the *Latin-American continent*, we see a cruel escalation of guerilla warfare, which aims, without discrimination, at institutions and persons. Such a recourse to violence, as well as tactics which consist in striking blindly, in order to kill, to make an impression, or to instill fear, deserve the most rigorous condemnations.

Without any doubt, we could cite other examples of conflicts, guerilla warfare, and tensions. In mentioning some of them, I evidently did not want to accentuate the somber aspects of the international situation, or to nourish additional fears, or aggravate the burden of humiliating sufferings of countries which are very dear to me, but, on the contrary, I wanted to show my solicitude for their peoples, and understanding and encouragement for the positive efforts of their governments, convinced that there is hope for peace everywhere, and that we must oppose a certain internationalism of violence and guerilla warfare with an internationalism of the will for peace.

Growth in cooperation

Precisely – and this is the second stage of my reflection – peace is a value without frontiers because it can be established in a just and lasting manner only where there is growth in cooperation in a region, on a continent, and among the totality of nations.

5. The growth of cooperation does not mean that diverse initiatives for peace are negligible when taken by certain personalities, by certain interventions, by certain governments; nor must it await a global consensus of all the parties involved to map out the way for peace. On the contrary, the solution of situations that are apparently inex-

tricable, or of conflicts and latent tensions, often comes from *courageous personal initiatives*, bold and prophetic, which break the sterile cycle of violence and hatred, and really change the situation, by beginning dialogue and negotiation in a spirit of understanding and in respecting the honor of each partner. Persons who act in this way merit to be called, in the evangelical sense of the term, "peacemakers." The originality of their action does not come from a position of force, but from a realistic, human conception of peace; it may be inspired by love, as Mahatma Gandhi said.

However, peace would unfortunately remain fragile and precarious if it were not sought by *all the partners of the region*, taking into account the rights and duties of each one; or if the other peoples of the earth were not interested and were not concerned about encouraging and consolidating this peace; or if the great powers continued to interfere and even oppose a just peace, depending on whether it suited their interests.

So, peace takes on a universal dimension, not only because various spheres of interdependence exist among peoples, on the political and economic level, but also by virtue of a higher and larger consideration of the common destiny of the peoples who make up the human family. It is difficult to see how most of the situations of which we have spoken could find a just solution only in bilateral agreements or in arrangements concluded solely with those directly concerned in the conflict. There would then be a great risk of arriving at an impasse or even at injustices. On the contrary, a more extensive entente and disinterested mediation or agreement with other powers can offer better guarantees.

6. The extended solidarity of which we have been speaking is also verified on the level of all the countries which have many points in common due to neighboring geographical positions, the proximity of their cultures, the convergence of their interests, and shared responsibilities for human and physical realities of a wider scope than states or nations. Continental solidarity is today a necessary step toward universal solidarity.

Such is the case, among others of the *Latin-American continent*. At Santo Domingo, on October 12, 1984, before my brothers of CELAM, I inaugurated the novena of years of preparatory to the fifth centenary of evangelization. There I invited the countries concerned to recognize each other in the unity of one large Latin-American family, free and prosperous, and founded on a common religious and cultural substratum. This can be grounded upon a natural dynamism marked by the Gospel to overcome together the injustices and self-interests of certain privileged parties, to thwart the seduction of certain ideologies, and to reject the ways of violence, to avoid rivalries between nations, and the interference of foreign powers, in order to grow in respect for the identity of ethnic groups and for the good of all.

Likewise, as I said to the civil authorities of Cameroon and to the members of the Diplomatic Corps at Yaoundé on August 12 last, the *African Continent* must be respected and helped in achieving a certain number of common objectives to which your Dean has given special attention: true independence, an economic autonomy rightly understood, the elimination of fratricidal wars and the setting aside of ethnic and regional rivalry, the struggle against drought and hunger, respect for man, whatever the race, and the development of human and spiritual values which are proper to the African nations.

Continental and universal solidarity

I again had occasion to speak at a Symposium of the European bishops on October 11 last of the common roots of their continent in the Christian faith, and also of the necessity of dispelling the confusion that Europe permitted to extend over the metaphysical certitudes or ethical standards which had constituted its strength, so as to continue to bring to the world the witness of values that make up the finer part of the European heritage. That is a service which requires a certain unity, an effective solidarity, all the more difficult to realize the more history has accentuated the particular character of each culture and tradition. One can only rejoice to see this solidarity progressing. In Western Europe, the economic community, as of now, comprises twelve countries which on this point are committed to opening their frontiers. At Brussels, on May 20 last, at the headquarters of the Institutions of the European Communities, I praised the founders for not having resigned themselves to the breaking up of Western Europe. But there remains *the great rupture which separates the peoples of the East and West.* Whatever may be the historical, political, or ideological events that caused this – to a great extent independently of the will of the peoples involved – it remains "unacceptable for a conscience formed by human and Christian ideals which presided over the formation of the continent," as I said to the European bishops. We continue to hope that the Helsinki process, which will have an important meeting in Vienna this year, will permit a further development of the spirit of mutual solidarity, free and fruitful communication of ideas and of persons, and cooperation between states. On the level of Christian communities, we intend to guard well and to foster fraternal bonds between the East and the West following in the path of Saints Benedict, Cyril and Methodius.

Our consideration obviously extends also to the *great Asiatic continent* where diversity is undoubtedly more accentuated and situations more complex, to the extent that this is a question of very vast countries, with very distinct antique traditions, and very dense populations. The human problems that these countries have to resolve are equally immense and the Church views their efforts with sympathy. I had occasion to express this while visiting Japan, and when I stopped in Thailand. And I am happy now that I shall soon be welcomed in India.

Finally, I think of the vast world of Oceania, where I shall visit Australia and New Zealand this year.

Yes, each continent has its problems, its destiny, and its responsibilities in regard to itself and to the whole human family. World peace presupposes that consistency be maintained on each of these levels, respecting the personality of each people and its responsible participation.

In this sense, I wish that regional or continental political organizations would help this process of cooperation and peace. I am thinking especially of the Organization of American States (OAS) and the Organization of African Unity (OAU).

7. The rupture of which I spoke between Eastern and Western Europe is spread over much of the continent. On the level of political, economic and ideological systems, it has profoundly characterized these last forty years, and it continues to polarize attention on two blocs, with the threat of wars and a ruinous and dangerous race toward an arms build-up. A hope arises each time that tension relaxes that dialogue will be resumed, that confidence will be manifested, and that a balanced and controlled

process of general disarmament will be decided upon (cf. my message to the UN,, October 14, 1985). The Geneva Meeting of November last between the highest representatives of the United States of America and the Soviet Union, was an interesting step on the necessary path of dialogue. The mutual exchange of wishes directly to the people themselves at the beginning of this year contributes a certain note of humanity and openness. But these new relations will bring peace only if, beyond symbolic gestures, they are translated into a real willingness for disarmament, without continuing to cover up situations of injustice by other means. As your Dean well said, the world waits with impatience for the fruits of these meetings.

In any event, our contemporary history should not be confined to the East-West polarization.

A certain number of countries – and sometimes great countries- have shown this in choosing the way of non-alignment, even though in different degrees and according to quite different forms. A difficult position, which does not prevent opportune reconciliation and even agreements, and which must not neglect solidarity on essential human problems, but which can also manifest a way of serving peace in the perspective of reaching beyond the opposition of the blocs. Above all, as I do not cease to say, North-South relations should concern the partners of the human family as much as relations between East and West. There it is a question of taking part together, no longer in unrestrained competition in the arms race, but of meeting the essential needs of an immense portion of humanity. That is what I mean when, in my message of January 1, 1986, I speak of peace as "a value with no frontiers, North-South, East-West."

8. Underdevelopment is, in fact, an ever increasing danger for world peace. Solidarity among all nations must always be more manifest there. Certainly, no country today is spared a certain economic crisis, which brings with it the social scourge of unemployment. But one must face squarely the primary needs of countries that have no solution at present for the daily problems of nutrition and health of their children; one must understand their difficulties for a better instruction of youth with a view to the future, to organize better their economic and social structures, with respect for the authentic values of their traditions. Some efforts along the lines of bilateral or multilateral cooperation are being pursued; some international moves tried to make progress in North-South relations in the framework of UNCTAD or of the Convention of Lome. It is true that the necessity of a new international economic order becomes more and more obvious wherein man will be the real measure of the economy, as I hoped in the Encyclical *Laborem Exercens*. But are not the reforms too slow or too timid to reduce the socio-economic gap which is developing?

In regard to this, the problem of *the global indebtedness of the Third World* and of the relationships of dependence that this has created is a matter of concern to all men of good will, as Mr. Amichia has emphasized. Beyond economic and monetary aspects, it has become a problem of cooperation and of an economic ethic. It is necessary at any cost to escape from inextricable situations and humiliating pressures. There, as elsewhere, justice and the interest of all require that on the world level, the situation should be seen in its global aspect and in all its dimensions (cf. Message to the UN of October 14, 1985).

9. Peace is not only the fruit of an arrangement, a negotiation, or a joint cooperation which is still larger. More profoundly, it is a universal value, because it must *everywhere be based on justice and identical respect for the rights of man* which are obligatory on all. The two demands go together: *justice and peace*. As Pius XII stated it "*Opus justitiae pax*, peace is the fruit of justice."

Every *injustice* puts peace in danger. It is a cause or a potential factor of conflicts. It is true in the interior of a country, when an elite formed by the wealthy or the powerful exploit other citizens. It is true between countries, when under new and subtle forms, there is a socio-economic exploitation of one country by another, and likewise, when one country imposes its political system on another.

Respect for human rights

But man does not live by bread alone. It is a serious matter to endanger the dignity of man, *his fundamental rights*, his freedom of political opinion, his inalienable freedom of conscience, his freedom to express his faith while respecting the convictions of others. The enforced massive displacements of populations, the limits placed on the possibilities of disinterested help, torture, imprisonment and summary executions without the guarantees of justice, arbitrary restrictions imposed for motives of racism or apartheid, religious vexation and persecution, even carried out in secret, are so many inadmissible outrages to the ethical imperatives which are binding on every conscience to guarantee the dignity of man and to assure true peace among men. Such rights are not to be defined, bestowed or limited by a state. They transcend every power. Certainly the rights of the human person are inseparable from his duty to respect the rights of others and to cooperate for the common good. But the violation of fundamental human rights can never become a means for political goals. A regime which stifles these rights cannot pretend to be working for peace; a détente which would wish to cover up such abuses is not a true détente. Man must be sure of man and nations sure of nations (cf. Homily of January 1, 1986). There is today in our world a large number of prisoners for reasons which are solely matters of conscience. It is to be hoped that an international juridical document of the United Nations will remedy such abuses.

10. Among the obstacles to peace which I have just spoken of, there is one to which our present world is sadly exposed and which creates a climate of insecurity; *terrorism within a country or international terrorism*. We are faced with a dreadful network of people who do not hesitate to kill a great number of innocent victims, and that often occurs in countries which are foreign to them, and not involved in their problems, in order to disseminate panic and draw attention to their cause. Our reprobation cannot but be absolute and unanimous. We must condemn just as much the barbaric process of taking hostages for purposes of blackmail. This is a question of crimes against humanity. Certainly, situations exist where a just solution has been refused over a long period of time. Then there are feelings of frustration, hatred, and temptations to vengeance to which we must remain very attentive. But the reasoning – or rather the behavior ruled by passion – is totally out of place when one uses means of injustice or the massacre of innocents to plead a cause; and when, moreover, they are prepared and carried out cold-bloodedly, with the complicity of certain movements and the help of

certain powers of the State. The UN must not tolerate member States reject[ing] the principles and rules contained in its Charter by compromising themselves with terrorism. The commandment "Thou shalt not kill" is, first of all, a fundamental unchangeable principle of religion: those who honor God must be in the first rank of those who fight against all forms of terrorism. I expressed that in the prayer that ended my address to young Muslims at Casablanca: "O God, do not permit us to invoke your name to justify human disorders" (August 19, 1985).

Reprisals which also strike indiscriminately at the innocent and which continue the spiral of violence, merit, in our view, the same reprobation; they are illusory solutions and prevent the moral isolation of the terrorists.

Sporadic terrorism which rightly arouses horror in upright consciences (cf. Angelus of December 29, 1985), should not make us forget another form of *systematic terrorism*, almost institutionalized, which is based on a secret police system, and utterly destroys the freedom and elementary rights of millions of individuals, "guilty" of not bringing their thought into line with the triumphant ideology, and generally unable to attract the attention and support of international public opinion.

Eliminate terrorism
Dialogue and negotiation are finally the arm of the strong, as your Dean expressed it. Moreover, while leading a concerted and firm action to ban terrorism from the human race, it is necessary, by negotiation, to seek, before it is too late, to get rid of everything, as far as possible, that would hinder the satisfying of the just aspirations of peoples.

In particular, do we not find here the noose of injustice that must be untied to arrive at a just and equitable solution of the entire question of the *Middle East*? One continues to build up hypotheses of negotiations, but one never arrives at the decisive point of truly recognizing the rights of all the interested peoples.

In my message to the United Nations on October 14, 1985, I said: "By its nature and vocation your organization is the world forum where problems should be examined in the light of truth and justice, while renouncing narrow egoisms and threats of recourse to force." Messrs. Ambassadors, your noble missions converge on this goal; despite the general bilateral character of the relations that you have to maintain, you are asked to have the same openness to the universal, to truth and justice.

11. In ending this discourse on the universal requirements of peace, do I need to make more precise the contribution that the Church wants to bring to peace in carrying out its specific mission, its spiritual mission? This enhances the importance of the ethical imperatives about which we have spoken, and which guarantee to the utmost the accomplishment of humanitarian and political tasks. You are at the Holy See to observe constantly its discourse and initiatives. Certainly, in history, the contribution of certain Christians, of certain "Christian Nations" to peace was not always at the high level of the message of which they were the bearers. The universal vision was sometimes restricted by particular interests and egoisms. But the Christian message presented by the Church has not ceased to bring a light and strength to establish a just peace.

Permit me to recall some *doctrinal documents* which are essential stakes along the path to peace. In the course of the last decades, the Church, strengthened by experience and animated by her solicitude for the human person, presented a teaching which is a real "education for peace." In his great messages of peace in a world ruined by war, Pius XII opened the perspectives for a solid construction of peace. John XXIII, in his encyclical, *Pacem in Terris* (addressed to all men of goodwill), based on a peaceful life of men together on the central place that the human person occupies in the order willed by God, that is to say, on the dignity of the person. The rights and duties of the person correspond to the rights and duties of the community. "There is an immense task incumbent on all men of good will, namely the task of restoring the relations of the human family in truth, in justice, in love, and in freedom: the relations between individual human beings; between political communities themselves; between individuals, families, intermediate associations and political communities on the one hand and the world community on the other hand" (no. 163).

Paul VI, particularly in the encyclical *Populorum Progressio*, developed the analysis begun by his predecessor on the disorders which reign in the world because truth, justice, love, and liberty are violated. He draws attention to the situations which prevent or wreck the integral promotion of man and the joint development of peoples, keeping humanity in a state of division and conflict. Paul VI presented the development of persons and of peoples as "the new name for peace" (no. 87).

In the same perspective, Vatican Council II, in the pastoral Constitution *Gaudium et Spes* said "Peace is not merely the absence of war. Nor can it be reduced solely to the maintenance of a balance of power between enemies. Nor is it brought about by dictatorship. Instead, it is rightly and appropriately called "an enterprise of justice" . . . "and is never attained once and for all, but must be built up ceaselessly" (no. 78).

For my part, in the encyclical *Redemptor Hominis*, I emphasized the grandeur, dignity, and value which are proper to the human person. Man is "the path of the Church, the path of its life and it daily experience, its mission, and its labor." That is why the Church is attentive to the "situation of man" and to all that is contrary to the effort aimed at giving man "a human life which is always more human" (cf. no. 14; cf. Paul VI, *Populorum Progressio*, no. 21).

The concrete work of the Church
12. *In practice*, the Church – that is to say the Holy See and local Churches in communion with it – is willingly committed to encourage all true dialogues for peace, all forms of sincere negotiation and loyal cooperation. She wishes to work so that there will be an end to passions that blind one's view, and in order to rise above frontiers, dissolve hatred, and draw men near to one another; to help them and to bring them hope in the very heart of their trials in the conflicts she cannot prevent. Recently, I entrusted to Cardinal Etchegaray the mission of visiting the Iraqi prisoners in Iran, and then the Iranian prisoners in Iraq. In the name of the whole Church, I wanted to bear witness that the Holy See never abandons hope that there will be found a political solution to usher in an era of peace. The Church also wants to lend its voice to the poor, to the abandoned victims of war, to the victims of torture, and to displaced persons. Above all, the Church wishes to *educate consciences* to an openness to others, to respect for others, to a tolerance which goes hand in hand with the search for truth, and to solidarity (cf. discourse at Casablanca, August 19, 1985). Besides she knows that the root of evil, of reliance on self alone, of hardness, violence, and hate is in the heart of man; to cure it, she proposes the salvific remedies of Christ.

In this year when, we hope, all peoples will devote their attention and their efforts to the theme of peace chosen by the UN, the Church has a particular contribution to propose. She wishes to invite men, her Catholic sons, but also all Christians and all believers who would like to do so, *to a great movement of prayer for peace*. This solidarity in prayer to the Most High which is made up of confident supplication, sacrifice and commitment of one's conscience, will be very efficacious in obtaining from God the inestimable gift of peace.

13. Your Excellencies, Ladies and Gentlemen, I thank you for the attention and good will that you show and will continue to show for the Holy See's work for peace. I assure you of the Holy See's attention and good will for all the efforts of your governments in the cause of peace.

We all hope that wherever there are still raging wars, guerilla warfare, threats or situations of injustice, steps toward peace will at last be taken, for the benefit of the populations concerned. We would like strong hope to be given to populations that have been brought to humiliation, to those living in their own lands and to those who are deprived of, or driven from their land. We hope that attempts toward peace which are taking form in several places on the earth at this beginning of the New Year will be successful and will have sufficient guarantees.

But I also offer my wishes for peace to each one of you, and to your families. I have already presented them to the Lord in my prayer. I implore his blessings and protection on each one of you. Peace on earth to men whom the Lord loves, and to men of good will.

January 10, 1987
(*OR*, January 19, 1987, pp. 5–8)

1. The good wishes just expressed in your name by your Dean, His Excellency Ambassador Joseph Amichia, constitute a moving and always very much appreciated testimony from a diplomat alert to the endeavors of the Holy See and committed with it to the search for better solutions to the great problems of the world. I thank him very much, and I thank all the members of the Diplomatic Corps who have wished to associate themselves therewith.

I am pleased to meet you on the threshold of a new year for which I in my turn offer you my *cordial good wishes*, for each of you, for your families, for the countries which you represent. I have visited a certain number of those countries, which have thus become more familiar to me, but all are assured of finding here the same consideration. Each of your nations is esteemed by the Holy See, not only for its cultural heritage, its achievements or its capabilities, but in the first place because it forms a human community whose full blossoming and development I desire, with a properly recognized place in the midst of the great family of peoples. It is my wish that here too the members of the Diplomatic Corps accredited to the spiritual entity that is the Holy See should manifest among themselves a mutual openness in respect and solidarity, and that they should share in their own way in the quest for the common good of all, namely peace. I greet especially the Ambassadors attending for the first time this ceremony of the exchange of good wishes, above all those that are just beginning the mission of representing their countries to the Holy See. I am pleased also to greet your spouses and families and the members of your Embassies accompanying you.

A concerted effort
2. Your representative, after expressing kind words about some of the important activities of my Pontificate during the past year, rightly emphasized certain grave aspects of the life of today's world which urgently call for progress and a concerted effort on the part of the peoples: the injustice of racial discrimination, the dangerous situation created by the stockpiling or sale of certain weapons, the indebtedness of numerous poor countries, the scourge of drug abuse, and terrorism. These are all among the challenges that rise from the heart of every sensible person who is anxious for peace, and which the Holy See also listens to, as it tries to bring to them its own witness and contribution.

Your governments, and yourselves as diplomats, exercise an activity whose *raison d'être* and nobility consist in creating bonds of peace between nations, in asserting and defending what seems just for your country, in listening to and understanding the needs of others, in reconciling their points of view, in waging a joint struggle against those things which threaten and degrade human relationships and the dignity of life. Do I need to [tell] you, your Excellencies, that the Holy See, being a member of the international community and having established diplomatic relations with your countries, is always ready to play its part in this matter, by concerning itself with your efforts, encouraging them, sharing in them, and sometimes instigating them?

But you know also that the Holy See is primarily and essentially a religious institution, called to deal with the problems of peace in their spiritual and ethical dimension. In this spirit, I took the initiative of a gathering of religious leaders by inviting them to *Assisi on October 27 last*. His Excellency the Dean in fact referred to this event as the most characteristic of the year. Thus today I would like to dwell upon this event in particular, in order to see with you what importance it has, not only for a dialogue between religions but for the achievement in depth of the justice and peace which it is part of your duty to promote.

3. Certainly, the meeting in Assisi of the leaders and representatives of the Christian Churches or Ecclesial Communions and of the World Religions had a *fundamentally and exclusively religious character*.

It was not a matter of discussing or deciding upon concrete initiatives or plans of action which might seem useful or necessary for the strengthening of peace. I repeat that this deliberate choice of engaging solely in prayer in no way diminishes the importance of all the efforts undertaken by politicians and Heads of State for improving international relations. But the Assisi initiative had a duty to exclude all possibility of exploitation in favor of a particular political plan.

In a word, the Catholic Church, the other Churches and Ecclesial Communions and the non-Christian Religions, by responding in their own way to the decision of the United Nations to establish 1986 as a "Year of Peace," wished to do so by using *their own language*, by approaching the cause of peace in the dimension which for them is the essential one: the spiritual dimension, and more precisely *through prayer*, accompanied by fasting and by pilgrimage.

Common aspiration
Nor was it a matter, on the part of the representatives of the great religions, of negotiating upon convictions of faith in order to arrive at a syncretistic religious consensus among ourselves. On the contrary, it was a matter of together turning, in a disinterested way, toward the capital objective of peace among men and among the peoples, or rather it was a matter of turning, all of us, toward God, in order to implore this gift from him. Prayer is the first duty of religious people, their typical expression.

Thus, the representatives of these religions showed in their own way their concern for the basic good of humanity. They have manifested the irreplaceable position which the religious sense retains in the hearts of people today. Even if unfortunately religion has sometimes been the occasion of divisions, the Assisi meeting expressed a certain common aspiration, the appeal of all to journey toward one final end, God; the personalities who were present there affirmed their intention of now fulfilling a decisive role in the construction of world peace (cf. General Audience of October 22, 1986).

4. Perhaps certain diplomats will ask themselves: in what way will prayer for peace advance peace?

The fact is that peace is first of all a *gift of God*. God is the one who establishes it, for it is he who gives to humanity the whole of creation in order to administer and develop it in a united way. It is God who inscribes in man's conscience the laws which require him to respect life and the person of his neighbor. God does not cease to call man to peace; he is the guarantor of man's rights. He desires men to live together in such a way as to express mutual relations founded on justice, respect and solidarity. He also helps them interiorly to attain peace or recover it, through his Holy Spirit.

From man's point of view, peace is also *something good on the human level*, of a rational and moral nature. It is the fruit of free wills guided by reason toward the common good to be achieved. In this sense it seems within the reach of the well-educated and mature man who thinks about the means of living – in truth, justice and love – a wider solidarity, in contrast to "the law of the jungle," the law of the strongest. But to be more precise, one does not see how this moral order could ignore God, the first source of being, essential truth and supreme good. Prayer is the way to acknowledge humbly that Source and to submit to it. Far from stifling man's responsibility it stimulates it. Experience shows that where man has thought it good to free himself from God, it is possible for him to preserve for a time the ideals of truth and justice which are inherent in his rational nature, but he risks losing touch with them by interpreting them to please his immediate interests, desires and passions.

Yes, history bears witness that men left to themselves have a tendency to follow their irrational and selfish instincts. They thus experience the truth that *peace is beyond human powers*. For it requires additional light and strength, a liberation from aggressive passions, a faithful commitment to building a society together, indeed a world community, founded on the common good of each and of all. Reference to the truth of God gives man the ideal and the energy needed to overcome unjust situations, to free himself from ideologies of domination and hatred, and to make an advance toward true universal brotherhood.

A religious attitude frees man by putting him in contact with the transcendent. To those who believe in a personal God who is all-powerful, man's friend and the source of peace, prayer appears to be truly necessary in order to ask him for the peace which they cannot give to themselves, that is, peace among men, the peace which begins in men's conscience.

Prayer changes hearts

5. Authentic prayer *already changes man's heart*. God is fully aware of what we need. If he invites us to ask for peace, it is because this humble approach mysteriously transforms the people who pray and puts them on the path to reconciliation and brotherhood.

Indeed, the person who prays to God sincerely, as we tried to do in Assisi, *contemplates* the harmony desired by God the creator, the love which is in God, the ideal of peace among men, that ideal which Saint Francis embodied in an incomparable way. For this the person who prays gives thanks to God. He senses that the human family is one in its origin and in its destiny, that it comes from God and will return to God. He knows that every man and woman bears within himself or herself the image of God, despite the limits and failures of the human spirit tempted by the spirit of evil. The person who accepts the Christian revelation goes further in this contemplation: he knows that Christ has united himself in some way with every man, has redeemed him, making him a brother, and gathers together in himself the scattered children of God. The person who prays thus feels a profound unity with all those who seek in religion spiritual and transcendent values in response to the great questions of the human heart.

Then, as he looks at himself, he recognizes his prejudices, his deficiencies, his failures; he easily sees how selfishness, jealousy and aggressiveness, in himself and in others, are the real obstacles to peace. For this *he asks forgiveness* of God and his brethren, he fasts, he does penance, he seeks purification.

He understands finally that he cannot ask for peace if he stands idly by. His prayer becomes an expression of his willingness to work in order to overcome these obstacles, by making a *resolute commitment* to promote peace.

These are not the benefits that prayer brings. Is not this what resulted from all the prayers uttered in Assisi? No self-justification, no plea on behalf of a particular ideology, no acceptance of violence, deflected those prayers away from their goal: the search for peace as God would have it. Men who pray in this way either remain or become peacemakers. They can no longer accept or go back to unjust or hateful behavior toward their fellowmen *without a flagrant contradiction*. Certainly, this contradiction can always arise, for temptations remain. That is why at Casablanca I prayed to God in these words "Do not permit it to happen that in invoking your name we should resort to justifying human disorders." That would be a sign that the prayer was not deep enough, true enough, long-lasting enough. It would be a sign that fanaticism has distorted it and manipulated it. But in itself the authentic act of prayer puts one on the path of true peace, because it signifies and brings about conversion of heart.

6. By showing that peace and religion go hand in hand, the Assisi event underlined once again that *peace is fundamentally ethical in nature*. I mentioned this fact on that occasion in the presence of my brothers and sisters of all religions: "In the great battle for peace, humanity, even with its diversity, must draw upon the deepest and most enlivening sources where conscience is formed and upon which human action is based" (First Address, no. 2). Besides the basic conviction that peace surpasses human efforts and must be sought in the Reality which is beyond us all, an element common to all religions is in fact "a profound respect for conscience and an obedience to conscience which teaches all of us to seek the truth, to love and to serve every person and all peoples," to respect, protect and promote human life, to overcome selfishness, greed, and the spirit of revenge (cf. *Final Discourse at Assisi*, nos. 2 and 4). That is to say that the Catholic Church recognizes the spiritual, social, and moral values which are found in the various religions. During my visit to India I stressed the value of Mahatma Gandhi's teaching on "the supremacy of the spirit and truth-force (*satyagraha*) which triumphs without violence by the intrinsic dynamism of just action" (Discourse of February 1, 1986, at Raj Ghat, no. 2.) In the presence of the young Muslims at Casablanca, I said that when we invoke God "we must also respect, love and help every human being because he is a creature of God and, in a certain sense, his image and representative" (August 19, 1985, no. 2). At the Rome Synagogue, I emphasized the fact that "Jews and Christians are the depositaries and the witnesses of an ethic marked by the Ten Commandments, in obedience to which man finds his truth and his liberty," and I noted that "Jesus carried to the ultimate limit the love demanded by the Torah" (April 13, 1986, nos. 6 and 7).

Religions worthy of the name, the open religions spoken of by Bergson – which are not just projections of human desires but an openness and submission to the transcendent will of God which asserts itself in every conscience – such religions permit the establishment of peace. This is also true of *philosophies* which recognize that peace is a reality of the moral order. Philosophies of this kind show the need to rise above the instincts; they affirm the radical equality of all the members of the human family, the sacred dignity of life, of the person, of the conscience, and the unity of the human family which demands true solidarity.

Without an absolute respect for man founded on a spiritual vision of the human being, there is no peace. This is the witness of Assisi. It was given by religious representatives in the spirit of the whole world, so that the world might find there light and support. I hope that this conviction also inspires your activity as diplomats.

7. In the concrete, respect for man entails respect *for his fundamental rights*. To the great question "how can peace be maintained?" one must respond "*within the framework of justice* among individuals and among peoples." Today we are lucky enough to see the rights of man being catalogued more and more clearly and being claimed ever more strongly: the right to life at every stage of its development; the right to respect, whatever the individual's race, sex or religion; the right to the material goods necessary for life; the right to work and to a fair share of the fruits of labor; the right to education; the right to freedom of spirit and of creativity; the right to respect for conscience and particularly to freedom of relationship with God.

Nor must one forget *the rights of nations* to preserve and defend their independence, their cultural identity, the possibility of sound organization, running their own affairs and freely determining their destinies, without being at the mercy, either directly or indirectly, of foreign powers. You know as well as I do the cases in which this right is clearly violated.

Such rights are the expression of the demands of the dignity of man. Those rights, worked out especially in the West by consciences which had been formed by Christianity, have become the heritage of all humanity, and are claimed in every part of the world. However, as well as being a claim they are also a duty for individuals and for States to create conditions which ensure that they can be exercised. Countries that wish to suspend these duties, under various pretexts – such as a totalitarian concept of power, an obsession with security, a desire to maintain privileges for certain categories, ideology, fears of every kind – damage peace. They live a false peace which also risks leading to sad awakenings. When these countries move out of dictatorship without preparation for a democratic life, as we have seen with certain countries during the past year, the road is difficult and slow. Each one then has to become aware of what is required by the common good, while avoiding individual excesses in the exercise of freedom. But these countries deserve encouragement, along this path of peace, which is the only one of value.

Mediation between conscience and actual life

The ethical imperative of peace and justice of which I have just spoken presents itself as both a right and a duty first of all on the level of the well-formed conscience, among people of good will, in communities which are sincerely interested in seeking peace and in truthfully training people for it. It then helps to influence *public opinion*. But it must also find expression, support and *a guarantee in appropriate juridical instruments* of civil society, in declarations, or rather in treaties, agreements and institutions, at the level of the nation, region, continent, and world community, so as to avoid as much as possible situations in which the weak fall victim to the ill will, force or manipulation of others. The progress of civilization consists in finding the means to protect, defend and promote, at the level of structures, that which is just and good for the conscience. Diplomacy too finds its field of action in this mediation between conscience and actual life.

If these efforts fail, whether at the level of individual conscience or at the level of structures, then true peace is no longer secure. It is fragile or else it is false. It then risks being reduced to the temporary absence of war, to tolerance, including tolerance of abuses which injure man, and to opportunism. It gives way before the concern to preserve at any price particular advantages while closing in on self. It gives way especially before the instincts of aggression or xenophobia, before the anticipated effectiveness of the class struggle, before the temptation to rely for strength solely on the superiority of weapons which intimidate the adversary, before the law of the strongest, before terrorism or the methods of certain guerillas who are prepared to use every violent means, even against the innocent; or before clever attempts to destabilize other countries, efforts to manipulate, before lying propaganda, all under the appearances of seeking something good or just.

9. When one sees the absurd ravages caused by wars and the major peril of widespread and very severe destruction which would be caused by the use of weapons possessed by certain countries, one may think that the world situation calls for the *most radical refusal possible of war* as a means of solving conflicts.

It is in this perspective that for October 27, I had invited all those engaged in hostilities to observe a complete ceasefire, at least on that day. A good number accepted the proposal favorably, and I congratulate them. It was a significant gesture which associated them with our religious supplication for peace, and I believe in the spiritual efficacy of signs. It was also a pause which permitted the sparing of human lives, which are all precious; it was an occasion given to each to reflect on the vanity and inhumanity of war for solving tensions and conflicts which could be settled by the means offered by the law; it was an invitation to renounce once and for all the violence of arms.

Instruments of dialogue
Of course, this does not mean the total setting aside of the principle whereby each people, each Government, has the right and duty to protect by proportionate means its own existence and liberty against an unjust aggressor. But war appears more and more to be the most barbaric and most ineffective means of solving conflicts between two countries or of gaining power in one's own country. It is necessary rather to do everything possible to acquire instruments of dialogue and negotiation, with the arbitration if needs be of impartial third parties, or of an international Authority endowed with sufficient powers.

10. In any case, a fundamental threat is posed by the *development of weapons of every sort* with a view to ensuring domination over others or at the expense of others. Should not arms be reduced to a level compatible with legitimate defense, with the abandonment of those which can be in no way be included in this category?

Is there any need to repeat that such an arms race is dangerous, destructive and scandalous in the eyes of those countries which cannot ensure for their own people the food and health care needed for survival? This is one of the *key problems of North-South relations,* and it seems, from the ethical point of view, even more fundamental than the problem of East-West relations. Another crucial point is that of external debt and of balance of exchange, which are matters that particularly concern the Holy See, for, in a word, what really matters is the united development of peoples. *Solidarity is by nature ethical* and a fundamental key to peace. It presupposes that one sees things from the point of view of the people which is in need and of seeking what is good for that people, while considering the people as an active agent of its own development. This solidarity is based upon the realization that we make up a single human family. This is the purpose of the Message for the World Day of Peace that I entrusted to you this year.

While aiming for the development of the peoples as a whole, means must be found to come to the aid of *the smaller groups* which are left aside, in a poverty or danger unworthy of humanity. They are legion. For example, I am thinking of those who are affected by the famine in Ethiopia or the Sudan; and I am thinking of the tragic plight of so many refugees. Admirable private initiatives have concerned themselves with these people; but what will they be able to do if Governments and the international community do not make their contribution?

11. From the Peace Message for this year I repeat this one sentence in order to conclude these words: "As solidarity gives us the ethical basis to act upon, development becomes the offer that brother makes to brother, so that both can live more fully in all the diversity and complementarily that are the hallmarks of human civilization" (no. 7).

Very frequently, in speaking of the rights of man, we have in view only the equality of men and their liberty. Men's equality in dignity is to be guaranteed always and everywhere; it does not necessarily require the equality of all situations, which risks being a snare and which continually creates conflicts. What is of capital importance is *brotherhood*. It appears as the keystone of the ever fragile edifice of democracy, as the goal of the ever difficult journey toward peace, as its decisive inspiration. It removes the contradiction so frequently pointed out between equality and liberty. It transcends strict justice. Its driving force is *love*. The Fathers of the Second Vatican Council emphasized this aspect: "Hence peace is likewise the fruit of love, which goes beyond what justice can provide" (Constitution *Gaudium et Spes*, 78). This love is at the heart of the Gospel of Jesus Christ, who in an incomparable manner gave the world a taste of it when he invited us to become the neighbor of every man, as a brother. This love presupposes a rising above self, which is favored by a religious attitude but which is in any case necessary to life in society. A world without fraternal love will never know anything but a fragmentary peace, a peace that is fragile and threatened. In case of war, the belligerent countries will be incapable of renouncing the desire to dominate, even at the price of a tragic massacre or senseless destruction, because this would be humiliating for them. Only the spirit of brotherhood will lead them to accept and offer a truce or rather a peace which is not humiliating for the other side.

Your Excellencies, Ladies and Gentlemen, it is not within my competence to propose more precise technical solutions for the grave problems of peace and development which we have evoked. But I have considered it appropriate to reflect with you upon the spirit which opens the door to viable solutions: humility, dialogue, respect, justice, brotherhood. The experience of Assisi, at the level of the representatives of the religions, was inspired by this spirit. May you be enabled to find in it light for your noble mission as ambassadors! And may the world drink from the same source, in order to know the peace that God destines for it!

January 9, 1988
(*OR*, January 25, 1988, pp. 6–8)

1. I am very grateful to your Dean, His Excellency Mr. Joseph Amichia, for having just expressed your best wishes to me with great tact and with deep trust in the successor of Peter. With a sensitivity conferred by faith he was able to evoke some events of great importance to the Church, while suggesting their connection with the present history of humanity. As an observer who is both wise and concerned for the good of all countries, particularly the most needy, he also noted the human problems that continue to trouble so many people. These difficulties in effect are like so many shadows and handicaps to be overcome so that the populations concerned may live this new year in peace. We also well know that it is a question of all peoples working in solidarity.

For my part, I too wish to express my wishes within this context of present realities. But first I want to extend *cordial good wishes* to all the members of the Diplomatic Corps here present, with a special word of welcome to the Ambassadors who are taking part in this gathering for the first time. I would like to note that the first Ambassador from Guinea-Bissau has just recently begun his mission. On Christmas and New Year's Day, I remembered all of you in prayer as well as your families and the nations you represent. Your governments have sought to establish stable diplomatic relations with the Holy See, which has an essentially spiritual mission, that is to say, one oriented toward the total good of individuals and of peoples in accordance with God's plan. May God preserve all of you and your compatriots in peace.

Conflicts still exist
2. I will develop this annual message for the New Year around some international events, including the negotiations on disarmament at the end of last year in Washington, and the fortieth anniversary of the Universal Declaration of Human Rights which we celebrate this year. Disarmament, justice in safeguarding the rights of individuals and of peoples and development are, in effect, three conditions for peace.

But these important points cannot allow us to forget the harsh conflicts that still split apart peoples or entire regions. No one can remain indifferent in the face of these conflicts that every day threaten or extinguish human lives, destroy the social or cultural patrimony of an entire people, stifling it or hindering it from freely progressing toward its development. Certainly the first responsibility belongs to the governments directly involved. But they must know that all of humanity suffers and is humiliated by the evils which overwhelm one part of its members, and that with them it seeks a favorable and humane solution.

Some of the peoples involved can invoke the reasons they have for an armed response to attacks, resorting to the morally acceptable distinction between legitimate defense and unjustified aggression. But motives are often very complex, and in any case, situations arise in which the escalation is such that it surpasses all limits and finally proves to be unjust because it is deadly and ruinous for the different parties.

All of us are mindful of the conflict between Iraq and Iran, where it is urgent to put an end to an inhumane combat that is terribly destructive, we may even say senseless. In fact, many other countries are concerned with this conflict. It is time for them to cooperate sincerely so that hostilities may cease, especially with the help of the institutions of the international community.

Afghanistan merits equal attention. For eight years we have witnessed the tragedy of its people whose life, formerly peaceful, has been subjected to incredible changes and to considerable human losses, while the peace of the whole region has been affected by it. We cannot fail to hope that the repeated prospects for negotiations may finally succeed, and that a just solution may be reached which corresponds to the wishes of the people.

We may also think of *Central America* where bloody antagonisms continue seriously to trouble the peace in many countries. Proposals for re-establishing peace are the object of a specific plan. The commitments that have been given are finally a source of hope. May they find among all parties a loyal adherence and an effective application that does not neglect any of the elements, including the right of populations to live under a regime that is freely chosen!

Nor may we forget all of the *Near East*, the populations that live in the land of *Palestine*, within a political and social context that is always precarious: *Lebanon*, where economic [hardship] is added to division and insecurity, at a time when it is absolutely necessary to assure its sovereignty and integrity.

We are thinking equally of *internal situations of conflict* which in bloody fashion are affecting so many countries like Ethiopia, Angola, Mozambique, and Sri Lanka, often to the extent of hampering aid to populations that are dying of hunger or that lack basic care. Other countries continue to suffer in silence from an unjust situation that violates the aspirations of a majority of citizens, as in Cambodia, or even, as often happens, the aspirations of a minority.

We must always remember that civilian populations are the first to suffer from these prolonged crises, with all the human tragedy that this entails. That is why I wish, once again, to appeal to all those who can contribute to the alleviation of these conflicts, particularly through diplomacy. The Holy See remains convinced that it is possible in all these cases to arrive at a solution without the belligerents finding themselves humiliated as a result. With the peaceful support of figures from international life, may they show courage in finding those paths that lead without delay to true peace, the essential conditions of which I now wish to recall.

Encouraging prospects
3. The will to put an end to the arms race, or still better, the will for effective disarmament, is obviously one of the conditions for peace.

Among international events of the past year, one must note especially the negotiation and signing by the United States and the Soviet Union of an agreement for *the elimination of intermediate range nuclear weapons*. This event, the importance of which I emphasized from December 8 last (cf. Angelus of December 8, 1987, *L'Osservatore Romano*, December 9, 1987), was generally welcomed with satisfaction and relief, because it represents the outcome of continued effort and at the same time opens up encouraging prospects for the consolidation of the disarmament process and for the future of peace. Thanks to their political will, the two great powers were able to create a new situation in which they agreed no longer just to limit but to destroy physically an entire class of weapons.

The stockpiling of these weapons in itself constitutes a threat to peace, as well as a provocation to the peoples that lack the essentials for survival and development. The fact that a portion of these weapons is being destroyed is praiseworthy today. It only emphasizes better the foolishness of the spiral in which we were allowing ourselves to be led, to the point of excessively diverting to this sector the wealth that should have been used to eliminate hunger in the world and to promote much needed humanitarian projects, notably in the areas of health and education, by activating the positive possibilities of science and technology.

Nuclear disengagement, which for the time being still involves only a very limited proportion of the respective arsenals, may now be pursued without the global military balance being called into question, to the point of reaching the lowest level compatible with mutual security. The detailed control measures put into place by the treaty show a realistic desire to have the guarantees necessary to ensure that the commitments entered into will be effectively respected. This mutual surveillance, freely agreed to, can help to overcome the climate of suspicion and can contribute to the long-term growth in trust that is required. Only a climate of growing trust can guarantee the success of the disarmament process and open up new possibilities for the future.

4. Further progress is awaited by all, as your Dean has just mentioned. According to the protagonists, the agreement on the intermediate nuclear weapons is more a point of departure than an end in itself. It was the occasion for the two signatories to affirm their determination to accelerate the negotiations taking place on *ballistic nuclear weapons*, which are the most menacing of all. It is important not only to mitigate but to remove definitively the threat of a nuclear catastrophe. It is certainly the wish of the entire international community that such talks succeed as soon as possible, inspired by the same principles.

It seems no less urgent to proceed to the elimination of another class of weapons that are especially cruel and unworthy of humanity, and that some belligerents have used again recently. I am referring to *chemical weapons*. I implore the political leaders involved to add this subject to the objectives that can be achieved without delay. An important step would thus be taken for the morality of international relations that would help improve the climate of dialogue to which the great powers and their respective allies now have to get accustomed.

Probably still more arduous will be the discussion on the subject of *the reduction of conventional weapons* and tactical nuclear arms, as they are called, connected with them. Here again, security ought to be ensured at the lowest level of weapons and forces compatible with reasonable requirements for defense, and on the basis of a balance between the parties facing each other. On this last point, one can understand that political leaders move forward with prudence and realism so as not to compromise the future of their fellow citizens for lack of sufficient guarantees. But there is need to avoid at all cost a new form of escalation in conventional weapons which would be hazardous and ruinous.

5. Equally one would hope that all countries, and especially the great powers, will perceive more and more that the fear of "mutually assured destruction," which is at the heart of the doctrine of *nuclear deterrence*, cannot be a reliable basis for security and peace in the long term. The Holy See, for its part, has always affirmed the deterrence

based on a balance of terror cannot be considered an end in itself, but only a stage toward progressive disarmament (cf. Message to the second special session of the General Assembly of the United Nations on disarmament, June 7, 1982, no. 8, *AAS* 74 [1982], p. 880). It is only on the condition of remaining fundamentally transitional and oriented toward the search for another type of international relationship that this strategy can be considered. Such a strategy, applied in a context of détente and cooperation, must lead to a progressive search for a new balance at the lowest possible level of weapons, so as to arrive eventually at the elimination of the atomic weapon itself. In this matter one must move toward total disarmament. May the protagonists understand that their mutual security is always furthered by an interpenetration of interests and vital relations!

A point of no return for the international community
6. If the recent disarmament agreement was able to be concluded it was also thanks to the intense international work undertaken over the *years by the United Nations*, notably by the Commission on Disarmament and by the Conference for Disarmament in Geneva. This work makes it possible to appreciate all the elements that come together to secure peace among nations, as well as the long road that remains to be traveled. If the agreement in Washington constitutes a beginning for the benefit of the international community, may it also represent for that community *a point of no return*! A return to the arms race would without doubt be fatal for all. Nations that live under different political or social systems now understand better that they must learn to live together, find grounds for cooperation, and deepen their peaceful relations. And it is your honor, ladies and gentlemen in the diplomatic service, to devote your skills to preparing these relations and to maintaining them.

To achieve these relations, certain ethical values and norms of law must be respected.

7. *Disarmament, then, is not all there is to peace*. It is not even an end to itself. It is one of the elements in the process of seeking a more stable security, looking in the end to establish mutual relations based on fair dialogue, on more intense cooperation and on greater trust.

In this sense, peace takes root in a *renewal of moral and spiritual convictions*. Humanity is invited to change its attitude. It must believe that peace is possible, that it is desirable, that it is necessary. In order to survive, humanity is called to a turnabout, to conversion, even if it means detaching itself from a part of its history – its history of war, filled with violence and oppression, in which men and nations were reduced to the mercy of the stronger party in defiance of the justice and moral order willed by God.

Peace is not only the absence of conflict, but the peaceful resolution of differences among nations, and the driving force of a social and international order founded on law and justice. More specifically, it is necessary to secure the foundations of peace by basing them on the *protection of the rights of man and also on the rights of peoples*.

8. Indeed, justice travels the road of *respect for the right of peoples and nations* to self-determination. A lasting peace cannot be imposed upon peoples by the will of the

strongest, but must be agreed to by all, with respect for the rights of each, particularly the weak and minorities.

There are still peoples who do not see *their right to independence* being recognized. There are also those who suffer under a protectorate, indeed an occupation, that undermines their right to self-government in conformity with their cultural values and their history.

Short of these extreme cases, which are unanimously condemned, one must take into account a desire that is more and more widespread and legitimate, that every nation, even the least powerful, be responsible for its own affairs, that it be *the subject of its own development* and not only the object of negotiations of interest to others or of condescending solicitude on the part of other nations.

In both the East and the West, the right of peoples to determine their destiny and to cooperate freely with others for the international common good cannot fail to foster peace to the extent that each feels better respected, and thus a full partner in the dialogue among nations.

9. The same principle holds for *relations between North and South*. Inequality of access to economic and social progress likewise has profound causes that demand to be carefully examined. The pronounced imbalances between abundance and poverty can be the seeds of future conflict. A great many countries – about sixty – are today in a critical situation that is growing worse. All of humanity must recognize in conscience its responsibilities in the face of the serious problem of *hunger* that it has not succeeded in resolving. This is truly the emergency of emergencies!

Efforts made over the decades to foster *development* must constantly be refocused on their original goal, that is, always to enable needy countries to take greater charge of themselves, to utilize their resources, to exchange their raw materials for a fair price, to have access to technology and to world markets, and reasonably to free themselves from debt, as your Dean has pointed out. This process makes an appeal to the responsibility of the more prosperous nations, but also to the responsibility of the leaders of the countries in question. It is incumbent upon them to manage available resources better, to forego certain expenditures for prestige purposes, to move away from the oligarchic structures that perpetuate social immobility, and to promote productive initiative, while at the same time respecting the rights of individuals and of their communities.

Yes, one of the profound conditions for peace over the long term is *development*, understood as the transition from being less to being more, encompassing all of man in his economic dimension certainly, but in his cultural, moral and spiritual dimensions as well. One can never say often enough that "development is the new name for peace," to use the beautiful expression of my predecessor Paul VI. I will return to this major theme in a future encyclical to be published in commemoration of the twentieth anniversary of *Populorum Progressio*.

The two processes of disarmament and development must continue until they are joined together and support one another. It would be especially absurd if aid for development became aid for weapons in Third World countries, even if these countries need the means to defend themselves. The power politics of industrial countries must not cancel with one hand the contribution granted by the other for the authentic development of peoples.

Climate of peace

10. The independence and freedom of States among themselves does not suffice to establish a climate of peace in the world. Peace is also *social peace*, order founded on *justice within sovereign States*, to which it fails to guarantee by just laws the conditions for a human life worthy of the name for all their citizens. It seems to me toady that what the teaching of the Church calls the "natural order" of co-existence, the "order willed by God," finds its expression partly in the culture *of the rights of man*, if one can thus characterize a civilization founded on respect for the transcendent value of the person. The person is in effect the foundation and the goal of the social order. The person is the subject of inalienable rights and of duties of conscience, guaranteed by the Creator, and is not first and foremost the object of "rights" granted by the State, at the whim of the public interest as determined by the State. The person must be able to fulfill himself or herself in freedom and in truth.

This year we are celebrating the *fortieth anniversary of the "Universal Declaration of Human Rights."* Although it is given different interpretations, the lofty principles that it contains merit universal attention. This document may be considered "a milestone on the long and difficult path of the human race" (Discourse to the United Nations, October 2, 1979, no. 7). The principles contained in the Declaration, if faithfully put into practice in the legislation of the different countries, can lead nations to authentic progress, with the understanding that this progress is identified above all with "the primacy given to the spiritual values and by the progress of moral life" (cf. ibid.).

11. The Declaration is of such importance in our eyes that it transcends the **racial**, cultural and institutional **differences** of peoples, and affirms beyond every kind of boundary *the equal dignity of all members of the human community*. It is a dignity that every constituted society, whether national or international, must respect, protect and promote.

The happiness of individuals depends on it, as does the peace of the world. The fact is that peace is indivisible. It cannot be secured on the international level if it is not rooted in social peace within nations. Every unjust situation inflicted upon a human community carries the risk of one day exploding and even assuming international dimensions that no one will any longer be able to control. "The spirit of war," as I said to the United Nations General Assembly in 1979, "in its basic, primordial meaning springs up and grows to maturity where the inalienable rights of man are violated" (ibid., no. 11).

These human rights are individual rights as well as social rights, such as those that assure an active participation in public life. In today's context of violence, I consider it my duty to recall *the right of absolute respect for human life*, in all its stages and whatever the state of health, from conception until its last moments. I equally condemn all forms of *terrorism* which attack the life of innocent people, and also State terrorism which stifles fundamental liberties.

I am especially mindful of *freedom of conscience*. As you know, I devoted my most recent Message for the World Day of Peace to this major theme. The right to religious freedom, that is, the power to comply with the dictates of one's conscience in the search for truth and to profess publicly one's faith by freely belonging to an organized religious community, is, as it were, the *raison d'être* for the other fundamental freedoms of man. To the extent that the profession of a conviction touches the conscience most intimately, it cannot fail to influence the choices and commitments of man. This being so, believers are led to contribute effectively to public morality, to solidarity among individuals, and to peace among peoples. That is why the Catholic Church has not ceased to exercise vigilance in order to ensure that everything is done to put an end to persecution and to discrimination against believers and their communities. In doing this, she is conscious of serving humanity by defending the dignity of the person.

True artisans of peace

12. In the final analysis, peace is inseparable from **justice**, from **freedom**, rightly understood, and from **truth**. It presumes a climate of trust. It is something more complex than disarmament alone, even though the latter is still very important process for building a world of peace and as a test of the will for peace.

In this context, I would like to express here my best wishes for a successful conclusion to the meeting of the Conference on Security and Cooperation in Europe, now taking place in Vienna. The final document now in preparation should represent a notable contribution in securing and furthering together the military and humanitarian aspects of peace.

For her part, **the Church** recognizes her responsibility in building peace. Not only does she recall the principles drawn from the Gospel, but she also seeks to form people capable of being true artisans of peace in the places where they live.

God's plan is a plan of peace for all of humanity. Most **believers** know that God is the Creator, the source of life, the guarantor of justice, the defender of the oppressed, the One who ceaselessly calls men to live in fraternity, or to be reconciled, to be forgiven, to rebuild in peace that which has been destroyed and divided by thoughtless and sinful men. True believers must be in the front line of those who work for peace and who, at the same time, await it from God as a gift while seeking his will.

Your Excellencies, ladies and gentlemen, as diplomats you too have a select part to play in the building of peace, in the disarming of prejudices, suspicions and rigidity, in the soothing of tensions, in the search for peaceful solutions, in the climate of trust and cooperation to be established, with the necessary prudence.

May the God of peace inspire your mission and bestow his blessing upon each of you, your families, and your countries!

January 9, 1989
(*OR*, February 13, 1989, pp. 1–3)

1. Your Dean, Ambassador Joseph Amichia, has just voiced the respectful greetings that you wished to convey to me, as well as the sentiments evoked in you by the most notable aspects of the Holy See's mission in the world. I thank him most cordially for this. At the same time, I wish to express my gratitude to all of you who have desired to associate yourselves with his remarks.

It is also my pleasure to welcome the Ambassadors who have been recently accredited, as well as their staff members who have begun their duties in the course of the year just ended. Their experience will be invaluable for us all. We likewise hope that their experience will in turn be enriched by the Apostolic See's views on international life.

For the Pope, the New Year meeting with the Diplomatic Corps accredited to the Holy See is a special moment for reflecting on some of the major matters at stake in the world, matters for which you and he share a common concern.

The Church's views on the challenges of our time are not always of course those of the nations. But the experience of centuries and the constant reference to the same values and ethical criteria make it possible for the views of the Holy See – situated as they are above political, economic or strategic interests – to offer a point of reference to the impartial observer who seeks to broaden the basis of his judgments. For her part, the Catholic Church is convinced that she is serving humanity in accordance with the plan of her Founder when she endeavors to dispense freely the treasure of wisdom and doctrine which has been entrusted to her so that each generation can derive from it the light and strength needed to guide its choices.

2. The international community has *a number of reasons to rejoice* at the strengthening of détente between East and West, as well as the progress made in the area of disarmament, both on the bilateral level between the Union of Soviet Socialist Republics and the United States of America with regard to strategic weapons, and on the multilateral level with regard to chemical weapons. On this subject, the Holy See hopes that the Conference being held in Paris on the banning of chemical weapons will bear lasting fruit.

The willingness to tackle with determination the question of reducing conventional weapons in Europe, shown by both NATO and the Warsaw Pact, allows us to think that soon the negotiators of the countries concerned will be duly mandated to define a common approach and to propose concrete measures and effective control mechanisms for the purpose of really freeing the peoples of Europe from the fear caused by the presence of offensive weapons and the possibility of surprise attacks.

In this context, the Holy See has followed with great interest the meeting of the Conference on European Security and Cooperation now taking place in Vienna, and it hopes that these efforts will be quickly concluded with a substantive and balanced final document which will take into account simultaneously the military, economic, social and humanitarian aspects of security, without which the "old" continent cannot know lasting peace. Human rights and religious freedom have been the subject of detailed discussion in Vienna, and they should be given a prominent place in the future closing document of the meeting, which from this fact will be of special importance.

The removal of obstacles which one has been able to note recently testifies to a growing awareness of the urgency which respect for these rights and this freedom and their effective exercise presents.

Let us hope then, Ladies and Gentlemen, that the developments which have taken place recently in the Soviet Union and other countries of Central and Eastern Europe will help to create favorable conditions for a change of climate and for an evolution of national legislations, so as to move effectively from the stage of a proclamation of principles to one which guarantees the fundamental rights and freedoms of every person. Such a process in these countries should lead in particular to the emergence of a concept of religious freedom understood as a true civil and social right.

Democratization, pacification and cooperation

Looking beyond Europe, I would also like to mention a region racked by many years of endemic national and regional struggles, the peoples of which ardently desire a true and lasting peace. I refer to Central America. It is now more than a year since the Heads of State of five countries signed the "Esquipulas II" Accord, with a view to ending the sufferings of their peoples. The concepts of democratization, pacification and regional cooperation which are at the basis of this agreement ought to find an ever greater response among political leaders. We must hope then that all the interested parties will courageously resume the path of sincere and constructive dialogue, that the commitments provided for in the Accord – as for example the "national commissions of reconciliation" – will be effectively implemented, and that the reinsertion of all political forces in the public life of these countries will be promoted.

The past year also very happily witnessed the beginning of a negotiated settlement of several conflicts in other regions. I am thinking first of all of the long-awaited cease-fire signed between Iran and Iraq. Their decision to begin talks under the aegis of the United Nations Organization is encouraging, to the extent that these discussions foster dialogue and strengthen the desire for peace of the two parties.

In this regard, however, there is one aspect which I cannot pass over in silence: the return of the prisoners of war to their homelands. At the beginning of the New Year, which is an occasion everywhere for family reunions, how can we forget all those who have spent these holidays far from their loved ones? How can we fail to express the hope that the Authorities of these two countries, assisted by the competent International Organizations, will come to an agreement concerning the methods of repatriation, and thus shorten the sufferings of these men and give many families the joy of reunions so impatiently awaited?

Still further East, the effective withdrawal of foreign troops from Afghanistan should be the prelude to an honorable solution enabling each interested party to promote a fresh stage in the reconstruction and development of that country.

Initiatives and persevering efforts on the part of various countries – particularly the nations of South East Asia – permit us to hope for a comprehensive settlement of the problem of Cambodia, the population of which has been sorely tried for so many years.

Still in that same region, certain recent gestures by the Vietnamese Authorities – also with reference to religious matters – holds forth the promise of a readiness on the part of that noble nation to resume an increasingly fruitful dialogue in the concert of nations.

We must also express the wish that the necessary dialogue and understanding will promote a solution to the very complex Korean problem. In this sense, the efforts of the Authorities involved deserve every encouragement.

It is also encouraging to think that the conflicts which have torn apart certain countries of Southern Africa will soon come to an end thanks to the Brazzaville Protocol and the New York Accord with a view to the process of independence for Namibia and the pacification of Angola. The inhabitants of these regions have suffered too cruelly for their fate to leave the international community indifferent.

Finally, as the latest sign of "good will," I would like to mention the immense movement of solidarity manifested on the occasion of the tragic earthquake which occurred last December in Soviet Armenia. It is to be hoped that this solidarity which people are capable of showing in such tragic circumstances – a solidarity which transcends borders and political or ideological divisions – will increasingly become their common rule of action.

Causes for concern
3. Unfortunately, however, *causes for concern* are certainly not lacking and somewhat dampen our confidence. In these last few days, tension in the Mediterranean has shown, yet again, how fragile the international equilibrium is.

I have repeatedly had occasion to express my dismay at the tragedy being experienced by Lebanon and to express the hope that the national unity of that country will be restored, in particular as a result of a reaffirmation of its sovereignty and at least through a resumption of the normal functioning of the institutions of the State. We cannot resign ourselves to seeing that country deprived of its unity, territorial integrity, sovereignty and independence. It is a question here of rights which are fundamental and incontestable for every nation. Once more, with the same conviction, before this authoritative assembly, I invite all countries friendly to Lebanon and her people to join forces in helping the Lebanese to rebuild in dignity and freedom, the peaceful and exemplary homeland to which they aspire.

In this tortured region of the Middle East, new elements have recently appeared on the horizon of the destiny of the Palestinian people. They appear to favor the solution long recommended by the United Nations Organization, namely the right of the Palestinian and Israeli peoples to a homeland. I also wish to express here my hope that the Holy City of Jerusalem, which is claimed by both these peoples as the symbol of their identity, can one day become a place of peace and a meeting place for each of them. This City, unique among all others, which evokes for the descendants of Abraham the salvation offered by the mighty and merciful God, should indeed become a source of inspiration for fraternal and persevering dialogue between Jews, Christians and Muslims, with respect for special characteristics and rights of each.

Nor can we forget certain of our brethren who in other parts of the world feel threatened in their existence of their identity. The difficulties which they find themselves facing are often complex and longstanding. The Holy See does not have the technical competence needed to resolve these serious questions, but it nevertheless considers it its duty to emphasize before this assembly that no principle, no tradition, no claim – however legitimate – gives authority to inflict upon peoples – all the more when they are made up of innocent and vulnerable civilians – repressive acts or inhuman treatment. It is a matter here of humanity's honor! In this context, I would recall the serious problem of minorities, which is the theme of my recent Message for the 1989 World Day of Peace: Not only do individuals have rights, but also peoples and human groups; there exists "a right to a collective identity" (no. 3).

4. How could we resign ourselves to so many situations of distress, when last December 10 marked the fortieth anniversary of the proclamation by the United Nations General Assembly of *the Universal Declaration of Human Rights*?

This text, presented as "the common ideal to be achieved by all peoples and nations" (Preamble), has certainly helped humanity to become aware of its shared destiny and patrimony of values belonging to the whole human family. To the extent that it was meant to be "universal," this Declaration applies to all people in every place. Despite the hesitations, admitted or not, of certain States, the 1948 text highlighted a set of ideas – imbued with the Christian tradition (I am thinking in particular of the notion of the dignity of the person) – which has become accepted as a universal system of values.

At the end of the excesses which had oppressed the human person at the hands of totalitarian regimes, the Paris Declaration sought to "protect" man, whoever and wherever he may be. In order to avoid a repetition of the horrors which all of us can remember, it seemed essential that the inviolable sphere of the freedoms and faculties proper to the human person should in the future be protected from possible physical or psychological constraints which the political power might be tempted to impose on it. From man's very nature there flows respect for the life, physical integrity, conscience, thought, religious freedom, and personal freedom of every citizen. These elements essential for each person's existence do not represent a "concession" by the State, which in fact only "recognizes" these realities, which preexist its own juridical system, and the State has a duty to guarantee their enjoyment.

These rights are those of the person, who is necessarily a part of a community, since man is social by nature. The inviolable sphere of freedoms must therefore include those which are indispensable for the life of the family and communities of believers, which are society's basic units. It is within them that this social dimension of man is expressed. It falls to the State to ensure that they receive adequate juridical recognition.

5. On the basis of these fundamental freedoms and rights there develop, like concentric circles, the rights of man as a citizen, as a member of society, and more broadly as an integral part of an environment to be humanized. In the first place, *civil rights* guarantee a person his or her individual freedoms and oblige the State not to interfere in the sphere of the individual conscience in any way. Then there are *political rights*, which enable the citizen to play an active part in the public affairs of his own country.

Undoubtedly there is interaction and mutual conditioning between fundamental rights and civil and political rights. When the rights of the citizen are not respected, it is almost always to the detriment of fundamental human rights. The separation of powers within the State and democratic control are essential conditions for the effective respect of these rights. The fruitfulness of the notion of human rights is also manifested in the development and progressively more precise formulation of *social and cultural rights*. And the guaranteeing of these latter depends upon the extent to which their application is subjected to impartial verification. A State cannot deprive its citizens of their civil and political rights, even under the pretext of wishing to ensure their economic or social progress.

Interdependence with nature

A right to development and [a right] to the environment are also beginning to be spoken of today. In this "third generation" of human rights, it is often a question of demands which are still difficult to translate into binding juridic terms so long as no authority is capable of ensuring their application. But, in the end, all of this shows humanity's growing awareness of interdependence with nature, whose resources – created for all, but limited – must be protected, especially through close international cooperation.

Thus, despite regrettable shortcomings, an evolution has taken place in favor of the elimination of arbitrariness in the relations between the individual and the State. And in this regard, the 1948 Declaration represents a reference which cannot be disregarded, for it unequivocally calls upon all nations to organize the relationship of the person and of society to the State on the basis of fundamental human rights.

The idea of "government by law" is thus seen to be implicitly required by the Universal Declaration of Human Rights, and is in harmony with Catholic doctrine, for which the function of the State is to enable and help people to achieve the transcendent ends for which they have been destined.

6. Among the fundamental freedoms which the Church must defend, first place naturally goes to *religious freedom*. The right to freedom of religion is so closely linked to the other fundamental rights that it can rightly be argued that respect for religious freedom is, as it were, a touchstone for the observance of the other fundamental rights.

The religious aspect, in fact, has two specific dimensions which show its originality in relation to the other activities of the spirit, notably those of conscience, thought or conviction. On the one hand, faith recognizes the reality of the Transcendence which gives meaning to the whole of existence and which is the basis of the values which behavior takes as its guidelines. On the other hand, religious commitment implies membership of a community of persons. Religious freedom goes hand in hand with the freedom of the community of believers to live according to the teachings of its Founder.

It is not for the State to pronounce on matters of religious faith, nor can it substitute for the various Confessions in matters of organizing religious life. The State's respect for the right to freedom of religion is a sign of respect for the other fundamental human rights, in that it is an implicit recognition of the existence of an order which transcends the political dimension of existence, an order which belongs to the sphere of voluntary membership of a community of salvation preceding the State. Even if for historical reasons a State accords special protection to one particular religion, it also has the obligation to guarantee religious minorities the personal and communal freedoms which flow from the common right to religious freedom in civil society.

Unfortunately this in not always the case. From more than one country there continue to arrive appeals from believers – notably Catholic believers – who feel oppressed in their religious aspirations and in the practice of their faith. Indeed it is not rare to find systems of legislation or administrative norms which obscure the right to religious freedom or which lay down such drastic restrictions as to have the effect of reducing to nothing the reassuring declarations of principle.

On the present occasion, I appeal once more to the consciences of the leaders of nations: there is no peace without freedom! There is no peace unless one finds in God the harmony of man with himself and with his fellowmen! Do not fear believers in any way! This is what I said last year, on the occasion of the World Day of Peace: "Faith brings people together and unites them, makes them see others as their brothers and sisters; it makes them more attentive, more responsible, more generous in their commitment to the common good" (Message for the Celebration of the 1998 World Day of Peace, no. 3).

7. It has been rightly pointed out that the 1948 Declaration does not present the *anthropological and ethical foundations of the human rights* which it proclaims. It is clear today that at that time such an undertaking would have been premature. It is thus the task of the various schools of thought – in particular the communities of believers – to provide the moral bases for the juridic edifice of human rights.

In this domain, the Catholic Church – and perhaps other spiritual families – has an irreplaceable contribution to make, for she proclaims that it is within the transcendent dimension of the person that the source of the person's dignity and inviolable rights is to be found, and nowhere else. By educating consciences, the Church forms citizens who are devoted to the promotion of the most noble values. Although the idea of "human rights," with its twofold claim to the autonomy of the person and of the rule of law, is in some way inherent in Western civilization marked by Christianity, the value upon which this idea rests, namely, the dignity of the person, is a universal truth destined to be accepted more and more explicitly in every cultural climate.

For her own part, the Church is convinced that she serves the cause of human rights when, with fidelity to her faith and mission, she proclaims that the dignity of the person has its foundation in the person's quality as a creature made in the image and likeness of God. When our contemporaries seek a basis upon which to establish human rights, they should find in the faith of believers and in their moral sense the indispensable transcendent foundations for ensuring that those rights are protected from all efforts at manipulation on the part of human powers.

Human rights are values
One can see that human rights are not just juridical norms but first and foremost values. These values must be maintained and fostered in society, otherwise they also risk disappearing from the texts of the law. And so the dignity of the person must be protected in society before being protected by law. I cannot fail to mention here the disquiet caused by the poor use which certain societies make of this freedom so ardently desired by others.

When freedom of expression and of creation is no longer directed toward the search for the beautiful, the true and the good, but takes pleasure, for example, in the production of plays and films containing scenes of violence, cruelty or horror, such abuses, when frequently repeated, threaten the prohibitions of inhuman or degrading treatment sanctioned by the Universal Declaration of Human Rights, and bode ill for a future secure from a return to the excesses which that solemn document opportunely condemned.

The same is true when the faith and religious sensibilities of believers can be held to ridicule in the name of freedom of expression or for propaganda purposes. Intolerance threatens to reappear in other forms. Respect for religious freedom is a criterion not only of the consistency of a juridical system but also of the maturity of a free society.

8. Your Excellencies, Ladies and Gentlemen, in closing I can only invite you to unite your daily efforts to those of the Holy See in order to meet the great challenge of the end of this century: to give back to man reasons for living!

As for the Church, she does not cease to be optimistic, for she is sure that she possesses a message which is ever new, received from her Founder, Jesus Christ, who is Life itself and who came among us, as the celebration of Christmas recently reminded us, so that people "may have life, and have it abundantly" (Jn 10:10). She never tires of inviting all those who are willing to do so to meet this God who made himself "the neighbor" of each of us and who suggests that we work, where we are and with our talents, in building a better world; a world in which people will live in friendship with God who sets free and who brings happiness.

It is to him that I entrust in prayer the fervent good wishes which I formulate for all of you, as I invoke upon you, your families, your noble mission and your countries an abundance of blessings from on high.

January 13, 1990
(*OR*, January 29, 1990, pp. 1–3)

1. I would like to extend my *best wishes* for a happy and prosperous New Year to you and your families, and to the peoples and governments that you represent. These sentiments of mine are expressed in prayer to the One who "became flesh and dwelt among us" (cf. Jn 1:14). May he bless you and make your labors fruitful in the service of greater understanding among men; may he comfort those among you who have experienced sorrow or who have faced trials.

2. I wish to express once again my joy in welcoming the *diplomats recently accredited* to the Holy See and to assure them that I and my collaborators depend very much on their cooperation.

I am also pleased to note the presence among you of the *Ambassador of Poland*, a country, which, after a long interruption, has renewed diplomatic relations with the Holy See.

3. Finally, I must *cordially thank your Dean*, the Ambassador of Cote d'Ivoire, who with his usual courtesy has voiced your thoughts and hopes. Besides the positive developments, often unexpected, which have left their mark on the international situation during the past year, you also mentioned, Mr. Ambassador, the efforts of the international community to remedy the crises and situations of injustice from which too many people still suffer today, often among the most deprived. I am grateful to you for the warm words of appreciation which you expressed with regard to the activity of the Catholic Church and of the Apostolic See, which, by spreading the Gospel, seek to make their own specific contribution to the cause of justice and the search for peace.

4. Ladies and Gentlemen, your presence clearly shows that for your peoples and their leaders *the Church and the Holy See* are by no means strangers to their achievements and their hopes, much less to the problems and adversities that mark their path. As you know from personal experience, the Church, by her presence in the world, and the Holy See, by its diplomatic activity in particular, seek to make *a contribution to strengthening and perfecting the unity of the human family*. You will recall the words of the Second Vatican Council in this regard, in the Pastoral Contribution *Gaudium et Spes*, "By her mission and nature the Church is not bound to any one culture or to any political, economic or social system. Hence by her very universality she can be a very close bond between the various communities of men and nations, provided they have trust in the Church and acknowledge her right to true freedom to carry out her mission" (no. 42).

5. By reason of this solicitude and interest in the spiritual and material well-being of all people, the Holy See has welcomed with satisfaction *the great transformations which have recently marked the life of many peoples, especially in Europe.*

The irrepressible thirst for freedom which we have witnessed there has accelerated the process of evolution; it has brought down walls and opened doors. All this has the appearance of a veritable overthrow. And you will no doubt have noted that the point of departure or rallying point has often been a church.

Little by little candles were lit, forming, as it were, a pathway of light, as if to say to those who for many years claimed to limit human horizons to this earth that one cannot live in chains indefinitely. Before our eyes a "Europe of the spirit" seems to be coming to birth, in direct correspondence to those values and symbols which brought her into being, to "that Christian tradition which unites all her peoples" (Address to Members of an International Study Group on Martin Luther, March 24, 1984).

Even as we point to this happy evolution which has led so many peoples to recover their identity and their equal dignity, we must remember that nothing is ever achieved once and for all. The after-effects of the Second World War which broke out fifty years ago call for vigilance. Ancient rivalries can always reappear, conflicts between ethnic minorities can be sparked off anew; forms of nationalism can increase. That is why a Europe conceived as a "community of nations" must be firmly established on the basis of the principles adopted in such timely fashion at Helsinki in 1973 by the Conference on Security and Cooperation in Europe (CSCE).

6. That Conference ended by insisting, in effect, on the fundamental conviction that the peace of the Continent depends not only on military security but also, and perhaps above all, on *the trust that every citizen must be able to have in his own country and on trust between peoples*. Furthermore, the year 1989 began with the adoption on January 19 in Vienna of the Final Document of the Third Follow-up Meeting of that same Conference. The text which the thirty-five participating countries adopted was an important one. By means of concrete agreements and by the balance it established between the military, humanitarian and economic aspects of security, the text clearly emphasized that stability within the community of European nations rests upon shared values and upon a rigorous code of conduct. That code does not permit national leaders to become the masters of thought over their fellow citizens, nor does it permit stronger nations to impose themselves on more vulnerable nations and show contempt for their dignity.

7. Warsaw, Moscow, Budapest, Berlin, Prague, Sofia and Bucharest, just to mention the capital cities, have become as it were the stages on *a long pilgrimage toward freedom*. We must honor those people who, at the cost of immense sacrifices, have courageously undertaken this pilgrimage; we must also honor the political leaders who have assisted it. What is admirable in the events that we have witnessed is the fact that whole peoples have spoken up: women, young people and men have overcome their fear. The human person has shown the inexhaustible resources of dignity, courage and freedom concealed within itself. In countries where for years a party has told people what to believe and the meaning to be given to history, these brothers and sisters have shown that it is not possible to stifle the fundamental freedoms that give meaning to human life: freedom of thought, conscience, religion, expression, and political and cultural pluralism.

8. These aspirations, expressed by the various peoples, must be satisfied *through the rule of law in every European nation*. Ideological neutrality, the dignity of the human person as the source of rights, the fact that the person comes before society, respect for democratically agreed juridical norms, pluralism in the organization of society: these are the irreplaceable values without which it is impossible to build in any last-

ing way a common home from East to West, one accessible to all and open to the world. In that home there can be no society worthy of man unless there is respect for transcendent and permanent values. When man makes himself the sole measure of all things, without reference to him from whom all things come and to whom this world returns, he very soon becomes a slave of his own finiteness. As for the believer, he knows from experience that man is truly man only in accepting himself from God and in agreeing to cooperate in the plan of salvation: "to gather into one the children of God who are scattered abroad" (Jn 11:52).

9. The time has come for *Western Europeans*, who have the advantage of having lived for many years in freedom and prosperity, to help their brothers and sisters in Central and Eastern Europe to regain fully their due place in the Europe of today and tomorrow. Yes, the moment is ripe to gather up the stones of the walls that have been torn down and to build together a common home. Unfortunately, too often the western democracies have not known how to use the freedom won not so long ago at the cost of bitter sacrifices. One can only regret the deliberate absence of any transcendent moral reference in the administration of the so-called "developed" societies. Side by side with generous impulses toward solidarity, with genuine concern for the promotion of justice and a constant concern for the effective respect for human rights, one has to note the presence and the spread of such counter-values as selfishness, hedonism, racism and practical materialism. It should not happen that those who have newly arrived at freedom and democracy should be disappointed by those who in a certain way are "veterans" of these things. All Europeans are providentially called to rediscover the spiritual roots which made Europe. In this regard, I wish to repeat before this distinguished assembly the words I spoke in October of 1988 to the Members of the Parliamentary Assembly of the Council of Europe in Strasbourg: "If Europe wants to be faithful to itself, it must be able to gather all the living forces of this continent, respecting the original character of each region, but rediscovering in its roots a common spirit. In expressing the ardent wish to see intensified the cooperation, already taking shape, with other nations, particularly those of the Center and East, I have the feeling of gathering together the desire of millions of men and women who know that they are bound together by a common history and who await a destiny of unity and solidarity on the scale of this continent" (Address to the Parliamentary Assembly of the Council of Europe, Strasbourg, October 8, 1988). Ladies and Gentlemen, this, it seems to me, is not only what Europeans hope for, but it is also what the whole world expects of a continent that has given so much to others.

10. For this reason, I confidently welcome *the efforts being made by the leaders of the United States of America and the Union of Soviet Socialist Republics* out of concern for dialogue and peace. My contacts with them have enabled me to note their desire to put international cooperation on more solid foundations, so that the two countries will be considered more and more as partners and not rivals.

This will be so only if all the members of the community of nations, especially those with a greater influence and therefore a greater responsibility for safeguarding peace, make efforts to respect scrupulously the principles of international law which have so happily contributed to strengthening harmonious cooperation between States.

The new climate which has thus been progressively establishing itself in Europe has fostered substantial progress in negotiations on nuclear, chemical and conventional disarmament. The year 1989 may well have marked the decline of what was called "the Cold War," of the division of Europe and the world into two ideologically opposed camps, of the uncontrolled armaments race, and of the confinement of the communist world in a closed society. Thanks be to God, whose will it has been to inspire people with those "thoughts of peace" which Christ, in coming among us on Christmas Night, bestowed on each individual as a heritage and a leaven capable of changing the world!

Progress toward peace

11. *Very happily, this new atmosphere has also spread well beyond Europe.* Peacemaking efforts have made progress, thanks especially to the far-sighted action of the United Nations, which I am glad to honor here.

Free elections have taken place in *Namibia*, which should soon attain the independence so eagerly awaited by the population.

Negotiations in *Angola* and *Mozambique* are to be encouraged, so that the goodwill of all may make it possible to remove the stubborn obstacles which hinder a resolution. Thus will there be an end to the cruel trials suffered by peoples, already materially disadvantaged, who will be better able to shape their own development.

The political and constitutional reforms toward which the *Republic of South Africa* seems to be heading need to be further transformed into reality, so that the climate of trust and dialogue for which all the population feels an urgent need may be fostered.

Burundi too now seems to be making progress toward a definitive settlement of the ethnic conflicts which until recently were tearing it apart.

Also of the African continent, we must note the birth of the *Arab Maghrebine Union*, a starting-point for necessary regional cooperation with a view not only to economic changes but also toward the peaceful solution of existing problems and beneficial relations with the European Economic Community.

Finally, a long way from there, in *Latin America*, the holding of democratic elections, most recently in Chile and Brazil, represents an important stage in the progress of the nations of this region toward greater freedom and democracy, a stage which others have still to reach.

12. But just as at dawn, when the sun begins to rise on some countries while others are still in darkness, so it is with the international scene: while some progress can be noted here or there, *numerous countries still remain in the grip of trial and uncertainty.*

I think first of *the Middle East*, which is still a prey to injustice and violence. *The future of Lebanon*, despite the great number of efforts made on her behalf, remains precarious. It is now urgently necessary that the Lebanese should be allowed to decide their own future with sovereign freedom, in fidelity to the civilized values which have shaped the distinct features of that country.

Not far from Lebanon, the people of *the West Bank and Gaza* are still subjected to sufferings that are hard to accept. How can I fail to repeat, yet again, that negotiation alone can adequately guarantee for the opposing parties respect for their legitimate aspirations, immediate peace and security for the future?

In the Gulf, now that the war between Iraq and Iran has ended, the problem of repatriating the prisoners of war still remains. This is a human problem par excellence. With the New Year celebrations, a time of happy family gatherings, just ended, we cannot forget the lot of those, mostly young people, who are still kept far from their own people without justifiable reason.

Farther east, a similar problem is posed by *the Afghan* refugees waiting to be able to return to their land. The international community cannot ignore their situation, nor, for that matter, the situation of the people inside Afghanistan who are daily experiencing the devastating effect of violent conflict. There, too, it is high time that the parties concerned redouble their efforts to ensure that, in respect for the legitimate aspiration of all, the persistent hostilities and the sufferings imposed on innocent civilians come to an end.

13. A rapid glance at the vast area of *Eastern Asia* shows us great peoples, with noble cultural and religious traditions, who should be able to make a greater contribution to the harmonious progress of international life. Unfortunately, side by side with positive and hopeful signs, painful situations continue to exist.

I think of *Cambodia*, where, despite a first attempt at negotiation, we are still awaiting a peaceful transition toward a future in which all can trust. Let us hope that effective international cooperation will prevent the return of the fearful ordeals already suffered by an entire people.

Sri Lanka unfortunately continues to be torn by conflicts of every sort. These have taken their toll in numerous victims, practically throughout the whole of last year, and they dangerously threaten the cohesion of a nation which is nevertheless so peace-loving.

Mention must likewise be made of *Vietnam*. I would like to encourage the modest signs of openness which have recently appeared, including those within the sphere of religious freedom. The Church and the Holy See are obviously well-disposed to any dialogue capable of improving the situation in this area. The international community, for its part, should further encourage the brave people of Vietnam by helping them ever more effectively to take their proper place within the community of nations. And the serious question posed by the refugees from this country will only be resolved by the same international solidarity.

Finally, I could not leave this region without mentioning *the Chinese nation*. The grave events of June 1989 left me deeply moved, and from the beginning, acting as it were as the voice of all who are concerned for the fate of mankind. I did not fail to express, along with my feelings of sorrow, my sincere wish that so much suffering should not be in vain, but rather should help to renew the national life of that noble land. On the threshold of the New Year, I cannot fail to express this same wish once more, convinced as I am that the problems of peace in today's world are so great that they concern all men and women of good will. All the peoples of the world, in fact, are called to work for peace while respecting truth, justice and freedom.

The Latin American situation
14. In *Central America*, the prospects of beginning the peace process anew under the auspices of the United Nations, prospects which aroused so much hope, have been somewhat dampened. Recently, *El Salvador* was the scene of violent strife which mainly affected the civilian population. We recall in particular the barbarous murder

of six religious of the Society of Jesus. The desire to solve society's problems through violence is quite simply an illusion – a suicidal illusion. For this reason, I welcomed the summit held last month in San Jose, Costa Rica by the Presidents of the countries of Central America. These leaders declared in a timely way their deep conviction that "it is indispensable to rouse in people's conscience the need to reject the use of force and terror as a way of attaining political ends and objectives" (San Isidro de Coronado Declaration, December 12, 1989).

The plague of violence and terrorism, aggravated by the detestable narcotics trade which is often its cause, has ravaged *Peru* and *Colombia*, to the point of endangering the social stability of those countries. In this climate of anarchy, we must deplore the cowardly murder of a bishop, the pastor of the Colombian Diocese of Arauca, Monsignor Jesus Jaramillo Monsalve.

The crisis in *Panama* has very recently been added to these concerns. There too, it is the civilian population which has suffered most. It is to be hoped that the Panamanian people will be able to return without delay to a normal life, marked by the dignity and freedom to which all sovereign peoples have a right.

15. Finally, in completing this survey of the world scene, it seems appropriate to pause on *the continent of Africa*, where for years two peoples in particular have been suffering a tragic fate. *The Sudan*, in fact, has seen added to natural calamities the event more dreaded ones arising from the war in the South of the country. The devastation of villages and the exodus of their inhabitants have caused tragic suffering, including that of the many refugees. It is clear that international aid is urgently needed, yet such aid can only be ensured if a truce is observed, as we await the resumption of what had been very promising peace talks. To the cease-fire there must be added genuine respect for the fundamental rights of all members of Sudanese society, particularly the minorities, in power-sharing and in the production and use of natural resources. All this must be accomplished with full freedom and without discrimination by reason of race or religion.

No less worrying is the situation of the people of *Ethiopia*, whom the Catholic Church has not ceased to assist through its charitable organizations, in cooperation with the initiatives of the local bishops and the efforts of governments and non-governmental organizations. There too, the tragic effects of drought, sickness and famine have exacerbated the effects of internal conflicts. Let us hope that assistance to the inhabitants of Tigre can be resumed so that a tragedy of immense proportions may be averted. Furthermore, the current negotiations with Eritrea and Tigre should likewise contribute to strengthening the conviction that a military solution to the conflict cannot be found. It goes without saying that any solution must take into account the legitimate aspirations of the beloved Eritrean people who have already suffered so much.

16. Your Excellencies, Ladies and Gentlemen: such is the setting, with its alternating lights and shadows, in which *the Catholic is called by her Lord to bring the witness of faith, hope and love*. It is brightened by the good will of her most humble laity, by the untiring devotion of her bishops and priests, and by the unconditional commitment of her men and women religious. As a pilgrim to the Far East and the island of Mauritius, I was recently able to note once again the abundant fruits brought forth by

the apostolic labors and perseverance of so many workers of the Gospel both yesterday and today. Thanks be to God for them!

I fervently hope that in the new climate of freedom which seems to be spreading
everywhere believers will be able not only to practice their faith – since certain countries and certain majority religions do not always permit them to do so – but also to
participate actively and with full right in the political, social and cultural progress of
the nations to which they belong.

Unbelief and secularization pose challenges which must be taken into account by
all believers, who are called to bear joint witness to the primacy of God over all things.
For this reason, besides the freedom of religion which the State must guarantee them,
it is essential that better understanding and better cooperation should exist between
religions. In this regard, I was recently able to note the beneficial effects of such inter-
confessional understanding in Indonesia, where the principles of "Pancasila" enable
Islam and the other religions practiced by the inhabitants of that country to come
together in a harmonious dialogue which benefits the whole of society. Unfortunately,
such is not always the case. I cannot remain silent about the disturbing situation experienced by Christians living in *certain countries where Islam is the majority religion.*
Expressions of their spiritual distress constantly reach me: often deprived of places of
worship, made the object of suspicion, prevented from organizing religious education
or charitable activities in accordance with their faith, they have the painful feeling of
being second-class citizens. I am convinced that the great traditions of Islam, such as
welcoming strangers, fidelity in friendship, patience in the face of adversity, the
importance given to faith in God, are the principles which ought to enable unacceptable sectarian attitudes to be overcome. I express my earnest hope that if Muslim
believers nowadays rightly find in countries of Christian tradition the facilities needed for satisfying the demands of their religion, then Christians will similarly be able
to benefit from a comparable treatment in all countries of Islamic tradition. Religious
freedom cannot be limited to simple tolerance. It is a civil and social reality, matched
by specific rights enabling believers and their communities *to witness without fear to
their faith in God* and to live out all the demands of that faith.

17. Never has the contribution of believers been so valuable as it is today, in a world
where so many people are searching for the real meaning of existence and history. I
am particularly convinced that *the witness of prayer, of community life within the
Church and of effective charity is as necessary to the development of this world as is
technological progress or material prosperity.* This is the point I wished to make in a
message to the European Ecumenical Assembly in Basel last May: "Political agreements and negotiations are necessary means to arrive at peace, and our gratitude is
great toward those who devote themselves to these matters with conviction, perseverance and generosity. But to be lastingly fruitful, these measures need a soul. For us, it
is a Christian inspiration which can supply them with one through an intrinsic reference to God, Creator, Savior and Sanctifier, and to the dignity of every man and every
woman, created in his image" (*L'Osservatore Romano*, May 18, 1989).

Yes, may the power of the Spirit gain for mankind everywhere a renewed spiritual energy which will draw it nearer to its Creator! In our age where material gain is so
important, where there is such concern for freedom, may there never be lacking signs

of transcendence, of concern for the most defenseless and of respect for the aspirations of others!

18. The year 1990 begins the decade which will bring us to the end of the second millennium of the Christian era. *For every individual, for every people, for our earth, let us make this time an "advent."* Let us prepare the way of God who never ceases to come to us, as on Christmas Night, so as to enrich us by his life and by his presence. There always remains a space in the heart of man which he alone can fill. May we be able, each of us in our own place and fulfilling the duties entrusted to us be Providence, to help the men and women of our time to discover ever more clearly, in wonder and trust, that God is their highest good!

These are my wishes for you, Your Excellencies, Ladies and Gentlemen, for your fellow-citizens, and for the entire human family! With all my heart, I entrust them "to him who by the power at work within us is able to accomplish far more than all we ask or imagine" (Eph 3:20). May his blessing be with you all!

January 12, 1991
(*OR*, January 14, 1991, pp. 1–3)

1. *The traditional exchange of good wishes* at the beginning of the New Year gives me a pleasant occasion to meet you and thus to strengthen the bonds between the Pope and the Representatives of the nations which desire to maintain diplomatic or official relations with the Holy See.

The words of your Dean, Ambassador Joseph Amichia, have touched me deeply and I thank you for those good wishes which were so kindly expressed, and for your friendly understanding of the Holy See's activity on behalf of international relations ever more inspired by the supreme values of good, truth and justice.

2. This year we have *the joy of having among us Ambassadors from some of the countries which have recently regained freedom* after a long "winter," and whose people are discovering or rediscovering the rules of democratic life and pluralism. I am particularly pleased to welcome the Ambassadors of Poland, Hungary and the Czech and Slovak Federative Republic; soon I expect to receive the Representative of Romania and the representative of Bulgaria, a nation which, for the first time in its history, has chosen to establish diplomatic relations with the Holy See.

With similar satisfaction I greet the Representative of the Union of Soviet Socialist Republics, whose Government has chosen to establish official relations with the Apostolic See. I also wish to mention the presence of the Personal Representative of the President of the United States of Mexico, and I cordially welcome the Heads of Mission and their associates who have recently been accredited. With your families, you form a veritable "community" which reflects the rich diversity of the peoples of the earth in whose midst the Church seeks to give her witness of faith, hope and charity.

Ever since the first Christmas, Christ has been united to every person; for that reason the Church in turn shares His concern for each person. Therefore the Pope, who presides over the communion of Churches, wants to serve all people, whatever their beliefs may be, and he cannot be indifferent to their happiness or to whatever threatens them.

3. As your Dean quite rightly recalled, the world has just experienced a year which was especially rich in special events. The whole of Europe has felt effects of the regenerating winds of freedom, a freedom which was won at the price of difficult sacrifices by peoples who today see how demanding is the ideal represented by the constitutional state.

The Summit of the Heads of State or Government of the 34 countries participating in the Conference on Security and Cooperation in Europe (CSCE) which was held recently in Paris, provided an eloquent image of *a Europe reconciled with itself.*

Elections have allowed the peoples of Central and Eastern Europe to express themselves. Germany has rediscovered its territorial and political unity. Disarmament negotiations have been accelerated. In the majority of European situations, there is a felt need to give "structure" to the forms of collaboration already existing. Soon we shall have before our eyes a "renewed Europe," as is witnessed to by the declaration of the participants in the Paris meeting which I just mentioned, "In Europe the era of confrontation and division is over. We declare that henceforth our relations will be based on respect and cooperation. Today it is up to us to fulfill the hopes and expectations which our people have nurtured for decades: a steadfast commitment to democracy based on human rights and fundamental freedoms; prosperity through economic freedom and social justice, and equal security for all" (*Paris Charter*).

We must thank the citizens and leaders who, through their faith in mankind and their perseverance, have achieved these results, which are so much in keeping with Europe's great traditions. However, please allow me, Ladies and Gentlemen, first of all to give thanks to "the Lord of History," in whom we "live and move and have our being" (Acts 17:28) who has willed an in-depth transformation of Europe which, perhaps for the first time, is not the result of war.

Now that this "new day" has dawned, each country of Europe is called to bring about what political change has allowed: a resolute commitment to democracy, effective respect for human rights and basic freedoms, prosperity through economic freedom and social justice, and equal security for each nation.

In Western Europe these goals have already been more or less obtained, but the citizens of this part of the continent seem to be affected by a certain lack of idealism. In the 19th century many Europeans placed their trust in reason, science and money. At the beginning of our century, an ideology sought to show that the State alone incarnated the scientific truth of history and could therefore determine the values to believe in. In recent decades people believed that by an improvement in the standard of living, industrialization and production would ultimately help to assure happiness. Today's young people are aware that "one does not live by bread alone" (Lk 4:4). They are looking for meaning: those in authority in society have the serious obligation not only to hear their voice, but also to respond to their hopes. All too often Western societies indulge in fads and passing fashion and, in a certain sense, are becoming dehumanized. The men and women of affluent societies must face the challenges of tomorrow's world; they must lay solid foundations for their construction. May they learn again how to be silent, to meditate, to pray! This is where, you can imagine, believers, and Christians especially, have something specific to say. They should always make themselves heard better, make their difference understood, in order to give to the projects of the societies they belong to that "extra spirit" which many people eagerly seek, sometimes without even being really aware of it.

The countries of Central and Eastern Europe are, in their own way, subject to the same difficulties. It is not enough to reject the monopoly of one party, they must also have reasons for living and working to build something else. Elections have taken place in these countries, but perhaps sometimes the candidates' programs have not been explicit about what actions should be given priority. In these countries whose moral and social fabric is in shreds, the family and school must once again become, places for forming consciences; people must develop a taste for work that is done well because it serves the common good.

In the face of all these tasks, *a duty becomes evident: European Solidarity.* Nothing would be worse for Europe's equilibrium – one can even say for maintaining peace on the continent – than a new duality: a Europe of the rich opposed to the Europe of the poor; modernized regions opposed to backward areas. Technological and cultural cooperation must go hand in hand with common economic projects. This means that the European countries which are accustomed to thinking and producing freely should have a certain understanding for their partners who, unfortunately, for more than a half century, have been forced to suffer the constraints of systems in which creativity and initiative were thought to be subversive.

These days we are following with concern the political changes in certain countries of Central and Eastern Europe, including Albania. In all the societies there is upheaval and expectations are being forcefully expressed. I am thinking of the Baltic Countries, especially the beloved country of Lithuania. Now that the European continent is seeking to regain its stride, it is essential that the solidarity of all should help these nations to remain faithful to their traditions and heritage and that, in dialogue and negotiation, they may find new solutions which will open doors and abolish prejudices.

If 1990 was the year of freedom, 1991 should be the year of solidarity!

However, Europe cannot be concerned about itself alone. It must resolutely turn toward the rest of the world, especially toward poorer countries or those with more problems. The Europe of 1990 has shown that it is possible to change the shape of societies without encountering opposition; today a reconciled Europe is able to express a message of hope.

4. My thoughts now turn to *Latin America*. While there is a certain unity to this vast continent, this unity hardly conceals the deep differences existing among the large groupings that form it. Poverty remains the experience of many peoples there; its tremendous natural resources are still far from being wisely exploited and equitably distributed.

Moreover, one can only deplore the ravages inflicted on certain societies by all kinds of violence and by drug trafficking, even to the point of disrupting the administration of justice. I think in particular of murders, kidnappings and the disappearance of innocent people. It is urgently necessary to find solutions to the serious social and economic problems which lead to the marginalization of a large part of the population in these countries. Everything ought to be begin with the restoration or with the safeguarding of family values, for the family is the nucleus of every society worthy of the name. As you know, the Catholic Church is seriously concerned about this, and seeks to be of service to all families.

I am particularly concerned with the countries of *Central America*, where the growth of democracy and peace is advancing at a very slow pace, despite praiseworthy efforts. The momentum of the Esquipulas Agreements, the initiative for a Central American Parliament, and the Antigua Declaration for creating a regional economic community are good examples of the cooperation among neighboring nations which I addressed in the Encyclical *Sollicitudo Rei Socialis* (no. 45).

There are also some attempts at dialogue between governments and guerilla forces, especially in Guatemala and El Salvador, but unfortunately, as recent sad events have confirmed, innocent people continue to be the first victims of these fratricidal conflicts.

There are certainly other obstacles as well, since various oligarchies hinder the road to normalization. But the time has come for all to work together in building up nations in which those who are "least" will be heard and respected with regard to their legitimate aspirations. The good of citizens is the only reason for the existence of political life: the rights that are theirs must be respected without exception.

Not far from this region, a people already severely tried has for some days been experiencing a dramatic situation. I refer to the *nation of Haiti*. Riots, murders, acts of revenge and violence of every kind have taken a deadly toll. Here I cannot fail to mention the destruction of the Apostolic Nunciature in Port-au-Prince, and particularly the treatment given to the Apostolic Nuncio, whose dignity was held in contempt, and to his Secretary, who was seriously wounded. Acts of violence such as these do not, in any event, promote the political and social stability desired by the people. The attack on the old cathedral and the offices of the Episcopal Conference are a source of consternation not only to Catholics but to all people of good will.

5. Turning our attention to *Asia*, we must again this year deplore the fact that certain problems remain unresolved. I will mention some of these.

Cambodia. It is true that negotiations are continuing, but with results that tend to vary. It is to be hoped that a determination to seek the good of the people, who for so many years have been burdened with cruel trials, will prevail over party interest or the desire for power. How can we not be reminded that force never finally resolves a dispute? Thus the Holy See hopes that an honorable solution can be found which will respect the needs of the Cambodian people, with the help of the international community and even possibly, as some have suggested, through the direct cooperation of the United Nations Organization.

The situation in *Afghanistan* remains unstable. A great number of people have had to abandon their homes; they are suffering and live without knowing what tomorrow may bring. There too, I invite the great powers, which have traditionally taken interest in events occurring in this country, to make every effort to prevent negotiations from becoming bogged down, and above all to ensure that peaceful solutions have priority over a recourse to force.

Vietnam also occupies a special place among my concerns. An official delegation of the Holy See has traveled to that country for the first time in many years in order to discuss with government authorities some problems regarding the life of the local Church and certain questions of common interest. The positive atmosphere of these exchanges is undoubtedly a sign of the will of the government both to guarantee the citizens of that noble country the religious freedom for which they yearn and to take its proper place once more on the international scene. I trust that it will not fail to find support from those throughout the world who admire the courage and the tenacity of a people striving to rebuild their country at the cost of great sacrifice.

I would also like to express my good wishes for reconciliation and peace in *Sri Lanka*, where civil war continues to take many victims. Ethnic and community differences must never be a factor of opposition but rather a treasure to be shared!

In addition to all the political and economic difficulties which affect the peoples of these areas there is also a problem which I cannot pass over in silence. I refer to the scarcely favorable conditions often reserved to the Christian communities.

Frequently the object of ostracism on the part of followers of the great traditional religions, Christians also have to endure contempt and various obstacles placed in their way by the authorities. I am thinking of certain particular Churches which are forbidden to profess their faith fully and openly and to communicate on a regular basis with the Pope and the Apostolic See, as is the case with the Catholics of continental China. I am also thinking of those members of the faithful who are exposed to discrimination in their work or in society because they do not belong to the religion of the majority, and of the difficulties encountered when recourse must be had to missionaries so as to satisfy the spiritual needs of the faithful. In these cases there are often subtle yet very real violations of basic human rights – primarily the right of professing one's faith, alone or in association with others, according to the rules of one's own religious family. Your Excellencies, Ladies and Gentlemen: I would hope that you understand my concerns in this regard. As I stressed in my recent Message for the World Day of Peace, intolerance is a threat to peace. There can be no concord and cooperation among peoples when men and women are not free to think and to believe in accord with their conscience, and obviously with respect for the legal norms which safeguard the common good and social harmony in every society.

6. The *Continent of Africa* must equally hold our attention. In addition to the tragic economic situations which affect practically all the peoples living there, Africa too is prey to violence: how could we forget that more than ten conflicts are presently taking place on that continent?

In *Ethiopia* war is soaking up a great part of the nation's financial resources and forcing the exodus of a great number of refugees. Famine threatens the areas of the North, particularly Eritrea and Tigris, which are ravaged by combat and closed to humanitarian aid organizations by the fronts of liberation. News of the recent opening of the port of Massawa is to be welcomed with hope, inasmuch as this can permit urgent assistance to begin to reach peoples barely at the level of survival. After thirty years of war, the time has come to establish a truce in order to favor dialogue and enable the various components of Ethiopian society to find a *modus vivendi*.

The Sudan has not fared better. The inhabitants there, victimized by combat, ecological crises and the collapse of the economy, seem to be hostage to a domestic conflict which has lasted all too long. The Christians of that country have shared their anguish with the Holy See. Living in fear of tomorrow, desirous of being accepted and recognized as a specific religious group, they ask that their voice be heard, that their missionaries be able to carry out their normal apostolate, so esteemed and so necessary to their communities, and that assistance and help from humanitarian Organizations reach them without hindrance.

Mozambique, which has often been at the center of our concerns, seems to have embarked upon the road to peace. The Government and the armed opposition, with the assistance of friendly countries and impartial organizations, have arrived at a preliminary, partial accord. This should lead, we strongly encourage, to a definitive ceasefire. It will thus be possible for this young nation to undertake the work of material and spiritual reconstruction, to give itself a constitution and institutions which allow all its citizens to feel that their convictions are respected and that they can thus look to the future with greater confidence.

We must also express our pleasure in the direct talks which seem to be in progress between the conflicting parties in *Angola*. The involvement of countries such as the United States of America and the Soviet Union, can positively influence the political development of that country, which has quite literally been torn apart by struggles which have divided families, destroyed economic structures and inflicted cruel trials upon the Catholic Church, trials which she continues to endure.

Finally, the institutional renewal going on in *South Africa* bodes well for the very stability of this vast area of the continent. The legalization of opposition parties, the release of their leaders after so many years of confinement, the numerous meetings between government leaders and other parties represent the seeds of reconciliation and brotherhood, seeds which may still be fragile but need to be protected and allowed to grow. It is especially necessary that episodes of violence, like those which have even recently brought death in their wake, should not cause people to lose hope after so many years of yearning for the day when their country would at last be reconciled.

The Holy See is also aware that many of the countries of Africa are still marked by ethnic rivalries. I think in particular of *Rwanda* and *Burundi*, whose Bishops, in a recent joint communiqué, recalled in a timely way that ethnic differences should not be a cause of division but of enrichment, since all people are children of the same Father.

Nor may we forget *Somalia*, whose inhabitants in these days are experiencing conflict and bloodshed. May God inspire them, so that all may strive to let reconciliation prevail over armed confrontation.

No less could we neglect the beloved country of *Liberia* whose people are experiencing unspeakable suffering. It is time that Liberians rediscover mutual trust and that the community of nations help them to avoid what would be a genuine disaster for a country which was once so peaceful and tolerant.

Your Excellencies, Ladies and Gentlemen: I wish to call your attention to the future of the continent of Africa, so rich in human resources, yet suffering from serious shortages: a famine once more threatening to affect millions of people, unemployment, great numbers of refugees, and illnesses of which AIDS is undoubtedly the most deadly. As I stated last September on the occasion of my meeting with the Diplomatic Corps in Burundi, many African countries have the feeling that they are undervalued by nations which only help them to serve their own interests. I believe that the urgent duty of solidarity toward the most defenseless demands greater efforts at a cooperation which would be above all an "encounter" between peoples, and more than a mere exchange of goods and the search for profit, however legitimate that may be. Obviously, as I recalled during that same Apostolic Journey in Africa, all such cooperation would demand free, intelligent and responsible participation by the beneficiaries themselves, together with effective support from the regional Organizations whose job it is to coordinate the various interests involved.

7. Finally, to complete this overview of the international scene, we must pause at a region somewhat nearer to us: the *Middle East*, where once there shone the Star of Peace.

These lands, filled with history, the cradle of three great monotheistic religions, ought to be places where respect for the dignity of man as a creature of God, and for reconciliation and peace are self-evident. Unfortunately, dialogue between spiritual families often leaves much to be desired. The Christian minority there, for example, is in some cases tolerated at most. At times, Christians are prohibited from having their own places of worship and from gathering for public celebrations. Even the symbol of the Cross is prohibited. We are referring here to flagrant violations of fundamental human rights and of international law. In a world like ours, where it is rare that the inhabitants of a country belong to the same ethnic group or to a single religion, it is absolutely essential for domestic and international peace that respect for each person's conscience be a principle without exception. The Holy See awaits the commitment of the whole international community to ending these cases of religious discrimination, which harm all of humanity and constitute a serious obstacle to the pursuit of inter-religious dialogue as well as fraternal collaboration for the sake for the sake of an authentically human, and thus peaceful society.

Remaining in this same region of the Middle East, what should be said of the presence of weapons and soldiers in truly terrifying proportions?

In addition to those conflicts which have already for so many years plunged peoples into despair and uncertainty – I am thinking of the conflicts in the Holy Land and of Lebanon – there has also been, for some months now, the so-called "*Gulf crisis*."

We find ourselves in fact confronting certain situations which demand rapid political decisions and the creation of a climate of genuine mutual trust.

For decades now, *the Palestinian people* has been sorely tried and unjustly treated; bearing witness to this are the hundreds of thousands of refugees scattered throughout the region and in other parts of the world, as well as the plight of the inhabitants of the West Bank and Gaza. Here is a people which demands to be heard, even if one must acknowledge that certain Palestinian groups have chosen to make their point by methods that are unacceptable and worthy of condemnation. On the other hand, however, we are forced to recognize that all too often a negative response has been given to proposals coming from various sources which might have enabled at least the first steps in a process of dialogue aimed at ensuring both to the State of Israel the just conditions of its security and to the Palestinian people their own indisputable rights.

Furthermore, within the Holy Land, there is *the City of Jerusalem*, which continues to be the occasion of conflict and discord between believers, Jerusalem, the "Holy," the "City of Peace."

Nearby, *Lebanon* has fallen to pieces. For years, it lay dying before the eyes of the world, without anyone ever helping it to overcome its domestic problems and to be freed from foreign elements and powers which wished to use it for their own ends. It is time that all non-Lebanese armed forces commit themselves to evacuating Lebanese territory and that the Lebanese be in a position to choose the forms of their co-existence in fidelity to their history and in continuity with their heritage of cultural and religious pluralism.

The *Gulf area*, finally, has been in a state of siege since August; it has become quite clear to all that when one country violates the most elementary rules of international law, the entire coexistence of nations is put to the test. One cannot allow the law of the stronger to be brutally imposed upon the weaker. One of the great advances in the development of international law has been precisely to establish that all countries are equal in their dignity and that all have equal rights.

It is fortunate indeed that the United Nations Organization has been the international instance which quickly took over the management of this grave crisis. Nor should this be surprising, if we recall that the Preamble and the first article of the *Charter of San Francisco* assign it as a priority the will to "preserve future generations from the scourge of war" and to "check every act of aggression."

This is why, faithful to this heritage and conscious of the risks – I would say even of the perilous venture – which a war in the Gulf would represent, true friends of peace know that now more than ever is the time for dialogue, for negotiation, and for affirming the primacy of international law. Yes, peace is still possible; war would be a decline for all humanity.

Your Excellencies, Ladies and Gentlemen; I wish you to know my deep concern about the situation which has been created in this area of the Middle East. I have expressed this concern on a number of occasions, and most recently yesterday, in addressing a telegram to the Secretary General of the United Nations. On the one hand, we have before us the armed invasion of a country and a brutal violation of international law as defined by the UN and by moral law. These are unacceptable facts. On the other hand, while the massive concentration of men and arms which has followed it has been aimed at putting an end to what must be clearly defined as aggression, there is no doubt that, should it end even in limited military action, the operations would be particularly costly in human life, to say nothing of the ecological, political, economic and strategic consequences, whose full gravity and import we have perhaps not yet completely assessed. Finally, without entering into the profound causes of violence in this part of the world, a peace obtained by arms could only prepare new acts of violence.

8. In fact, there is *a relationship between force, law and values* which international society cannot afford to neglect.

States are today rediscovering, especially as a result of the various structures of international cooperation which unite them, that international law does not constitute a kind of extension of their own unlimited sovereignty, or a protection of their interests alone or even of their attempts to increase their sphere of power and influence. Instead, it is truly a code of behavior for the human family as a whole.

The law of nations, the ancestor of international law, took shape over the centuries by distilling and codifying certain universal principles which are prior to and higher than the domestic law of States and which were commonly acknowledged by those taking part in international life. The Holy See is pleased to see in these principles an expression of the order willed by the Creator. We may recall, by way of example, the equal dignity of all peoples, their right to cultural existence, the juridic protection of their national and religious identity, the rejection of war as a normal means of settling conflicts; and the duty to contribute to the common good of humanity. As a result, States came to the conviction that it was necessary, for their mutual security and for the safeguarding of a climate of trust, that the community of nations be endowed with universal rules of coexistence applicable in all circumstances. These rules represent an indispensable point of reference for harmonious international activity, as well as a precious heritage to be preserved and developed. Otherwise, the law of the jungle would prevail, with consequences that can easily be foreseen.

Your Excellencies, Ladies and Gentlemen. Allow me, in this regard, to express the hope that the norms of international law will be increasingly and effectively furnished with coercive provisions adequate to ensure their application. In the domain of applying international laws, the inspiring principle must be that of justice and equity. Recourse to force for a just cause would only be admissible if such recourse were proportionate to the result one wished to obtain and with due consideration for the consequences that military actions, today made more destructive by modern technology, would have for the survival of peoples and the planet itself. The "needs of mankind" (St. Petersburg 1868; The Hague 1907, Convention IV) today require that we proceed resolutely toward outlawing war completely and come to cultivate peace as a supreme good to which all programs and all strategies must be subordinated. How can we fail to echo here the warning of the Second Vatican Council in the Constitution *Gaudium et Spes*: "The capability for war does not legitimize every military and political use of it. Nor does everything automatically become permissible between hostile parties once war has regrettably commenced" (no. 79).

International law is the privileged means for building a more human and peaceful world. It enables the weak to be protected against the despotism of the strong. The progress of human civilization is often measured by the progress of law which makes possible the free association of the great powers and others in that common enterprise which is cooperation between nations.

9. Your Excellencies, Ladies and Gentlemen, having come to the end of our meeting, I wish to renew my best wishes for the peoples whom you represent, for the Authorities who have appointed you, and for your families and colleagues.

We live in an age which is not lacking in signs of progress and hope. It is also an age marked by disappointments and dangers which demand a response from all people of good will.

How can one fail to mention at this point the great barrier which continues to separate rich peoples from poor ones? This widening gap and the frustration of millions of our brothers and sisters who live without hope for the future does not only constitute an imbalance but also represents a threat to peace. In the light of this reality, the entire international community owes it to itself to set about making economic and social changes, and particularly to resolve the problem of foreign debt by those countries least prepared to face the demands being placed upon them. The search for the common good must guide the efforts of all, in a spirit of solidarity. Money should not become the principal criterion of behavior. May there be a renewed effort on the part of all to restore confidence to those people and nations who are most in need!

Each of us according to his or her place – the place which God's Providence has assigned to us, according to our abilities – *has to change the world*, and to take up once again one of its most ancient challenges, the challenge of peace.

Some days ago, Christians awaited and celebrated a light. It shone forth from a stable where a tiny infant lay, the Light of the world!

In the presence of this God given as a gift to mankind, in the presence of this God who appears so vulnerable, we must lay down our arms. He invites us to place ourselves at the service of others and to rediscover that a man is never so great as when he allows the other – be it an individual or people – to grow and develop.

May you, who in a special way have a part to play in the present moment of history, open the door of hope!

This is my wish; this is my prayer!

May the God of Peace be with you throughout the year which is now beginning!

January 11, 1992
(*OR*, January 15, 1992, pp. 1–3)

1. I am very grateful for the expression of good wishes which your Dean, Ambassador Joseph Amichia, has just presented in your name and on behalf of the Governments which you represent. I thank you most sincerely.

Your presence here this morning brings to mind the achievements and expectations of the peoples of the earth. Providence has given me the joy of visiting a great number of them; at this moment I picture once more all those I have been able to meet, and the others are close to my heart.

For my part, I *would offer you my fervent good wishes* for your own happiness and that of your families, as well as for your success in carrying out the important duties entrusted to you. Nor do I forget your Governments or your fellow-citizens; may God enable them to achieve their shared aspirations, so that each society will know greater justice, greater spiritual and material well-being, and consequently greater peace. Such is my hope. Such is my prayer.

I am likewise pleased to welcome the diplomats who have taken up their duties in recent months, and I am gratified to see the family of nations ever more fully represented at the Holy See. I am all the more satisfied because this increased presence is the sign, for many peoples, of a return to democracy. For the Catholic Church, this is always an occasion to manifest to each country desirous of maintaining diplomatic relations with the Apostolic See the Church's resolve to stand beside those nations which are working wholeheartedly for the progress of peoples.

Ambassador Amichia has perceptively set forth a panorama of the principal events of 1991, as well as the more notable activities of the Catholic Church and the Holy See. In fact, the past year was filled with foreseeable developments, but also with unexpected events.

1991: The year of wars
The Gulf War
2. Unfortunately, 1991 was to be *a year in which war played a leading role.*

As you recall, the so-called "*Gulf War*" broke out only a few days after our meeting on January 12. Like every war, it left behind a sinister wake of dead and wounded, of devastation, hostility and still unresolved problems. The consequences of the conflict cannot be forgotten, even today the people of Iraq continue to suffer terribly. The Holy See has recalled, as you know, the ethical imperatives which must prevail in all circumstances: the sacredness of the human person, of whatever side; the force of the law; the importance of dialogue and negotiation; respect for international agreements. These are the only "weapons" which do honor to humanity, according to God's plan.

Yugoslavia
3. The year 1991 likewise ended amid the clash of arms. Disturbing images have shown us to civilian populations literally crushed by *the battles rending Yugoslavia and particularly Croatia.* Houses destroyed, inhabitants forced to flee, an economy wiped out, churches and hospitals systematically bombed; who is not appalled by these actions which reason condemns? My numerous appeals for peace and for dia-

logue are known to you. The position of the Holy See regarding the recognition of States newly emerged from the changed situation in Europe is familiar to you. Today I will limit myself to stressing that peoples have the right to choose their own way of thinking and living together. It is their right to endow themselves with the means which enable them to attain their legitimate aspirations, determined freely and democratically. Moreover, the community of nations has produced juridic documents and instruments which appropriately define each one's rights and duties, just as they foresee structures of cooperation geared to balancing essential relations between sovereign States, on both the regional and international level. Bombs are certainly not the way to build the future of a country or a continent.

Northern Ireland

4. We must also recall another conflict to which it seems we have become accustomed: I am thinking of *Northern Ireland*. For years, the continuance of violence has counteracted attempts to reach a political solution. Can one be resigned to this calamity which disfigures Europe? No cause can justify the degree to which human rights, respect for legitimate differences and the observance of the law in that land have been trampled on. I invite all those involved to reflect before God on their way of acting.

At this time I recall the words of a "European" saint whom I recently canonized, Father Raphael Kalinowski. When Poland was fighting to preserve its national dignity and independence in the last century, although taking part himself in this struggle, he dared to exclaim: "Our homeland needs sweat, not blood!" Your Excellencies, Ladies and Gentlemen: Europe needs men and women ready to come together to work in order that hatred and the rejection of others will no longer be tolerated on this continent which has raised up saints, models of humanity – on this continent which has been a source of productive thinking and has spread institutions which honor the genius of man.

Africa and Sri Lanka

5. In addition to these uncurbed wars, other situations of conflict still disturb the life of the earth's peoples. Since it is not possible to cite them all, I will mention the ethnic rivalries which characterize *the Horn of Africa*. While the Eritreans have obtained their autonomy, other centrifugal forces continue to undermine *Ethiopia*. In nearby *Somalia*, the State has collapsed and the fragmentation of society is making humanitarian aid practically impossible. The federal system is still a promise in *the Sudan*, debilitated by a war which began in 1983. Still farther from us, *Sri Lanka* continues to agonize amid offensives and reprisals which reap victims by the thousands.

We must not resign ourselves to this state of affairs. Political leaders most especially have the grave duty to favor everything that can end fratricidal conflicts. They must support the growth of dialogue, promote plans for society which are in harmony with their people's aspirations and increase necessary humanitarian assistance. Fortunately diplomacy, especially in its multilateral aspect, enables exchanges and agreed solutions in an increasingly interdependent world; in this regard the United Nations Organization has an importance and a significance recognized by all. I express the hope that after the able leadership of Mr. Javier Perez de Cuellar, the new Secretary General, Mr. Boutros Boutros-Ghali, drawing on his international experience, can continue to make this irreplaceable Institution a privileged form for the promotion of peace and the negotiated settlement of disputes.

Looking to the future
6. When a new year begins, a year filled with uncertainties, each of us is prompted *to chart our position and to look to the future.*

The persistence of the conflicts and tensions which I have just called to mind gives rise to a *sense of sadness*. Sadness at having to acknowledge that the lessons of history, long past or recent, are never fully learned. In the end, to place one's trust solely in armed conflict in order to impose one's point of view, to appeal to situations inherited from the past in order to feel dispensed from opening new paths of understanding and of justice, to destroy systematically all that constitutes the richness of the societies one opposes, or openly to flout law and humanitarian conventions the better to dominate one's adversary, all this represents a step backwards. Peace and reconciliation always begin with a benevolent outlook which respects in others – individuals or peoples – their dignity.

Europe's responsibilities
7. In this context, *Europe has a specific responsibility* precisely by reason of its high degree of civilization. Europe is on the path toward unity. It possesses a whole juridic patrimony and rules of international conduct which should permit it to face the uncertainties of the immediate future with a certain confidence.

The changes taking place in *Yugoslavia* or in what was until a few weeks ago *the Soviet Union* appear to demand the establishment of new structures of political cooperation. It is also likely that a greater solidarity will be required of all so as to come to the assistance of increasingly impoverished populations and to ensure that the changes taking place do not occur against a backdrop of poverty.

Security, cooperation and the safeguarding of the human dimension must be the pillars on which the future of peoples will rest. This is the case for the Baltic Republics which have regained their independence, for Albania which has taken its place once again in the wider European family, as well as for the new reality which has emerged in the Soviet Union. The affirmation of national particularities poses and will continue to pose problems which will need to be resolved with wisdom so that all can have trust in their future, can walk at their own pace, see themselves respected in their uniqueness and take their place in the Europe of tomorrow, a community with a common destiny.

These are tasks which involve all Europeans. Now that the walls have fallen, no one can appeal to lack of information about the living conditions of his neighbor in order to justify indifference: solidarity in the broadest sense of the term has at this stage become a prime duty. Either Europeans will be saved together or they will perish together!

The place and role of Christians
8. *Christians – Catholics, Orthodox and Protestants – will find themselves on this path*; they are called to play a leading role and desire to keep the place which theirs. Many of the values typical of the modern age have their roots in Christianity and today

as in the past the disciples of Jesus, faithful to the teaching of their Master, owe it to themselves to be the "salt of the earth" (Mt 5:13). Still, it is necessary that they be given the possibility of doing this.

One can observe, in fact, even in countries of established Christian tradition, that the Churches do not always find help and understanding for their projects and their efforts. The Catholic school, for example, is at times more tolerated that considered a partner in the national enterprise of education. But who could deny the services which it renders to society, if only for its contribution to the formation of consciences? In government schools, religious instruction is too often marginalized. If information is at once a right, a duty and a good, we must without a doubt be grateful for the importance and the accomplishments of the means of social communication. Often they are a decisive factor in people's personal and social maturity. Nevertheless, it is not uncommon – and this is altogether regrettable – that information about religion is reduced to folklore, or that religion and its noblest expressions are treated with derision. Who, today, can think of Europe without Christians? This would be to cut her off from one of her fundamental dimensions, to impoverish her memory and to forget the crucial role played by Christians in the changes which took place in Central and Eastern Europe in 1989 and in 1990.

I am confident that, despite the temporary difficulties affecting ecumenical dialogue, the great spiritual families rooted in this "old" continent will be able to rise to the historic tasks which lie before them, so as to give Europe a "reinforcement of spirit," the indispensable condition for this continent's harmony and growth. In this regard, the gathering of young people at Czestochowa last August and the recent Special Assembly of the Synod for Europe fill me with hope.

Trusting in man: signs of hope
Madrid Peace Conference
9. One cannot, in fact, despair of man! *We need to trust in his good will*, in his creativity. First and foremost, because he is capable of love, having been "made in the image of God" (cf. Gen 1:26). Secondly, because he possesses a capacity for good which is perhaps not always fully appreciated. The various international agencies, including Catholic ones, bear striking witness to this desire for effective brotherhood. Their work to alleviate suffering as well as to promote the spirit of tolerance and of service contributes to harmony in human relationships and to the solution of pressing problems. Thanks to them, many people rediscover joy and hope. The Holy See for its part follows all these activities with interest, thanks especially to some of its agencies which have been present in the past year on many humanitarian "fronts." Here I would mention the activity of the Pontifical Council for Justice and Peace, the Pontifical Council *Cor Unum* and Pontifical Council for Pastoral Assistance to Health-Care Workers.

If we consider the activity carried on in the diplomatic sector, there too we perceive some *promising signs*. I am thinking, for example, of last autumn's *Madrid meeting*, where for the first time Arabs and Israelis were seated at the same table and agreed to speak of subjects which until then had been considered prohibited. The perseverance of enlightened people who desire to work for peace resulted in a structure of dialogue and of negotiations being set in place, one which will enable the peoples of the region – in particular the most exposed, the Palestinians and the Lebanese – to face the future with greater confidence. It is the entire international community which ought to mobilize itself in order to accompany these peoples of the Middle East on the arduous paths of peace. What a blessing it would be if this Holy Land, where God spoke and Jesus walked, could become a special place of encounter and prayer for all peoples, if the Holy City of Jerusalem could be a sign and instrument of peace and reconciliation!

There too, believers have a mission of primary importance to accomplish. Forgetting the past and looking to the future, they are called to repentance, to reexamine their behavior and to realize once again that they are brothers and sisters by reason of the one God who loves them and invites them to cooperate in his plan for humanity. I consider dialogue between Jews, Christians and Muslims to be a priority. In coming to know each other better, in growing to esteem one another and in living out, with respect for consciences, the various aspects of their religion, they will be, in that part of the world and elsewhere, "artisans of peace." As I wrote in my Message for the XXV World Day of Peace, "a religious life, if it is lived authentically, cannot fail to bring forth fruits of peace and brotherhood, for it is in the nature of religion to foster an ever closer bond with the Godhead and to promote an increasingly fraternal relationship among people" (no. 2).

Unfortunately, I know also how difficult this fellowship between believers can be. How many appeals arrive at the Holy See to deplore situations where Christians in particular are the object of outright and unjustifiable discriminations, both in the Middle East and in Africa! There are countries, for example, where Islam is the majority religion and where Christians still today do not even have the possibility of having a single place of worship at their disposal. In other cases, it is not possible for them to take part in the political life of the country as equal citizens. In still other cases, they are advised simply to leave. In this regard I appeal to all the leaders of countries which have had the beneficial experience of interreligious dialogue to deal with this problem seriously and realistically. At stake is respect for the conscience of the human person, peace in society and the credibility of international agreements.

Progress in Asia
10. If we shift our attention to *Asia*, we recognize the emergence of a regional identity which is becoming more and more strengthened, thanks especially to the persevering action of regional organizations, which promote cooperation and friendship between peoples and civilizations, often quite diverse. Thus, in the course of the past months some courageous political actions have been made possible: the two *Koreas* have drawn closer together, and in *Cambodia* an accord has been reached, allowing the current factions to set out together on a path which friendly and disinterested countries are helping to delineate.

Two other countries have also drawn the attention of public opinion. The immense country of China has been very present on the world scene. Let us hope that fruitful international cooperation can be established with it. The Holy See looks sympathetically upon this vast country, with its highly developed culture and extraordinary human and natural resources. The Holy See also strives to follow the life of the small Catholic community which lives there. The Pope encourages his Chinese sons and daughters to continue to live their faith in fidelity to the Gospel and to Christ's Church. He exhorts them to serve generously their nation and their brothers and sisters, as they have always done.

A word also for beloved *Vietnam*, whose efforts toward economic openness should be supported. In that nation also there is a Catholic community whose apostolic vigor is praiseworthy. The Holy See ardently desires that the dialogue undertaken with the government leaders be intensified and that the situation and growth of the local Church, so close to the aspirations of the country, be acknowledged.

In calling to mind the condition of these enormous populations, we must not forget the men and women who are, perhaps, the most deprived and most exposed to uncertain circumstances of every sort: expatriates and refugees. Let us recall, for example, the tragedy being undergone by those among them who are in camps in Hong Kong, Thailand, Malaysia and other countries or by those who have been forcibly repatriated. In this regard, while reaffirming that these individuals have the same rights as other people, it is necessary to insist on the duty of the international community to accept its responsibility to welcome them and, at the same time, to promote in the countries from which they come socio-political conditions which permit them to live with freedom, dignity and justice.

I would not wish to bring to a close this brief look at Asia without mentioning a place of persistent tension: *East Timor* – which I have had the great joy of visiting. A persevering dialogue, which I have called for in the past, is needed so that all the parties which play a role in the life of Timor will lay the foundations for a political and social life in harmony with the aspirations of the people. The Holy See for its part has taken every opportunity, both on the ecclesial level and on the diplomatic level, to invite those responsible and concerned for the well-being of this region to strive to put an end to contrasts which have endured too long.

Africa moving toward democratization
11. We must now pause at *Africa*, where the winds of democratization are blowing. One fact seems to capture our attention, and it represents a great step forward: those who are working to bring about new societies are striving to strengthen freedom of expression, freedom of assembly, and the possibility of freedom of action. There, it is a question of an evolution which should be encouraged both from the point of view of political assistance, as well as from the point of view of economic and technical assistance. As I wrote in the Encyclical Letter *Centesimus Annus*, it is necessary "to abandon a mentality in which the poor – as individuals and as peoples – are considered a burden, as irksome intruders trying to consume what others have produced. The poor ask for the right to share in enjoying material goods and to make good use of their capacity for work, thus creating a world that is more just and prosperous for all" (no. 28).

There are other positive signs in Africa to take note of. *South Africa*, for example, has not allowed itself to be overwhelmed by the difficulties which accompany its transformation into a society without "apartheid." *Angola* is taking its first steps as an independent nation, and *Mozambique* seems to be committed to a peace process. All of this has been accomplished because of the tenacity of those who act within their own nations, as well as through the mediation and assistance of friendly countries. This is a good example of international solidarity, and one would like to see it applied to other centers of tension which cause grave concern.

12. Nevertheless, the welcome changes which I have pointed out in Africa are far from being the case in all the countries of that continent. How can one forget the ethnic rivalries which trouble *Rwanda*, or *Burundi*, where a process of national reconciliation has been initiated? I have appealed to the international community not to abandon these peoples to themselves. *Zaire* is of intense interest at present. The breakdown of structures of government there does nothing to make it easier to set out a plan for society which corresponds to the aspirations of the majority. Sadly too, the people of *Chad* in these last weeks have experienced troubles which threaten its already precarious civil peace. Elsewhere, hesitation over democracy in *Togo* is a cause of preoccupation, and everything must be done to avoid disastrous confrontations. *Liberia*, too, continues to be assailed by a civil war which has not only destroyed the entire infrastructure of the country, but has likewise forced many people to flee. *Madagascar*, where for many months a deep political, social and economic crisis seems to have held the whole population hostage, again appears to be in the grip of changes which are cause for concern. May the peoples of these countries, already tried by so many natural disasters, by a stormy history and by endemic poverty, not be abandoned! This is the call which I issue in their name to the whole international community!

Some notes of optimism

13. To leave Africa on a more optimistic note, I would like to go back to a small nation which, after thirty years of war, is only now enjoying the first months of peace. I refer to *Eritrea*. The fruits of this peace have, it is true, a bitter taste when one thinks of the orphans, of the food shortages, and of the great task of reconstruction. But, with the return of peace and the support of good friends, all becomes possible. May these people no longer lack help and understanding! Obviously, neighboring *Ethiopia* should not be overlooked. For Ethiopia it is a matter of creating institutions capable of dealing with the diversity of peoples which make it up.

Africa is stirring, therefore she is alive. Her peoples are more and more aware of their dignity, and also better informed. They have a right to our concern. They look forward to it. The Catholic Church, as you know, has been realizing on that continent a patient and persevering work which often receives little recognition on the part of public opinion. This is the work of exemplary missionaries, whose detachment and self-denial are admirable, and who often pay with their lives for their apostolic commitment. Here, before this audience, I am pleased to pay homage to them and to encourage them in their witness of faith and love, which brings honor to the whole Church.

Latin America

14. Our last stop takes us to *Latin America*, which in this year, 1992, will celebrate the Fifth Centenary of Christopher Columbus's odyssey to the Americas. It is also the anniversary of the first evangelization. God willing, I shall have the joy of presiding in Santo Domingo next October at the General Assembly of the Latin American Bishops. These lands have been made fruitful through the Gospel, and my Pastoral Visits have enabled me to ascertain that these communities live in a deep faith and are motivated by the resolve to bear witness to Christ in every circumstance.

In Latin America, too, there is no lack of positive things for us to consider. Democratization has made progress. The countries of the region now have elected governments and armed groups – with the exception of Peru – have laid down their arms or are negotiating such a move. I have in mind *El Salvador, Guatemala and Colombia*. Numerous projects exist to put into effect programs which respect the right of indigenous and Afro-American people to their own cultural identity. In addition, economic integration, along with the broad movement of regional and international solidarity which this presupposes, is going forward. All of this shows that it is possible to move from confrontation to cooperation.

Although all of this ought to be spreading, there remain, nonetheless, some areas of shadow. I particularly have in mind *Haiti*, where a whole population finds itself in the grip of poverty, a victim of an implacable logic of violence and hate, which does not allow it to express its aspirations toward peace and democracy. Here again I would hope that the international community might exert itself especially to help Haitians to be the builders of their own future. Nor do I forget *Cuba*, still isolated. The Holy See would like to see its people experience, under prosperous living conditions, the joy of being able to build a society where each individual more and more thinks of himself as a partner in a common project which has been freely undertaken. Other, more general, problems affect some countries, for example, drug production and trafficking which affect the countries of the Andes, or the armed struggle which is subverting and destroying the political and social life of Peru and does not spare even the Church. Poverty and foreign debt are also serious stumbling blocks to a peaceful and progressive development.

15. Happily, all these societies, imbued with the Christian tradition, possess moral and human resources which should not be overlooked, but rather should be made to bear fruit. The Catholic Church is very conscious of her mission on the "continent of hope" and her members are in the forefront of the vital forces of the countries that constitute it. They strive to bear witness to Christ. I had the privilege of seeing this for myself on my recent Apostolic Visit to Brazil. Catholics contribute to the advancement of that huge country, with such enormous potential, by their commitment to the political and social renewal which is so needed in order to achieve increased justice and greater development. During this year in which a broad range of observances will mark the celebration of the Fifth Centenary of the First Evangelization, they, in profound union with their Pastors, are called to make more intense their commitment to the renewal of society, to integral human development, and to safeguarding family values which, sad to say, some legislation aims at weakening.

Attentive listening to others, taking into account their needs and respecting their rights are the only civilized means whereby it is possible to get beyond self-interest and to be open to the needs of the whole community. I refer, for example, to the urgent need for better and more peaceful collaboration between *Ecuador* and *Peru*. I strongly encourage the leaders of these countries, which are so deeply marked by the Gospel message of peace and charity, to avoid anything which might exacerbate their differences, and to commit themselves courageously to the path of a clarifying dialogue and eventual contacts. The meetings between the Presidents of Ecuador and Peru, which are taking place in Quito during these days, represent a significant step. I pray that God will strengthen their resolution and shed light upon their exchanges.

Conclusion

16. Your Excellencies, Ladies and Gentlemen, we have come to the end of our meeting. We have called to mind the fortunes and the hopes of today's world, for which each one of us – in the place to which God has assigned us – is responsible. In the months ahead, let us together attempt to contribute to the temporal and spiritual good of individuals and of society. I ask God to give us wisdom, foresight and compassion, so that no suffering will leave us insensitive, no injustice will leave us indifferent, and no division leave us resigned to it.

Christians find a source of new vitality for their faith and hope in the inexhaustible Christmas mystery, which can be summarized in one word, "Peace"! Peace to those whom God loves and has visited. May God be with you in the months ahead, and may he bless those who are dear to you.

January 16, 1993
(*OR*, January 20, 1993, pp. 1–2)

I

1. At the beginning of the year 1993, it is a particular pleasure for me to receive the good wishes which in your name His Excellency Ambassador Joseph Amichia has so courteously expressed. I thank you warmly for your presence here today, as also for the interest and benevolent understanding with which you follow day by day the activity of the Holy See.

Please accept, in your turn, the earnest good wishes which I entrust to God in my prayers for you personally and for your families, for your noble mission as diplomats and for the peoples to which you belong.

One hundred and forty-five countries at present maintain diplomatic relations with the Holy See. In the year 1992 alone, 16 nations expressed the desire to establish this type of cooperation, and I am happy to see among you this morning, for the first time, the Ambassadors of Bulgaria, Croatia, Mexico and Slovenia. In this manner, the expectations and hopes of the greater part of the peoples of the earth make themselves felt in the very heart of Catholicism. And I hope that circumstances will make it possible for other countries to join those represented here. I am thinking of, among others, China and Vietnam, and Israel and Jordan, to mention but a few.

Listening to the wise reflections of your Dean and seeing your faces, I recalled many of the countries I have visited on my apostolic journeys. It gives me pleasure to call to mind that marvelous world, its nature and cultural heritage, it gives me pleasure to call to mind those hard-working peoples, often lacking material goods, but able to resist the temptation to despair, and it certainly gives me pleasure to call to mind the sons and daughters of the Church, with their inexhaustible spiritual resources and daily Christian commitment – sometimes in an environment of religious indifference and even hostility – they bear witness to the fact that God "so loved the world that he gave his only Son, that whoever believes in him should not perish but have eternal life" (Jn 3:16). What human and spiritual riches in the various different nations!

The light of Christmas has illuminated this world with an incomparable brightness, and it continues to show human achievements in their true nature, revealing the good that has been done and the efforts made to improve certain situations. But this light also shows up the mediocrities and the setbacks affecting the life of individuals and societies. This year, as we consider the human family which God loves and which he does not cease to sustain in its existence and growth (cf. Acts 17:28), we must once more, alas, note that two sorts of evil still hold it in their grip: war and poverty.

II

2. *War* is tearing apart many of the peoples of Africa. In *Liberia*, for example, the path to reconciliation is proving hard to find. Despite the efforts of the Economic Community of West African States, this country is continuing to be a theatre of unheard-of violence which spares neither the Church nor her personnel. It is becoming vital to put an end to these battles, to the ceaseless influx of armed men roaming the territory, as also to put an end to personal ambitions and rivalries. In 1992, the Yamoussoukio Accord had been considered a good basis for rapid peace-making. Is it impossible to manage to put it into practice?

The sinking of *Rwanda* into a disguised form of war has not made it possible for the transition to democracy, yet to achieve its objectives, while military expenditure is weighing heavily on an already precarious economy. It is now clear that in a multiracial nation a strategy of confrontation can never achieve peace.

The Sudan is still divided by a war, which sets the peoples of the North and South against one another. I hope that the Sudanese, with the freedom to choose, will succeed in finding a constitutional formula which will make it possible to overcome contradictions and struggles, with proper respect paid to the specific characteristics of each community. I cannot fail to make my own the words of the local Bishops: "Peace without justice and respect for human rights cannot be achieved" (*Communiqué* of October 6, 1992). I entrust to God my plan to make a brief stop in Khartoum next month. It will give me the opportunity to take to all those who are suffering a message of reconciliation and hope, and above all it will be an opportunity for me to encourage the sons and daughters of the Church who, despite trials of every kind, are bravely continuing their journey of faith, hope and charity.

The humanitarian aid brought to *Somalia* by the international community has revealed to the eyes of the world the unbearable distress of a country long plunged into anarchy, to the point of compromising the very survival of its inhabitants. It must be stated that the claims of clans or individuals will not lead to peace. Let us then hope that international solidarity will intensify – it is the whole balance of the African continent which will thereby be consolidated.

In fact, Africa cannot be left to itself. On the one hand, urgent aid is essential in several areas of conflict or of natural disasters, and on the other hand the vast movement toward democracy which has spread there calls out for support. There too, the link between democracy, human rights and development is more clearly seen to be of prime importance. I express the hope that the countries of Africa which have happily taken the path toward political renewal will be able to continue their journey. That path is of course strewn with hazards and slowed down by those who prefer to look backwards, but it is the only road leading to progress, since the aim of democratization is respectful service of the peoples and of the choice which they have freely expressed. I am thinking in particular of *Togo* and *Zaire*, which are continuing to experience moments of grave political uncertainty. In the latter country especially, it would be desirable for the parties involved to make a courageous choice of the path of dialogue and of unselfish efforts to ensure that the transition period leads to a social plan that will respect the legitimate aspirations of the people. Quite clearly, this will only happen if there is an avoidance of intolerance and violence in the different regions of Zaire, which could drag this great country into an adventure with fatal consequences.

3. Nor is the Mediterranean region exempt from strong tensions causing violence and death. I am thinking of the grave events which have affected *Algeria*, and the serious difficulties which are endangering the *peace process in the Middle East*, begun just over a year ago in Madrid. Since fresh violence and armed interventions could compromise the efforts of dialogue and peace which have been made in recent months, to all those engaged in the process, I renew my appeal to renounce the acts of force and *fait accompli* policy. In this way it will be easier to progress along the path of peace, thanks to negotiation and sincere and trusting dialogue, in order to go beyond the stage of mere meetings. A new climate of respect and understanding is proving more than

ever needed in this part of the world. Moreover, it will be a factor of equilibrium and pacification for the neighboring countries, for example Lebanon and Cyprus, where unsolved problems are still preventing the people from looking to the future with confidence. Nor can we forget that war has long-term consequences, and that it forces innocent civilians to endure heavy sufferings. Such is the case of the peoples of *Iraq*, who, by the simple fact of living in that country, are still continuing to pay a heavy price in the form of cruel privations.

4. But it is nearer to us, Your Excellencies, Ladies and Gentlemen, that war is exercising its ruthless brutality. Obviously I am thinking of the *fratricidal battles in Bosnia-Hercegovina*. The whole of Europe is being humiliated by them. Its institutions are being ignored. All the peace efforts of recent years have been as it were destroyed. After the disaster of the last two World Wars which had originated in Europe, it had been agreed that States would never again take up arms and support their use in order to solve their internal or mutual differences. The Conference on Security and Cooperation in Europe (CSCE) has even worked out principles and a code of conduct, adopted by consensus by all the States taking part. Now, before our very eyes, these principles and the ensuing commitments are being systematically transgressed. Humanitarian law, a laborious achievement of this century, is no longer being respected. The most elementary principles governing social life are being scoffed at by veritable hordes spreading terror and death. Ladies and Gentlemen, how can we fail to think of those children forever marked by the sight of so much horror? Those families separated and thrown out into the street, dispossessed and without resources? Those women dishonored? Those people shut up and ill-treated in camps which we thought had forever disappeared? The Holy See is constantly receiving anguished appeals from the Catholic and Orthodox Bishops and the Muslim religious leaders of these regions, appeals that this collective martyrdom might cease, and that at least the humanitarian law might be respected. I echo those appeals before you this morning.

The international community ought to show more clearly its political will *not to accept aggression and territorial conquest by force*, nor the aberration of "ethnic cleansing." This is why, in fidelity to my mission, I believe it necessary to say here once again, in the most solemn and firm manner possible, to all the leaders of the nations which you represent, and also to all those who, in Europe and elsewhere, have in their hands a weapon in order to attack their brothers and sisters

* war of aggression is unworthy of man;
* the moral and physical destruction of the enemy or stranger is a crime;
* practical indifference in the face of such forms of behavior is culpable omission;
* finally, those who indulge in such actions, and those who excuse them or justify them, will answer for it not only before the international community but still more before God.

Let the words of the Prophet Isaiah resound here. "Woe to those who call evil good and good evil, who put darkness for light and light for darkness" (Is 5:20)! Peace can rest only upon truth and freedom. This demands today much clear-sightedness and courage. The Catholics of Europe implored this grace in Assisi, at the moving prayer meeting held on January 9 and 10. By means of prayer and purifying penance, we asked pardon of God for the many offences against peace, the many occasions on which brotherhood has been scorned, and we implored him to spare Europe these waves of hate and pain which man seems unable to stem.

5. *Europe*, torn between community integration and the temptation to nationalist and ethnic disintegration, is in fact experiencing *a painful transformation*. The sources of violent tension which are battering several Republics of the former Soviet Union (I mention in passing Georgia and the Caucasus region), as well as the destiny of the Balkan area, will weigh heavily on the future of the continent. These tragic uncertainties challenge peaceful and prosperous Western Europe, which on January 1 entered the phase of the "single market." Strengthened by the unity of a political and economic project and by the sharing of common values, this Western Europe must continue to increase the contacts and gestures of solidarity and openness toward the rest of the continent. Genuine and lasting progress cannot be made by some without the others, not by some against the others, still less with weapons in their hands.

III

6. The other great trial affecting the life of peoples and hindering their development is *poverty*, both *material and moral*.

Never has the earth produced so much and never has it counted so many hungry people. *The fruits of growth continue to be divided unfairly*. Added to that is the growing division between North and South. As you know, I wished to draw the attention of people of good will to this problem with my Message for the World Day of Peace on January 1, in which I wrote "Destitution is a hidden but real threat to peace. By impairing human dignity, it constitutes a serious attack on the value of life and strikes at the heart of the peaceful development of society" (no. 3).

In the face of this growing destitution which is causing the poor to become more numerous and ever poorer, faced with forms of exclusion such as the unemployment which is so sadly affecting the younger generation, illiteracy, racism, broken families or illness, those in positions of political responsibility are the first to be questioned. The world possesses the technological and structural capabilities to improve conditions of life. Today, even more than yesterday, every individual should have the opportunity to participate worthily and fairly in the banquet of life. The sharing of natural resources, the just distribution of profits, a sound reaction against the excesses of consumption, and the preservation of the environment are some of the priority tasks incumbent upon public authorities.

The United Nations Conference on the Environment and Development, held in Rio de Janeiro last June, tried to pave the way. Now it is necessary to go beyond good intentions. Involving citizens in society's projects gives them confidence in those who govern them and in the nation to which they belong; these are the bases on which the harmonious life of human societies rests. Very often, phenomena such as street protests or an atmosphere of suspicion which the print and broadcast media report are simply a manifestation of dissatisfaction and helplessness due to the frustration of basic needs, not seeing legitimate rights guaranteed, not feeling that one is regarded as a partner in political and social planning, not discovering the beginning of a solution to difficulties that have lasted for years. Basically, all problems of justice have as their main cause the fact that the person is not sufficiently respected, taken into consideration or loved for what he or she is. People must learn or learn anew to look at one another, to listen to once another, to walk together. That obviously presupposes that people share in common a minimum of human values, the recognition of which is able to motivate convergent choices.

7. This brings me naturally to that other form of poverty: *moral destitution*. The reception currently being given to the *Catechism of the Catholic Church* of itself shows our contemporaries' felt need for references. Reflecting currents of opinion and fashion, the means of social communication often transmit indulgent messages which excuse everything and result in an unrestrained permissiveness. Thus the dignity and stability of the family are not recognized or are changed. Many young people are coming to consider almost everything as objectively indifferent: the only reference is what suits the convenience of the individual, and quite often the end justifies the means. Now, as we can see, a society without values rapidly grows "hostile" to the individual who becomes the victim of personal profit, of a brutal exercise of authority, of fraud and crime. Today, too many people have a bitter experience of this and I know that statesmen are conscious of these serious problems which they must face each day.

I would like to restate here the *Church's readiness* to cooperate in the authentic moral development of societies by her witness of faith, the contribution of her reflection and the aid of her activities. She must still be given a place in public dialogue: one sometimes has the impression of a desire on the part of some people to relegate religion to the private sphere, under the pretext that believers' convictions and norms of behavior are synonymous with reaction or an attack on freedom. The Catholic Church, present in every nation of the earth, and the Holy See, a member of the international community, in no way wish to impose judgments or precepts, but merely to give the witness of their concept of man and history, which they know comes from a divine Revelation. Society cannot afford to forgo this original contribution without becoming the poorer for it and without violating the freedom of thought and expression of a large part of its citizens.

If the Gospel of Jesus Christ does not offer ready-made responses to the many social and economic problems assailing contemporary man, it nevertheless shows what is important to God, and therefore for human destiny. This is what Christians propose to those who are willing to hear their voice. Despite difficulties, the Catholic Church for her part will continue to offer her disinterested cooperation so that at the end of this century man will be better enlightened and able to free himself from the idols of this age. Christians' only ambition is to show that they understand personal and collective history as a meeting between God and mankind, of which Christmas is its most shining expression.

IV

8. That is why, with vigilance but also in solidarity with initiatives and advances which help man grow, the Church rejoices at everything which in recent months has represented *a peaceful victory over violence and disorder*.

In *Europe*, despite the uncertainties mentioned earlier, a new chapter in the history of the continent opened on January 1. With the single market coming into effect, a good many Europeans have gained a heightened awareness that they form one family, sharing values coming from their recent and more distant history. This is important, because the future cannot rest solely on the bases of economy and trade. Let us hope that, centuries-old conflicts having become a thing of the past, solidarity and a sense of community will be established once and for all. From now on, thanks to common structures and permanent mechanisms of concerted action, life will be more harmonious for much of Europe.

In this context, I would like to encourage the two new European countries which saw the light of day on January 1, *the Czech Republic and the Slovak Republic.* May the peaceful character of the dissolution of the former Czech and Slovak Federative Republic, the result of persevering dialogue, be a good omen for the development of each of the two new States and for the quality of their mutual relations!

9. Farther away from us, peace efforts have succeeded, as in *Angola*, where we hope that the difficulties of recent days will not endanger the gains of the peace accord signed in Lisbon on May 31, 1991. The choice of the voters must be respected by all! This sorely-tried people, whom I had the joy of visiting recently, is waiting for peace. They deserve it! The fratricidal conflicts which are devastating certain regions will bring victory to no one. They will only serve to exhaust the fragile human and moral resources of a country which had nevertheless taken the right path.

Again in Africa, in *Mozambique* the negotiations happily concluded in Rome allow us to hope that the parties concerned will from now on act as partners in national dialogue and together carry forward the process of pacification and democratization desired by all the Mozambicans. No one can do that for them.

One cannot help but rejoice at seeing the desire of the African peoples to build their societies on new bases whereby exercising the right to opinion and to initiate legislation makes it possible to transform the political profile of the whole continent. Even though at times the changes which have begun are still disappointing, it is nonetheless true that the movement toward democracy is irreversible. In this new Africa, it is important that the central role should be left to the population, which must be able to participate fully in development. For this purpose, the population needs regional and international cooperation to help to prevent crises on the one hand, and for this cooperation to support the process of democratization as well as economic growth on the other.

10. In Asia, *Cambodia* has gradually emerged from its isolation and begun its reconstruction, thanks to the persevering efforts of the United Nations Organization and friendly countries. The commitments made in the Paris Accords mapped out a path which can lead to true democracy and national reconciliation. It should not happen that new difficulties call everything into question. Peace will not be viable unless yesterday's foes are inspired today by a sincere desire for peace. Let us hope that this country, too, which has suffered so much, can benefit from the long-term aid of unfailing international solidarity.

11. In *Latin America*, again this year, the desire for regional dialogue has remained strong. The year 1992 was an important anniversary for the continent. Latin Ameri-

cans recalled the great human and spiritual epic of discovery and evangelization, with its lights and shadows. They have become more aware of their immense moral capacities for meeting the challenges of the hour, in particular those of social justice. The Catholic Church, so strongly present in this part of the world, will continue to offer her specific cooperation by proclaiming "the truth of Christ which must enlighten minds and hearts by the active, tireless and public proclamation of Christian values," as I emphasized at the opening of the fourth General Conference of the Latin America Episcopate on October 12 last in Santo Domingo. By so doing, the Catholic faithful and their Pastors will promote the moral renewal of the peoples of this vast continent, thus facilitating the construction of a more just and prosperous society with respect for their noble traditions.

Among the comforting signs which have marked the life of these peoples, one should note the fact that *armed groups have laid down the arms*, except alas in Peru, or at least are on the point of doing so, as in Colombia. The most eloquent example is provided by *El Salvador* where, on December 15 last, after 12 years of war, the government and the guerrillas officially put an end to the armed conflict. It remains to be hoped that the reconciliation which has been proclaimed will be affirmed more and more by the facts.

May this happy conclusion inspire another neighboring country which is also being torn by too much violence, Guatemala! There as elsewhere, a harmonious common life can be built only on respect for human rights and public morality.

12. I hope that other countries of the hemisphere will likewise make progress from both the social and political points of view. My thoughts turn first to *Haiti*, where a serious, generalized crisis continues. Let us hope that Haitians too may live in civil peace and experience anew the dignity of citizens who are the artisans of their own destiny. The urgent needs of this sorely-tried people must be faced without delay. We must help them, as the local Bishops and many people of good will are trying to do.

Not far from there is another people particularly dear to me, *the people of Cuba*. The economic difficulties they are enduring and their international isolation are daily increasing the sufferings of the whole population. The international community cannot ignore this country. I likewise hope that the desire of Cubans for a society renewed in justice and peace will become a reality. Without claiming special privileges, Catholics wish to make their contribution to this internal evolution by the light of their Gospel witness.

V

13. This broad survey of the international scene, which has become traditional in the framework of our annual meeting, has above all highlighted the fact that *the very heart of international life is not so much States and man*. Here we take note of what is doubtless one of the more significant developments of the law of nations during the 20th century. The emergence of the individual is the basis of what is called "humanitarian law." There exist interests which transcend States: they are the interests of the human person, his rights. Today as in the past, despite the more or less compelling documents of international law, man and his needs unfortunately continue to be threatened, to such an extent that in recent months a new concept has emerged, that of "humanitarian intervention." This term says much about the precarious state of man and of the

societies he has established. I myself have had occasion to speak on this subject of *humanitarian assistance* during my visit to the headquarters of the United Nations' Food and Agriculture Organization on December 5 last. Once the possibilities afforded by diplomatic negotiations and the procedures provided for by international agreements and organizations have been put into effect, and that, nevertheless, populations are succumbing to the attacks of an unjust aggressor, States no longer have a "right to indifference." It seems clear that their duty is to disarm this aggressor, if all other means have proved ineffective. The principles of the sovereignty of States and of non-interference in their internal affairs – which retain all their value – cannot constitute a screen behind which torture and murder may be carried out. For this is what it means. Jurists will still of course have to examine this new phenomenon and refine its contours. But, as the Holy See often seeks to remind the international bodies to which it belongs, the organization of society has no meaning unless the human dimension is made the principal concern, in a word made by man and for man.

14. Your Excellencies, Ladies and Gentlemen, at this beginning of the year, amidst the clamor of arms and of events too often tragic, the angels' hymn on Christmas night still rings out, "Glory to God in the highest, and on earth peace among men with whom he is pleased!" All the greetings we exchange are summed up in this heavenly message. In this violent world, so ready to suspect and to strike, in which interests sometimes seem to stifle the most generous aspirations, the Child in the crib of Bethlehem brings the sweetness of his innocence. He is the sign, offered to man, of God's infinite compassion! To you, your countrymen, your Authorities, to all our brothers and sisters in humanity, I offer from my heart this "Good News" in its perennial freshness. I ask you to accept it! In it is found human happiness, for today and for tomorrow.

January 15, 1994
(*OR*, January 19, 1994, pp. 1–3)

1. "For I know the plans I have for you, says the Lord, plans for welfare and not for evil, to give you a future and hope." Thus the Prophet Jeremiah reports words received from God himself (cf. 29:11).

A future and hope. Such are my good wishes for you, Your Excellencies, Ladies and Gentlemen, for your families and your homelands. You represent the greater part of the peoples of the earth. Thus, through you, it is all your compatriots whom I greet and to whom I offer my prayerful good wishes that each one of them may be granted happiness and prosperity, in freedom and justice. These wishes I likewise address, with the same goodwill, to all the nations which are not yet represented at the Holy See, but which certainly have a place in the heart and prayer of the Pope.

Your Dean, dear Mr. Joseph Amichia, has been good enough to recall with his customary delicacy, my various activities during the year which has just ended. I thank him warmly for his words of esteem and for the cordial good wishes which he has expressed in your name. I see in them an encouragement for the whole Catholic Church to pursue her task as a witness to faith in the "goodness of God" (Ti 3:4), that goodness which the feast of Christmas has manifested to us, once more, in its astonishing freshness.

The Middle East

2. For *Christmas is simply the revelation of the divine love, offered to all men and women.* It is the light which illuminated the night of Bethlehem; it is the Good News proclaimed to all the peoples, on the day of the Epiphany. These recent celebrations have naturally turned our thoughts toward the *Holy Land*, where Jesus was born and to which we have been on a spiritual pilgrimage.

For the first time in very many years, *peace seems possible*, thanks to the good will of the people who live there today. Yesterday's enemies are talking to one another and talking together about the future. The dynamism of the Madrid Conference, begun in 1991, continues to inspire all those bravely striving to ensure that dialogue and negotiations will triumph over every sort of extremism and selfishness. Israelis and Palestinians, the children of Isaac and of Ishmael, have begun a journey: all their friends have a duty to help them continue it to the end. It is a question of an imperious duty, for to perpetuate a situation of uncertainty and especially of heavy sufferings for the Palestinian population – trials which are well known to us – makes even more serious the present difficulties and risks putting once more out of reach the longed-for practical results of the dialogue which has been begun.

It is this background of hope and frailty which is the setting for the *conversations which have enabled the State of Israel and the Holy See to sign an accord* on a number of fundamental principles suitable for regulating their mutual relations and of guaranteeing for the Catholic Church in that country conditions for a normal existence. There is no doubt that all believers will also draw benefits from the accord. Furthermore, the Holy See is convinced that this new form of relationship with the State of Israel will enable it, while safeguarding its specific spiritual and moral nature, to help consolidate the desire for justice and peace entertained by all those who are involved in the peace process. Without renouncing any of the principles which have inspired its activity in the past, the Holy See will therefore continue to work to ensure that, in respect for the law and the legitimate aspirations of individuals and peoples, it will be possible to find without delay solutions to other questions which so far have received only partial answers. It is impossible to over-emphasize that among these questions there figures the status of the Holy City of Jerusalem, which greatly interests believers in the religions of the Book.

In fact, it is the whole region which should benefit from this happy development. I am thinking in particular of *Lebanon*, the sovereignty and unity of which are not yet adequately ensured. Nor do I forget, not far from there, *Iraq*, whose inhabitants are still paying very dearly the price of war.

The East

3. Looking farther East, I would like to call *Afghanistan* to your attention. Perhaps some have forgotten the sufferings of these peoples, hostages of divisions and violence which know no truce. I take the opportunity offered to me today to invite the international community not to lose interest in that country, and to work toward a regional solution which could give it some guarantees for the future.

In the *continent of Asia* live hardworking peoples striving to develop their economy, at the cost of great sacrifices on the material and human levels. I am thinking about the great people of *China*, of course, but also the *nation of Vietnam*, whose efforts at opening up and rejoining the international community should be welcomed.

I salute the progress peacefully made by *Cambodia*, with the support of the United Nations, and which allows a more serene outlook on the future.

Unfortunately, areas of shadow still linger in that part of the world. The ethnic groups of *Sri Lanka* confront each other ruthlessly. The people of *East Timor* aspire to see their cultural and religious identity increasingly safeguarded. The inhabitants of the *Island of Bougainville*, tragically isolated from the rest of the world, are the victims of bloody rivalries. We cannot forget their trials.

In this vast region of the Far East live *devout Catholic communities* of remarkable apostolic vigor. Several of them, and I say this with profound sorrow, are today still deprived of their most fundamental freedoms and are victims of intolerable discrimination. Some have been reduced to a precarious existence, unable, for example, to have recourse to the aid of missionaries whose entry is made almost impossible by administrative measures. Other communities are prevented from gathering for worship or making religious writings freely available.

Yet others are denied the right to organize themselves in conformity with the law of the Church or to maintain normal contacts with the Apostolic See. The same is true for those experiencing the difficult condition of living in secrecy. In calling your attention to these sad situations, I would hope that the leaders of the nations will generously cooperate in finding necessary solutions, for it is also a question of justice.

Latin America

4. Last year, *Latin America* still remained a region of contrasts. It is certainly true that, with few exceptions, the governments in power are the result of democratic elections. Inflation and the weight of debt have diminished slightly, even though the social costs have been high and the absolute index of poverty has grown.

The beginning of this year is unfortunately marked by serious tensions and violence which have spread in certain regions of *Mexico*. Let us hope that there too dialogue will prevail so that a common effort will make it possible to discover the causes of these sad events and so that it will be possible to respond to the legitimate desires of the peoples involved in a spirit of mutual esteem.

There is no doubt that the American countries of the Southern Hemisphere have human and material possibilities still insufficiently developed. Cooperative structures are to be encouraged, like those which already exist (I am thinking, for example, of the Contadora Group or the Common Market of the Southern Cone). Regular summit meetings between Heads of State, and the recent signing of the free trade agreement between the United States, Mexico and Canada have been added to those traditional institutions. Let us hope that real benefits for all these deprived peoples will result.

It is also urgently necessary to speed up the normalization of political situations which are still precarious. In *Guatemala* and *El Salvador*, the disarming of the armed factions, the reintegration of former combatants, and political and social reforms are only going ahead slowly, and sometimes suffering setbacks. A true CULTURE OF PEACE has not yet been established in this region, despite the sustained efforts of many leaders, in particular of the Catholic Church and her pastors. *Nicaragua* too is experiencing a worrying situation, for the different sectors of society do not always manage to agree upon a model for society resting on values shared by all.

Great countries continue to be the prey of endemic evils such as the ever wider gap between rich and poor, administrative corruption, terrorism and drug trafficking. All these nations, large and small, need a fresh impulse of moral vigor, which should not be impossible, since their peoples profess the Christian faith.

To say that the Catholic Church knows that she is invested with a particular responsibility is a point I have had the opportunity to emphasize during my apostolic visits to that part of the world. Moreover, the Episcopates continue vigorously to express the basic principles of Catholic social teaching. It is necessary that the common good should be the one goal of both governors and governed, "the good of all and of each individual, because we are all really responsible for all" (*Sollicitudo Rei Socialis*, no. 38).

We cannot leave this region of the globe without mentioning two countries suffering in a particular way: Cuba and Haiti.

The people of *Cuba* are experiencing especially serious material difficulties, caused by both internal and external factors. It is important that this country should not be left isolated; Cubans should be helped to regain confidence in themselves. In their courageous message, "Love Hopes All Things," the Bishops have indicated a priority: "To revitalize the hope of Cubans." We must all help them to rediscover their unity on the path toward a society ever more marked by solidarity and respectful of the innate values of each individual. At any rate, the Catholic Church in Cuba has convincingly shown its desire to make a spiritual and moral contribution to the country by fostering education in forgiveness, reconciliation and dialogue, which are the foundations on which is built a society in which everyone feels at home.

Not far from there, *Haiti* continues to go through endless ordeals. In their recent Christmas message, the Bishops of Haiti clearly described the "physical and moral sufferings which beset the people, eat away at society and bring destruction to the country." In Haiti too, the complete reconciliation of minds and the renunciation of divisions which have grown worse over the last two years ought to become a reality. And this will only happen through a dialogue of all sectors of society. An honest, respectful dialogue, without prejudice, with one single goal: to seek unselfishly the true good of the nation. I can only invite the international community to contribute as far as possible to a speedy realization of this aim. Ready-made political models cannot be imposed on the Haitian people, at the risk of giving rise to fresh divisions. It is the Haitians themselves who must build their future, in accordance with the principles restated in so timely a manner by the Bishops in the message mentioned above: the end does not justify the means; force cannot be set above right; political life cannot be dissociated from morality.

Africa

5. Let us take the time to consider the situation in *Africa*, a continent which is changing and going through a decisive period of its history. In recent months numbers of its peoples have once more expressed their legitimate claims to democracy and pluralism. This is a positive development, and it must be taken into account. There can be no going back! It is a hopeful sign that several nations have undertaken, by peaceful means, a major effort for institutional renewal.

The peace process in *Mozambique* is taking hold, albeit slowly, but with the prospect of elections in the autumn of 1994. *South Africa* has courageously overcome the final obstacles inspired by racial relations to building a multi-racial society in which every person should feel responsible for the well-being of others. Nearby in the Indian Ocean, *Madagascar* has been able to bring about a peaceful transition toward a democratic society. Let us hope that these examples catch on, for too many African nations are still prevented from setting out on to the path of political and social renewal.

The case of *Angola* is a tragic one. Elections have been followed by a return to hostilities between factions, and this is in defiance of the people's choice. Recent news nevertheless speaks of a return to dialogue. May the Angolans understand that no one will emerge victorious from such fratricidal conflicts! In any case, the people can only suffer from them, reduced as they are to living conditions unworthy of man.

Burundi has recently seen a fresh outbreak of ethnic rivalries, which have plunged it once more into the horrors of barbarism and poverty, gravely weakening its most basic institutional structures. After the killings of last autumn, the moment for forgiveness and reconciliation has come. God expects this from the Burundi people. The election of a new President of the Republic, just two days ago, is a hopeful sign.

Not far from there, a vast country of considerable human and material resources is in the process of dissolution: *Zaire*. It is going through a political crisis which could easily degenerate into an uncontrollable civil war. Here I would like to issue a fatherly but firm appeal to all those who have some responsibility in prolonging and aggravating the situation: things must change quickly. No cause, no ambition, can justify the state of institutional and material decay in which almost thirty million citizens are forced to live. The interests of individuals and groups must give way before the common good and before the legitimate aspirations of the national community as a whole. Otherwise chaos will prevail, international isolation will become more rigid, and finally the country's future will be mortgaged for many years to come.

In nearby *Congo*, and in *Togo*, we are forced to note with regret that there too the wishes expressed by the people have not yet succeeded in prevailing. Certainly it is not political ploys or recourse to force which can make a credible order spring up and lead the peoples to work together in planning a society.

Let us hope too that the process of democratization being undertaken in *Gabon* will not be definitively brushed aside and that those in power will have the farsightedness to allow the Gabonese themselves to be the artisans of a better future.

Similarly, let us hope that *Nigeria* will find a way to avoid drifting into authoritarianism, so that the people can freely find their way again on the basis of common values. This would finally make possible the development of the economic potential of this great country, within an ordered and stable context.

Let us hope that *Liberia*, which is trying to emerge from the war that has despoiled it since 1989, can be helped by its traditional partners in its first steps along the road to peace and reconstruction!

If we turn our attention to the East of the continent, we rejoice to see *Eritrea* increasing in stability and experiencing a certain growth, even if it is still modest.

Sadly, two sources of war remain, sowing death and desolation: I am obviously thinking of the conflicts still devastating *Somalia* and the *Sudan*. To the dead are added the wounded and the tragedy of the displaced persons, condemned to material and moral insecurity. How can one not fail to invite the parties in these conflicts, which too often assume a tribal character, to enter into a serious dialogue? I hope that the competent International Organizations will take steps to appeal to the local individuals and groups most committed to peace, and that at the same time they will support the institutions which are capable of bringing about in these countries the acceptance of a courageous and necessary process of a return to brotherhood. For peace and security can only come from the Somalis and Sudanese themselves.

I must mention again the grave crisis rocking *Algeria*. The combination of armed violence and the escalation in terrorism seem to have brought that country to a political stalemate. The various sections of the Algerian people must come together. The friends of that great country should help it to establish a frank dialogue between all parties, so as to break out of the vicious circle of hatred, revenge and killings. May the Mediterranean, the home of civilization *par excellence*, be spared a fresh wound!

In many countries of Africa we find ourselves face to face with new ways in which people are working for their future. It is often admitted that it is a question of an irreversible trend. But it is important that the political alternative should not be translated into ethnic changeover: that would be proof that nothing is changing. I am convinced that the uniqueness of the ethnic, cultural and social structures of Africa will enable each nation to develop its own state of law and democracy. What is urgently necessary is to put an end to the state of lawlessness which is spreading in too many African countries. It would be fitting to take note of this factor in the establishment of programs of cooperation with these states. For cooperation is still necessary: Africans have to be able to rely on the many different forms of help provided by their friends – especially of their European partners – so that their material and technical development can keep up with their democratic development. It is clear, in particular, that they need support in the face of the plague constituted by the AIDS epidemic, and, apart from that, for the acceptance and feeding of displaced persons and of the great number of refugees in this continent.

It is in this tormented context of the continent that the Catholic Church is shortly going to celebrate a special assembly for Africa of the Synod of Bishops. With the help of God, this will be a great moment of prayer and reflection which will help the Catholics of those regions, pastors and faithful, to place themselves once more in the presence of God, in order to refocus their lives, personally and collectively, and to look around themselves and learn to see in every African the human being which he is and not just his ethnic identity. It is necessary to build bridges, not walls, between people, as well as between nations and the different groups which comprise them.

Europe
6. And here we are on the shores as it were of the "old continent," pulled between integration and fragmentation. On the one hand, in fact, *Europe* possesses a network of multi-state institutions which ought to help it to bring to fulfillment its noble community project. But on the other hand, this same Europe is as it were weakened by growing tendencies to individualism which are giving rise to reactions inspired by the most primitive forms of racism and nationalism. The conflicts which are steeping the Caucasus and Bosnia-Hercegovina in blood are proof of this.

The European contradictions seem to have left political leaders at a loss, unable to control these paradoxical tendencies in a global manner and through negotiation.

It is certain that the barbarous and unjustifiable war which for nearly two years has been staining *Bosnia-Hercegovina* in blood, after devastating *Croatia*, has considerably eroded the goodwill which Europe used to enjoy. The fighting goes on. The most iniquitous forms of extremism are still being seen. The peoples are still in the hands of torturers [without] morals. Innocent civilians are systematically being made the target of hidden snipers.

Mosques and churches are being destroyed. The villages, emptied of their inhabitants, cannot be counted any more.

This morning, before you, Ladies and Gentlemen, I would like once more to condemn in the most categorical manner, the crimes against man and humanity which are being perpetrated before our very eyes. I would like once more to appeal to the conscience of everyone: – to all those carrying a weapon, I ask them to put it down; what is taken or destroyed by force will never do honor to a man or to the cause he claims to uphold; – to the humanitarian organizations, I express my admiration for the work they are accomplishing at great cost, and I ask them to continue without becoming discouraged; – I ask European political leaders to redouble their efforts to persuade the warring factions so that reason will finally prevail; – to the peoples of Europe, I ask them not to forget, through the weariness or selfishness, their brothers and sisters trapped in conflicts which have been imposed on them by their leaders.

To everyone, I would like to make them share the firm conviction which I have: war is not inevitable; *peace is possible*! It is possible because man has a conscience and a heart. It is possible because God loves each one of us, just as each one is, so as to transform and make him or her grow.

Thus it is that, after so many years, peace in *Northern Ireland* could become a reality. Let no one reject it! It depends on the goodwill of every person and of every group that today's hope may be something more than an illusion.

It would in fact be a scandal to see Europe resign itself and accept that the law is ultimately scorned, that international order is ridiculed by the actions of armed bands, that society's objectives are conceived as a means to the supremacy of a particular nationality. The fact that the United Nations Organization has set up a tribunal to judge war crimes and crimes against humanity in the former Yugoslav Federation is a sign that the ignominy perpetrated there is being recognized more and more. Some are even calling for the establishment of a permanent International Tribunal to judge crimes against humanity. Does this not show that, far from progressing, international society is running a serious risk of regressing?

A vision of the whole

7. If we reflect on what is at the bottom of the collective behavior which we have just described in Africa and Europe, we shall easily discover the presence of *exaggerated forms of nationalism*. And it is not a question of legitimate love of country or of esteem for its identity, but a rejection of others because they are different, in order more easily to dominate them. Every means is good: the exaltation of race which goes so far as to identify nation and ethnic group; the glorification of the State which thinks and decides for everyone; the imposition of a uniform economic model; the leveling out of cultural differences. We are faced with a new paganism: the deification of the nation. History has shown that the passage from nationalism to totalitarianism is swift and that, when States are no longer equal, people themselves end up no longer being equal. Thus the natural solidarity between peoples is destroyed, the sense of proportion is distorted, the principle of the unity of mankind is held in contempt.

The Catholic Church cannot accept such a vision of things. Universal by nature, she is conscious of being at the service of all and never identifies with any one national community. She welcomes into her bosom all nations, races and cultures. She is mindful of – indeed she knows that she is the depositary of – God's design for humanity: to gather all people into one family. And this because he is the Creator and Father of all. That is the reason why every time that Christianity – whether according to its Western or Eastern tradition – becomes the instrument of a form of nationalism, it is as it were wounded in its very heart and made sterile.

My predecessor Pope Pius XI had already condemned these serious deviations in 1937 in his Encyclical Letter *Mit Brennender Sorge*, when he wrote: "Whoever exalts race, or the people, or the State, or a particular form of State, or the depositories of power, or any other fundamental value of the human community . . . and divinizes them to an idolatrous level, distorts and perverts an order of the world planned and created by God" (*AAS* 29 [1937], no. 8, p. 149).

Europe is now made up for the most part of States of small and medium size. But they all have their patrimony of values, the same dignity and the same rights. No power can put limits on their fundamental rights, unless they endanger the rights of other nations. If the international community cannot come to an agreement on the means to deal at the source with this problem of nationalist claims, it is foreseeable that whole continents will be as it were poisoned and that there will be a progressive return to relationships based on force, in which the first to suffer will be people themselves. In fact, the rights of peoples go hand in hand with human rights.

A final wish

8. In this regard, I would like to recall before you who are experienced diplomats *the great responsibility incumbent on those who administer public life*. They are in the

first place the servants of their brothers and sisters and, in an uncertain world such as ours, people look to them as points of reference. In my latest Encyclical I recalled that "openness in public administration, impartiality in the service of the body politic, respect for the rights of political adversaries, safeguarding the rights of the accused against summary trials and conviction, the just and honest use of public funds, the rejection of equivocal or illicit means in order to gain, preserve or increase power at an cost – all these are principles which are primarily rooted in . . . the transcendent value of the person and the objective moral demands of the functioning of States" (*Veritatis Splendor*, no. 101).

In too many societies, including in Europe, those in positions of responsibility seem to have abdicated in the face of the demands of a political ethic which takes into account man's transcendence and the relative nature of systems of social organization. It is time that they joined together and conformed to certain moral demands which concern the public powers just as much as the citizens. In this regard, I wrote in the same Encyclical: "In the face of serious forms of social and economic injustice and political corruption affecting the entire peoples and nations, there is a growing reaction of indignation on the part of very many people whose fundamental human rights have been trampled upon and held in contempt, as well as an ever more widespread and acute sense of *the need for a radical* personal and social *renewal* capable of ensuring justice, solidarity, honesty and openness" (ibid., no. 98).

In this difficult but so necessary work of moral resurgence, Catholics, together with other believers, are called to accept their responsibility to bear witness. The presence of Catholics in the running of societies is part of the social doctrine of the Church, and civil authorities and citizens alike should be able to count on them. It is a question here of a form of proclaiming the Gospel and the values which it contains that is helpful, indeed necessary, for the building of a more human society. I am convinced that, just as they were once capable of doing in so many countries of the Europe of old, Christians will again be capable of a political and social involvement enabling them to state and, even more, to demonstrate by their generosity and unselfishness that we are not the creators of the world. On the contrary, we receive the world from God who creates it and creates us. Therefore we are just stewards who, in respect for God's plan, are meant to increase goods in order to share them. Here I would like to quote the forceful words of Saint Paul: "You are called, as you know, to liberty . . . Serve one another, rather, in works of love . . . If you go snapping at each other and tearing each other to pieces, you had better watch or you will destroy one another" (Gal 5:13, 15).

9. Having for too many years experienced a division imposed by reductive ideologies, the world should not now be experiencing a season of exclusions! On the contrary, now should be the season of coming together and of solidarity between East and West, between North and South. Glancing at the world today, as we have just done, we can only state with deep regret that too many human beings are still the victims of their brothers. But we cannot resign ourselves to this.

Having begun the year which the United Nations Organization has dedicated to the Family, let us act in such a way that humanity will more and more resemble a genuine family in which each individual knows he is listened to, appreciated and loved, in which each is ready to sacrifice self for the benefit of the other, and no one hesitates to help the weaker one. Let us listen to the challenge of the Apostle John: "If any one has the world's goods and sees his brother in need, yet closes his heart against him, how does God's love abide in him?" (1 Jn 3:17).

In this Christmas season, the unheard of tenderness of God is offered to all mankind; how clearly this is shown by the Child in the crib! Each one of us is invited to the *boldness of brotherhood*. This is my heartfelt wish for each of you, for each of your fellow-citizens, for all the nations of the earth.

January 9, 1995
(*OR*, January 11, 1995, pp. 6–7)

1. The traditional New Year meeting with the members of the Diplomatic Corps accredited to the Holy See is always for me a *source of great satisfaction*.

Once more, your worthy spokesman, Ambassador Joseph Amichia, has expressed in elegant terms the good wishes which you desire to offer me. They go straight to my heart and are a source of comfort. I thank you cordially.

2. Again this year *the number of countries with representatives to the Successor of Peter has increased*: in fact 10 nations have established diplomatic relations with the Holy See: the Republic of South Africa, the Kingdom of Cambodia, the State of Israel, the Hashemite Kingdom of Jordan, the former Yugoslav Republic of Macedonia, the Federated States of Micronesia, Western Samoa, the Republic of Suriname, the Kingdom of Tonga and the Republic of Vanuatu. I am very pleased to see thus increased the number of representatives to the Apostolic See.

3. The destiny of the great human family, of which these widely differing peoples form part, is certainly marked by many successes, but also by too many setbacks. Your Dean has evoked before us, a few moments ago, *the lights and shadows which go with us*. Yet believers know that man, created in the image and likeness of God, is capable of doing good. This is why, as I in my turn address to you my fervent good wishes for a good and happy New Year, I address them also to your fellow-countrymen and all your leaders. To each one I say, in the very words of the Apostle Paul: "Do not be overcome by evil, but overcome evil with good" (Rom 12:21)! Yes, for the happiness of all, it is my wish that at the threshold of the year 1995 the path of the people of the world should be illuminated by that divine light and serenity which the crib at Bethlehem reflects in such a marvelous way.

Too many cries of despair and pain
4. Alas, there are still rising today from this world *too many cries of despair and pain*, the cries of our brothers and sisters in humanity, crushed by war, injustice, unemployment, poverty and loneliness.

Very near to us, in the winter cold, the peoples of *Bosnia-Hercegovina* continue to suffer in their own flesh the consequences of a pitiless war. While it is still fragile, the recent ceasefire could lead to the resumption of serious negotiations. Faced with this tragedy, which in a way seems like the shipwreck of the whole of Europe, neither ordinary citizens nor political leaders can remain indifferent or neutral. There are aggressors and there are victims. International law and humanitarian law are being violated. All of this demands a firm and united reaction on the part of the community of nations. Solutions cannot be improvised at the whim of conquests by either side. And may law never reach the point of sanctioning results obtained by force alone! That would be the ruin of civilization and a fatal example for other parts of the world.

The conflicts tearing apart the *Caucasus* and very recently once more the Russian Federation, in *Chechnya*, pose to the international community serious questions about the means to be taken in order to ensure genuine coexistence between different peoples. Yet again it has to be remembered that negotiation, if necessary with the help of international institutions, is the only possible path for overcoming obstacles to harmony in these ethnic, religious and linguistic mosaics of our world, in such a way that the original character of each of the separate parts will be respected.

5. *For too many peoples, violence and hatred remain a temptation and an easy solution*. Thus I am thinking of *Africa*, with its still smoldering fires: *Liberia, Somalia* and *Southern Sudan*, where no one is yet able to think about the future. *Angola*, which remains a land where violence and devastation still reign. *Rwanda*, which is struggling to emerge from the abyss into which it has been plunged by systematic and barbarous genocide, while neighboring *Burundi* could itself blunder into the senseless adventure of a further ethnic conflict. A great country like *Zaire* has still not attained the hoped-for restoration of democracy. And we are witnessing, on the shores of the Mediterranean, ravages being perpetrated in *Algeria* by a brute force which is not even sparing the small Catholic community. There too, it is necessary that a way be speedily found to work out means for indispensable national dialogue.

Urgent need for international solidarity
Ladies and Gentlemen, we cannot allow a great continent like Africa to go adrift. Yes, for Africa *I ask for a major effort of international solidarity*: in the first place, to make those confronting one another with arms in their hands for reasons of race, power or prestige to listen to reason; secondly, to bring an end to the ignoble arms trade, which encourages those who trust in violence alone; finally, to come to the aid of the peoples living below the poverty level. In fact, one cannot fail to feel concern, for international aid for Africa has gone down considerably this year. And it has been noted that of the 40 poorest countries in the world 30 are in Africa.

6. International solidarity becomes all the more urgent as the world in these first days of 1995 appears sharply divided into *areas of wealth and peace and regions plagued by crisis, poverty and even war*. All this represents a continuing threat to global stability.

For example, we know that in *Latin America*, with a few exceptions, democracy has made real progress. Let us hope that the *people of Haiti* and the *people of Cuba* too will find, in their respective situations, the most appropriate paths to consolidate democratic life in these countries, which have already endured so much. But, on the other hand, it must be stated that although this continent has experienced the beginnings of economic growth, vast social reforms are still needed in order that the real cancers of poverty and injustice may be eliminated. These are the cause, among other things, of such phenomena as drug trafficking and crime, which are as subversive as the guerrilla movements of the past.

Asia and the Pacific are becoming increasingly aware of their distinctiveness and their human and economic potential. This is a good thing. But in order to contribute to peace-making and peace itself, co-operation, which is taking place above all in the economic sphere, must also be translated into a solidarity which takes into account the great diversity of countries and their languages, ethnic groups, cultures and religions, so that material growth will never come about at the expense of human rights and people's legitimate aspirations.

In the vast expanse of our world, my attention now turns to the people of *Sri*

Lanka and of *East Timor*, still being subjected to distressing trials. Nor do I forget the great peoples of *China* and of *Vietnam* who are engaged in a vast economic and social renewal. I think particularly of the sons and daughters of the Catholic Church who live in these countries and generously contribute to them; unfortunately they still do not enjoy satisfactory conditions for practicing their faith fully.

7. In today's interdependent world, a whole network of exchanges [is] forcing nations to live together, whether they like it or not. But there is a need to pass from simply living together to partnership. Isolation is no longer appropriate.

The embargo in particular, clearly defined by law, is an instrument which needs to be used with great discernment and it must be subjected to strict legal and ethical criteria. It is a means of exerting pressure on governments which have violated the international code of good conduct and causing them to reconsider their choices. But in a sense it is also an act of force and, as certain cases of the present moment demonstrate, it inflicts grave hardships upon the people of the countries at which it is aimed. I often receive appeals for help from individuals suffering from confinement and extreme poverty. Here I would like to remind you who are diplomats that, before imposing such measures, the humanitarian consequences of sanctions [must be taken into account], without failing to respect the just proportion that such measures should have in relation to the very evil which they are meant to remedy.

Spirit of reconciliation and compromise must prevail

8. These considerations are not utopian, for we are very happy to know of situations where the international community has shown itself to be far-sighted and effective. I wish to take this occasion in particular to encourage all involved in the Middle East peace process. Here we have proof that when people talk to one another the course of history can change.

We know of course that, in the Holy Land where Jesus was born almost 2,000 years ago, confrontations and restrictions still exist. The Palestinian people is still waiting to see its aspirations completely fulfilled. *Lebanon* has not recovered its full sovereignty. But let us not see those situations as inevitable.

Courageous men and women, ready to look at one another and listen, will never be lacking. They will be capable of finding fitting tools for building societies where each person is absolutely necessary to the others, and where diversity is recognized above all as a source of enrichment. One does not write peace with letters of blood, but with the mind and the heart!

South Africa shows us that this is so. This great country has been able to accept in a mature manner the challenge of multiracial elections. It provides an example to many other nations in Africa and elsewhere, by causing the spirit of reconciliation and of compromise to prevail over the tensions which are an inevitable element of transition.

The ceasefire declared in *Northern Ireland*, followed by negotiations between representatives of the two sides which have been in conflict for decades, represents a happy development. I wish to encourage the parties concerned to devote themselves wholeheartedly to the search for a political solution, which can only be based on forgiveness and mutual respect.

Yes, Ladies and Gentlemen, I am convinced that though war and violence are alas

contagious, peace is equally so. Let us give it every chance! In the face of the disintegration of societies once made compact whether people liked it or not, in the face of
predatory nationalism, in the face of overt or covert attempts to dominate, the members of the international community must be of one mind in order that the forces of
moderation and brotherhood which open the way to dialogue and co-operation may
finally triumph.

Holy See seeks to be voice of human conscience
9. In a few months we are going to celebrate the 50th anniversary of the foundation of
the United Nations Organization: how could we fail to want the Organization to
become ever more the instrument par excellence for promoting and safeguarding
peace? In recent years it has increased the number of its peace-keeping operations, as
also its interventions aimed at easing the transition to democracy in States rejecting a
single-party regime. It has set up tribunals for trying those held to be responsible for
war crimes.

These are significant developments which foster hope that the Organization will
provide itself with means ever more suitable and effective, capable of sustaining its
ambitions. In the end, the achievements of an Organization like the United Nations
clearly demonstrate that respect for human rights, the demands of democracy and
observance of the law are the foundations upon which must rest an infinitely complex
world, the survival of which depends upon the place attributed to man as the true goal
of all political activity.

10. It is in this spirit that the Holy See acted on the occasion of the recent Conference
on Population and Development held in Cairo in September 1994. In the face of an
attempt to demote the person and his motivations, in a sphere as serious as that of
human life and solidarity, the Holy See considered that it was its duty to remind the
leaders of the nations of their responsibilities, and to make them realize the risk that
there could be forced on humanity a vision of things and a style of living belonging
to a minority. In doing so, the Holy See considers that it has defended man. Allow me
to quote to you in this regard the unforgettable words of my predecessor Pope Paul VI,
in his Christmas message of 1973: "Woe to the person who lays his hand on man: for
man is born sacred in this life, from his mother's womb. He is born ever endowed with
the perilous but divine prerogative of freedom. This freedom can be trained but is inviolable. Man is born as a person sufficient in himself, yet needing social companion-
ship; he is born a thinking being, a willing being, a being destined for good but capable of error and sin. He is born for truth and he is born for love."

Many of those taking part in the Cairo Conference were expecting this statement
and this witness from the Holy See. Such in fact is the reason why the Holy See has a
place in the midst of the community of nations: to be the voice which the human conscience is waiting for, without thereby minimizing the contribution of other religious
traditions. Being a spiritual and worldwide authority, the Apostolic See will continue
to provide this service to humanity, with no other aim than tirelessly to recall the
demands of the common good, respect for the human person, and the promotion of the
highest spiritual values.

What is at stake is the transcendent dimension of man: this can never be made
subject to the whims of statesmen or ideologies. It is equally the service of man that

must concern the leaders of societies: their fellow-citizens, by giving them their trust, expect from them an indefectible attachment to what is good, persevering effort, honesty in the conduct of government, and the ability to listen to everyone, without any discrimination. There is a morality of service to the earthly city which excludes not only corruption but, even more, ambiguity and the surrender of principles. The Holy See considers itself at the service of this reawakening of conscience, without the least temporal ambition, the small Vatican City State being merely the minimum support necessary for the exercise of a spiritual authority which is independent and internationally recognized. Your presence here, Ladies and Gentlemen, bears witness to the fact that it is precisely thus that your leaders regard the Holy See.

11. It only remains for me to express to you my gratitude for the wisdom with which you carry out your duties, Ladies and Gentlemen, and to express to you once more my affectionate good wishes for yourselves, your families and the peoples whom you represent. With all my heart I hope that we shall co-operate ever more closely in the creation of a climate of brotherhood and trust between individuals and peoples, in order to prepare a world more worthy of humanity in the eyes of God. May God bless you and your fellow-citizens, he "who by the power at work within us is able to do far more abundantly than all we ask or think" (Eph 3:20)!

I have not finished yet; I have finished in part. A substantial part is over already. Now I just want to say goodbye and happy New Year: happy New Year to your families, to your countries, to the whole world. Thank you.

January 13, 1996
(http://www.vatican.va/holy_father/john_paul_ii/speeches/1996/documents/hf_jp-
ii_spe_13011996_diplomatic-corps_en.html)

1. I thank you for your presence and for the good wishes formulated by your Dean with such refinement of sentiment and expression. Please accept in return my own fervent wish that God will bless you, your families and your nations; may he grant to everyone a year of happiness!

It is with joy that each year I see an increase in the number of countries which maintain diplomatic relations with the Holy See. Today there are more than a hundred and sixty. Such a development seems to us to show the genuine esteem which many have for the Apostolic See and its mission among the nations. This constitutes, for the Pope and those who assist him, a constant reminder to cooperate ever more intensely with the greatest number of people and organizations who, out of respect for morality and law, endeavor to ensure that justice and peace reign on our earth. I wish to say how much I appreciate the words of Ambassador Joseph Amichia, who in your name has kindly emphasized some of the initiatives thanks to which the Pope and, with him, the Holy See have given voice to all those people throughout the world who ardently yearn for peace, tranquility and solidarity.

2. Today we cannot but rejoice to see here, for the first time, the Representative of the Palestinian People. For more than a year, as you know, the Holy See has enjoyed diplomatic relations with the State of Israel. We had been looking forward to this happy state of affairs, because it is the eloquent sign that the Middle East has resolutely taken the path of peace proclaimed to mankind by the Child born in Bethlehem. May God assist the Israelis and Palestinians to live from now on side by side, with one another, in peace, mutual esteem and sincere cooperation! Future generations demand this and the whole region will benefit from it.

But allow me to confide that this hope could prove ephemeral if a just and adequate solution is not also found to the particular problem of Jerusalem. The religious and universal dimension of the Holy City demands a commitment on the part of the whole international community, in order to ensure that the City preserves its uniqueness and retains its living character. The Holy Places, dear to the three monotheistic religions, are of course important for believers, but they would lose much of their significance if they were not permanently surrounded by active communities of Jews, Christians and Muslims, enjoying true freedom of conscience and religion, and developing their own religious, educational and social activities. The year 1996 should see the beginning of negotiations on the definitive status of the territories under the administration of the National Palestinian Authority, and also on the sensitive issue of the City of Jerusalem. It is my hope that the international community will offer the political partners most directly involved the juridical and diplomatic instruments capable of ensuring that Jerusalem, one and holy, may truly be a "crossroads of peace."

This serene and resolute quest for peace and brotherhood will contribute without any doubt to providing other still existing regional problems with solutions which will respond to the aspirations of peoples still worried about their fate and their future. I am thinking especially of Lebanon, whose sovereignty is still threatened, and of Iraq, whose peoples are still waiting for the chance to lead a normal life, safe from all arbitrary action.

3. A climate of peace also seems to be advancing in certain parts of Europe. Bosnia-Hercegovina has been able to benefit from an agreement which should – we hope – safeguard its territorial integrity while taking into account its ethnic composition. Sarajevo especially, another city of symbolic significance, should likewise become a crossroads of peace. Is it not in fact called the "Jerusalem of Europe"? If the outbreak of the First World War is linked to this city, from now on its name ought to be synonymous with a city of peace, and cultural, social and religious meetings and exchanges ought to foster its multi-ethnic harmony. This involves a process which will be long and is not without difficulties. In this regard I would like to point out that an enduring peace in the Balkans can only be achieved if certain conditions are met: the free flow of people and ideas; the unhindered return of refugees to their homes; the preparation of truly democratic elections; and finally, sustained material and moral reconstruction, in which not only the international community but also the Churches and Religious Communities are called to take part unreservedly. Although this war, which I have often described as "useless," seems to be over, the work of building and consolidating peace looms as a great challenge in the first place to Europeans – but not only to them, – to ensure that indifference or selfishness do not reach the point of causing the shipwreck of a whole region of Europe, with unforeseeable consequences.

Northern Ireland also continues to move toward a more serene future and the peace process offers hope of a stable and permanent peace. From now on all are called upon to banish forever two evils which are in no way inevitable: sectarian extremism and political violence. May the Catholics and Protestants of that region respect one another, build peace together, and cooperate in everyday life!

Among the encouraging signs, I cannot fail to mention the political evolution of South America, where the majority of the people are Catholics, and whose spiritual vitality is a treasure for the Church. Numerous elections have taken place in recent months and have been conducted in conditions which international observers have judged to be normal. But social inequalities are still very marked, and the problem of the production of drugs and drug-trafficking remains unsolved. These are factors which ought to spur political and economic leaders of that Continent to manage public affairs and the economy in a way which is ever more attentive to the aspirations and real needs of the people. This kind of approach, let us not forget, has enabled the peace process in Central America to go forward. In Nicaragua and El Salvador arms have fallen silent. In Guatemala reconciliation is going well. To be sure, the end of hostilities does not always mean social peace. Demilitarization is difficult to impose, and respect for human rights is not absolute. But there too a new climate is gradually emerging. For her part, the Catholic Church does not fail to contribute to this process.

This new climate, offering hope, which is developing thanks to the strenuous work of courageous negotiators to whom gratitude is due, must not only be a truce. Between threatening forms of extremism, peace must become a reality. And if this is achieved, it will be contagious.

4. But there are still too many hotbeds of conflict, more or less disguised, which keep people under the unbearable yoke of violence, hatred, uncertainty and death.

I am thinking of course of Algeria, very near to us, where blood is spilled almost daily: we cannot but ardently hope to see established at last, in a just respect for differences, a reasonable settlement and a national plan in which everyone can be considered a partner.

Still in the Mediterranean region, I would like to mention an island which has been divided since 1974: Cyprus. No solution has yet been found. Such a situation, which prevents people who are separated or dispossessed of their property from building their future, cannot be maintained indefinitely. May the negotiations between the parties involved be intensified and inspired by a sincere desire to bring them to a successful conclusion!

Cooperation in the Mediterranean is an indispensable factor for European stability and security, as was stated by those taking part in the recent European Summit in Barcelona. In this context, we must not overlook questions of identity, territory and neighbors, as well as of religion: these are all elements to be reconciled in order to make this Mediterranean zone an area of cultural, religious and economic cooperation which could benefit all the peoples of the countries bordering it.

5. If we look toward the East, we must again note, unfortunately, that fighting is continuing in Chechnya. Afghanistan is still in a political stalemate, with the people being treated without respect and plunged into the greatest distress. In Kashmir and Sri Lanka fighting has continued to take its toll among the civilian populations. The people of East Timor too are still waiting for proposals capable of allowing the realization of their legitimate aspirations to see their special cultural and religious identity recognized.

We must admire and support the courage of the many men and women who manage to safeguard the identity of their peoples and who hand on to the younger generations the torch of memory and hope.

6. Turning to Africa, we are compelled to deplore the continuing presence of hotbeds of war and ethnic conflicts which constitute a permanent handicap for the Continent's development. The situation in Liberia and in Somalia, to which international assistance has not succeeded in bringing peace, is still governed by the law of violence and of special interests. Widespread armed activity has also plunged Sierra Leone into a situation of tension and increased insecurity. The Southern Sudan remains a region where dialogue and negotiation are not welcomed. We would also like to see more decisive progress in Angola, where political antagonisms and social disintegration prevent normalization. Rwanda and Burundi are still affected by a wave of ethnic and nationalist rivalry, the tragic consequences of which the people have already experienced in the extreme.

Last year, on this same occasion, I had asked for more international solidarity for Africa, and in the present circumstances I cannot but earnestly renew this appeal. But today I would like to direct my comments most particularly to the consciences of Africa's political leaders: if you do not commit yourselves more resolutely to national democratic dialogue, if you do not more clearly respect human rights, if you do not strictly administer public funds and external credits, if you do not condemn ethnic ideology, the African Continent will ever remain on the margin of the community of nations. In order to be helped, African governments must be politically credible. The

Bishops of Africa, meeting in the Special Assembly of the Synod of Bishops, under-lined the urgent need for the competent management of public affairs and the proper training of political leaders – men and women – who "profoundly love their own peo-ple and wish to serve rather than be served" (Post-Synodal Apostolic Exhortation *Ecclesia in Africa,* 111).

7. These situations of conflict which I have just mentioned briefly are not inevitable. The positive developments which certain regions have experienced, regions them-selves caught up in the meshes of violence, show that it is possible to restore trust in others, which is really trust in life. A guaranteed and courageously safeguarded peace is a victory over the ever lurking forces of death.

In this spirit, I cannot but encourage the work which will resume in Geneva in a few days, of the Conference on revising the Convention on conventional arms which are the cause of so much suffering, and the conclusion, during 1996, of the treaty on the banning of nuclear tests. In this regard, the Holy See is of the opinion that, in the sphere of nuclear weapons, the banning of tests and of the further development of these weapons, disarmament and non-proliferation are closely linked and must be achieved as quickly as possible under effective international controls. These are steps toward a general and total disarmament which the international community as a whole should accomplish without delay.

8. As I have had occasion to recall several times, what the International Community brings together is not just States but Nations, made up of men and women who weave a personal and collective history. It is their rights which must be defined and guaran-teed. But, as happens in the family, these rights have to be qualified on the basis of the importance of corresponding duties. On the occasion of my recent visit to the head-quarters of United Nations Organization in New York, I used the expression "family of nations." I pointed out that: "the ideal of 'family' immediately evokes something more than simple functional relations or a mere convergence of interests. The family is by nature a community based on mutual trust, mutual support and sincere respect. In an authentic family the strong do not dominate; instead, the weaker members, because of their very weakness, are all the more welcomed and served" (Address to the Fiftieth General Assembly of the United Nations Organization, October 5, 1995, no. 14).

This is the true meaning of what international law proposes in theory as the con-cept of "reciprocity." Each people must be ready to accept the identity of its neighbor: this is the exact opposite of the despotic nationalistic ideologies which have torn apart Europe and Africa, and continue to do so! Each nation must be prepared to share its human, spiritual and material resources in order to help those whose needs are greater than the needs of its own members. Rome is preparing to host next November the World Summit on Food, called by the Food and Agriculture Organization of the United Nations. I hope its work will be inspired by a sense of solidarity and sharing, espe-cially as 1996 has been declared by the United Nations Organization the "Year for the Eradication of Poverty."

9. Recognition of others and of their heritage, this latter term being understood in a broad sense, is obviously applicable as well to a specific area of human rights: that of

freedom of conscience and of religion. In fact I consider it my duty to return once more to this fundamental aspect of the spiritual life of millions of men and women, for the situation – and I say this with genuine sadness – is far from being satisfactory.

Just as countries of Christian tradition welcome Muslim communities, certain countries with a Muslim majority also generously welcome non-Muslim communities, allowing them even to build their own places of worship and to live in those countries in accordance with their beliefs. Others however continue to practice discrimination against Jews, Christians and other religious groups, going even as far as to refuse them the right to meet in private for prayer. It cannot be said too often: this is an intolerable and unjustifiable violation not only of all the norms of current international law, but of the most fundamental human freedom, that of practicing one's faith openly, which for human beings is their reason for living.

In China and Vietnam, in contexts which are certainly different, Catholics face constant obstacles, especially with regard to the external manifestation of the bonds of communion with the Apostolic See.

Millions of believers cannot be indefinitely oppressed, held in suspicion or divided among themselves, without this involving negative consequences not only for the international credibility of those States but also for the internal life of the societies concerned: a persecuted believer will always find it difficult to have confidence in a State which presumes to regulate his conscience. On the other hand, good relations between Churches and the State contribute to the harmony of all members of society.

10. Ladies and Gentlemen, the purpose of these simple remarks has been to make the good wishes which we exchange more relevant. They have sketched a picture made up of lights and shadows, a reflection of the human soul.

But it is the pressing duty of the Successor of Peter to remind national leaders, whom you so worthily represent here, that world stability cannot be achieved if certain values are disregarded, values such as respect for life, conscience, fundamental human rights, concern for the most needy, solidarity, to name but a few.

The Holy See, being sovereign and independent among the nations, and for this reason a member of the international community, wishes to makes its specific contribution to this common commitment. Without political ambition, it is eager above all that humanity's path should be illuminated by the light of the One who, in coming into this world, became our traveling companion, the One "in whom are hid all the treasures of wisdom and knowledge" (Col 2:3).

To him once more I commend your persons, your families and your nations, in particular the younger generation of whom I thought when I launched the appeal: "Let us give children a future of peace!" (Message for the Celebration of the World Day of Peace, 1 January 1996). Upon everyone, for the year now beginning, I invoke abundant divine blessings.

January 13, 1997
(http://www.vatican.va/holy_father/john_paul_ii/speeches/1997/documents/hf_jp-
ii_spe_13011997_diplomatic-corps_en.html)

1. Your Dean, Ambassador Joseph Amichia, has just presented to me your cordial greetings with his usual serenity and graciousness. He has done this for the last time, since after more than twenty-five years he will soon return definitively to his beloved Côte-d'Ivoire. In your name I would like to offer to him, to his wife and family and to all his fellow-citizens, our best wishes for a future which will enable them to realize their most cherished aspirations.

To all of you, Your Excellencies, Ladies and Gentlemen, I offer cordial thanks for your greetings and good wishes; and I am grateful for the signs of appreciation which you so often show for the international activity of the Holy See. I will shortly have the opportunity to greet you personally and to express to you my sentiments of esteem. Through you, I would also like to send my affectionate and prayerful good wishes to the leaders of your countries and to your fellow-citizens. May the year 1997 mark a decisive stage in the establishment of peace and a prosperity more fully shared by all the peoples of the earth!

In my Message for the 1997 World Day of Peace, I invited all people of good will to "set out together on a true pilgrimage of peace, starting from the concrete situation in which we find ourselves" (no. 1). How better to begin if not with you, Ladies and Gentlemen, who are expert and attentive observers of international life? At the beginning of this year, what is the state of hope and peace? This is the question which, together with you, I would like to answer.

2. Hope. Very fortunately, hope is not absent from the horizon of humanity. Disarmament has taken important steps forward with the signing of the Treaty completely banning nuclear testing, a Treaty which the Holy See also signed, in the hope that it will be accepted by everyone. From now on the nuclear arms race and the proliferation of nuclear weapons have been banned from society.

This must not however make us less vigilant with regard to the production of increasingly sophisticated conventional and chemical weapons, or indifferent to the problems caused by anti-personnel mines. Regarding the latter, I express the hope that a juridically binding agreement with appropriate provisions for inspection will see the light of day at the meeting scheduled in Brussels next June. Everything must be done in order to build a safer world!

Almost all Governments, meeting in Istanbul under the auspices of the United Nations Organization for the Second Conference on Human Settlements and in Rome for the World Summit of the UN Food and Agricultural Organization, have made concrete commitments with a view to better reconciling development, economic growth and solidarity. The right to housing and the equitable sharing of the earth's resources emerged as priorities for the future: these represent decisive steps forward.

We must likewise take note of the agreement reached at the end of the year in Abidjan for peace in Sierra Leone, while at the same time expressing the hope that disarmament and the demobilization of the armed forces will take place without delay. May the same come true in neighboring Liberia, itself engaged in a difficult process of normalization and of preparation for free elections.

In Guatemala, peace seems finally to be at hand after too many years of fratricidal conflict. The agreement signed on December 29 last, by creating a climate of trust, should favor the settlement, in unity and with courage, of the many social problems still to be resolved.

Turning our gaze toward Asia, we await the date of July 1, 1997, when Hong Kong will return under the sovereignty of Mainland China. By reason of the size and vitality of the Catholic community living in the territory, the Holy See will follow with very particular interest this new stage, trusting that respect for differences, for the fundamental rights of the human person and for the rule of law will accompany this new journey forward, prepared for by patient negotiations.

3. In the second place, peace. It still seems precarious in more than one place on the earth, and, in any event, it is always at the mercy of the self-interest and the lack of proper foresight on the part of many leaders of international life.

Quite near to us, Algeria continues to wallow in an abyss of unprecedented violence, giving a bleak impression of an entire people taken hostage. The Catholic Church in Algeria paid a heavy price last year, with the barbaric murder of the seven Trappist Monks of Notre-Dame de l'Atlas, and the brutal death of Bishop Pierre Claverie of Oran. Cyprus, still split in two, awaits a political solution, which ought to be worked out in a European context which would offer it a broader variety of possibilities. And then, on the Eastern shore of the Mediterranean, the Middle East continues to search uncertainly for the road to peace. Everything must be tried to ensure that the sacrifices and efforts of these past years, since the Madrid Conference, will not have been in vain. For Christians in particular, this "Holy Land" remains the place where there first was heard the message of love and reconciliation: "Peace on earth to men of good will!"

All people together, Jews, Christians and Muslims, Israelis and Arabs, believers and non-believers, must create and reinforce peace: the peace of treaties, the peace of trust, the peace in people's hearts! In this part of the world, as elsewhere, peace cannot be just nor can it long endure unless it rests on sincere dialogue between equal partners, with respect for each other's identity and history, unless it rests on the right of peoples to the free determination of their own destiny, upon their independence and security. There can be no exception! And all those who have accompanied the parties most directly involved in the difficult Middle East peace process must redouble their efforts to ensure that the modest capital of trust already accumulated is not wasted, but rather increases and bears interest.

In recent few months, a hotbed of tension has dramatically enveloped the entire region of the Great Lakes in Africa. Burundi, Rwanda and Zaire in particular have found themselves trapped in the deadly cogs of unbridled violence and ethnic rivalry, which have plunged entire nations into human tragedies which should leave no one indifferent. No solution will ever be worked out until the political and military leaders are seated around the negotiating table, with the help of the international community, in order to study together how their necessary and unavoidable relationships should take shape. The international community, and I include here the regional organizations of Africa, must not only find a remedy for the indifference recently shown with regard to the humanitarian tragedies which the entire world has witnessed, but also increase its political activity lest new tragic developments, the carving up of territories or the displacement of populations, create situations which no one will be able to control. The security of a country or region cannot be founded on the accumulation of risks.

In Sri Lanka, hopes for peace have been shattered in the face of fighting which has again devastated entire regions of the Island. The persistence of these clashes is an obvious obstacle to economic progress. There too negotiations must be taken up anew in order to arrive at a cease-fire which will allow the future to be planned in a more serene manner.

Looking finally at Europe we can see that the forging of European Institutions and the deepening of a European concept of security and defense should ensure for the citizens of this continent's countries a more stable future, because it will rest on a patrimony of shared values: respect for human rights, the primacy of liberty and democracy, the rule of law, the right to economic and social progress. All of this, of course, with a view to the integral development of the human person. But Europeans too must remain vigilant, for it is always possible to drift off course, as the Balkan crisis has made clear: persisting ethnic tensions, exaggerated nationalism, intolerance of every sort constitute permanent threats. The hotbeds of tension remaining in the Caucasus tell us that the contagion of these negative influences can only be checked by the establishment of a true culture of peace and of a true education in peace. For the moment, in too many areas of Europe one has the impression that people are coexisting rather than cooperating. We must never forget what one of post-war Europe's "Founding Fathers" wrote as the inscription to his memoirs, I am quoting here Jean Monnet: "We do not make coalitions of States, we unite people!"

4. This rapid panorama of the international situation suffices to show that between the progress already made and the problems still unresolved, political leaders have a broad field of action. And what the international community perhaps lacks most of all today is not written Conventions or forums for self-expression – there is a profusion of these! – but a moral law and the courage to abide by it.

The community of nations, like every human society, cannot escape this basic principle: it must be regulated by a rule of law, valid for all of them without exception. Every juridical system, as we know, has as its foundation and end the common good. And this applies to the international community as well: the good of all and the good of the whole! This is what makes possible equitable solutions in which gain is not made at the expense of others, even when those who benefit are the majority: justice is for all, without injustice being inflicted on anyone. The function of law is to give each person his due, to give him what is owed to him in justice. Law therefore has a strong moral implication. And international law itself is founded on values. The dignity of the person, or guaranteeing the rights of nations, for example, are moral principles before they are juridical norms. And this explains why it was philosophers and theologians who, between the fifteenth and sixteenth centuries, were the first theorists of international society and the precursors of an explicit recognition of *ius gentium*. Moreover, we cannot fail to note that international law is no longer a mere law between States, but rather tends more and more to bring individuals together by international definitions of human rights, of the international right to health care or the right to humanitarian aid, to mention but a few examples.

There is thus an urgent need to organize the post-Cold War peace and the post-

1989 freedom on the foundation of moral values which are diametrically opposed to that law which would see the stronger, the richer or the bigger imposing on others their cultural models, economic diktats or ideological models. In this sense, attempts to form an international criminal justice system are evidence of real progress in the moral conscience of the nations. The development of humanitarian initiatives, whether intergovernmental or private, is also a positive sign of a re-awakening of solidarity in response to intolerable situations of violence or injustice. But, in this same regard, we must be careful to ensure that these acts of generosity do not rapidly become a kind of justice of the victors, or conceal ulterior motives of domination which would base decisions on concerns of spheres of influence, the preservation of control or the reconquest of trade markets.

For a long time international law has been a law of war and peace. I believe that it is called more and more to become exclusively a law of peace, conceived in justice and solidarity. And in this context morality must inspire law; morality can even assume a preparatory role in the making of law, to the extent that it shows the path of what is right and good.

5. Your Excellencies, Ladies and Gentlemen, these are the reflections which I wished to share with you at the beginning of the New Year. Perhaps they can inspire your own reflection and activity in the service of justice, solidarity and peace between the nations which you represent.

In my prayers, I entrust to God the well-being and prosperity of your fellow citizens, the plans of your Governments for the spiritual and temporal good of their peoples, and the efforts of the international community to ensure that right and law prevail.

On our pilgrimage of peace, the Christmas star guides us and shows us mankind's true path as it invites us to follow the path of God.

May God bless you and your countries; may he grant you all a happy year!

January 10, 1998
(http://www.vatican.va/holy_father/john_paul_ii/speeches/1998/documents/hf_jp-
ii_spe_10011998_diplomatic-corps_en.html)

1. The collective homage of the Diplomatic Corps, on the threshold of the New Year, always takes on the character of moving solemnity and heartfelt familiarity. I cordially thank your Dean, Ambassador Atembina-Te-Bombo, who has courteously presented your friendly good wishes and delicately evoked certain aspects of my apostolic mission.

At the beginning of this year 1998, let us allow to shine for all of today's men and women the light which rose over the world on the day of the birth of the Divine Child. By its very nature, that light is universal, its brightness illumines everyone without exception. It reveals both our successes and our setbacks in the management of creation and in our mission at the service of society.

2. Very fortunately there is no lack of positive achievements. Central and Eastern Europe have continued their progress toward democracy, gradually freeing themselves from the burdens and conditionings of the totalitarian regime of yesterday. Let us hope that this progress will prove effective everywhere!

Not far from us, Bosnia-Hercegovina is experiencing a more or less relative peace, although the recent local elections have shown the precarious nature of the peacemaking process between the different communities. In this regard, I would like to extend an earnest invitation to the international community to pursue its efforts in favor of the return of the refugees to their homes, and in favor of respect for the fundamental rights of the three ethnic communities which make up the country. These are preconditions necessary for the vitality of the country: my unforgettable pastoral visit to Sarajevo, last Spring, made me even more clearly aware of this.

The enlargement of the European Union eastwards, and its efforts to achieve monetary stability, should lead to an ever greater complementarity among the peoples involved, in respect for each one's identity and history. In a way it is a question of sharing the heritage of values which each nation has succeeded in bringing into being: the dignity of the human person, his inalienable fundamental rights, the inviolability of life, freedom and justice, the sense of solidarity and the rejection of discrimination.

Also within this continent, we cannot but encourage the resumption of dialogue between the parties which for so many years have been opposed to one another in Northern Ireland. May all parties have the courage to persevere in order to overcome present perils, there as in other regions of Europe!

In Latin America, the process of democratization has continued, even though here and there pernicious reactions have hindered its advance, as shown by the tragic events which occurred in the Mexican Province of Chiapas, a few days before Christmas. At the end of this month, God willing, I will make a Pastoral Visit to Cuba. The first visit of a Successor of Peter to that Island will give me an opportunity to strengthen not only the courageous Catholics of that country but also all their fellow-citizens in their efforts to achieve a homeland ever more just and united, where all individuals can find their rightful place and see their legitimate aspirations recognized.

As regards Asia, where more than half of humanity lives, we must applaud the talks being held in Geneva between the two Koreas. Success here would considerably reduce tension in the whole region, and would undoubtedly encourage constructive dialogue between other countries in the region which are still divided or hostile, and would thus encourage them to undertake a dynamic process of solidarity and peace. The financial fluctuations which have recently occupied center-stage in certain countries of that part of the world call for serious reflection on the morality of the economic and financial markets which have led to the considerable development of Asia in recent years. Greater sensitivity to social justice and more respect for local cultures could in the future avoid unpleasant surprises, the victims of which are always the local peoples.

I do not need to insist in order to remind you of the interest with which the Pope and his collaborators are following the evolution of the situation in China, hoping that that evolution will favor the establishment of more friendly relations with the Holy See. This would enable Chinese Catholics to live their faith fully inserted into the communion of the whole Church as she approaches the Great Jubilee.

My thoughts likewise go to the Church in Vietnam which is still aspiring to better conditions of existence. I cannot forget the people of East Timor, and in particular the sons and daughters of the Church there, still awaiting more peaceful conditions in order to be able to look to the future with greater confidence.

At this point I would like to address a cordial greeting to Mongolia, which has expressed the desire to establish closer links with the Apostolic See.

3. In a more general way, I would consider as being among the positive aspects of our review the increase of sensitivity in the world to questions connected with the preservation of an environment worthy of man, and the international consensus which made possible, just a month ago in Ottawa, the signing of a treaty banning antipersonnel mines (which the Holy See is preparing to ratify). All this shows an ever more concrete respect for human beings, considered individually and as members of society, as well as in their role as stewards of creation; and this also corresponds to the conviction that true happiness can only come about when we work with one another, not against one another.

The initiatives undertaken by the leaders of the international community on behalf of children, who are all too frequently victimized in their innocence, the battle against organized crime and drug trafficking, the efforts to oppose every form of contemptible trafficking in human beings: these clearly show that, with political determination, it is possible to strike at the causes of the disorders which too often disfigure the human person.

These advances are all the more in need of being consolidated, since the world around us is still so changeable and since its equilibrium can be compromised at any moment by an unexpected conflict, a fresh economic crisis or the baneful effects of the disturbing spread of poverty.

4. The fragility of our societies is painfully demonstrated by the "crisis spots" which are in the forefront of the news and which have once more cast a shadow over the joyful atmosphere of the celebrations of recent days.

I am thinking in the first place of Algeria, which practically every day is thrown into mourning by deplorable massacres. We see a whole country held hostage to an inhuman violence which no political cause, far less a religious motivation, could legitimate. I insist on repeating clearly to all, once again, that no one may kill in God's name: this is to misuse the divine name and to blaspheme. It would be appropriate for all people of good will, in that country and elsewhere, to unite in ensuring that the voice of those who believe in dialogue and fraternity is finally heard. And I am convinced that they are the majority of the Algerian people.

The situation in Sudan still does not permit us to speak of reconciliation and peace. Furthermore, the Christians of this country continue to be the object of grievous discriminations which the Holy See has time and again brought up with the civil authorities, unfortunately without any notable improvement.

Peace seems to have moved further away from the Middle East, since the peace process begun in Madrid in 1991 is practically at a standstill, when it is not altogether endangered by ambiguous or even violent incidents. My thoughts turn at this time to all those – Israelis and Palestinians – who in recent years had hoped that justice, security, peace and a normal everyday life would finally dawn on this Holy Land. Today, what remains of this desire for peace? The principles of the Madrid Conference and the guidelines of the 1993 Oslo meeting paved the way to peace. They still remain the only effective means of moving forward. There is no need at all to attempt other paths. I would like to assure you and, through you, the whole international community, that the Holy See will for its part continue to dialogue with all the parties concerned in order to encourage the determination of both sides to salvage peace and to heal the wounds of injustice. The Holy See maintains a constant concern for this part of the world and it conducts its activity in accordance with the principles which have always guided it. The Pope, in particular, in these years preceding the celebration of the Jubilee of the Year 2000, turns his gaze toward Jerusalem, the Holy City par excellence, praying daily that it will become soon and forever, together with Bethlehem and Nazareth, a place of justice and peace where Jews, Christians and Muslims will finally be able to walk together before God.

Not far from there, an entire people is the victim of a constraint which puts it in hazardous conditions of survival. I refer to our brothers and sisters in Iraq, living under a pitiless embargo. In response to the appeals for help which unceasingly come to the Holy See, I must call upon the consciences of those who, in Iraq and elsewhere, put political, economic or strategic considerations before the fundamental good of the people, and I ask them to show compassion. The weak and the innocent cannot pay for mistakes for which they are not responsible. I therefore pray that this country will be able to regain its dignity, experience normal development, and thus be in a position to re-establish fruitful relations with other peoples, within the framework of international law and world solidarity.

We cannot pass over in silence the tragedy of the Kurdish peoples, which in these very days has drawn everyone's attention; the immediate demands of compassion toward refugees in extreme situations must not make us forget the quest of millions of their brothers and sisters who are also calling for secure and acceptable conditions of life.

Finally, it is my duty, unfortunately, to draw your attention to the drama of the peoples of the central part of Africa. In these last months we have witnessed a regional recomposition of ethnic and political balances. All of your chanceries know about the events which have taken place in Rwanda, Burundi, the Democratic Republic of Congo, and just recently in Congo-Brazzaville. I shall not therefore recall the facts here, but mention essentially the trials inflicted on these peoples: armed conflict, displacement of persons, the tragedy of refugees, deficient health conditions, a defective administration of justice. . . . Faced with such situations, no one's conscience can remain at peace. Today, in the greatest silence, intimidation and killing still continue. This is why I wish to address myself to the political leaders of these countries: if violent attainment of power becomes the norm, if insistence on ethnic considerations continues to override all other concerns, if democratic representation is systematically put aside, if corruption and the arms trade continue to rage, then Africa will never experience peace or development, and future generations will mercilessly judge these pages of African history.

I would also like to appeal to the solidarity of the countries of the continent. Africans ought not to rely on outside assistance for everything. Within their own ranks there are many men and women with all the human and intellectual aptitudes to meet the challenges of our time and to manage societies in an appropriate way. However, more "African" solidarity is needed to support countries in difficulty, and also to avoid discriminatory measures or sanctions being imposed upon them. They should all assist one another in the analysis and evaluation of political options, and should also agree not to take part in arms trafficking. Rather the countries of the continent should favor peace-making and reconciliation, if necessary through peace forces composed of African soldiers. In this way the credibility of Africa will be more real in the eyes of the rest of the world and international help would doubtless become more intensive, with respect for the sovereignty of nations. It is urgently necessary that territorial disputes, economic initiatives and human rights should mobilize the energies of Africans to arrive at equitable and peaceful solutions which will allow Africa to face the twenty-first century with better opportunities and more confidence.

5. In reality, all these problems show the vulnerability of the women and men of the end of this century. Certainly, it is fortunate that the International Organizations, for example, are concerning themselves more and more with indicating criteria to improve the quality of human life and with implementing concrete initiatives. The Apostolic See considers itself in solidarity with these activities of multilateral diplomacy, in which it willingly collaborates through its Observer Missions. In this regard, I would merely mention this morning that the Holy See is formally associated with the workings of the World Trade Organization, with the aim of promoting human and spiritual progress in a sector which is vital for the development of peoples.

However, we should not forget that modern men and women are often subject to ideologies which impose models of society or of behavior which claim to decide about everything, about life and death, about the private domain and even thought, about procreation and genetic heritage. Nature would be no more than simple matter, open to every experiment. One sometimes has the impression that life is appreciated only in terms of utility or the prosperity it can procure, that suffering is considered to be without meaning. The handicapped and the elderly are neglected because they are seen as an encumbrance, the child to be born is too often considered an intrusion into an existence planned in terms of subjective interests not marked by generosity. Abortion and euthanasia then rapidly come to be seen as acceptable "solutions."

The Catholic Church – and the majority of spiritual traditions – know from experience that man is unfortunately capable of betraying his humanity. He must then be enlightened and accompanied so that, in his wanderings, he can always find again the sources of life and order which the Creator has inscribed in the most intimate part of his being. Wherever man is born, suffers and dies, the Church will always be present in order to signify that, precisely at the moment when man experiences his limits, there is Someone who calls him in order to welcome him and give meaning to his fragile existence.

Conscious of my responsibility as Pastor at the service of the universal Church, I have often had the opportunity in the acts of my ministry to recall the absolute dignity of the human person from the moment of conception to his last breath, the sacred character of the family as the special place able to protect and ensure the proper development of the person, the greatness and beauty of responsible parenthood, and the noble aims of medicine and scientific research.

These are some of the questions which the conscience of believers must take into account. When man runs the risk of being regarded as an object which can be manipulated or made subject to one's will, when one no longer sees the image of God in man, when . . . love and self-sacrifice [are] deliberately obscured, when selfishness and profit become the prime driving-force of economic activity, then anything is possible and barbarism is not far away.

Your Excellencies, Ladies and Gentlemen, these reflections are not new to you who witness day by day the work of the Pope and his collaborators. But I wanted to put them before you once again for your consideration, because one has the impression at times that the leaders of society and the heads of International Organizations allow themselves to be influenced by a new language, which recent technologies seem to accredit and which certain legislative systems allow or even endorse. What we have, though, are ideologies finding a voice or pressure groups seeking to impose their ideas and their way of life on everyone. The social pact is then seriously weakened and citizens lose their points of reference.

Those who are guarantors of the law and of a country's social cohesion, or those in charge of organizations created for the good of the community of nations, cannot escape the duty of fidelity to the unwritten law of the human conscience, of which the ancients spoke and which is for everyone – believer and non-believer alike – the foundation and universal guarantee of human dignity and of life in society. Regarding this, I cannot but restate what I have already written: "If there exists no ultimate truth which guides and directs political action, then ideas and convictions can be easily exploited for the benefit of the powerful" (Encyclical Letter *Centesimus Annus*, no. 46). In the forum of conscience, "there are no privileges or exceptions for anyone. Whether one be the master of the world or the most wretched on the face of the earth, it makes no difference: faced with moral demands, we are all absolutely equal" (Encyclical Letter *Veritatis Splendor*, no. 96).

6. With this I conclude my presentation, Your Excellencies, Ladies and Gentlemen, and upon each of you, your families, the leaders of your countries and your fellow citizens I invoke divine protection throughout the year now beginning. May Almighty God help each of us to forge new paths where people may meet and walk together! This is the prayer which I raise to God each day for the whole of humanity, that it may be ever more worthy of this name!

January 11, 1999
(http://www.vatican.va/holy_father/john_paul_ii/speeches/1999/documents/hf_jp-
ii_spe_11011999_diplomatic-corps_en.html)

1. I am deeply grateful for the good wishes offered to me on your behalf by your Dean, the Ambassador of the Republic of San Marino, Signor Giovanni Galassi, at the beginning of this final year before the year 2000. They join the many expressions of affection which were sent to me by the Authorities of your countries and by your fellow citizens on the occasion of the twentieth anniversary of my Pontificate and for the New Year. To all, I wish to express once again my profound gratitude.

This yearly ceremony is like a family gathering and for this reason it is particularly dear to me. First, because through you almost all the nations of the world are made present here with their achievements and their hopes, but also with their difficulties. Secondly, because such a meeting affords me the pleasant opportunity to express my fervent and prayerful good wishes for you, your families and your fellow citizens. I ask God to grant each one health, prosperity and peace. You know that you can count on me and my collaborators whenever it is a matter of supporting what each country, with its best efforts, undertakes for the spiritual, moral and cultural uplifting of its citizens and for the advancement of all that contributes to good relations between peoples in justice and peace.

2. The family of nations, which has recently taken part in the joy of Christmas and with one accord has welcomed the New Year, has without doubt some grounds for rejoicing.

In Europe, I think especially of Ireland, where the agreement signed on Good Friday last has established the basis for a much awaited peace, which must be founded on a stable social life, on mutual trust and the principle of equality before the law for all.

Another reason for satisfaction for all of us is the peace process in Spain which for the first time is enabling the peoples of the Basque territories to see the specter of blind violence retreat and to think seriously of a process of normalization.

The transition to one currency and the enlargement toward the East will no doubt give Europe the possibility to become more and more a community with a common destiny, a true "European community" – this is in any case our dearest wish. This obviously presupposes that the member countries are able to reconcile their history with the same common project, so that they may all see themselves as equal partners, concerned only for the common good. The spiritual families which have made such a great contribution to the civilization of this continent – I am thinking especially of Christianity – have a role which seems to me to be more and more decisive. In the face of social problems which keep significant sectors of the population in poverty, and of social inequalities which give rise to chronic instability, and before the younger generations seeking points of reference in an often chaotic world, it is important that the Churches should be able to proclaim the tenderness of God and the call to fraternity which the recent feast of Christmas has caused to shine out once again for all humanity.

I would like to draw to your attention, ladies and gentlemen, further grounds for satisfaction in relation to the American Continent. I am referring to the agreement reached in Brasilia on October 26 last between Ecuador and Peru. Thanks to the per-severing efforts of the international community – especially on the part of the guar-antor countries – two sister nations had the courage to renounce violence, to accept a compromise and to resolve their differences in a peaceful way. This is an example for so many other nations still bogged down in divisions and disagreements. I am firmly convinced that these two nations, thanks particularly to the Christian faith which unites them, will be able to meet the great challenge of fraternity and peace, and thus turn a painful page of their history, which in fact dates from the very beginning of their existence as independent states. I address an urgent and paternal call to the Catholics of Ecuador and Peru to work with conviction for reconciliation through prayer and action, and thus to contribute to ensuring that the peace brought by the treaties enters everyone's heart.

We should also rejoice at the efforts of the great people of China, in a dialogue undertaken with determination and involving the peoples on both sides of the Strait. The international community – and the Holy See in particular – follows this felicitous development with great interest, in the hope of significant progress which, without any doubt, would be beneficial to the whole world.

3. However, the culture of peace is far from being universal, as the centers of persist-ent dissension testify.

Not far from us, the Balkan region continues to experience a time of great insta-bility. We cannot yet speak of normalization in Bosnia-Hercegovina where the effects of the war are still being felt in inter-ethnic relations, where half the population remains displaced and where social tensions dangerously persist. Again recently, Kosovo has been the scene of deadly confrontations for both ethnic and political rea-sons which have prevented a peaceful dialogue between the parties and hindered any economic development. Everything must be done to help the people of Kosovo and the Serbs to meet around a table in order to defuse without delay the armed suspicion which paralyzes and kills. Albania and Macedonia would be the first to benefit, since in the Balkans all things are closely related. Many other countries, large and small, in Central and Eastern Europe are also at the mercy of political and social instability; they are struggling along the road to democracy and have not yet succeeded in living in a market economy capable of giving everyone a legitimate share of well-being and growth.

The peace process undertaken in the Middle East continues to make uneven progress and has not yet brought the local peoples the hope and well-being which they have the right to enjoy. It is not possible to keep people indefinitely between war and peace, without the risk of dangerously increasing tensions and violence. It is not rea-sonable to put off until later the question of the status of the Holy City of Jerusalem, to which the followers of the three monotheist religions turn their gaze. The parties concerned should face these problems with a keen sense of their responsibilities. The recent crisis in Iraq has shown once more that war does not solve problems. It com-plicates them, and leaves the civilian population to bear the tragic consequences. Only honest dialogue, a real concern for the good of people and respect for the internation-al order can lead to solutions befitting a region where our religious traditions are root-ed. If violence is often contagious, peace can be so too, and I am sure that a stable

Middle East would contribute effectively to restoring hope to many peoples. I am thinking for example of the suffering peoples of Algeria and of the island of Cyprus, where the situation is still in deadlock.

Some months ago Sri Lanka celebrated the fiftieth anniversary of independence, but unfortunately it is still today divided by ethnic struggles which have delayed the opening of serious negotiations, which alone are the only way to peace.

Africa remains a continent at risk. Of its fifty-three States, seventeen are experiencing military conflicts, either internally or with other States. I am thinking in particular of Sudan where, in addition a cruel war, a terrible human tragedy is unfolding; Eritrea and Ethiopia which are once again in dispute; and Sierra Leone, where the people are still the victims of merciless struggles. On this great continent there are up to eight million refugees and displaced persons practically abandoned to their fate. The countries of the Great Lakes region still bear open wounds resulting from the excesses of ethnocentrism, and they are struggling amid poverty and insecurity; this is also the case in Rwanda and Burundi, where an embargo is further aggravating the situation. The Democratic Republic of Congo still has far to go in working out its transition and experiencing the stability to which its people legitimately aspire, as the massacres which recently occurred at the very beginning of the year near the town of Uvira testify. Angola remains in search of a peace which cannot be found and in these days is experiencing a development which causes great concern and which has not spared the Catholic Church. The reports regularly coming to me from these tormented regions confirm my conviction that war is always destructive of our humanity, and that peace is undoubtedly the pre-condition for human rights. To all these peoples, who often send me pleas for help, I wish to give the assurance that I am close to them. May they know also that the Holy See is sparing no effort to bring about an end to their sufferings and to find equitable solutions to the existing serious problems, on both the political and humanitarian levels.

The culture of peace is still being thwarted by the legitimation and use of armed force for political purposes. The nuclear tests recently carried out in Asia and the efforts of other countries quietly working on establishing their nuclear power could very well lead to a gradual spread of nuclear arms and consequently to a massive re-armament which would greatly hinder the praiseworthy efforts being made on behalf of peace. This would frustrate all policies aimed at preventing conflicts.

There is also the production of less costly weaponry, like anti-personnel mines, happily outlawed by the Ottawa Convention of December 1997 (which the Holy See hastened to ratify last year), and small-caliber arms, to which, I believe, political leaders should pay greater attention in order to control their deadly effects. Regional conflicts, in which children are frequently recruited for combat, indoctrinated and incited to kill, call for a serious examination of conscience and a concerted response.

Finally, the risks to peace arising from social inequalities and artificial economic growth cannot be underestimated. The financial crisis which has shaken Asia has shown the extent to which economic security is comparable to political and military security, inasmuch as it calls for openness, concerted action and respect for specific ethical principles.

4. In the face of these problems which are familiar to you, Ladies and Gentlemen, I

wish to share with you a conviction which I firmly hold: during this final year before the year 2000 an awakening of consciences is essential.

Never before have the members of the international community had at their disposal a body of such precise and complete norms and conventions. What is lacking is the will to respect and apply them. I pointed this out in my Message of January 1, in speaking of human rights: "When the violation of any fundamental human right is accepted without reaction, all other rights are placed at risk" (no. 12). It seems to me that this truth needs to be seen in relation to all juridic norms. International law cannot be the law of the stronger, nor that of a simple majority of States, nor even that of an international organization. It must be the law which is in conformity with the principles of the natural law and of the moral law, which are always binding upon parties in conflict and in the various questions in dispute.

The Catholic Church, as also communities of believers in general, will always be on the side of those who strive to make the supreme good of law prevail over all other considerations. It is likewise necessary for believers to be able to make themselves heard and to take part in public dialogue in the societies of which they are full members. This leads me to share with you, as the official representatives of your States, my painful concern about the all too numerous violations of religious freedom in today's world.

Just recently, for example, in Asia, episodes of violence have caused tragic suffering to the Catholic community: churches have been destroyed, religious personnel have been mistreated and even murdered. Other regrettable events could be mentioned in several African countries. In other regions, where Islam is the majority religion, one still has to deplore the grave forms of discrimination of which the followers of other religions are victims. There is even one country where Christian worship is totally forbidden and where possession of a Bible is a crime punishable by law. This is all the more distressing because, in many cases, Christians have made a great contribution to the development of these countries, especially in the area of education and health care. In certain countries in Western Europe, one notes an equally disturbing development which, under the influence of a false idea of the principle of separation between the State and the Churches or as a result of a deep-seated agnosticism, tends to confine the Churches within the religious sphere alone and finds it difficult to accept public statements from them. Finally, some countries of Central and Eastern Europe have great difficulty in acknowledging the religious pluralism proper to democratic societies and attempt to limit, by means of a restrictive and petty bureaucratic practice, the freedom of conscience and of religion which their Constitutions solemnly proclaim.

As I recall religious persecutions either long past or more recent, I believe that the time has come, at the end of this century, to ensure that everywhere in the world the right conditions for effective freedom of religion are guaranteed. This requires, on the one hand, that each believer should recognize in others something of the universal love which God has for his creatures. It requires, on the other hand, that the public authorities also – called by vocation to think in universal terms – should come to accept the religious dimension of their fellow citizens along with its necessary community expression. In order to bring this about, we have before us not only the lessons of history, but also certain valuable juridical instruments which only need to be applied. In a certain sense, the future of societies depends on the inescapable relationship between God and the Earthly City, for, as I stated during my visit to the seat of the European Parliament on October 11, 1988: "Wherever man no longer relies on the great reality that transcends him, he risks handing himself over to the uncontrollable power of the arbitrary and to pseudo-absolutes that destroy him" (no. 10).

5. These are some of the thoughts which have come to my mind and heart as I look at the world of this century which is coming to a close. If God in sending his Son among us took such interest in mankind, let us act in such a way as to correspond to such great love! He, the Father of all, has made with each of us a covenant which nothing can break. By telling us and by showing us that he loves us, he also gives us the hope that we can live in peace; and it is true that only the person who knows love can love in return. It is good that all people should discover this Love which precedes them and awaits them. Such is my dearest wish, for each of you and for all the peoples of the earth!

January 10, 2000
(http://www.vatican.va/holy_father/john_paul_ii/speeches/documents/hf_jp-
ii_spe_20000110_diplomatic-corps_en.html)

1. I wish before all else to express my deep gratitude to your Dean, Ambassador Giovanni Galassi, who has graciously offered greetings and good wishes in your name while at the same time pointing to a number of significant events in the life of our contemporaries, their hopes, their troubles and their fears. He has wished to underline the specific contribution of the Catholic Church on behalf of harmony between peoples and in support of their spiritual progress. I offer him heartfelt thanks.

2. Since we have just crossed the threshold of a new year, the Vicar of Christ strongly desires to offer to the peoples whom you represent his prayerful good wishes for this Year 2000 which so many have welcomed in "jubilation." Christians have entered into the Great Jubilee by commemorating the coming of Christ into time and human history: "In many and various ways God spoke of old to our fathers by the prophets; but in these last days he has spoken to us by a Son," as we read in the Letter to the Hebrews (1:1–2).

To God who desired to make a covenant with the world which he continues to create, to love and to enlighten, I most heartily entrust each one's noblest aspirations and their fulfilment, without overlooking the tragic trials and setbacks which so often thwart humanity's march forward. With our contemporaries I praise God for so many beautiful and good things, and I invoke his forgiveness for so many attacks on human life and dignity, on fraternity and solidarity. May the Most High help us to conquer in us and around us every form of resistance, so that the season of men and women of good will may dawn or return, a season which the recent feast of Christmas has proposed to us with the freshness of new beginnings! These are my prayerful good wishes for all men and women, of all countries and of all generations.

3. The century just ended has seen remarkable advances in science which have considerably improved people's life and health. These advances have also contributed to our dominion over nature and made easier people's access to culture. Information technology has made the world smaller and brought us closer to one another. Never before were we so quickly informed about the daily events which affect the lives of our brothers and sisters in the human family. But one question can be asked: was this century also the century of "brotherhood"? Certainly an unqualified answer cannot be given.

As the balance is made, the memory of bloody wars which have decimated millions of people and provoked massive exoduses, shameful genocides which haunt our memories, as well as the arms race which fostered mistrust and fear, terrorism and ethnic conflicts which annihilated peoples who had lived together in the same territory, all force us to be modest and in many cases to have a penitent spirit.

The life sciences and biotechnology continue to find new fields of application, yet they also raise the problem of the limits imposed by the need to safeguard people's dignity, responsibility and safety.

Globalization, which has profoundly transformed economic systems by creating unexpected possibilities of growth, has also resulted in many people being relegated to the side of the road: unemployment in the more developed countries and extreme poverty in too many countries of the southern hemisphere continue to hold millions of women and men back from progress and prosperity.

4. For this reason it seems to me that the century now beginning ought to be the century of solidarity.

We know one thing today more than in the past: we will never be happy and at peace without one another, much less if some are against others. The humanitarian efforts deployed during recent conflicts and natural catastrophes inspired praiseworthy initiatives of volunteerism which reveal a greater sense of altruism, especially among the younger generation.

The phenomenon of globalization has somewhat changed the role of States: citizens have become more and more involved, and the principle of subsidiarity has undoubtedly contributed to greater balance between the forces present within civil society; the citizen has become more a "partner" in the common effort.

This means, it seems to me, that the men and women of the 21st century will be called to a more developed sense of responsibility. First, their personal responsibility, in fostering a sense of duty and honest labor: corruption, organized crime or passivity can never lead to a true and healthy democracy. But there must also be an equal sense of responsibility toward others: an attitude of concern for the poor, participation in structures of mutual assistance in the workplace and in the social sphere, respect for nature and the environment, all these are required if we are to have a world where people live together in a better way. Never again must there be separation between people! Never again must some be opposed to others! Everyone must live together, under God's watchful eyes!

This also supposes that we must renounce idols such as prosperity at any price, material wealth as the only value, science as the sole explanation of reality. It also supposes that the rule of law will be applied and respected by everyone and in all places, so that individual liberties can be effectively guaranteed and equal opportunity become a reality for all people. It also supposes that God will have his rightful place in people's lives: the first place.

In a world more than ever in search of meaning, Christians sense the call, as this century opens, to proclaim with greater fervor that Jesus is the Redeemer of mankind, and the Church senses the call to show herself to be the "sign and safeguard of the transcendence of the human person" (Vatican Council II, *Gaudium et Spes*, no. 76).

5. Such solidarity calls for certain precise commitments. Some of these are quite urgent:

The sharing of technology and prosperity. In the absence of an attitude of understanding and readiness to help, it would be difficult to restrain the frustration felt by certain countries which see themselves condemned to founder in ever more serious precariousness and at the same time to have to compete with other countries. I myself have brought up on a number of occasions, for example, the issue of the debt of poor countries.

Respect for human rights. The legitimate aspirations of the most defenseless persons, the claims of ethnic minorities, the sufferings of all those whose beliefs or culture are in one way or another held in contempt are not merely optional issues to be dealt with as circumstances, or political or economic interests, dictate. Not to ensure these rights means quite simply to flout the dignity of persons and to endanger global stability.

Conflict prevention would avoid situations difficult to resolve and would spare much suffering. Appropriate international means are not lacking; they need only to be used, carefully distinguishing, without opposition or separation, between politics, law and morality.

Lastly, calm dialogue between cultures and religions could favor a new way of thinking and living. Despite their diverse mentalities and beliefs, the men and women of this millennium, in recalling the errors of the past, must find new ways of living together and respecting one another. Quality education, science and information represent the best means for developing in each of us respect for others, for their talents and beliefs, as well as a sense of universality worthy of man's spiritual vocation. This dialogue would also make it possible in the future to avoid arriving at an absurd situation: that of excluding or killing others in the name of God. This undoubtedly will be a decisive contribution to peace.

6. In recent years there has been much talk of a "new world order." The persevering action of far-sighted diplomats, and of multilateral diplomacy in particular, has resulted in a number of praiseworthy initiatives aimed at the building of an authentic "community of nations." At present, for example, the Middle East Peace Process is continuing; the Chinese people are speaking to one another; the two Koreas are in dialogue; certain African countries are attempting to arrange meetings between rival factions; the government and armed groups in Colombia are trying to remain in contact. All this demonstrates a real desire to build a world based on brotherhood, in order to create, defend and spread peace all around us. Regrettably, however, we must also acknowledge that the errors of the past are all too often being repeated: I am thinking of reactions based on group identity, of persecutions inflicted for religious reasons, of the frequent and at times rash recourse to war, of social inequalities, of the gap between the rich and the poor countries, of the exclusive trust in profit alone, to cite only some typical traits of the century just ended. At the beginning of the year 2000, what do we see? Africa, shackled by ethnic conflicts which hold entire peoples hostage, impeding their economic and social progress and often condemning them to a situation of mere survival.

The Middle East, constantly poised between war and peace, when we know that only the rule of law and justice will make it possible for all the peoples of the region, without distinction, to live together and to be free of endemic dangers.

Asia, a continent of immense human and material resources, gathers into precarious balance peoples of venerable and economically highly developed cultures and others who are becoming increasingly impoverished. I recently visited this continent in order to consign the Apostolic Exhortation *Ecclesia in Asia*, the fruit of a recent synodal assembly, which has now become a charter for all Catholics. I join the Synod Fathers in inviting once more all the Catholics of Asia and men and women of good will to unite their efforts in building a society more firmly based on solidarity.

America, an immense continent where one year ago I had the joy of promulgating the Apostolic Exhortation *Ecclesia in America*, inviting the peoples of the continent to an ever-renewed personal and communal conversion, in respect for the dignity of the person and love for the outcast, for the sake of promoting a culture of life.

North America, where economic and political concerns are often considered paramount, is home to many poor people, despite its manifold riches.

Latin America, which, with a few exceptions, has seen encouraging advances toward democracy, remains dangerously crippled by alarming social inequalities, the drug trade, corruption and in some cases movements of armed struggle.

Europe, following the failure of the ideologies, is finally on the way toward unity; it is struggling to meet the two-fold challenge of reconciliation and the democratic integration of former enemies. Europe has not been spared terrible forms of violence, as the recent Balkan crisis and the conflicts of recent weeks in the Caucasus have shown. The Bishops of the continent recently met in synodal assembly; they acknowledged the signs of hope, growing openness between peoples, reconciliation between nations, more frequent cooperation and exchange, and called everyone to a greater European consciousness.

Faced with this troubled world, at once magnificent and unstable, I am reminded of a commitment made at the end of the terrible Second World War, which everyone wanted to be the last. I am speaking of the Preamble to the Charter of the United Nations, adopted in San Francisco on June 26, 1945: "We, the peoples of the United Nations, determined to save succeeding generations from the scourge of war which twice in our lifetime has brought untold sorrow to mankind, and to reaffirm our faith in fundamental human rights, in the dignity and worth of the human person, in the equal rights of men and women and of nations, large and small . . . have resolved to combine our efforts to accomplish these aims."

This solemn text and this solemn commitment have lost nothing of their force and their timeliness. In a world structured around sovereign but de facto unequal States, it is indispensable for stability, understanding and cooperation between peoples that international relations be increasingly imbued with and shaped by the rule of law. Surely what is lacking is not new texts or juridical instruments; it is quite simply the political will to apply without discrimination those already in existence.

7. Your Excellencies, Ladies and Gentlemen, I speak to you as one who has himself been a fellow-traveler of several generations of the century just ended. I shared the harsh ordeals of my native people as the darkest hours experienced by Europe. Twenty-one years ago, when I became the Successor of the Apostle Peter, I felt myself charged with a universal fatherhood which embraces all the men and women of our time without exception. Today, in addressing you who represent practically all the peoples of the earth, I would like to share with each one something personal: at the opening of the doors of a new millennium, the Pope began to think that people might finally learn to draw lessons from the past. Indeed, I ask everyone, in God's name, to save humanity from further wars, to respect human life and the family, to bridge the gap between the rich and the poor, to realize that we are all responsible for one another. It is God himself who asks this, and he never asks what is beyond our abilities. He himself gives us the strength to accomplish what he expects of us.

The words which Deuteronomy puts on the lips of God himself come to mind: "See, I have set before you this day life and good, death and evil; . . . therefore choose life, that you may live" (Dt 30:15–19). Life takes shape in our daily choices. And political leaders, since they have the role of administering the *"res publica,"* can by their personal choices and their programs of action guide whole societies either toward life or toward death. For this reason believers, and the faithful of the Catholic Church in particular, consider it their duty to take an active part in the public life of the societies to which they belong. Their faith, their hope and their charity represent additional and irreplaceable energies to ensure that not only will there be unfailing concern for others, a sense of responsibility and the defense of fundamental rights, but also to ensure that there is a perception that our world and our personal and collective history are invested with a Presence. I therefore insist that believers be granted a place in public life because I am convinced that their faith and their witness can reassure our contemporaries, who are often anxious and disoriented, and can ensure that despite failures, violence and fear, neither evil nor death will have the last word.

8. The time has now come for our exchange of personal good wishes. I greet all of you most cordially and I ask you kindly to convey my best wishes to the leaders of the countries which you represent. The doors of the Great Jubilee have been opened for Christians and the doors of a new millennium for humanity as a whole. What is important now is to cross the threshold in order to make our journey. This is a journey on which God precedes us and in which he traces the path which will lead us toward himself. Nothing, no prejudice or ambition, should hold us back. A new history is beginning for us. The peoples whom you represent are going to write that history in their personal and collective life. It is a history in which today, like yesterday and like tomorrow, humanity has an appointment with God. And so to all I say: "Safe journey"!

January 13, 2001
(http://www.vatican.va/holy_father/john_paul_ii/speeches/2001/documents/hf_jp-
ii_spe_20010113_diplomatic-corps_en.html)

1. I cordially thank each one of you for the good wishes which your Dean, Ambassador Giovanni Galassi, has so thoughtfully expressed and presented on behalf of all of you. I extend heartfelt good wishes to each one of you. *May God bless you and your countries, and may he grant everyone a prosperous and happy New Year.*

But a question comes immediately to mind: what is a happy year for a diplomat? The world scene in this month of January 2001 could cause one to doubt the capacity of diplomacy to bring about the rule of order, equity and peace among peoples.

However, we should not resign ourselves to the inevitability of sickness, poverty, injustice or war. It is certain that without social solidarity or recourse to law and the instruments of diplomacy, these terrible situations would be even more dramatic and could become insoluble. I therefore wish to thank you, Ladies and Gentlemen, for your activity and persevering efforts to promote understanding and cooperation among peoples.

2. The inspiration of the Holy Year which has just ended, and of the different Jubilee events which brought together and motivated men and women of every race, age and condition, showed, if there was a need, *that the moral conscience is still very much alive and that God dwells in the human heart.* In your presence I shall content myself with recalling the Jubilee of Members of Government, Parliamentarians and Politicians which took place at the beginning of November. It was for me a source of great spiritual consolation to see so much good will and so much openness to God's grace. Once again it was possible to see the correctness of what the Second Vatican Ecumenical Council's Pastoral Constitution *Gaudium et Spes* magnificently proclaims: "The Church believes that Christ, who died and was raised up for all, through his Spirit offers man the light and the strength to respond to his supreme calling. Nor has any other name under heaven been given to man by which he should be saved. She likewise holds that in her Lord and Master can be found the key, the focal point, and the goal of all human history" (no. 10).

3. Following the shepherds and the wise men and all those who for the past two thousand years have hastened to the crib, today's humanity too has paused for a few moments on Christmas Day to gaze upon the Infant Jesus and to receive some of the light which accompanied his birth and continues to illumine all human darkness. *This light tells us that the love of God is always stronger than evil and death.*

This light signals the path of all who in our times in *Bethlehem* and *Jerusalem* are struggling on the road to peace. In this part of the world which received God's revelation to man there should be no resignation before the fact that a kind of guerilla warfare has become an everyday event, or in the face of the persistence of injustice, the contempt for international law or the marginalization of the Holy Places and the requirements of the Christian communities. Israelis and Palestinians can only think of their future together, and each party must respect the rights and traditions of the other. It is time to return to the principles of international legality: the banning of the acquisition of territory by force, the right of peoples to self-determination, respect for the resolutions of the United Nations Organization and the Geneva conventions, to quote only the most important. Otherwise, anything can happen: from unilateral rash initiatives to an extension of violence which will be difficult to control.

This same light is shed upon all the other regions of the planet where people have chosen armed violence in order to exact their rights or further their ambitions. I am thinking of *Africa*, a continent where too many weapons are circulating and where too many countries suffer from unstable democracy and devastating corruption, where *the drama of Algeria* and the war in southern *Sudan* are still mercilessly slaughtering people; nor can we forget the chaos into which the countries of *the Great Lakes region* have been plunged. That is why the peace agreement arrived at last month in Algiers between *Ethiopia and Eritrea* is a cause for satisfaction, as are the promising attempts to lead *Somalia* gradually back to normality. Nearer to us, I must mention – and with such a sense of sadness! – the murderous terrorist attacks in *Spain*, which sully the nation and humiliate the whole of Europe as it searches for its identity. Many people still look to Europe as a model from which to draw inspiration. May Europe never forget the Christian roots which have allowed its humanism to bear much fruit! May Europe also be generous toward those – individuals and peoples – who come knocking at its door!

4. The light of Bethlehem, shed upon "men and women of good will," also imposes upon us the duty of combating always and everywhere poverty, marginalization, illiteracy, social inequalities or the shameful treatment of human beings. None of these is beyond redress, and it is pleasing to note that various international meetings and agencies have brought at least a partial remedy to these wounds which disfigure humanity. Egoism and the will to power are humanity's worst enemies. In some way, they are at the root of every conflict. This is especially evident in certain parts of *South America*, where socio-economic and cultural differences, armed violence or guerilla warfare, and the turning back of democratic gains damage the social fabric and cause entire populations to lose confidence in the future. This immense continent must be helped to bring all its human and material heritage to fruition.

Distrust, conflicts and the vestiges of past crises can always be overcome through good will and international solidarity. Asia has shown that this is so, with the dialogue between *the two Koreas* and with *East Timor's* progress toward independence.

5. Believers – and especially Christians – know that another approach is possible. I will formulate it in words which may seem too simple: *every man is my brother*! If we were convinced that we are called to live together, that it is wonderful to come to know one another, to respect and help one another, the world would be radically different.

When we think of the century just ended, one thing is clear: history will judge it to be the century which saw the greatest conquests of science and technology, but also as the time when human life was despised in the cruelest ways.

I am certainly referring to the murderous wars which burgeoned in Europe and to the forms of totalitarianism which enslaved millions of men and women, but I am also referring to laws which "legalized" abortion or euthanasia, and to cultural models which have spread the idea of consumption and pleasure at any price. If people upset the balance of creation, forgetting that they are responsible for their brothers and sisters, and do not care for the environment which the Creator has placed in their hands, then a world determined by our designs alone could well become unliveable.

6. As I recalled in my World Day of Peace Message on January 1, we should all use this year 2001, which the United Nations Organization has declared the "International Year of Dialogue between Civilizations," as a time "for building the civilization of love . . . based upon the recognition that there are values which are common to all cultures because they are rooted in the nature of the person" (no. 16).

But what do we have more deeply in common than our human nature? *Yes, at the dawn of this millennium, let us save man*! Let us together, all of us, save humanity! It is up to the leaders of societies to safeguard the human race, ensuring that science is at the service of the human person, that people are never objects to be manipulated or to be bought and sold, that laws are never determined by commercial interests or by the selfish claims of minority groups. Every age of human history has seen humanity tempted to inhabit a self-enclosed world in an attitude of self-sufficiency, domination, power and pride. But in our own time this danger has become still greater in man's heart, as people believe that through the efforts of science they can become the masters of nature and of history.

7. It will always be the task of believing communities to state publicly that no authority, no political program and no ideology is entitled to reduce human beings to what they can do or produce. It will always be the imperative duty of believers to remind everyone in all situations of *the inalienable personal mystery of every human being*, created in the image of God, able to love as Jesus did.

Here I would like to say to you once more and, through you, to say once more to the governments which have accredited you to the Holy See, that *the Catholic Church is determined to defend the dignity, the rights and the transcendent dimension of the human person*. Even if some are reluctant to refer to the religious dimension of human beings and human history, even if others want to consign religion to the private sphere, even if believing communities are persecuted, Christians will still proclaim that religious experience is part of human experience. It is a vital element in shaping the person and the society to which people belong. This is why the Holy See has always been vigorous in defending freedom of conscience and religious liberty, at both the individual and social level. The tragic experience of the Christian community in Indonesia or the blatant discrimination suffered by believing communities, both Christian and non-Christian, in some countries under Marxist or Islamic control, summon us to vigilance and unfailing solidarity.

8. These are the reflections prompted by this traditional meeting which enables me in some way to address all the peoples of the earth through their best qualified representatives. I ask that you communicate to all your fellow countrymen and to your national governments the prayerful good wishes of the Pope. Through this history of which we are the protagonists, let us chart the course of the millennium now beginning. Together, let us help one another to live a life worthy of the vocation that is ours, *the vocation of forming a great family, happy in the knowledge that it is loved by a God who wants us to be brothers and sisters*! May Almighty God bless you and those who are dear to you!

January 10, 2002
(http://www.vatican.va/holy_father/john_paul_ii/speeches/2002/january/documents/h
f_jp-ii_spe_20020110_diplomatic-corps_en.html)

1. The good wishes which your Dean, Ambassador Giovanni Galassi, has just offered me in your name are all the more touching in that they are also extended in the name of the governments and peoples which you represent.

I in my turn extend to you, your families and dear ones my heartfelt good wish that God will bless you and grant all peoples *a year of serenity, happiness and peace*.

Mr. Ambassador, your thoughtful greeting has been accompanied by a penetrating analysis of the international scene during the past year. The horizon indeed appears dark, and many of those who have lived through the great movement toward freedom and the changes of the '90s are surprised to find themselves gripped today by fear of a future which has once again become uncertain.

But for those who have put their faith and hope in Jesus, born in Bethlehem to become one of us, the angelic message has rung out again in the stillness of Christmas night: "Be not afraid . . . I bring you good news of great joy which will come to all the people, for today is born a Savior" (Lk 2:10–11). *The future is wide open, God is with us on our way*!

2. *The light of Christmas gives meaning to all human efforts* to make our earth more fraternal and friendly, to make it a good place to live, and to ensure that indifference, injustice and hatred will never have the last word. Here we could quote a long list of actions successfully concluded by governments, negotiators and volunteers who in recent times have put their know-how and their dedication at the service of the cause of humanity.

Among reasons for satisfaction, one must surely mention the progressive unification of *Europe*, recently symbolized by the adoption of a single currency by twelve countries. This is a decisive step in the long history of this continent. But it is also important that the expansion of the European Union should continue to be a priority. I am likewise aware that the question has been raised about the expediency of a Constitution for the Union. In this regard, it is essential to make increasingly explicit the goals of the process of building up Europe and the values on which it must rest. Hence it is that, with some regret, I have noted that, no explicit mention was made of communities of religious believers among the partners who are to contribute to the reflection on the "Convention" instituted at the Laeken summit last month. The marginalization of religions, which have contributed and continue to contribute to the culture and humanism of which Europe is legitimately proud, strikes me as both an injustice and an error of perspective. To recognize an indisputable historical fact in no way means to disregard the modern demand for States to have an appropriate non-confessional character, and therefore Europe as well!

I am also pleased to mention the good news, so long awaited, of the beginning of a direct dialogue between the leaders of the two communities on the island of *Cyprus*. A legitimate parliament in *Kosovo* is another harbinger of a more democratic future in that region. Since last November, delegations of the People's Republic of *China* and the Republic of China have taken their seats in the World Trade Organization. May this positive development help prosper all the efforts which have been made on the difficult path of rapprochement! The conversations taking place between the parties in the conflict which has so long torn *Sri Lanka* apart undoubtedly must be encouraged. These certainly are significant advances on the path of pacification between individuals and peoples.

3. But likewise the light which has come from the stable in Bethlehem illuminates implacably *the ambiguities and setbacks in our undertakings*. At this year begins, we are tragically aware that humanity finds itself in a situation of violence, suffering and sin.

On Christmas night we were present in spirit at Bethlehem and were alas forced to note that the *Holy Land*, where the Redeemer was born, is still, through man's fault, a land of fire and blood. No one can remain indifferent to the injustice of which the Palestinian people have been victims for more than fifty years. No one can contest the right of the Israeli people to live in security. But neither can anyone forget the innocent victims who, on both sides, fall day after day under the blows of violence. Weapons and bloody attacks will never be the right means for making a political statement to the other side. Nor is the logic of the law of retaliation capable any longer of leading to paths of peace.

As I have already stated on many occasions, only respect for others and their legitimate aspirations, the application of international law, the evacuation of the occupied territories and an internationally guaranteed special status for the most holy places in Jerusalem can bring about a beginning of pacification in that part of the world and break the hellish cycle of hatred and vengeance. And I express the hope that the international community will be enabled to fulfill, through peaceful and appropriate means, its irreplaceable role and be accepted by all the parties in the conflict. One against the other, neither Israelis nor Palestinians can win the war. But together they can win peace.

The legitimate fight against terrorism, of which the abhorrent attacks of last 11 September are the most appalling expression, has once again let the sound of arms be heard. Barbarous aggression and killings raise not only the question of legitimate defense but also issues such as the most effective means of eradicating terrorism, the search for the factors underlying such acts, and the measures to be taken to bring about a process of "healing" in order to overcome fear and to avoid evil being added to evil, violence to violence. It is appropriate therefore to encourage the new government installed in Kabul in its efforts to achieve the effective pacification of all *Afghanistan*. Finally I must mention the tensions which have once more set *India* and *Pakistan* at odds, in order earnestly to request the political leaders of these great nations to give absolute priority to dialogue and negotiation.

We also need to heed the question which comes to us from the depths of this abyss: that of *the place and the use made of religion* in the lives of people and societies. Here I wish to say once again, before the whole international community, that killing in the name of God is an act of blasphemy and a perversion of religion. This morning I wish to repeat what I wrote in my Message for January 1: "It is a profanation of religion to declare oneself a terrorist in the name of God, to do violence to others in his name. Terrorist violence is a contradiction of faith in God, the Creator of man, who cares for man and loves him" (no. 7).

4. In the face of these outbreaks of irrational and unjustifiable violence, *the great danger is that other situations will go unnoticed* and leave whole peoples abandoned to their sad fate.

I am thinking of *Africa*, and the health emergencies and armed struggles which are decimating its peoples. Recently, during a debate in the General Assembly of the United Nations Organization it was observed that there were seventeen conflicts taking place on the African continent! In such a situation, the establishment of an "African Union" is in itself good news. This Organization should help to develop common principles capable of uniting all the member States, with a view to facing major challenges such as the prevention of conflicts, education and the fight against poverty.

And how can I fail to mention *Latin America*, which is always dear to me? In some countries of this great continent the persistence of social inequalities, drug trafficking, corruption and armed violence can endanger the foundations of democracy and discredit the political class. Most recently, the difficult situation in *Argentina* has given rise to public unrest which has painfully affected people's lives. This is yet another reminder that political and economic activity at the national and international levels must always be inspired by the pursuit of the authentic good of individuals and peoples. With insistence I wish to encourage the people of Latin America, and of Argentina in particular, to hold on to hope amid the present difficulties, and not to lose sight of the fact that, given the great human and natural resources available, the present situation is not irreversible and can be overcome with everyone's help. If this is to happen, private or partisan interests must be set aside, and the interest of the nation must be promoted by every legitimate means, through a return to moral values, open and frank dialogue, and the renunciation of what is superfluous in order to help those who are in any way in need. In this spirit, it should be remembered that political activity is above all a noble, demanding and generous service to the community.

5. The troubled situation of this world of ours at the dawn of the third millennium has one advantage, if I may say so: it makes us squarely face our responsibilities. *Everyone is forced to ask the real questions: the truth about God and the truth about man.*

God is not at the beck and call of one individual or one people, and no human venture can claim to monopolize him. The children of Abraham know that God cannot be commandeered by anyone: God is to be received. Standing before the crib, Christians can better realize that Jesus himself did not impose himself, and he rejected the use of power as a means of promoting his kingdom!

The truth about man, who is a creature. Man is true to himself only when he sees himself as coming from God, in an attitude of poverty. He is conscious of his dignity only when he acknowledges in himself and in others the mark of God who created him in his own image. For this reason I chose to put the subject of forgiveness at the heart of my traditional Message for the celebration of the World Day of Peace on January 1, 2002, for I am convinced that: "the help that religions can give to peace and against terrorism consists precisely in their teaching forgiveness, for those who forgive and seek forgiveness know that there is a higher Truth, and that by accepting that Truth they can transcend themselves" (no. 13).

This truth about God and man is a gift which Christians offer to all people, especially to their brothers and sisters who are followers of authentic Islam, a religion of peace and love of neighbor.

6. To you, Ladies and Gentlemen, I confide these reflections which rise from my prayer as well as from the things I hear from those who visit me. I ask you to pass them on to your governments. Let us not be overwhelmed by the distress of the present time. *Let us instead open our hearts and minds to the great challenges lying before us*:

* the defense of the sacredness of human life in all circumstances, especially in relation to the challenges posed by genetic manipulation;
* the promotion of the family, the basic unit of society;
* the elimination of poverty, through efforts to promote development, the reduction of debt and the opening up of international trade;
* respect for human rights in all situations, with especial concern for the most vulnerable: children, women and refugees;
* disarmament, the reduction of arms sales to poor countries, and the consolidation of peace after the end of conflicts;
* the fight against the major diseases, and access by the poor to basic care and medicines;
* the protection of the environment and the prevention of natural disasters;
* the rigorous application of international law and conventions.

Of course, many other demands could also be mentioned. But if these priorities became the central concerns of political leaders; if people of good made them part of their daily endeavors; if religious believers included them in their teaching, the world would be a radically different place.

7. These are the thoughts which I wanted to share with you. *Darkness can only be scattered by light. Hatred can only be conquered by love.* My most fervent wish, which I entrust to God in prayer and which, I believe, will be shared by all those taking part in the forthcoming meeting in Assisi, is that we should all carry in our unarmed hands the light of a love which nothing can discourage. May God grant that it be so, for the happiness of all!

January 13, 2003
(http://www.vatican.va/holy_father/john_paul_ii/speeches/2003/january/documents/h
f_jp-ii_spe_20030113_diplomatic-corps_en.html)

1. This meeting at the beginning of the New Year is a happy tradition which affords me the joy of welcoming you and in some way of embracing all the peoples whom you represent! For it is through you and thanks to you that I come to know their hopes and aspirations, their successes and their setbacks. Today I wish to offer your countries my *fervent good wishes of happiness, peace and prosperity.*

At the threshold of the New Year I am also pleased to offer all of you my best wishes, as I invoke upon you, your families and your fellow citizens an abundance of divine blessings.

Before sharing with you some reflections inspired by the present situation in the world and in the Church, I must thank your Dean, Ambassador Giovanni Galassi, for his kind words and for the good wishes which he has thoughtfully expressed, in the name of all present, for my person and for my ministry. Please accept my deep gratitude!

Mr. Ambassador, you have also pointed to the legitimate expectations of modern men and women, all too often frustrated by political crises, by armed violence, by social conflicts, by poverty or by natural catastrophes. Never as at the beginning of this millennium has humanity felt how precarious is the world which it has shaped.

2. I have been personally struck by *the feeling of fear which often dwells in the hearts of our contemporaries.* An insidious terrorism capable of striking at any time and anywhere; the unresolved problem of the Middle East, with the Holy Land and Iraq; the turmoil disrupting South America, particularly Argentina, Colombia and Venezuela; the conflicts preventing numerous African countries from focusing on their development; the diseases spreading contagion and death; the grave problem of famine, especially in Africa; the irresponsible behavior contributing to the depletion of the planet's resources: all these are so many plagues threatening the survival of humanity, the peace of individuals and the security of societies.

3. *Yet everything can change.* It depends on each of us. Everyone can develop within himself his potential for faith, for honesty, for respect of others and for commitment to the service of others.

It also depends, quite obviously, on political leaders, who are called to serve the common good. You will not be surprised if before an assembly of diplomats I state in this regard *certain requirements* which I believe must be met if entire peoples, perhaps even humanity itself, are not to sink into the abyss.

First, a "YES TO LIFE"! Respect life itself and individual lives: everything starts here, for the most fundamental of human rights is certainly the right to life. Abortion, euthanasia, human cloning, for example, risk reducing the human person to a mere object: life and death to order, as it were! When all moral criteria are removed, scientific research involving the sources of life becomes a denial of the being and the dignity of the person. War itself is an attack on human life since it brings in its wake suffering and death. The battle for peace is always a battle for life!

Next, RESPECT FOR LAW. Life within society – particularly international life – presupposes common and inviolable principles whose goal is to guarantee the security and the freedom of individual citizens and of nations. These rules of conduct are the foundation of national and international stability. Today political leaders have at hand highly relevant texts and institutions. It is enough simply to put them into practice. The world would be totally different if people began to apply in a straightforward manner the agreements already signed!

Finally, the DUTY OF SOLIDARITY. In a world with a superabundance of information, but which paradoxically finds it so difficult to communicate and where living conditions are scandalously unequal, it is important to spare no effort to ensure that everyone feels responsible for the growth and happiness of all. Our future is at stake. An unemployed young person, a handicapped person who is marginalized, elderly people who are uncared for, countries which are captives of hunger and poverty: these situations all too often make people despair and fall prey to the temptation either of closing in on themselves or of resorting to violence.

4. This is why *choices need to be made so that humanity can still have a future*. Therefore, the peoples of the earth and their leaders must sometimes have the courage to say "No."

"NO TO DEATH"! That is to say, no to all that attacks the incomparable dignity of every human being, beginning with that of unborn children. If life is truly a treasure, we need to be able to preserve it and to make it bear fruit without distorting it. "No" to all that weakens the family, the basic cell of society. "No" to all that destroys in children the sense of striving, their respect for themselves and others, the sense of service.

"NO TO SELFISHNESS"! In other words, to all that impels man to protect himself inside the cocoon of a privileged social class or a cultural comfort which excludes others. The life-style of the prosperous, their patterns of consumption, must be reviewed in the light of their repercussions on other countries. Let us mention for example the problem of water resources, which the United Nations Organization has asked us all to consider during this year 2003. Selfishness is also the indifference of prosperous nations toward nations left out in the cold. All peoples are entitled to receive a fair share of the goods of this world and of the know-how of the more advanced countries. How can we fail to think here, for example, of the access of everyone to generic medicines, needed to continue the fight against current pandemics, an access – alas – often thwarted by short-term economic considerations?

"NO TO WAR"! War is not always inevitable. It is always a defeat for humanity. International law, honest dialogue, solidarity between States, the noble exercise of diplomacy: these are methods worthy of individuals and nations in resolving their differences. I say this as I think of those who still place their trust in nuclear weapons and of the all-too-numerous conflicts which continue to hold hostage our brothers and sisters in humanity. At Christmas, Bethlehem reminded us of the unresolved crisis in the Middle East, where two peoples, Israeli and Palestinian, are called to live side-by-side, equally free and sovereign, in mutual respect. Without needing to repeat what I said to you last year on this occasion, I will simply add today, faced with the constant degeneration of the crisis in the Middle East, that the solution will never be imposed by recourse to terrorism or armed conflict, as if military victories could be the solution.

And what are we to say of the threat of a war which could strike the people of Iraq, the land of the Prophets, a people already sorely tried by more than twelve years of embargo? War is never just another means that one can choose to employ for settling differences between nations. As the Charter of the United Nations Organization and international law itself remind us, war cannot be decided upon, even when it is a matter of ensuring the common good, except as the very last option and in accordance with very strict conditions, without ignoring the consequences for the civilian population both during and after the military operations.

5. *It is therefore possible to change the course of events*, once good will, trust in others, fidelity to commitments and cooperation between responsible partners are allowed to prevail. *I shall give two examples.*

Today's Europe, which is at once united and enlarged. Europe has succeeded in tearing down the walls which disfigured her. She has committed herself to planning and creating a new reality capable of combining unity and diversity, national sovereignty and joint activity, economic progress and social justice. This new Europe is the bearer of the values which have borne fruit for two thousand years in an "art" of thinking and living from which the whole world has benefited. Among these values Christianity holds a privileged position, inasmuch as it gave birth to a humanism which has permeated Europe's history and institutions. In recalling this patrimony, the Holy See and all the Christian Churches have urged those drawing up the future Constitutional Treaty of the European Union to include a reference to Churches and religious institutions. We believe it desirable that, in full respect of the secular state, three complementary elements should be recognized: religious freedom not only in its individual and ritual aspects, but also in its social and corporative dimensions; the appropriateness of structures for dialogue and consultation between the Governing Bodies and communities of believers; respect for the juridical status already enjoyed by Churches and religious institutions in the Member States of the Union. A Europe which disavowed its past, which denied the fact of religion, and which had no spiritual dimension would be extremely impoverished in the face of the ambitious project which calls upon all its energies: constructing a Europe for *all*!

Africa too gives us today an occasion to rejoice: Angola has begun its rebuilding; Burundi has taken the path which could lead to peace and expects from the international community understanding and financial aid; the Democratic Republic of Congo is seriously engaged in a national dialogue which should lead to democracy. The Sudan has likewise shown good will, even if the path to peace remains long and arduous. We should of course be grateful for these signs of progress and we should encourage political leaders to spare no effort in ensuring that, little by little, the peoples of Africa experience the beginnings of pacification and thus of prosperity, safe from ethnic struggles, caprice and corruption. For this reason we can only deplore the grave incidents which have rocked Côte-d'Ivoire and the Central African Republic, while inviting the people of those countries to lay down their arms, to respect their respective constitutions and to lay the foundations for national dialogue. It will then be easy to involve all the elements of the national community in planning a society in which everyone finds a place. Furthermore, we do well to note that Africans are increasingly trying to find the solutions best suited to their problems, thanks to the activity of the African Union and effective forms of regional mediation.

6. Your Excellencies, Ladies and Gentlemen, it is vital to note that *the independence of States can no longer be understood apart from the concept of interdependence*. All States are interconnected both for better and for worse. For this reason, and rightly so, we must be able to distinguish good from evil and call them by their proper names. As history has taught us time and time again, it is when doubt or confusion about what is right and wrong prevails that the greatest evils are to be feared.

If we are to avoid descending into chaos, it seems to me that *two conditions* must be met. First, we must *rediscover* within States and between States *the paramount value of the natural law*, which was the source of inspiration for the rights of nations and for the first formulations of international law. Even if today some people question its validity, I am convinced that its general and universal principles can still help us to understand more clearly the unity of the human race and to foster the development of the consciences both of those who govern and of those who are governed. Second, we need *the persevering work of Statesmen who are honest and selfless*. In effect, the indispensable professional competence of political leaders can find no legitimation unless it is connected to strong moral convictions. How can one claim to deal with world affairs without reference to this set of principles which is the basis of the "universal common good" spoken of so eloquently by Pope John XXIII in his Encyclical *Pacem in Terris*? It will always be possible for a leader who acts in accordance with his convictions to reject situations of injustice or of institutional corruption, or to put an end to them. It is precisely in this, I believe, that we rediscover what is today commonly called "good governance." The material and spiritual well-being of humanity, the protection of the freedom and rights of the human person, selfless public service, closeness to concrete conditions: all of these take precedence over every political project and constitute a moral necessity which in itself is the best guarantee of peace within nations and peace between States.

7. It is clear that, *for a believer*, these motivations are enriched by *faith in a God who is the Creator and Father of all*, who has entrusted man with stewardship of the earth and with the duty of brotherly love. This shows how it is in a State's own interest to ensure that religious freedom – which is a natural right, that is, at one and the same time both an individual and social right – is effectively guaranteed for all. As I have had occasion to remark in the past, believers who feel that their faith is respected and whose communities enjoy juridical recognition will work with ever greater conviction in the common project of building up the civil society to which they belong. You will understand then why I speak out on behalf of all Christians who, from Asia to Europe, continue to be victims of violence and intolerance, such as happened recently during the celebration of Christmas. Ecumenical dialogue between Christians and respectful contact with other religions, in particular with Islam, are the best remedy for sectarian rifts, fanaticism or religious terrorism. As far as the Catholic Church is concerned, I will mention but one situation which is a cause of great suffering for me: the plight of Catholic communities in the Russian Federation, which for months now have seen some of their Pastors prevented from returning to them for administrative reasons. The Holy See expects from the Government authorities concrete decisions which will put an end to this crisis, and which are in keeping with the international agreements subscribed to by the modern and democratic Russia. Russian Catholics wish to live as

their brethren do in the rest of the world, enjoying the same freedom and the same dignity.

8. Your Excellencies, Ladies and Gentlemen, may all of us who have gathered in this place, which is a symbol of spirituality, dialogue and peace, contribute by our daily actions to the advancement of all the peoples of the earth, in justice and harmony, to their progress toward conditions of greater happiness and greater justice, far from poverty, violence and threats of war! May God pour out his abundant blessings upon you and all those whom you represent. A Happy New Year to everyone!

Chapter II
Speeches on the Occasion of the Presentation of Credentials:
The Culture of Peace as a Process of Collaboration

On December 2, 1978, Pope John Paul received the Letters of Credence of H.E. Paul Ndiaye, newly appointed Ambassador of Senegal. In keeping with long-established protocol, Ambassador Ndiaye delivered a formal statement in which he commented on concerns specific to his nation, especially in its relationship to the Holy See. There was reference, for example, to the economic emergence of the Third World, notably of Africa, and how this is interpreted respectively by both Senegal and the Holy See. However fragile its own economic status, Senegal can claim "many achievements," as "in the fields of education and health." In a carefully phrased passage, the Holy See's relief assistance during "these recent years of drought" was applauded (para. 10). Immediately, a discreet petition was inserted. No one, the Pope included, could miss the plea implied in the words, "a contribution to the maintenance of which remains desirable." The pontiff listened, himself mentioning "the drama of the drought." He then advanced a two-pronged recommendation. First, Senegal's crisis "must be remedied thanks to wide solidarity." Broad collaboration is a prerequisite. And secondly, while external intervention with humanitarian aims is laudable in conflict relative to peace and justice, Senegal must be cautious lest that intervention translate into self-interested foreign interference (para. 6). Now it became the Ambassador's turn to read between the lines. This would not prove difficult, since the Pope made no attempt to conceal his anxiety. Readers may deduce from the Pope's remarks his belief that the establishment of the culture of peace presumes *a priori* awareness of potential vulnerability. The temptation for Senegal is to resolve the desperation of short-term problems by methods which merely perpetuate long-term ones. Humanitarian assistance cannot be allowed to disguise proneness to exploitation.

The majority of papal addresses chosen for Chapter II are accompanied by the text of Ambassadors' speeches to the Pope. As with the preceding example of Senegal, readers are invited to determine the issues which each Ambassador poses to the pontiff. Next, it may prove a valuable exercise to analyze the manner in which the Pope responds to these issues, along with how he interjects themes that are his particular interest. Where there are addresses of the Pope which are not paired by an Ambassador's speech, the Pope's statements are so comprehensive that even standing alone they suggest multiple attributes of the culture of peace. Additionally, with Chapter II one recognizes that the culture of peace:

(11) . . . *espouses constructive reciprocity.*
Speaking to the first Ambassador of the Republic of the Congo (1980), the Pope reiterated that at the core of international legation lies the principle of reciprocity

(para. 1). Yet that reciprocity is neither transient nor mute. It is a forum in which States may inform each other of their deepest needs and preoccupations. And it is a forum in which to inaugurate cooperative endeavors on behalf of world improvement. For that reason Ambassador Jean-Pierre Nonault asserted how the Congo rejects "the narrow limits of a local diplomacy" and favors extensive global outreach. The Congo's basic criterion for the diplomatic embrace of another nation is identical with that of the Holy See – a culture of peace which struggles to replace "all forms of domination" with a vision of universal "freedom, peace and progress" (para. 4).

(12) . . . *adheres to a solidarity which fosters joint responsibility.*
Pope John Paul twice referred to the importance of responsibility in his 1981 message to the Ambassador of Austria, H.E. Johannes Proksch. First, there is that responsibility which pertains to "the competent State authorities" (para. 2). By implication, the Pope states that civil authority must be rooted in a legally recognized legitimacy. It is never a usurpation. In the culture of peace, the primacy of the common good is the guarantor of that legitimacy. Moreover, in the culture of peace there is search for a balance of the autonomies of the Church and the State. Simultaneously, there is a possibility to integrate their shared goal, the total and holistic development of humanity. This segues to the Pope's second reference to responsibility, that it is unequivocally ethical. Where there is "commitment for peoples in want" (para. 4), together with commitment to international unity, there is an ethical obligation to counter those "many internal and external threats" to the "inviolable dignity of man" (idem). According to Ambassador Proksch, inter-state agreement on how to move toward this objective is a genuine act of co-responsibility (para. 3). The culture of peace subscribes to equality of partnership.

(13) . . . *continues to revise its inherited outlook.*
When the first Ambassador of Togo, H.E. Vigniko A. Amedegnato, offered his Letters of Credence, he related that human rights, "though as old as the world, [now] acquires quite a new meaning" (1982, para. 4). For him, this is consequent to three factors: the need for a new international economic order, serious inequity in the distribution of global resources, and the lack of means to exercise those human rights. Ambassador Amedegnato lobbied for a version of the culture of peace in which the acquired legacy of attitudes and disposition can flexibly accommodate unprecedented circumstances. The Pope concurred, directly quoting the Ambassador as well as noting the work of the Convention of Lome. The Pope also "underlined the importance of an international juridical order" (no. 5). The culture of peace cannot prosper without adaptable and enforceable inter-State statutes, axioms and policies.

(14) . . . *accepts what is distinctive about the nature of a people.*
On January 10, 1985, Pope John Paul advised the Ambassador of Ethiopia that the reception of international aid should not discount the "original way which each country wants to safeguard according to the wish of the people" (para. 4). He

thereby not only appealed to the notion of popular sovereignty – consent of those governed – but insisted that what is intrinsic and native to a people's identity must not be attacked or obliterated. "The Holy See desires," the Pope said, "the independence of every country." The Holy See also seeks independence in the preservation of that same country's unique expression of civilization's patrimony.

(15) . . . *upholds the rightful place of pluralism.*
H.E. Jesus E. Calvo, when submitting his credentials in 1987, spoke of Spain's regard for pluralism "as an essential element in the make-up of Spanish society." The centrality of citizens' religious freedom, however, does not preclude the kinds of agreements which Spain and the Holy See ratified in 1979. Instead, those agreements augment a cooperation which grapples "with the concrete problems" of society (para. 9). The Pope's response acknowledged that Spain's constitutional disposition has never meant a denial of the Church's right of mission. Within a culture of peace mentality, a State's non-confessional position may reinforce religious practice and the profession of moral life. The pontiff also extolled the many positive "imprints" which Judaism and Islam have imparted to Spanish history.

(16) . . . *embodies a humanistic spirit in foreign policy.*
The structure of foreign policy was referred to on November 23, 1990, by the Ambassador of Canada, H.E. Theodore Arcand. When recalling the views of a predecessor, Paul Tremblay, Ambassador Arcand stressed that the formation of Canada's foreign policy involves the restoration of a humanistic or idealistic emphasis (para. 5). This accounts for Canada's consistent "support for international actions . . . in the Security Council of the United Nations" and for its willingness to act as an intermediary during instances of conflict. The Pope commended Canadian "tolerance and generosity," notably where it leads to "the expansion of the North-South dialogue." This is but another assurance that a culture of peace is one which is cognizant of the common good, sensitive to the heritage of minorities and adamant to protect the earth's environment.

(17) . . . *nourishes a climate of trust.*
Pope John Paul, when receiving Ambassador F.X. Halos of the Czech and Slovak Federative Republic, talked about how the resolution of problems flows not only from the process of dialogue, but from the trust which imbues that dialogue. Doubtless, the Pope recalled a period of rupture and strain between the nation and the Holy See. This is evident in the controversy surrounding the issue of "the restitution of Church property." But the renewal of trust may neutralize such obstacles and permit the Church's "educational and charitable activity" to once again flourish in the service of the republic's people (1991, no. 3b). Ambassador Halos elaborated. What he described was a culture of peace in which trust assumes the stance of reconciliation. When considering the "delicate balance between the spiritual and secular realms" in Czech and Slovak society, he related the biblical episode of the return of the prodigal son. "Solutions acceptable to both parties" will always be possible when trust permeates relationship.

(18) . . . *raises crucial and profound questions.*
Socrates is credited with the adage, "The unexamined life is not worth living." In his meeting on May 7, 1993, with Edward Tsu-yu Wu, Ambassador of the Republic of China, the Pope discussed the impressive record of Chinese philosophy and cultural achievement and its interface with Catholicism. The Jesuit missionary, Matteo Ricci (1552–1610), became renowned for a style of evangelization which demonstrated the compatibility between traditional Chinese wisdom and the Christian Gospel. The growth of the Church in China testifies to the success of Ricci and his incorporation of the breadth of Chinese intellectual experience. The history of that experience exhibits a natural willingness to deliberate upon "the level of the vital questions facing all individuals and societies" (1998, para. 8). The Pope implied that a culture of peace disdains the unexamined life and beckons the international community to probe the question of resource distribution, the question of human solidarity, the question of "the vision which underlies political policies and programs" (para. 6).

(19) . . . *refuses to authorize coercion.*
H.E. Mark E. Pellew presented his Letters of Credence on January 31, 1998, on behalf of the United Kingdom of Great Britain and Northern Ireland. In response, the Pope spoke about the connection between freedom of conscience and coercion. Although the context initially pertained to religious convictions, Pope John Paul's belief that the State must never apply coercion to implement its agenda was easily related to other key areas. For example, the "poorer countries" when burdened by "heavy . . . external debt" are coerced by hindrance to their "social, political and economic progress" (para. 7). Pressure to squander precious resources in the purchase of military technology is likewise a species of coercion. The Pope indicated that the European Union's efforts to formulate a Code of Conduct "to regulate the export of arms" helps to lessen this adverse trend (para. 8). The Ottawa Convention "banning anti-personnel land-mines" also promises to diminish the coercion inflicted by extremist political ideology (para. 9). By contrast, the culture of peace steadily reacts against any arsenal comprised of threat, intimidation and violence.

(20) . . . *interprets repetition as reinforcement of pivotal political and social doctrine.*
Readers will note that the papal addresses contained in Chapter II seem to continually repeat several themes: the merit of dialogue, the common good, cooperation, reconciliation, etc. Is it because there is nothing else to say? No. Is it because the Pope is convinced that States just don't get the point? No. By analogy, think of an Impressionist painting. After several visits to the art gallery, the probability is that the same picture will still reveal something new to the admirer. Full disclosure is never an all-at-once phenomenon. The apparent repetition of return to the gallery permits a greater penetration of the richness of the artist's gift. The same is true of the Holy Father's approach to diplomatic discourse. At first glance it may look like surface reframing. But that would be an inaccurate assessment,

because every repetition adds significant nuance, expands upon detail, broadens an application, deepens and diversifies the basis for perception. For example, in 2002 the Pope described "authentic peace-making" in his remarks to H.E. Dorkas Tomaskovic of the Federal Republic of Yugoslavia. It is a process which "goes forward" when a nation is able "to put aside ethnic and nationalistic introversion" (no. 2c). How appropriate when the milieu is the Balkans. A somewhat different perspective is evident in the Pope's words about the role of the U.S. in terms of the peace process in the Middle East. Ambassador R. James Nicholson of the United States heard the pontiff's view that such peace-making means the promotion of "a realistic dialogue" which fosters "security, justice . . . in full respect for . . . international law" (2001, para. 4).

December 2, 1978
(*L'Osservatore Romano*, December 14, 1978, pp. 5, 12)

H.E. Paul Ndiaye, Ambassador of Senegal:

Holy Father,

After the events that have followed one another at the Holy See, historic events owing to their spiritual and human dimension, it is with deep emotion that I have the honor and the agreeable duty to present to Your Holiness the Letters with which His Excellency Leopold Sedar Senghor, President of the Republic of Senegal accredits me to you in the capacity of Ambassador extraordinary and plenipotentiary as well as the Letters of recall of my distinguished predecessor.

At this solemn moment, I measure all the importance and nobility of my mission just as I feel even more deeply all the honor which falls upon me to represent my country to Your Holiness on the one hand, and on the other the outstanding privilege of being among the first Heads of mission accredited to you.

Meanwhile, I rejoice already at the ties that unite my country with the Holy See – ties the special character of which is the consequence of a century of Christian presence, marked by a fruitful cooperation which my honorable predecessors have developed so harmoniously. May the Lord preserve them for the constant strengthening of a mutual understanding of which the Senegalese people will always be proud.

Senegal, a land with an old Christian community, and a land of dialogue, and consequently of opening to all cultures and to spiritual values, has always followed with keen admiration the considerable work of the Holy See, particularly the opening brought forth by the late Holy Father Paul VI and his indefatigable efforts with regard to ecumenism, the dialogue of cultures as of religions, the disappearance of the gulf between the rich and poor as well as the armaments race, for the coming of a world more attentive to poverty, justice and peace.

Your predecessor, Pope John Paul I, of revered memory, had already applied himself to concerns just as noble, which the shortness of his pontificate and the suddenness of his decease make even more topical, in the spirit of continuity of Vatican II.

Holy Father, the message that President Leopold Sedar Senghor addressed to Your Holiness on the occasion of your election is an act of faith in the virtues of your illustrious predecessors whom you incarnate.

Moreover, this election, which the whole world hailed as one of the highest testimonies of the universality of the contemporary Church and the dawn of your sovereign pontificate so radiant with satisfactions already fill suffering humanity with a great hope.

In this regard, the authorities of my country attentive to the last messages of Your Holiness are convinced that the Holy See will persevere in particular in the pursuit of understanding and tolerance among beliefs in respect for their diversity.

But beyond these cultural and religious factors, the interest of which is as evident as their interferences are inevitable, there are the realities of the economic emergence of the Third World in general and Africa in particular.

In this connection, my country today still records many achievements, especially in the fields of education and health, the impact of which on its development holds all attention. It has appreciated all the more highly the contribution of the Holy See in these recent years of drought, a contribution the maintenance of which remains desirable.

Moreover, the nomination of two nuncios in Africa, one of whom is in Senegal, and the stress laid on the relevance of the Encyclical *Populorum Progressio* today, had borne witness, coinciding with your first decisions, to the interest of Your Holiness takes in Africa.

Holy Father, Senegal, whose relations with the Holy See have been excellent, maintains the hope that, during your pontificate, they will continually be strengthened.

Thus in carrying out my high mission, I cannot but implore the Lord to grant me the grace of clear-sighted lucidity asking Your Holiness to join in my prayer. I am convinced that my wishes will be fulfilled and that I will find in you and your worthy collaborators all the help necessary for the success of my mission.

May Your Holiness permit me, in conclusion, to transmit the wishes for good health for a fruitful pontificate which President Leopold Sedar Senghor charged me to present to you with the assurance of his respectful consideration.

Papal Response:

Mr. Ambassador,

I am very happy to receive you today. Senegal, which you now represent as Ambassador extraordinary and plenipotentiary, is a country with which the Holy See has long maintained friendly relations. Your President, His Excellency Mr. Leopold Sedar Senghor, who has charged you to transmit his good wishes to me, is a statesman whose visit my revered predecessor Pope Paul VI received several times with pleasure and whose interventions he appreciated. Kindly convey to him my sentiments of high consideration and deep esteem.

My thought goes spontaneously to the Church in Senegal, and particularly to dear Cardinal Hyacinthe Thiandoum and my other Brothers in the episcopate. But in this instance, it is for all your fellow countrymen that I formulate fervent wishes of happiness, peace and progress.

An essential condition of this progress – as Your Excellency stressed to my deep satisfaction – is respect for, and the promotion of, spiritual values. Certainly, the expansion of knowledge, the struggle for better conditions of health, and economic development, are necessary and deserve all our efforts: I am thinking of the drama of the drought, which must be remedied thanks to wide solidarity; I am thinking of the courageous achievements of your Government in the cultural field. But if this progress were to be accompanied by a materialistic conception of life, it would actually be a regression. Man would be mutilated and he would not be long in losing his dignity and his sacred character, at the same time as the ultimate meaning of his existence, which is to live in the presence of God and in brotherly relations with his neighbor. Every civilization must take care not to lose its soul!

It is the honor of your country, it is the honor of African tradition, to preserve the intuition of the sacred. The civilization of "negritude" (Negro civilization), which President Senghor himself has analyzed with penetrating insight, includes this deeply rooted religious sense and encourages it. It must, however, be deepened and educated in order to be able to deal without reduction with the whole of modern culture with its philosophies and its scientific and technical spirit.

Tolerance and peace among the disciples of the great religious confessions are facilitated by the institutions of your country, under the wise guidance of your President. With regard to these religious confessions, the State keeps the distance which permits the necessary impartiality and the normal distinction between political interests and religious matters. But this distance is not indifference, the State knows how to mark its esteem for spiritual values and encourages, with justice, the services that religious communities render to the populations, in the field of teaching or medical care.

Finally, peace among countries, and particularly on the African continent, is also a matter of concern, and rightly so, for the government and people of Senegal. Aware of the interdependence of nations and anxious about the human rights of your neighbors, your country wishes to help its African partners to subdue violence, which is always springing up again, to overcome the racial discriminations from which they suffer, to settle their conflicts in a reasonable way, and to establish a just and lasting peace among them, if possible without foreign interference.

The stake is an immense and redoubtable one for the happiness and development of African peoples. May God promote the wise and generous contribution which Senegal is capable of making to it! You know the constant solicitude of the Holy See in this field. I am touched by the way in which your Excellency paid tribute to it.

I wish you yourself, Mr. Ambassador, a happy and fruitful mission. And I invoke the assistance of the Almighty on your person, your fellow-countrymen and your rulers.

February 24, 1979
(*OR*, March 5, 1979, p. 10)

H.E. Dr. A. A. Peralta, Ambassador of Costa Rica:

Holy Father

It is an honor for me to have the privilege of presenting to your Holiness my Letters of Credence as Ambassador of Costa Rica under your noble Pontificate.

Our Democracy, built on Work, Freedom, and spiritual and moral values is the work of a people that cultivates relations of friendship with all countries in the world.

Our political Constitution, in article 76, declares that the Roman, Apostolic, Catholic religion is that of the State which contributes to its maintenance without preventing the free exercise within the Republic of other religions which are not contrary to universal ethics and good morals.

I wish to recall at this moment, Your Holiness, the memory of an illustrious former President of my country, Di Rafael Angel Calderon Guardia. With his Catholic social thought, forged at Louvain University, and a disciple of the late Cardinal Mercer, he succeeded in instilling into our country the spirit of struggle and the consolidation of social guarantees in the decade of the forties, with the precious collaboration of Archbishop Manuel Sanabera of San Jose.

Our interest in, and defense of human rights and the cause of peace is recognized all over the world. Our President, Advocate Rodrigo Carazo Odio on the occasion of the opening speech of his government, spoke as follows:

"Costa Rica has a rich and noble history of respect for human rights. Our democracy is based on the educative vision of our ancestors, and this preeminently spiritual vocation of our country has made respect for human rights a constant of our history, as we will manifest in international forums, in which my Government will speak with strong words and above all, with its example."

Thirty years ago, by constitutional mandate, our country decided to abolish the army, a unique event in the world.

On September 27, 1978, Your Holiness, Advocate Rodrigo Carazo Odio, President of the Republic of Costa Rica, put forward before the General Assembly of the United Nations the project of creating a University for peace. We are convinced that education for peace must be a permanent activity, and that was why the President of my country proposed, for this purpose, the creation of an Institution that would prepare men and peoples for peace.

We listened, moved, to your words, Your Holiness, on the occasion of the Day of Peace, on the first of January 1979. As Your Holiness so well says, "I take from the hands of my revered Predecessor, Paul VI, the pilgrim staff of peace, under the sign of education for peace. To reach peace, teach peace."

We will pray with Your Holiness and say with you that "peace will be the last word of history."

Your Holiness, on your recent journey to Mexico on the occasion of the Congress of CCLAM, we saw how the Latin-American people paid a rightful homage to you, knowing that you represent the genuine defense of the dispossessed, which incarnates on the plane of justice what must be a better world for everyone. I thank you for your affectionate expressions with regard to Costa Rica on the occasion of the conversation with our first lady, Dona Estrella Zeledon de Carazo.

Holy Father, on behalf of our President, our Foreign Minister, and the whole of the people of Costa Rica, on my own behalf and on that of my family, we raise a prayer to the Almighty for the glory of your Pontificate and for your personal happiness.

Papal Response:

Mr. Ambassador,

I have listened with deep pleasure to the words spoken by Your Excellency on presenting the Letters of Credence as Ambassador Extraordinary and Plenipotentiary of Costa Rica to the Holy See. I bid you in the first place a hearty welcome.

Your Excellency has just referred to the task carried out by the Church in favor of peace. It is certainly a cause to which the Church and the Holy See have dedicated and will continue to dedicate their best energies, in order that this incalculable good may preside over social life within the nations and in the international community. It is an aim which, following my revered predecessors, I have also made mine. For this reason, as I said recently, the Church "wishes to serve peace not by means of political activities, but by promoting the values and principles which are the condition for peace and human *rapprochement*, and are at the basis of [the] international common good" (Address to the Diplomatic Corps accredited to the Holy See, on January 12, 1979, no. 5).

I am happy to know that the people of Costa Rica is making effective efforts to cultivate these values and principles which promote and defend peace.

Another point to which Your Excellency has referred is respect for human rights in society today. A subject which in the present period of the history of humanity is becoming an increasingly pressing one as an irreplaceable element of social order, which must be governed by the requirements that spring from the dignity of persons, considered individually and collectively.

The teachings of the Second Vatican Council are clear in this connection: "The protection and promotion of the inviolable rights of man is an essential duty of every civil authority" (Declaration on Religious Liberty, no. 6). The Church in her doctrine and in her evangelizing activity, does not forget, but on the contrary makes every effort that all men (regardless of race, culture, religion, and social class) may see their rights respected as persons and as depositaries of a transcendent vocation to which God has called them, and which, therefore, no person or human power can suppress or ignore.

Serving this cause, the Church is well aware that she is serving the cause of man. With this conviction from the beginning of my Pontificate, I have laid stress on this line, in order to obtain that man may reach rightful freedom in truth: a truth concerning the human being, society and concerning his destiny. It is the cause of human dignity, to which I called attention in the third part of my address at the opening of the work of the recent Puebla Conference, and which the Latin-American Episcopate has included in the final Document. These are aims which I am sure the Authorities and people of Costa Rica will make their own, in accordance with the Christian and humanist tradition which they wish to pursue.

May the Blessed Virgin of the Angels, so venerated in Costa Rica, intercede in order that these aims may become a splendid reality.

Mr. Ambassador, before concluding this first meeting of ours, I wish to assure you of my constant and benevolent help in the promotion of these ideals and in the accomplishment of the high mission which is beginning today. Kindly convey to Mr. President and to the Authorities and people of Costa Rica, the most respectful and cordial regards of the Pope, who asks God to grant this noble nation his best blessings along the way to peace, common life, and pursuit of increasingly higher human and Christian aims.

April 28, 1980
(*OR*, June 23, 1980, p. 4)

H.E. Jean-Pierre Nonault, Ambassador of the Congo:

Sovereign Pontiff,

It is with immense joy that I have the great honor to present to Your Holiness the Letters of Credence through which Colonel Denis Sassou N'Guesso, the President of the People's Republic of the Congo, accredits me to you in the capacity of Ambassador Extraordinary and Plenipotentiary.

Sovereign Pontiff,

I am fully aware of the responsibilities conferred on me by this high office under the eye of one of the most eminent spiritual leaders of our time, and I can assure Your Holiness of the renewed will of my Government to do its utmost to maintain the relations between our two States at the highest level of the only service that is worth while: the service of man, to the future of whom the Holy See and Brazzaville remain attentive, each in the name of the moral, spiritual and ideological values on which its essential action is based.

The millenary message, the cornerstones of which sustain the prestigious edifice at the head of which 263 Vicars of Christ have preceded you after St. Peter, has never left the People's Republic of the Congo indifferent. Notwithstanding the choices it has made to guide its destiny, it has, whenever the opportunity occurred, paid due tribute through the most authoritative voice of its rulers to its Catholic population, available in the field of social action.

My Government has always attached real importance to the maintenance and consolidation of the relations so happily existing between our two States, in a spirit of mutual frankness, trust, friendship and respect. Firmly convinced that all peoples on earth aspire to peace, justice, happiness and education, the Government of my country has never accepted the narrow limits of a local diplomacy, and has always extended them to the whole world, where the fundamental principles of foreign policy found a favorable echo. That is why the People's Republic of the Congo has continually expanded its relations with all countries enamored of freedom, peace and progress; being of the opinion that its own battle to throw off all forms of domination is a part of the global struggle being carried out by the Third World to be the master of its riches and enjoy them as it likes.

My country is aware of the primary vocation of the Holy See, that of endeavoring especially to ensure that relations among peoples are imbued with moral values. My country also knows that in the field of bilateral relations with States and through the quality of its participation in the activities on international or regional governmental organizations, the Holy See also tries to make its contribution to the complete development of peoples.

Sovereign Pontiff,

In your illustrious person, President Denis Sassou N'Guesso, the Government and the whole Congolese people highly appreciate the exceptional qualities of a Missionary in the noblest sense of the word, who has succeeded in giving his apostolate a worldwide impact, following the ancient example of the chief engineer of bridges who was formerly a priest called Pontifex, from which the significant name attributed to your high office is derived. How could I forget your great open-mindedness, your solicitude for peoples in need and the constant attention you give to their problems, in the conciliar spirit of His Holiness John XXIII, whose thought you prolong through an itinerant *aggiornamento* which has already led you, in less than two years of pontificate, to erect a bridge between the Holy See and several continents.

How could I forget your tangible aims, deeply humanitarian and feasible, for peace in the world? The Congo has always gone in this same direction, condemning unequivocally all who undermine peace and all economic imperialism.

Sovereign Pontiff,

Is it necessary to recall the action carried out in the Congo by a Church that will soon celebrate its centenary, a witness to the particularly fruitful relations that our two States maintain?

I am convinced that the Holy See, which occupies a very special place in the heart of the Congolese people, will see to it that the relations between our two States will develop harmoniously in all fields. By appointing me as Ambassador to the Holy See, President Denis Sassou N'Guesso wished to show with this act the way to a new era between the Holy See and Brazzaville.

It is certainly a difficult and delicate task. However, I can assure Your Holiness that I will endeavor, within the limits of the frail human forces that are mine, to understand the realities and the concerns of your State, and to be inspired by the constant concern to strengthen understanding and mutual respect between the Holy See and the Congo. I venture to hope that during my weighty mission, Your Holiness will deign to grant me your full confidence and your benevolent support.

Allow me, in conclusion, to transmit to you the good wishes of happiness and long life expressed by Colonel Denis Sassou N'Guesso, the President of the People's Republic of the Congo, for your personal well-being and dignity, and of the prosperity for your closest collaborators.

Papal Response:

Mr. Ambassador,

Some time ago, wishing to provide themselves with the means of establishing permanently a constructive dialogue, the Holy See and your country decided by common consent to set up diplomatic relations with each other. An Apostolic Pro-Nuncio has already been accredited at Brazzaville. I am personally very happy to receive today the first representative sent by the People's Republic of Congo.

Kindly accept my good wishes, at the moment when you inaugurate your high mission. They are wishes of welcome, prosperity for your person, your family and your collaborators. They are in proportion to yours, the courtesy of which I appreciated.

I was also sensitive to the noble words you transmitted to me from H.E. the President, Denis Sassou N'Guesso. Tell him that I greet him respectfully, and how happy I am at the thought that I will soon enjoy his hospitality, how grateful I am to him for permitting this pastoral visit in the Congolese territory.

For such is the character that my African tour aims at having: a religious journey in the first place, to visit the local Christian communities, and a journey of friendship and brotherly love, to greet the populations and, getting to know them better, to be able to love them better. I will come to the Congo as a messenger of peace, as a man of God, to bring the testimony of my esteem for this People, to whom I wish a promising and prosperous future. It will be a rather short stay, but one which will certainly turn out to be fruitful and rich in memories on my return.

You have been kind enough to stress some of the initiatives taken by the Holy See in the international field. They are inspired by service of man, and of all the great causes connected with the service of man. No other aim animates, in this field, the Catholic Church, which wishes to be faithful on every point to the mission that God has entrusted to her. It is in this spirit, implying respect for the public authorities of each State, that I would like to see our ties with the People's Republic of the Congo become stronger. You will certainly endeavor, on your side, to consolidate them, and in this way you will meet my deep wish.

On your Excellency and on those who accompany you, I invoke the blessings of the Almighty, to whom I entrust also the dear Congolese nation.

January 10, 1981
(*OR*, February 2, 1981, pp. 11, 20)

H.E. Johannes Proksch, Ambassador of Austria:

Holy Father,

It is a great honor for me to present the Letters with which the Federal President accredits me as Ambassador Extraordinary and Plenipotentiary of the Republic of Austria to Your Holiness, and expresses the hope that in this function I will meet with esteem and confidence, for which I too ask.

I am charged by the Federal President to convey his respectful greetings and his sincere good wishes for the heavy task, and good health of Your Holiness.

I am aware of the great obligation that is connected with co-responsibility in fashioning the relations between the Republic of Austria and the Holy See in an authoritative way. I willingly express the assurance that it will be my endeavor to promote and develop these relations to the best of my ability, and that this also represents a personal desire on my part. All the more so in that the Church and State in Austria, fully aware of the difference of their tasks and after dividing by mutual agreement their spheres of activity, are endeavoring to reach even deeper mutual understanding and even better collaboration.

It would not do justice to the real foundations of these relations to consider them only from the standpoint of tradition. It is certainly true and can be regarded as a fortunate lot that the Austrian man was formed to a very great extent by the Catholic faith and his character determined by it. But in the last few decades – as also in other countries – a constant and deep process of change has occurred, the roots of which lie in technology and economy, and which has considerably influenced both habits of life and also the consciousness of men. In the area of man's conception of the world as well as in political discussion, answers are being sought to new questions, and a great many men indifferently stand aside since their traditional ties have been challenged. It is evident that in the pluralistic society of today a great deal of tolerance and patience is necessary, in order to find the necessary degree of agreement in freedom, which Your Holiness, in the message for the World Day of Peace 1981, proclaimed in such an impressive way as the foundation of peace.

It should be noted, in all modesty, that Austria has succeeded in developing a system of economic and social participation which, after the catastrophes of two world wars, guarantees our country successful reconstruction and continual development. So we hope, in peace and freedom, to find a way toward the future which will do justice to the heritage of our past and the demands of the present.

Already on obtaining full independence and choosing neutrality in the year 1955, our country recognized the obligation, of which it has become more and more aware, of making a contribution to international understanding and collaboration. By means of measures that create confidence, the premises must be laid for a true peace, which applies first of all to the relationship with neighbors and other nations. Not infrequently many of our contacts have been pointed out as "a model of the relations of States with different political and economic systems."

Austria is making special efforts in international organizations, to help the fundamental principles of the preservation of peace and of collaboration, which are also the main lines of its own foreign policy, to win recognition. Its committed participation in the work of this organization, including the sending of troops for measures to preserve peace, bear witness to this. Mention should also be made of Austrian efforts in the framework of the European Conference for Security and Collaboration as well as of the circumstance that Vienna has become a third seat of the UN. The close collaboration of the Delegations of Austria and of the Holy See in numerous international organizations, is seen to be very valuable.

No less weight than to political and diplomatic initiatives, goes, however, to the humanitarian efforts, as a result of which there reigns complete agreement between the population and the government, going far beyond what is customary. The ready welcome of a very large number of refugees, which sometimes represents a serious problem for a small country in an exposed situation, and the rapid, spontaneous [response] given on the occasions of natural catastrophes, would not be possible to this extent if there did not exist in Austria a deep feeling of solidarity with the unfortunate and the persecuted, a participation which is also being deeply manifested on the occasion of the recent tragic disaster in the south of Italy.

Your Holiness has brought faith in peace, freedom and human dignity in an unprecedented way to the wide world. This message was received also in our country with very great attention and deep joy. On it is based the certainty that a period of deep understanding and outstanding collaboration between Austria and the Holy See lies ahead.

Papal Response:

Mr. Ambassador,
With your official visit to the Vatican today, you begin your new and responsible mission as Ambassador Extraordinary and Plenipotentiary of the Republic of Austria to the Holy See. I congratulate you on this and bid you a hearty welcome. I thank you sincerely for the friendly words with which, on the occasion of the presentation of your Letters of Credence, you expressed appreciation for the friendly relations that have long existed between your country and the Holy See. I likewise warmly return the words of esteem and good wishes which you expressed to me on behalf of your distinguished Federal President.

You represent a land whose history bears the decisive stamp of a trusting collaboration between State and Church. Precisely under the various present circumstances, to which you briefly referred, the Church feels called upon in a particular way, also in the present day pluralistic society, to make her specific contribution, in solidarity and joint responsibility with the competent State Authorities, to the common good of citizens in the individual nations, and to the international community of peoples.

"The political community and the Church," as the Second Vatican Council stressed again, "are autonomous and independent of each other in their own fields. Nevertheless, both are devoted to the personal vocation of man, though under different titles" (*Gaudium et Spes*, no. 76). No political calculation or economic interests, no exterior claims to power or other selfish motives, but only her universal task of proclamation in the service of man and of the human community, cause the Church and the Holy See to strive also on the plane of official diplomatic relations and the international political collaboration between the States for the universal good of men, for peace and a just order in, the individual nations and between all peoples.

As I emphasized in my address to the United Nations, "in reality, what justifies the existence of any political activity is service to man, concerned and responsible attention to the essential problems and duties of his earthly existence in its social dimension and significance, on which also the good of each person depends" (Address of His Holiness Pope John Paul II to the XXXIV General Assembly of the United Nations Organization, 2 Oct 1979, para. 6). Today this service calls in particular for defense of the inviolable dignity of man and of his fundamental rights, the advancement of his complete development − including his ethical responsibility − commitment for peoples in want, and the safeguarding of peace between the nations, as well as the common effort for the progressive unity of the peoples of Europe and of the whole human family in the spirit of worldwide solidarity and fraternity. In this service for men and nations, such a vital one because of the many internal and external threats to it at present, those who are responsible in the State and society and in the international community of peoples find in the Church and in the Holy See a loyal ally and helpful companion.

As you emphasized in your words of greeting, Mr. Ambassador, your country too feels bound by these high ideals in national and international life. As an esteemed member of the international community of States, today Austria makes a considerable contribution, through political and diplomatic initiatives and through humanitarian aid, to worldwide understanding among peoples and collaboration in the service of peace and more and more extensive and just social progress among all nations. This is underlined also by the fact that important international organizations have chosen the capital of Austria as their seat.

I willingly express the wish that, through your diplomatic activity of representation, which you are now officially beginning as Ambassador to the Holy See, the good relations that have reigned up to now between your country and the Holy See, and the common endeavor for a more peaceful and just world tomorrow for all men and peoples of good will, may be deepened further and develop fruitfully. For this purpose I accompany your future activity here in the Eternal City with my best wishes and ask for God's special protection and assistance for you and your collaborators, for a successful accomplishment of your responsible mission.

March 11, 1982
(*OR*, May 10, 1982, p. 18)

H.E. Vigniko A. Amedegnato, first Ambassador of Togo:

Your Holiness,

The people of Togo, its great party of national unity, the Assembly of the People of Togo, and its Chief of State General Gnassingbe Eyadema, thank you deeply for having agreed to welcome in your presence, through my humble person, their representatives, who intend, with your considerate good will, to do all they can to strengthen the almost century-old ties that already exist between the Holy See and their country.

The People of Togo, who have known colonial domination by three successive powers (German, British and French) have also, following the independence achieved at great cost on April 27, 1960, experienced the bitterness of internal conflict, fratricidal struggle and, above all, the extortions of a regime of terror to which the army put an end by twice intervening in the political life of the nation. It is for this reason that the people today count themselves blessed for having regained the dignity and peace to which they have always aspired and which they consider to be the necessary condition for their socio-economic and cultural progress.

In rallying to the great movement of national unity, the people of Togo have established as basic principles of its policies both at home and abroad, unity, peace and solidarity through tolerance and dialogue.

It is in this new spirit that the Government of Togo, aware of the eminently positive role played by the Catholic Church in Togo since its official creation in 1892, involves this Church fully, as it does other religious communities, in conducting the affairs of the nation, and subsidizes its educational institutions by assuming responsibility for the salaries of the teachers. Indeed, all national holidays in Togo are officially inaugurated by religious services, celebrated before the same altar by all religious communities, in the presence of political and administrative authorities, with the aim of paying homage with one voice to a common God, and beseeching that "his will be done on earth"; this will being also a desire for happiness, peace and social justice for all men and for all the peoples of the earth.

Your Holiness,

The people of Togo and their Government know to what extent these principles of peace, solidarity, tolerance, ecumenism itself, are dear to your heart. Thus they entrust me with the task of relaying to your Holiness their enthusiastic approval and their whole-hearted support of the many initiatives you yourself have taken to establish a dialogue between peoples and religions; to permit entry into all international or national political decisions or actions that human dimension which is divine and without which all political action is doomed to chaos and grief.

We are above all honored and full of hope for the particular interest that Your Holiness has accorded our continent, Africa, which you have visited twice already since your accession to the throne of the Apostle Peter. Your latest visit particularly is evidence of your courage under any circumstances and your love for the peoples of

Africa, especially when we think of your state of health following the base and dia-bolical assassination attempt that nearly put an end to your noble and divine mission.

Let us add that for us in Togo, the position you have taken in favor of the Third World and above all in favor of a new international economic order, singularly serves to reinforce the concept of the rights of man which, even though as old as the world, acquires here quite a new meaning.

How indeed can we speak of the rights of man when a tiny proportion of the world's population lives in abundance while more than half live haunted by a fear of hunger, illness and death? While, as General Eyadema declared in 1979, there is "denied to this group of men that most elementary of rights, that of life itself, a right already recognized for animals which are protected by law."

What can "right" mean when a man is bereft or at a loss for the means to exer-cise this right?

This reflection leads us to tell the Holy Father that the whole of Togo is mobilized for development and peace, that it works toward and supports the participation of the Universal Church and the Holy See in struggles on behalf of the peoples of the Third World which are:

* the struggle for instruction, education, health and their own sufficient food resources,
* the struggles against the flagrant injustices of the present-day economic system.

The total commitment of Your Holiness in this matter no longer leads to be demon-strated, and the whole nation of Togo, praying as it does for your personal health, wish-es you equally much courage and a long reign at the head of the Roman Catholic Church, that the Church may be assured of full success in the onerous and noble mis-sion that Jesus Christ has entrusted to it: that of working for the coming, on our earth, of the Kingdom of God, which is the kingdom of justice, love and peace among peo-ples.

Finally we would be unable at this point to conceal the burning desire that the whole people of Togo one day see the Holy Father embrace and bless the soil of their nation, and in this way intensify in them the flame of faith in the building of a better world.

Papal Response:

Mr. Ambassador,

1. You are the first Ambassador Extraordinary and Plenipotentiary entrusted to repre-sent the Republic of Togo at the Holy See. This important event illustrated the signif-icance of the diplomatic relations that were established by mutual agreement in April of last year, and will invest these relations with their full effectiveness.

Above all, I express my joy in welcoming Your Excellency here. And, through your person, I welcome the people of Togo, beginning with the Chief of State, General Gnassingbe Eyadema, to whom you will be so good as to convey my respectful greet-ings, my gratitude and my cordial wishes for the achievement of his task in the serv-ice of his countrymen. In the eyes of the Church, all peoples have an equal dignity, and the Church indeed has a particular concern for those who have been tried and who have endeavored to develop their resources, however limited these might be, through strenuous effort. In the course of my two journeys in Africa I passed near Togo and though I was unable to stop there, in spite of the pressing invitations of the bishops of Togo, who came to meet me at Accra or Cotonou. I thought much of your country, which I was able to greet through the persons of these brothers.

2. Your Excellency's presence today gives me the opportunity to express my fervent wishes for the entire nation of Togo: may it continue to be free, in profound peace, a peace made possible by a spirit of tolerance, seeking at the same time to establish increasingly just relations between all the citizens who are called to participate actively in its development, and with a particular concern for the poorest.

3. In this context the Catholic Church takes its share in the common effort; in fact it brings together a large number of the people of Togo in the same faith, the faith of the Bishop of Rome, and of the universal Church. It is to be hoped that, in Togo as elsewhere, the Church, grouped around its pastors and under their authority, in communion with the successor of Peter, should enjoy all the freedom that corresponds to its spiritual mission, especially in as much as concerns the organization and conduct of the Catholic community, in such a way as to permit the teaching of their faith and the worship they must render to God, following their conscience, both individually and in common. I am convinced that this principle, fully understood and respected, cannot but always facilitate still further the good relationship existing today between the Church and the State, all the more so because Christians are committed to peace and, in their anxiety to serve their nation, do not wish to be sparing in their contribution to its leap forward.

4. You yourself, Mr. Ambassador, have been anxious to praise, among other things, the remarkable work of instruction, education and professional training possible today through Catholic institutions. Yes, the Church wishes to contribute to the formation of good citizens within the important area of schooling, but also in other domains. Even in the State schools the Church endeavors, thanks to the benevolent cooperation of the State, to give its children an adequate moral and religious formation, for the quality of the civilization that the people of Togo wish to construct depends not only on economic development for which I have the highest hopes, but also the quality of the relations among men and their relationship with God. This is tantamount to saying the formation of consciences, of their ethical and spiritual progress. I was happy to hear you say that the people of Togo are eager to give public worship to God.

5. Finally you have understood the importance of an international juridical order which would guarantee the respect of freedom and the rights of man, and also an international economic order which would assure all peoples of a true development. On this subject the Holy See has followed with interest the work that culminated in the Convention of Lome. And we will do our utmost to recall to men of good will in other countries and international organizations, weary of seeing the amounts wasted on preparations for war and traumatized with fear of such a war, that the true battle to wage is that of mutually responsible development, such that each human being be

freed from the miseries of ignorance, from hunger and from illnesses which scientific progress and technology and more just relations have permitted us to repel, according to the design of the Creator himself: "Fill the earth and subdue it." And here I think in particular of the human needs of Africa, which I referred to recently in Libreville on leaving the continent.

Of this action of the Church you will henceforth be a closer witness. In assuring you here of the warmest welcome, I extend cordial wishes for your noble mission in the service of ever-more fruitful relations between the Holy See and Togo. I pray God to assist you and inspire you in this high office.

November 14, 1983
(*OR*, December 12, 1983, p. 4)

H.E. Pierre Pompee, Ambassador of Haiti:

Most Holy Father,

To represent one's country at the Holy See is unquestionably a privilege; the name alone of the Vatican cannot fail to evoke, for every civilized person, images, ideas, and sentiments which, taken all together, help one to understand the Christian mind.

That this mission is exercised during the pontificate of His Holiness Pope John Paul II, how great an honor and a pleasure, for one is very pleased to find in his teaching that just balance "nova et vetera" which our era requires.

Today, then, an immense emotion fills my heart on meeting your Sovereign Pontiff thanks to this ceremony where diplomatic ritual finds a special importance in the context where Christian truth floats aloft, far from worn-out ideologies and exhausted hegemonies.

I know, Most Holy Father, that I would put your great humility to a severe test if I should begin to eulogize your virtues and the work of peace which you are in process of accomplishing throughout the world. I shall limit myself simply to uniting my humble voice to the lavish testimonies of so many countries to Your Holiness who has taken up the work of opening wide the doors through which pass world peace, support for the undeveloped peoples and the brotherhood of men of whom following your vocation, you have today made yourself the champion.

And so, it is with great interest that the Haitian Government, whose activity is inspired by the principles proclaimed in the motto: liberty, equality, fraternity, pursues the great movement of religious, moral and social renewal which you have taken the initiative to lead to a successful end.

And since the lesson which Your Holiness never ceases to make heard proclaims that development is the new name for peace, I may be allowed to point out that the new Haitian constitution, to which the mass media from overseas have given ample coverage, has now opportunely impressed on our activity new goals and horizons while seeing to it, among other things, that each individual discover his role in the national development.

Most Holy Father, I am pleased to transmit to you, along with this homage, the greeting of Haiti, the greeting of an entire people which treasures and reveres the indelible memory of your visit and whose attention follows you in the office you have assumed.

I likewise bring you the respectful greetings of the Haitian Government and, most especially, of the Head of the Government, His Excellency Mr. Jean-Claude Duvalier and of his dynamic wife for the marks of solicitude with which you have honored our country where spiritual and apostolic vitality is so well established.

As for me, Most Holy Father, I am extremely pleased to have been granted the distinction by the head of the Haitian State to fulfill this delicate mission of Ambassador Extraordinary to the Holy See.

May the Apostolic Blessing accompany me. Such are the sentiments that inspire me as I submit to Your Holiness these Letters which accredit me to you and to the Holy See.

Papal Response:

Mr. Ambassador,

1. You have just expressed to me the emotion with which you inaugurate your functions as Ambassador of the Republic of Haiti to the Holy See, a delicate mission which Your Excellency considers as a privilege. For my part, I thank you for your kind words, for the grateful memory you recalled, for the greetings you have conveyed and for the willingness you display to develop in a harmonious and fruitful way the good relations that exist between your Government and the Holy See.

When I received your predecessor on December 14, 1979, I alluded to the filial attachment of the Haitian people to the Pope and to its eager desire to receive him in their own country, and I added: "We will do everything in our power to realize the proposal."

Since last March 9 it has been an accomplished fact. To be sure, at the end of a very intense apostolic journey in nearly all the countries of Central America, my stay in Haiti had, alas, to be of short duration. But it left in my mind and in my heart a lasting souvenir which allows me henceforth to rejoin your dear country more easily on the level of pastoral concern and prayer.

Recalls visit
2. I had the opportunity of meeting at Port-au-Prince His Excellency President Jean-Claude Duvalier, whom I would ask you to thank for his respectful greeting. I was touched by the warm reception he gave me. I appreciated the willingness he expressed to proceed with an updating of the concordat terms, in the line generally adopted according to the spirit of Vatican Council II, and I hope that a happy conclusion of the transactions now in progress will soon be reached. You will kindly assure him of my gratitude for this display of goodwill, of my confidence with regard to the full realization of the project, and also of my best wishes for the discharge of his high office.

I likewise met with a significant segment of the Haitian people, and especially of Christians gathered around their bishops and priests. This was mostly within the framework of the great Eucharistic and Marian celebration, and I was very struck by the fervor and the dignity of the prayer, by the vitality of the ecclesial community, by its simple and warm reception, by the seriousness of its commitment. I read in this attitude the confidence of the Haitians in the Church, their good will, their desire for progress, their hope.

Continued development
3. I am aware of the heavy task that devolves on each individual, according to his responsibilities, to ensure the continuance of the human, social and spiritual development. Each family, each profession, each community should supply its share of initiative, of honest and persevering work, to the extent of its power and its means, and should also feel supported by an atmosphere of justice and of peace, according to the principles of liberty, equality and fraternity which Your Excellency recalled. The concern of all, as you very happily brought out echoing the new Constitution, is that "each individual discover his role in the national development." I know that those in authority are aware of what is at stake, which is the honor of their office.

Form consciences

4. The Church, as you know, whether in its bishops, its priests, its religious – of Haitian origin or those from other countries who have generously come to assist their brothers – and its laity, will continue to work according to its competence toward this development. Its primary role is to form consciences so as to allow them to deepen their faith, to enlighten and to strengthen their piety, to face up to their personal, family and social responsibilities. It pertains also to the Church to encourage and promote the works that assist people to nourish, instruct, care for themselves better, to be more responsible. In this way the Church responds to its universal mission at the service of man and of his full development. In this task it is sure of being able to encounter the understanding and the support it needs, for the honor of religion and the welfare of the country.

5. This is moreover what the Church would like to accomplish in a spirit of service, throughout the entire world. You mentioned in this regard a few of the great objectives it has at heart: world peace, the development of the less favored peoples, brotherhood among men, religious, moral and social renewal. You will henceforth be the close witness of the specific contribution the Holy See endeavors to make toward these aims, even as you yourself echo here the desires and the efforts of your country at the national and international levels.

I am happy for this occasion which is offered me of reiterating my regard and my sympathy for all the Haitian people, and my sincere good wishes to its government Authorities. As for you, Mr. Ambassador, I welcome you cordially in this House, I offer you my best wishes for the fulfillment of your high mission, praying God to assist and bless you.

March 2, 1984
(*OR*, March 20, 1984, pp. 4–5)

H.E. Ali Kaiser Hasan Morshed, Ambassador of Bangladesh:

It is for me a profound honor to present to you the Letters accrediting me as the Ambassador of the People's Republic of Bangladesh to the Holy See. This honor conferred on me by the Government of Bangladesh implies that to some modest degree, I shall be a participant in the ongoing dialogue and exchange between the Church of Rome and the 95 million people of Bangladesh – a dialogue which my Government recognizes has been of historical significance and will continue to be so.

While Bangladesh is amongst the most populous Muslim countries in the world we are not unmindful of the areas of convergence with other religions that stems from our common faith in a single transcendental Divinity. The Constitution of Bangladesh guarantees to every faith, every sect, full and nondiscriminatory protection.

After centuries of oppression and exploitation the people of Bangladesh are embarked upon a quest for a better life. Under the inspiring leadership of Lt. General H.M. Ershad, President and Chief Martial Law Administrator, we are engaged in the colossal task of developing our country to ensure to our people certain minimum basic necessities of human life – necessities without which the concept of human rights and human dignity become meaningless slogans that serve only to mock the misery of millions of the world's poor and downtrodden.

A program of decentralization has been completed with a view to bringing the Government closer to the people and to foster local initiative for development. Under the new administration, elections will take place in the Upazillas (Sub-districts) on March 24th involving the entire electorate.

Your Holiness, I am inspired by your words in your address to the Committee of Presidency of the International Institute of Human Rights on March 22, 1979, which I seek permission to quote: "It is no secret that the abyss separating the minority of the excessively rich from the multitudes of the destitute is a very grave symptom in the life of any society. This must also be said with even greater insistence with regard to the abyss separating countries and regions of the earth. Surely the only way to overcome this serious disparity between areas of satiety and areas of hunger and depression is through coordinated action by all countries."

The Church of Rome has been in the vanguard of those that have recognized that this abyss poses a fundamental challenge to peace as well as the very survival of human values, both moral and spiritual. Bangladesh, till recently Chairman of the Group of 77, has striven not without success to further the North-South dialogue and to bridge the gap between rich and poor in a spirit of conciliation and not of confrontation.

Your Holiness, the Roman Catholic Church has made significant contributions to the social, cultural and human progress in my country. A number of Catholic organizations, such as Camtas, and a number of Roman Catholic orders have made and continue to make significant contributions in the educational, medical and social fields in Bangladesh.

In this context the continuing exchange and interaction between the Roam

Catholic Church and Bangladesh, which acknowledges amongst its citizens almost one million Christians, is of enduring significance and promise. We believe this dialogue will contribute to a deeper understanding in the world community of the problems of development and of the fight against disease, ignorance and human misery.

Permit me in the end to convey to you the greetings and the sincere good wishes from the President and Chief Martial Law Administrator of Bangladesh, Lt. General H.M. Ershad.

Papal Response:

Mr. Ambassador,

I am pleased to accept the Letters of Credence which accredit you as the Ambassador Plenipotentiary and Extraordinary of the People's Republic of Bangladesh. I thank you for the kind greetings which you have just now conveyed on behalf of the highest authorities of your country, and for the noble expression of the inner dispositions of heart and mind with which you begin your mission to the Holy See.

You have made reference to the presence of the Catholic Church in Bangladesh and to the contribution made by Catholic institutions and personnel in various fields of service to the people. You have also referred to the assistance rendered to refugees. In all of this the Church seeks to follow the teaching and example of her divine Founder, whose whole concern was to serve and not to be served. Such service, whether it be on a personal and individual level or on the level of the various organizations and institutions involved, is the fruit of a conviction that every human being is a unique image of the Creator called into existence *through love* and *for love* (cf. *Familiaris Consortio*, no. 11).

Consolidating our good relations

The Church is fully at the service of the dignity of man. In this she seeks to cooperate with other private associations and public authorities throughout the world which uphold the values that constitute and adorn this unique dignity. It is in this context that the Holy See is pleased to extend a cordial welcome to you as the representative of your country and its Government and people. Your presence here consolidates still further the good relations already existing between the State and the Church in your country, and offers further opportunities for dialogue and collaboration. In promoting relations with the governments and international organizations, the Holy See is following the intentions of the Second Vatican Council when it indicates that "in their proper spheres, the political community and the Church are mutually independent and self-governing. Yet, by a different title, each serves the personal and social vocation of the same human beings. This service can be more effectively rendered for the good of all insofar as both institutions practice better cooperation according to the local and prevailing situation" (*Gaudium et Spes*, no. 76).

Today, moreover, as you rightly suggested, no country or people can hope to promote true development and progress in isolation from the world community. For this reason, the Holy See endeavors to encourage greater international cooperation at all levels, conscious of the truth that for peace to be achieved and maintained it is necessary that peoples be free from excessive inequalities and from every form of undue dependence. Again it is the Second Vatican Council which succinctly enunciates the vision that lies behind the Church's activities in the area of international cooperation and development: "If an economic order is to be created which is genuine and universal, there must be an abolition of excessive desire for profit, nationalistic pretensions, the lust for political domination, militaristic thinking, and intrigues designed to spread and impose ideologies" (ibid., no. 85). This statement was made by the Council almost twenty years ago, but it is still valid today.

On essential values

Mr. Ambassador, as you are well aware, your mission to the Holy See is not to a power in the temporal and worldly order. The heart of that mission is centered on the essential values that give meaning to man's efforts to create a better life in peace and harmony. I wish you every success and invoke abundant divine blessings upon you in the fulfillment of your task.

Finally, I would ask you to convey my greetings to the President of Bangladesh and to the President of the Council of Ministers. Be assured, Mr. Ambassador, of my deep respect and love for the people of your country.

January 10, 1985
(*OR*, February 18, 1985, p. 9)

H.E. Gatechew Kebreth, Ambassador of Ethiopia:

Most Holy Father,
It is a great honor for me to present to Your Holiness the letters of accreditation by which President Mengistu Haile Mariam, Secretary General of the Ethiopian Worker's Party, President of the Provisional Administrative Military Council, and Commander-in-Chief of the Revolutionary Army, accredits me to Your Holiness in the capacity of Ambassador Extraordinary and Plenipotentiary of Socialist Ethiopia, as well as the letters of recall of my predecessor.

Most Holy Father,
The Holy See and Ethiopia have always maintained close and friendly relations, based on mutual trust and respect. It is the ardent desire of Socialist Ethiopia to see these relations further strengthened. And for me there could be no more noble a responsibility than to have been chosen to work for this strengthening.

Most Holy Father,
As you know, for more than ten years Ethiopia has been involved in a process of profound socio-economic change in order to establish a new society of liberty, equality, justice and democracy, in which Ethiopians can find their full development. Ethiopia knows that in order to prove victorious in the struggle which she is waging in this regard – against exploitation in all its forms, famine, disease, and ignorance – she has need of peace. But she also knows that peace can only result when everyone everywhere respects the great principles which must direct relations among independent countries. Ethiopia for her part is faithful to her commitment to peace, and is working to establish relations of friendship and co-operation with all countries and all peoples.
My country, which, because of the exceptionally severe drought which is affecting it and of the resulting famine, now more than ever has need of understanding, sympathy, and of good will from all sides.
Allow me, Holy Father, to express to you the gratitude of the Ethiopian people for the concern which you have shown in the face of the misfortune which has afflicted them, and for the repeated appeals which you have made for international solidarity in favor of the victims of these natural calamities. I am sure that I shall benefit from the help and agreement of Your Holiness, and your close collaborations as I fulfill my assignment.

Most Holy Father,
In conclusion, I should like to transmit to you, on behalf of President Mengistu Haile Mariam and the Government and people of Ethiopia, most sincere good wishes for Your Holiness's happiness and health, and for the triumph of the values and ideals common to the Holy See and Ethiopia, namely liberty, peace, progress and prosperity for all peoples.

Papal Response:

Mr. Ambassador,

The sentiments which you have expressed as you inaugurate your high office at the Holy See are welcomed here with great attention. I thank you for them and I see in them the sign of a new stage, a happy and fruitful one, in our relations.

The Holy See is glad to see you take your place here today as Ambassador Extraordinary and Plenipotentiary in the diplomatic corps accredited to the Holy See, a place which has been empty for some time. And I have no doubt that this event corresponds to a desire of your Government to strengthen the ties which have for a long time existed between Ethiopia and the Holy See. Please express to your President, His Excellency Lieutenant-Colonel Mengistu Haile Mariam, my gratitude for the good wishes which you have transmitted and my own good wishes for your country and for those who have the heavy responsibility of caring for its welfare.

Esteem and sympathy

The Holy See's esteem and sympathy for Ethiopia increase when it considers your country's long and glorious history, parallel to biblical history. It knows of the stubborn efforts of your country, repeated again and again over several thousand years, in the face of internal difficulties and in spite of foreign interventions, to safeguard the identity of its civilization and the ties among its provinces, each of which has its own particular cultural riches. Even though the Catholic faithful in your country form only a small minority – an active one and very attached to its native land – the Catholic Church nevertheless feels an affinity with the faith and the spiritual witness of the Coptic Orthodox Church of Ethiopia, which has so profoundly marked the soul of the country, its customs and its art. As she expressed it in the Second Vatican Council, the Church also regards with respect and good will all those who profess their faith in the one God, and those who follow the voice of conscience and sincerely seek the welfare of their neighbor. This means that the Church does not consider any human society truly foreign; rather, she regards each one with fraternal concern.

Common ideals

Your Excellency has emphasized certain ideals common to the Holy See and Ethiopia, concerning how to conceive the well-being of this nation or international relations. In what concerns us, I can give you this assurance, to which many countries could testify: in its declarations as in its actions the Holy See desires the independence of every country, as I said last year when I received the diplomatic corps. The Holy See wishes that the sovereignty of each country should be recognized and respected by all the others, without interference, direct or disguised; that international aid itself should respect the civilization and the original way which each country wants to safeguard according to the wish of the people. The Holy See considers as essential the acknowledgement and exercise of fundamental human rights, liberty, respect for the spiritual values which belong to the culture of a country, and the guarantee that all citizens can profess and live their religious faith according to the requirements of their community.

The Holy See is equally attached to those things which establish and develop justice among men and among social groups, recognizing an equal dignity in each person of whatever sex, race, nationality or religion. Likewise the Holy See values that which promotes people's responsibility according to their talents, respecting and serving the common good. The Holy See is convinced that the practice of justice is the most solid foundation for establishing and maintaining peace, that peace, interior and exterior, which is so necessary in order to undertake true reforms, to face vital needs, and to allow citizens to come to a prosperity which provides a level of nutrition, health, and education which conforms with their dignity. The Holy See is not unaware that this peace can be threatened by unjust violence and that it is proper to defend peace in the common interest; but we think that one must always try to replace violence with negotiated solutions, just and honorable ones, taking account of the legitimate demands of the parties involved; for violence engenders violence, and it leads to ruin. Such are the ideals which the Holy See proclaims in a clear voice; it seeks to promote them among all friendly countries. It hopes to arouse the acquiescence of the greatest possible number of them by a reasonable evaluation of the true interests of the peoples and by an appeal to conscience.

Present suffering

At this moment Ethiopia is living out a great drama, like many countries of Africa: the drama of a drought which is becoming even more severe and which brings famine in its train. Here and there armed conflicts continue to prevent solutions to the problem. Millions of people are suffering from this vital lack of food. They will remain marked by it for a long time, while thousands of them die each day, among them a large number of children. Throughout the world international organizations, governments, and aid agencies have been moved and are organizing help to meet the immediate need, while hoping to see the implementation of long-term solutions. How could the Pope not raise his voice to echo and amplify this appeal? Through the Pontifical Council *Cor Unum*, through *Caritas* organizations, through many initiatives the Catholic Church thus participates on site in this work of solidarity, as you have had the goodness to emphasize. She is ready to continue and to develop this humanitarian action to the extent that her means – alas too limited – permit, for the benefit of all the starving populations, without the distinction of religion or allegiance.

The Church is grateful to the Ethiopian government for the confidence which it has in her with regard to these aid distribution efforts.

Church's efforts

But, as your Excellency well knows, such participation in emergency aid, conforming as it does to that charity which is at the heart of the Christian message, does not express the total contribution which the Church offers to the world. As I mentioned above, the Church wants to work to advance the good of human beings, integrally and jointly, wherever men trust her, respecting the persons and institutions with which each country is endowed: she favors the development of everything which ensures the dignity of persons, their health, education, culture, family values, social justice and fraternity, moral integrity, their relationship with God himself. This shows the importance which the Church accords to education, to which she gladly devotes her efforts. As regards her spiritual mission through the witness of her children and the international action of the Holy See, she has this ambition: that everywhere men and women may be better prepared for the responsibility which they must exercise, with competence and in the spirit of impartial service, for the good of their fellow countrymen and for the common good of all nations. May all men and women of good will come together in this common endeavor!

This, Mr. Ambassador, is what you will witness in the special relations which you will from now on have with the Holy See, in the name of your Government. And you yourself will share with us the problems and desires of your compatriots, in the assurance that the Holy See wishes the greatest good of your nation and of all those who form it in their diversity. We entrust this mutual openness to the grace of God who probes the will and inspires upright hearts. And I offer you, Mr. Ambassador, my wishes for a happy and a fruitful mission.

January 20, 1986
(*OR*, February 3, 1986, p. 10)

H.E. Ketel Borde, Ambassador of Norway:

Your Holiness,

I have the honor of presenting to you the letters by which His Majesty King Olav V accredits me as Ambassador Extraordinary and Plenipotentiary to the Holy See as well as the letters of recall of my predecessor.

His Majesty charged me to transmit to Your Holiness the expression of his high esteem as well as his most sincere good wishes for your health and personal well-being.

When in 1982 it was decided to establish diplomatic relations between Norway and the Holy See, a new chapter was opened in our common history. The relations between Norway and the Holy See had in the past played a decisive role in the development of a Norwegian nation. When in 1152 Norway became an archdiocese, this new statute was in effect the occasion for the promotion of the national government structures, inspired and sustained by the representatives of the Church. The first Norwegian Archbishop, Oystein Erlendsson, thus contributed in large measure to placing this Church in the foreground of a struggle which would one day end with the establishment of a modern and unified national state. So it was that the Holy See was for our country a source of inspiration and a spiritual home throughout the 13th and 14th centuries, at a time when Norway was playing an active role in the intellectual life of Europe. At this time, thousands of pilgrims, coming from all the countries of Europe, had to follow the road to Nidaros where Saint Olav, Rex Perpetuus Norvegiae, was buried.

The course of history however saw the break off of these close relations between Norway and the Holy See. If it is right to rejoice in the establishment of diplomatic relations and of the strengthening of ties between Norway and the Holy See, this is not only because of the important role played by the Holy See in Norwegian history. The present historical situation shows that today, more than ever, the states are dependent on one another and that a concerted effort is absolutely necessary if we wish to be able to defend the common values that constitute the foundation of our culture and upon which our future rests. At this level that fact should be underlined that our two states, although we have found ourselves separated by the course of history, are both depositaries of the basic values of the West.

National Norwegian policy is based on certain values and convictions among which are democracy, social equality and solidarity. These ideals are likewise pursued in our activities at the international level.

The policy of the Holy See on behalf of the rights of man as also its engagement aimed at the bettering of the life conditions of all the peoples of the world are admired and highly appreciated in Norway. They receive the unconditional support of my Government. The free exercise of religion is one of the fundamental rights of which my country also makes itself the ardent defender, especially in the framework of the current negotiations relative to security and cooperation in Europe.

The role played by Your Holiness in the efforts to rouse the spiritual and moral values of humanity, to maintain peace and security and to better the human condition is of inestimable importance and the work you contribute in these domains is followed with respect and admiration by my Government.

The bilateral relations between Norway and the Holy See reflect a number of mutual interests and common commitments. The decision, made by common accord and resting on the already existing friendly ties, to establish diplomatic relations between our two states has then been very well received in my country. The meeting between Your Holiness and the Norwegian Minister of Foreign Affairs, Mr. Svenn Stray, on July 5, 1983, roused profound interest in this and it was followed on July 31, 1985, by discussions at Helsinki between Mr. Stray and His Excellency Archbishop Silvestrini. As new Ambassador to the Holy See, I express the hope that these contacts be deepened and developed in the future.

Allow me finally to express my great personal joy at the honor conferred on me by my Government in naming me Ambassador to the Holy See. I shall strive to accomplish the important mission entrusted to me with all the care it requires and deserves. In the exercise of my functions, I confidently request the benevolence of Your Holiness to whom I address my most sincere and respectful good wishes.

Papal Response:

Mr. Ambassador,

1. At the moment when you are inaugurating your mission as Ambassador Extraordinary and Plenipotentiary of the Kingdom of Norway to the Holy See, I am happy to express to you, with my welcome greeting, my cordial best wishes for the accomplishment of your exalted diplomatic task, and for the well-being of all those whom you represent here.

I am thinking especially of His Majesty King Olav V. Please thank him for the kind message he charged you to convey. I wish him and his family the very best of health and serenity, praying the Lord to help him to preside over the destiny of the Norwegian people, to whom I am happy to express likewise my sympathy and my cordial good wishes.

When your predecessor presented his Letters of Credence as first Ambassador of Norway to the Holy See, on February 18, 1983, I spoke of an historical moment of great importance in our relations. These relations, at the diplomatic level, are now well rooted, and your Excellency will contribute, I am sure, to making them ever more profound and fruitful.

2. You mentioned the period characteristic of the Middle Ages, when the religious and cultural vitality of Norway – I am thinking especially of the epoch of the sagas – exercised a notable influence on Scandinavia and on a large part of Europe, continuing, at another level, the victorious expeditions of your Norman compatriots. And you had the goodness to point out the peaceful and fruitful relations which then existed with the Bishop of Rome and which, by enhancing the role of the Church in your country, facilitated the conscious assimilation of your own values and of the national identity.

These human values are rooted in a patrimony common to all of Europe, profoundly marked by the Christian faith; in particular, the beautiful figure of Saint Olav II, King, symbolizes forever the belonging of the Norwegian people to Christ, after the baptism of their nation almost a thousand years ago. Today, after the unfortunate division among Christians that followed the Reformation, Christianity, within the framework of the Lutheran confession, remains tied to the social structures of the country.

3. Your State had to fight many a time in the course of history to maintain its independence and to seek with tenacity the prosperity of the country in every respect. Henceforth, it is as a modern State that Norway has wished to establish diplomatic relations with the Holy See, as have a great number of countries in the world. In fact, Norway and the Holy See – recognized with its *sui generis* juridical personality in the international community – can agree on many similar objectives, very crucial for the truly human development of the peoples, for the service of the common good incumbent on governments, and for the relationships of equity and of peace that must be established or strengthened among the nations.

You yourself mentioned democracy, equality, solidarity; you made special mention of the free communication of ideas and of persons, in the line of the Helsinki report, and notably of the free exercise of religion. I am grateful to Norway for contributing its support on this point which is so important to the Holy See, as it is to all the countries attached to a just conception of liberty. It is a matter of the fundamental rights of man, which demand to be respected by all in all things, and without which a civilization would not be worthy of the name.

New international economic order
4. This exigency of the dignity of the person does not allow one to neglect, rather – contrary to the individualism encouraged by certain consumer societies – it calls for the promotion of the people of other countries who are floundering under the heavy difficulties of development and of peace. Solidarity should not remain a word that makes us dream; it requires courageous actions aimed at a new international economic order; it requires cooperation with all of the nations represented at the Organization of the United Nations, and in the first place at the level of the region and of the continent. My recent meeting with the Diplomatic Corps accredited to the Holy See (January 11, 1986) offered me the opportunity of developing at length this aspect of the universal value of peace. And I know that Norway is concerned with extended cooperative activity, in the framework of the Nordic Council and of the Council of Europe.

5. But all the human projects regarding the well-being of the peoples and the equity of their relations must rely for support on spiritual and moral values in the consciences of the citizens and in those of their leaders at the various levels – from the educators to the governments. You have emphasized the importance of these values, Mr. Ambassador. To be precise, you know well that it is the proper role of the Holy See to help to promote these values, since its mission is above all of the spiritual order, as witness of the evangelical message entrusted by Christ to the Apostle Peter and to his brothers. With the Catholic bishops of Europe recently assembled in symposium, I recalled the "model" of the present European society with its positive aspects and with its shadows; sometimes man, in the midst of a superabundance of goods and of knowledge, no longer recognizes the meaning of his life and of his dignity as a being created in the image of God, no longer sees the requirements of love and of stability in the

family. He should never forget that his Christian roots are an integral part of his identity part of his identity and summon him to a new creative synthesis between the Gospel and the present conditions of his life. It is a matter here, beyond that of fidelity to the faith received, of an eminent service to be rendered to our Western societies, in the respect of consciences. For my part, I invite all Catholics to engage themselves in this way, including those who live with you, in the diocese of Oslo, in the prelacies of Trondheim and of Tromsø, and whom I greet with particular affection; they are few in number, but well integrated into Norwegian society. Moreover, moral and spiritual values are certainly the object of the same preoccupation in the other Christian Churches. And this is a further reason to promote ecumenism, which helps all Christians to understand one another better, to respect one another, to work together for the good of their brothers, while at the same time working toward full unity among them. It is also for this reason that I greet here your compatriots, almost all of whom belong to the Lutheran Church.

6. Mr. Ambassador, you represent your country and its major interests. I think that the reflections expressed here are fundamentally at one with these interests. Once again I express to you my fervent good wishes for your mission with the Holy See, for all the Norwegian people, for its Sovereign and all its government officials. In the midst of the long winters that make your compatriots await with eagerness the return of sunnier days, may God never cease to fill them with his Light and with his many gifts so as to allow them to live in happiness and in peace, in conformity with his will and with his love!

October 17, 1987
(*OR*, November 16, 1987, pp. 7, 12)

H.E. Jesus E. Calvo, Ambassador of Spain:

Holy Father,

I have the honor of presenting to Your Holiness the Letters of Credence by which His Majesty the King of Spain has appointed me his Ambassador Extraordinary and Plenipotentiary to the Holy See. I convey to you the expression of the respect and loyalty of His Majesty King Juan Carlos I.

I am conscious of the great honor it is to be Ambassador of Spain to the Holy See as I am also conscious of the grave responsibility placed upon me by the Spanish Government in entrusting this diplomatic mission to me. At this moment I am reminded of the simple words expressed by Your Holiness at the time of your election: "Do not be afraid." I will be faithful to this advice as I take up my duty and I will count on your generous understanding in order to maintain and, where possible, improve the already very good relations between Spain and the Holy See.

The admirable example left by those who have preceded me in this office throughout its long history will be an inspiration and guidance to me in carrying out my responsibilities.

It would not be easy, maybe even impossible, to understand the history of my country without taking account of the history of the Church and of the religious convictions of the Spanish people. As a European nation, and even more, as a nation situated on the frontiers of Europe, thereby in contact with many other civilizations, the Spanish Nation has formed its understanding of the world with deep roots in the Christian vision of humanity and of life. A great regard for freedom and the dignity of the human person is something which has always been present in Spanish culture and political endeavors, a sentiment which also exists most certainly in the religious convictions of so many of my fellow countrymen.

In a few more years, in 1992, we will be celebrating the fifth centenary of the discovery of America. This undertaking was brought to completion through the combined efforts of Church and State, it brought into being in modern history nations and peoples who today are fully integrated into the culture and political modes which originated in Europe.

This kind of historical undertaking has penetrated deeply into the consciousness of the Spanish people who today follow with attention and interest the socio-cultural, economic and political development of our sister nations in whose lives so many Spaniards still play a part; among these we find so many religious, to whom I render profound homage on this solemn occasion.

You yourself referred to this when on the occasion of your visit to Zaragoza in October 1984, on the eve of your journey to Santo Domingo, you said: "As I set out on this missionary journey, and on behalf of the whole Church, I wanted to come personally to thank the Church in Spain for the steadfast work of evangelization which it has done throughout the world and especially in the Americas and in the Philippines." . . . "As we begin the preparations for the celebration of the fifth centenary of the evangelization of America, I wanted to make a stop at El Pilar de Zaragoza in order to highlight the significance of this journey."

In the world in which we live, with all its hurts and tensions and in which violence, selfishness and terrorism are ever present, producing all kinds of misery, in this
world in which the relations between nations are frequently imbued with values which
are alien to justice and mutual respect, I would like to refer to the work Your Holiness
has done in defense of human rights, which as you have said, are "the basis of everything." I am happy to note that Spain has among the guiding principles of its foreign
policy that same concern for the defense of and the promotion of human rights. Thus
there is an obvious convergence with the position of the Holy See. My country, which
looks to the future with hope, and begins from a pride in its past, which it assumes in
full without any sterile attempts to revise it, wishes to make clear to the world its firm
intention of confronting the present conflicts. In the international arena, that will mean
a willingness on Spain's part to be associated with all those initiatives which have as
their objective the defense of peace and justice among nations and states, every project which defends the dignity of the human person and seeks the establishment of
more just and balanced political and economic relations. Spain, which recently
became a member of the European Economic Community, is aware that no one State,
turned in on itself in a selfish nationalism, can hope to resolve on its own the great
problems which face the modern world. Therefore, she shares the desire of Your
Holiness to stimulate cultural, economic, social, human and political contacts among
the nations of this continent. Every day, she becomes more aware of the urgent need
to promote and defend her traditional values among which religious freedom holds a
special place.

"All of us make up one human family . . . By the fact of coming into this world
we share in the same inheritance and we are members of the one human race," as you
reminded us in your Message for the World Day of Peace, 1987. The message is the
same as that given by the symbolism of the Day of Prayer for Peace which took place
a short time before in Assisi.

I wish to refer also, Your Holiness, to the Agreements signed in 1979 between
Spain and the Holy See in the preparation of which I had the honor to take part. These
agreements have given us the juridical framework of the understanding between both
parties beginning from a mutual respect for principles and competencies. I believe that
these agreements have given us the juridical framework of the understanding between
both parties beginning from a mutual respect for principles and competencies. I
believe that these agreements have been applied in a satisfactory way for some time
and they have provided a high degree of development in terms of norms, in their various aspects, in a process that goes on even to the present day. The Spanish
Government, out of the strict application of the constitutional principles in operation,
which regard pluralism as an essential element in the make-up of Spanish society, and
the religious freedom of the citizens as a basic principle in terms of liberties and
human rights, does not limit the possibilities for cooperation with the Catholic Church
strictly to the areas indicated in the Agreements of 1979. Rather it is disposed to look
for ways of cooperation in an effort to deal with the concrete problems with which the
Spanish society is faced.

Your Holiness, the Spanish people are giving ample proof of their moral courage
in the struggle against terrorism, without sacrificing the inalienable values of freedom
and democracy, established in our Constitution. For this reason, they deeply appreciate the firm words uttered by you against anyone who, inspired by ideals of fratricidal

destruction, commit crimes against the freedom of people to live together in peace and against humanity itself.

Holy Father, in presenting my Letters of Credence to you I wish to express the filial loyalty of the Catholics of Spain and I convey to you the respectful good wishes of His Majesty the King and the Royal Family. I ask your blessing for all of us, especially the members of the Spanish Embassy to the Holy See, for me and for our families.

Papal Response:

Mr. Ambassador,

I wish to thank you for the kind words you expressed on presenting your Letters of Credence as the Ambassador Extraordinary and Plenipotentiary of Spain to the Holy See.

First of all I would like to reply to the sentiments of friendship from His Majesty, King Juan Carlos I, by asking you to convey to him my respectful greeting and good wishes for peace and prosperity.

In your address, Mr. Ambassador, you alluded to the profound and widespread presence of the Catholic faith in the life of the Spanish people and in the history of Spain. Indeed, within a few years we will celebrate the 14th centenary of the Council of Toledo. From that Council onwards the Catholic faith began to take deep root among the people of Spain, as an essential part of their spiritual and cultural heritage. Even though other religions such as Judaism and Islam have played an important role in your country and have left significant imprints on it there is little doubt that it is the Catholic faith which has left the deepest mark on the spirit and the customs of your nation and has had a decisive influence on the more important events of your history. Among the many distinguished men and women that Spain has given to the world we find a number of saints, bishops, founders, missionaries, doctors and martyrs who at the same time bring honor both to Spain and to the Catholic Church.

Indeed in my journeys to the Americas I was able to see for myself the immense work of evangelization and human and cultural endeavor which the Spanish missionaries carried on, and how they played a part in the establishment of a political and social order based on the recognition of the dignity of the human person as a citizen and child of God.

In the recent past your country has seen important transformations in the institutions and social and political structures. In the State the full and effective recognition of religious freedom is at one and the same time the result of and the guarantee of all the other civil liberties. In this juridical framework then, the non-confessional position of the State does not mean that the civil authorities should not guarantee, in the area of their competence, the practice of religious faith and of the moral life as they are professed and freely lived by the people. There we see one of the deepest manifestations of the freedom of the person and a contribution of primary importance to the right exercise of social life and the achievement of the common good.

I wish to make clear to you, Mr. Ambassador, the desire of the Church, in accordance with the mission which she has received from Jesus Christ, to cooperate with the authorities and the various institutions in your country, in the interests of peace and the welfare of the people, both spiritual and material. Therefore the areas in which this cooperation can be effected are both many and important, following the Agreement signed in 1979. The Church would hope that by following this Agreement faithfully a relationship of mutual respect and understanding may be fostered, bearing in mind both the constitutional dispositions in your country and the nature of the mission of the Church.

Cooperation between Church and State

There is no denying that the presence and the work of the Catholic community in Spain is already an important contribution to the welfare of Spanish society. It should not be forgotten that many problems of a political nature find their roots in the moral order which is promoted in a respectful way by the evangelizing and educational work of the Church. Hence we see that the Christian life consolidates the family, gives dignity to human relations, brings people together, and educates for freedom under the headings of justice and mutual respect. Spanish Catholics, therefore, to the extent that they are faithful to the Gospel and the teachings of the Church, will at the same time be sincere defenders of justice and peace, freedom and honesty, respect for life in all circumstances and of solidarity with those who are most in need. All of this will bring great benefits of Spanish society; they will be all the greater for the loyal cooperation between the Church and State, always in respect and freedom.

I want to take this opportunity to express the hope that the Spanish Nation, which contributed so much to the spread of the Christian faith, especially in America, still finds in its deep-rooted piety valuable help for dealing with and resolving its internal problems; it is thus able to express itself in the area of international relations in support of human rights, the pursuit of justice, development and the consolidation of a stable and lasting peace among all the nations of the earth. These are the noble causes which this Apostolic See, with no authority other than that which was given to it by its Founder, tries to defend in every international forum in which it is present. Thus it will be a source of satisfaction and consolation to be able to work together with Spain in this peaceful and generous struggle in pursuit of spiritual values.

Mr. Ambassador, before bringing this meeting to a conclusion I wish to assure you of my esteem and support as well as my best wishes for the success of the important mission which you take up today. Please convey my hopes and good wishes to their Majesties, the King and Queen of Spain, to the Government and civil authorities. I invoke the blessing of God and the gifts of the Holy Spirit upon you, your family and your colleagues and above all, upon the beloved Spanish Nation.

June 13, 1988
(*OR*, August 15, 1988, p. 7)

H.E. Selcuk Korkud, Ambassador of Turkey:

Your Holiness,

I have the honor to present to Your Holiness the Letters by which the President of the Republic of Turkey, His Excellency Mr. Kenan Evren, accredits me to you in the capacity of Ambassador Extraordinary and Plenipotentiary of the Republic of Turkey, as well as the Letters recalling my esteemed predecessor.

The President of the Republic of Turkey has likewise charged me to convey his personal greetings and good wishes for the well-being of Your August Person.

On this solemn occasion, allow me to assure Your Holiness that I am fully aware of the honor conferred on me and of the responsibilities which devolve on me. During this exalted mission, I shall seek to maintain and to develop still more the links of mutual esteem and friendship which happily exist between Turkey and the Holy See.

The Turkish Nation and its Government are profoundly attached to human values as well as to independence and liberty, emulating with all due respect the great example Your Holiness has set for the realization of an ever better world by bringing peoples and believers together on the basis of impartial understanding and brotherly co-operation.

In keeping with its glorious past, Turkey, committed as it is to progress, imbued with profound humanism, with a spirit of tolerance and respect for the human person, loathes all religious and racial discrimination; it carries out tirelessly the international plan to promote harmony and cooperation in its territory and in the world in accordance with the high principles of the modern family of nations to which it belongs.

In fact, Your Holiness knows that the fundamental elements of our national attitude come from rich historical experience. That is why my country, while putting all its resources into development, spares no efforts to make its contribution to the solution of international difference by pacific means, notably by constructive dialogue. We shall also continue to attach importance, and contribute positively, to efforts undertaken to create favorable conditions for the realization of world security through true and durable co-operation. Because we firmly believe that when wills positively converge, they can help to surmount the difficulties and problems that concern our world.

We consider Your Holiness's work as the great messenger of international peace with admiration and respectful affection. We are particularly grateful for your activity as regards defense and to human rights, justice and international morals in the context of the tide of human development.

On this occasion I equally wish to pay homage to the memory and work of your illustrious predecessors, principally Pope John XXIII and Pope Paul VI, who made an inestimable contribution to our relations.

I also wish to evoke the precious memory of your visit to our country, a visit which by its historic significance marked a new stage in the evolution of our relations. It is a great pleasure to express our joy in the continued development of our relations in mutual respect, confidence and reciprocal understanding.

With these thoughts I ask Your Holiness to accept the expression of my sentiments and most respectful good wishes.

In assuming my duties I dare to hope that Your Holiness will accord me your full confidence and that I may count upon the benevolent support of your collaborators in the fulfillment of my mission.

Papal Response:

Mr. Ambassador,

I am happy to receive you at the very beginning of the high mission the President of Turkey has entrusted to you to the Holy See. The content of your address testifies to the noble sentiments you bring to your office. I thank you most sincerely for your words, and I shall be grateful if you will express my heartfelt gratitude to His Excellency Mr. Kenan Evren for the greetings and good wishes he entrusted you to convey to me.

In welcoming Your Excellency, as Ambassador Extraordinary and Plenipotentiary accredited to the Holy See, I sincerely hope that your mission, a continuation of that carried out by your distinguished predecessors, may contribute not only to maintaining the good relations to which you alluded just now, between the Apostolic See of Rome and your Government, but, that it may be a new and valuable stone in the, as yet, unfinished edifice of these bilateral relations. We all know that the art of diplomacy, if it is worthy of the name and able to promote the general and particular good of the populations concerned, demands an unceasing search for the truth, loyalty, and continuous dialogue, so as to bring about an improvement in those situations still in need of it, a fortiori to dispel misunderstandings and to regulate situations of conflict.

Every diplomat, whatever his religious or cultural tradition, cannot but be a person prepared to dialogue, one who hopes for peace. The essential work of peace, precious and fragile, is indispensable for the happiness of every human being and nation.

I experienced real satisfaction as I listened to you stress the importance your Government and your nation attach to the human values of tolerance and respect, to the exclusion of all racial or religious discrimination. Equally you stress the efforts your country is making to cooperate in world security measures, which are often compromised by conflict and the terrorist methods we condemn. This cooperation is directed equally toward the least privileged peoples. You may be pleased to know, Mr. Ambassador, that the Holy See and its Head carry out an extensive and disinterested activity in the defense and promotion of human rights, justice, morals, and international peace. I am all the more sensitive to your assurances as I have the certitude that Your Excellency will fulfill your mission for peace with ardor and discretion in all the areas where your diplomatic intervention may prove both useful and necessary.

Allow me, Mr. Ambassador, to name an area of concern which I have especially at heart, and which I often mention to diplomats accredited to the Holy See. I mean religious freedom, because respect for this liberty is of fundamental importance for peace. On the traditional Day of Peace instituted by Pope Paul VI, I wished to make it the theme of a message destined to all government authorities. Actually, when one considers the events taking place in the world one cannot but notice that forty years after the Universal Declaration of Human Rights, millions and millions of people in numerous regions of our universe still suffer from the consequences of oppressive legislation, sometimes from persecution, but more often from subtle forms of discrimination. This state of affairs is a heavy mortgage on peace. Certainly, in your country Catholics are a small minority. More precisely, Mr. Ambassador, your Government, noticing that these Christian minorities abide by the legitimate laws of your nation, will honor themselves by assuring their religious freedom. These Catholics of different rites are happy to live on your soil insofar as they feel safe, have the use of adequate places and premises where they may deepen and celebrate the faith they have received and which they have the sacred right to hand on to their children. Every State, especially once it has opened diplomatic relations with the Apostolic See of Rome, distinguishes itself highly by a clear attitude of justice in regard to believers who have legitimately made a choice of religion. I am confident, Mr. Ambassador, that your mission will serve to bring to the communities mentioned the happiness of living in peace in your land. Your country's welcome to me in 1979 is engraved in my memory. Pope Paul VI also visited it and Pope John XXIII demonstrated his zeal and kindness there when he was Apostolic Delegate to Ankara.

In thanking you again for your words full of respect and hope, I wish, Excellency, that you may experience much moral and spiritual satisfaction in the fulfillment of your high mission to the Holy See. Do I need to add the assurance, Mr. Ambassador, that the understanding and support you may rightly expect from the Apostolic See will always be at your service? Please be so good as to convey this same assurance to the President of the Republic of Turkey, His Excellency Mr. Kenan Evren, with my homage and very high esteem and my wishes for the prosperity and peace of the whole Turkish nation. On your person, your mission and those who are dear to you, I invoke the light, the strength and the protection of Almighty God.

March 3, 1989 (A)
(*OR*, March 20, 1989, pp. 4–5)

H.E. F. Rodriquez Paz, Ambassador of Cuba:

Your Holiness,

Allow me to express to Your Holiness the deep satisfaction, joy, and great responsibility that I feel in presenting to you my Letters of Credence as Ambassador Extraordinary and Plenipotentiary of Cuba to the Holy See.

On this occasion, it is my duty to recall the great work done by my predecessors, the Ambassadors Luis Amando Blanco, Jose Antonio Portuondo and Manuel Estevez, who over the past thirty years have carried out an outstanding diplomatic effort that has helped to develop the existing relations between the Holy See and Cuba.

According to the mandate given me by my Government, and my personal desire, I will commit myself diligently to maintaining and increasing, as much as possible, the relations and exchange that happily exist between our States in the mutual understanding and respect that have characterized them. This objective and charge, among those I bear, are related to the efforts and actions of the Vatican, and particularly of Your Holiness, as well as those of the Government which I represent, that humanity may reach a solid and lasting peace, that a full easing of the tension in international relations may be achieved, that the conditions for peace, independence, and development may prevail for all nations, great or small, weak or powerful, rich or poor; and that all people may reach the universally desired goals of well-being, health, security, and integral development.

With regard to this, allow me, Your Holiness, to point out that in an interview given to an Italian journalist in June 1987, the President of the State Council and Government of the Republic of Cuba, Commander Fidel Castro, said: "We proclaim something to which Christian teaching also subscribes: the brotherhood of all men, solidarity, selflessness, generosity, to which we add a high level of education, a high level of technical preparation, a patriotic consciousness, and an international consciousness."

More recently, during his visit to Caracas, during a meeting with a hundred Venezuelan religious, President Fidel Castro highlighted the moral and ethical values that inspire thousands of Cuban internationalists to be ready to offer their lives for other peoples, a motive that he compared with the faith of the religious missionaries.

In these days of crisis, of serious worries mixed with tidings of peace and the easing of tensions, a painful, dangerous, and lamentable fact weighs upon the less developed nations and peoples, which slows and impedes their progress and development. We refer to the smothering burden of foreign debt, which paralyses and crushes the peoples of the Third World and particularly of Latin America.

It is right to recall the preoccupation and appeals of Your Holiness that a solution be found to this grave situation. We also must recognize the efforts, actions, and warnings of the Cuban Government, and especially of its President, seen in various international fora, so that the depth, complexity, and danger of this situation may be known, and that a true solution to the problem of the foreign debt may be sought, that it, its abolition and the establishment of a New International Economic Order.

We are aware of the need to join forces in these labors. In this first decade of your Pontificate, Your Holiness has discharged an active role, which has led you to visit numerous countries and to speak with peoples of varying levels of economic development, ethnic make-up, and customs, in a quest for the goals of peace, understanding and well-being among men.

It falls to me to assume my functions at a favorable moment in our relations, demonstrated, among other deeds, by the recent visits of His Excellency, the Most Reverend Florenzo Angelina and His Eminence, Cardinal Roger Etchegaray, who left a positive balance of perspectives made even greater by all the collaboration in our relations. As well as the act that almost simultaneously inaugurates the new Apostolic pro-Nuncio of Your Holiness in Cuba, His Excellency the Most Reverend Faustino Sainz Munoz; these are precedents which, we are sure, will help my in my future work.

I would also like to take advantage of this opportunity to communicate to Your Holiness the warm greetings of our President Dr. Fidel Castro, and his best wishes for your personal health and well-being.

In the tasks that I assume today and in all my future duties, the longings and desires of the Cuban people – a simple, hard-working, proud people, with a sublime and proven sense of universal brotherhood – are and always will be in my heart.

I would like to end my remarks expressing my conviction that I will find in my new responsibility, the support and understanding of Your Holiness and your distinguished co-workers.

Papal Response:

Mr. Ambassador,

I have listened with pleasure to the words of friendship that you have desired to express to me as you present your Letters of Credence which accredit you as the Ambassador Extraordinary and Plenipotentiary of Cuba to the Holy See. In extending to you a warm welcome on the occasion of this solemn act, I also wish to reiterate before you the sincere affection I bear toward all the people of the Cuban nation.

I would also like to respond to the kind of greetings that the President of the State Council and Government of Cuba, Dr. Fidel Castro Ruz, wished to send to me through you, and I ask you to send him my very best wishes for the material and spiritual prosperity of the nation.

You alluded, Mr. Ambassador, to the supreme good of peace and to the work that the Holy See carries out to contribute to the solution of the grave problems that exist in the international community, and to build a more just social order that would make our world a more welcoming and fraternal place, where the values of peaceful coexistence and solidarity would be a constant point of reference. The Church, faithful to the command she received from her divine Founder, commits herself to the noble cause of the service of all peoples without distinction, inspired only by her irrevocable option on behalf of the dignity of man and the protection of his legitimate rights. The spiritual and religious character of her mission allows her to carry out this service free from earthly motivations and particular interests, for, as the Second Vatican Council teaches, "not committed to any one culture or to any political, economic or social system, the Church can be a very close bond between the various communities of men and nations, provided they have trust in the Church and guarantee her true freedom to carry out her mission" (*Gaudium et Spes*, no. 42).

Peace between individuals and peoples is an arduous task in which we must all work together generously. It is not to be attained through intransigence or egocentrism, either national, regional, or of blocs. Rather, it is to be reached through the nurturing of hope, understanding and solidarity, which bind men together as brothers in this world that was created by God so that all of us might share in an equitable way in its goods.

However, there is a cause to worry about the international scene in general, and that of Latin America in particular, due to the great antagonisms and differences that some countries face; countries which geography itself, cultural roots, language and the Christian faith have united in the course of history.

The Holy See – without any other force than the moral authority conferred upon her in her mission in the great causes of mankind – will continue supporting all initiatives undertaken to overcome confrontation and create solid foundations for a more stable and peaceful coexistence.

Among the factors that today work against just international relations, you mentioned, Mr. Ambassador, the serious problem of the foreign debt that hampers many developing peoples. In this regard, the Holy See, with a document from the Pontifical Commission "*Justitia et Pax*," has sought to offer its contribution by laying out the criteria of justice, equity, and solidarity. These inspire initiatives on the regional and international levels in an effort to arrive at acceptable solutions that do not frustrate the legitimate aspirations of so many countries whose development is overdue. In the face of the great challenge that the debt of developing countries represents today, it is becoming necessary to share.

It must not be forgotten that many economic, social, and political problems find their roots in the moral order, to which, in a respectful way, the Church responds through her work of education and evangelization. For this reason, the Church considers as her specific mission "the necessary projection of the Gospel into all areas of human life; in society, in culture, in economic life, and in education" (Address to the Bishops of Cuba, August 26, 1988). Faced with the profound crisis of values that today affects institutions as well as the family, or broad sectors of the population such as youth, the Church, in a spirit of reconciliation and love, offers reasons to hope for the good of the entire human community.

Mr. Ambassador, I want to reiterate the firm desire of the Church in Cuba to collaborate, within her own religious and moral mission, with the authorities and various institutions of your country on behalf of the higher values and the material and spiritual prosperity of the nation. In this regard, we must take pride in the climate of dialogue and greater understanding which has been growing between the ecclesiastical hierarchy and the civil authorities in the past few years. This has been made clear by the recent visits of various ecclesiastical personalities to Cuba, as you yourself have pointed out. I pray that the positive signs that are now becoming evident, such as the admission of a certain number of priests and religious sisters to minister among the Cuban ecclesial communities, may continue to develop and be strengthened into the necessary level of effective freedom that the Church requires to carry out her mission of evangelization.

It is also inspiring to see the respectful dialogue with the culture and the social situation that led to the Cuban National Ecclesial Meeting that took place in February 1986. It is to be hoped that it may facilitate a more active presence of Catholics in public life, contributing to the great task of the common good. In the measure in which they are faithful to the teaching and demands of the Gospel, they will also be sincere defenders of justice, peace, freedom, honor, respect for life, and solidarity with the most needy. The Cuban Catholic, as a citizen and a child of God, cannot refuse to participate in the development of the civil community, nor remain aloof from the social program.

Mr. Ambassador, before finishing our meeting, allow me to assure you of my good will and support, that you may carry out joyfully the noble mission that has been entrusted to you. I also ask that you extend my respectful and cordial greetings to the President, Government, Authorities and people of Cuba, while I invoke the gifts of the Most High on you, your family and co-workers, and all my beloved children of the Cuban nation.

November 23, 1989 (B)
(*OR*, January 22, 1990, p. 4)

H.E. T. Arcand, Ambassador of Canada:

Most Holy Father,

I have the great honor of presenting to Your Holiness the letters accrediting me as Ambassador Extraordinary and Plenipotentiary of Canada to the Holy See as well as the Letters of Recall of my predecessor, His Excellency Mr. Eldon P. Black.

I would like to express, Most Holy Father, the warmest greetings of Her Excellency the Governor General of Canada and her good wishes to Your Holiness. I also bring you the greetings of our Prime Minister, who has an unforgettable memory of the visit which he paid to Your Holiness on January 26, 1987.

Several years ago I had the privilege of serving my country within this same Embassy which is entrusted to my direction today; you can certainly understand my special emotion on finding in these familiar places both the memory of His Holiness Pope Paul VI and the challenge of an important task to accomplish in collaboration with your person.

Your Holiness knows my country through the two pastoral visits which you have made (I had the joy of participating in the preparation for the one at Fort Simpson and was present at it), as well as in your former visits to meet the Polish immigrants, and also through your contact with the many Canadians who come to Rome. Among these I recall especially the Canadian bishops who made their "ad limina" visit last year, of my Minister, Mr. Joe Clark whom you received in private audience at the beginning of the new year, and of so many distinguished visitors or private citizens who attend your Wednesday audiences.

One of my predecessors, Mr. Paul Tremblay, in an article published in 1984 and referring directly to Canada, said, "Would not the recognition of the growing importance of spiritual forces in the life of the nations be, in the long run, the best means for restoring to our foreign policy its humanistic (others say idealistic) character, which gave it its value and explains its dynamism during the period following the war?" Most Holy Father, in that perspective, your messages of peace and brotherhood are heard throughout the whole world. The Canadian Government recognizes their full meaning and appreciates their true value. These messages attest to the very wide agreement of views and are often a very important support for international actions either in the Security Council of the United Nations or in the discussions which we have with the parties involved in the various conflicts which still afflict the world. Your compassion and that of the whole Church for the poor, your appeals for the respect of basic freedoms and for dialogue and tolerance are of primary importance for the international community.

At the beginning of each year Your Holiness issues a message for the celebration of the World Day of Peace. This year you emphasized the importance of respect for minorities in building peace, and you wrote that "the increased awareness which is found today at every level regarding the situation of minority groups constitutes for our own times a hopeful sign for the coming generations and for the aspirations of minority groups themselves. Indeed, in a sense, respect for minorities is to be considered the touchstone of social harmony and the index of the civic maturity attained by a country and its institutions." It makes me proud to say that my compatriots continually seek to improve the lot of the members of the great Canadian mosaic and, in cases of failure, to repair the injustice. Unfortunately I know that some nations seem to have remained deaf to your appeal, and that many States continue to violate their citizens' freedom and dignity, or to oppress a part of their population because of ethnic or religious affiliation. Canadians firmly believe in the defense and promotion of human rights throughout the world and the struggle against racism in all its forms, especially against apartheid. The Canadian Government will continue to seek to extend these principles of basic justice for all wherever it can make itself heard. For this goal it is necessary to increase the dialogue between the countries of the North and South. Furthermore, as our Prime Minister, Mr. Brian Mulroney, emphasized during the third summit of the Francophone countries at Dakar in May, "it is to be feared lest our hopes for peace and our dreams of justice be wrecked in the gap which continues to widen between the two worlds."

Besides our duties toward mankind, we have a responsibility to our earth and our environment. Once again I quote our Prime Minister: "It is essential for economic development to be continued. Nevertheless, the classic model of economic development of growth at the expense of the environment is no longer acceptable. We know its consequences, and they are often disastrous." Most Holy Father, Canada acknowledges that the rich countries which are primarily responsible for the degradation of our environment must work to promote the concept of a lasting development and to draft a body of international agreements relative to the atmosphere. Otherwise, man, who must live in harmony with nature, will cause irreparable damage to the environment, and jeopardize his entire future.

Holy Father, we are at the dawn of a new era in which differences between nations are becoming less important that the dangers which they must face together. It is an era in which we can dream of the reduction of poverty, the protection of our common environment, the reduction of arsenals, and a greater justice of man toward man. It is this positive outlook which spurs me on.

I know that my task will not be easy, but I am confident that it will be facilitated by the great convergence of views between my country and the Holy See on the basic subjects which are dear to us. I am certain that I can count on your support and that of the members of the Curia. I assure you, Most Holy Father, of my full collaboration.

Papal Response:

Mr. Ambassador,

With pleasure I welcome Your Excellency and receive the Letters accrediting you as Ambassador Extraordinary and Plenipotentiary of Canada to the Holy See. I am all the more appreciative of the greetings which you convey to me from Her Excellency the Governor General and from the Prime Minister, because of the treasured memories linking me to your country. I would be obliged if you express my gratitude for the messages which they have asked you to convey.

You mentioned the years which you spent in the past in Rome as a member of Canada's Embassy to the Holy See; I am happy at your return as head of the mission. That experience, to which are added the various high responsibilities you have held in various posts, will make your task easier in the context of the harmonious relations which Canada enjoys with the Apostolic See. You know that you can count on the assistance of my collaborators who will try to facilitate your mission.

Mr. Ambassador, you have just recalled several major concerns which to a large measure respond to the Church's own point of view concerning the positive signs or elements of concern marking the world's current situation. The desire for peace and its strengthening go hand in hand, as is so often clearly expressed, with the desire for the development of a generous spirit of fraternity among the peoples, with the safe-guarding of the spiritual and cultural heritage of every human group, even of minorities, and with the need for greater dialogue and cooperation among the nations of all regions of the world.

The Holy See, in conformity with its specific mission, works for the ever greater acceptance of the conditions of a peace truly founded on the respect of the person in all his dimensions. The exchange and reflection which diplomatic relations permit are greatly useful in contributing not only to increasing the knowledge of current situations, but also to promoting the analysis of the moral principles without which the solutions of the problems would not be just.

Canada's history and traditions have caused it to face the difficulties of a nation forged by men and women coming from different cultural horizons. This centuries-old experience seems to have disposed your country to participate with a spirit of tolerance and generosity in international life. As you have pointed out, it is in joining forces and not in confrontation, that the world must face the considerable problems confronting it. Canada is making a contribution appreciated by its partners, particularly through the expansion of the North-South dialogue so that the common good may eventually have a global dimension. This path certainly involves practical activity on behalf of development, the true freedom of peoples, the protection of the environment, respect for all that is precious in man, beginning with his person and his life. For its part, the Holy See does not fail to participate in these efforts, as you know.

In welcoming you, Mr. Ambassador, I turn in thought to all your compatriots who gave me such a warm welcome five years ago. My wish is that they do not cease strengthening the harmony and peaceful coexistence which I was able to witness. Undoubtedly, the considerable changes which have occurred during recent decades still cause concern for the future. I know particularly that the members of the Catholic Church are very much aware of it, and that they seek to assume their share of the concerns of the whole of Canadian society. They cannot forget the role which the Church's first apostles played in your country, their example of holiness, their sense of charity practiced with effectiveness and delicacy, and their skill as educators, to mention only a few of their characteristics. They want to continue to serve the nation in a spirit of fraternity under the forms which have evolved, and in harmony with their compatriots of other Christian confessions.

Your Excellency, through you I want to express my warmest best wishes to all of Canada, and the assurance of my vivid memory of my visits to that beautiful country. Please convey my respectful greetings to Her Excellency the Governor General and to the Prime Minister.

I express my best wishes for the fulfillment of your mission to the Holy See, and I assure you once again, also in the name of my collaborators, that you are welcome here.

December 21, 1990
(*OR*, January 7, 1991, p. 4)

H.E. F. X. Hulas, Ambassador of the Czech and Slovak Federative Republic:

Most Holy Father,

Accredited by Mr. Vaclav Havel, President of the Czech and Slovak Federative Republic, a diplomatic representative once again presents himself before the Head of the Catholic Church, in my person, after a gap of more than 40 years, to represent our country to the Holy See, from the time of the presentation of the Letters of Credence.

The Ambassador is not the only new thing, an entirely new period is opening up on the level of relations between my country and the universal Church. This is an important event in the history of Czechoslovakia and the Vatican, an event which evokes emotions of joy but, at the same time, invites us to serious reflection. For some time I have thought about this moment and dreamed about how to express its importance. In the end, all my reflections crystallized in a single main idea which I submitted to the President of the Republic for his consideration. A writer and philosopher, Vaclav Havel thought my idea was right and good, he let me know that it was close to what he himself felt, and allowed me to use it to describe the moment which marks the renewal of diplomatic relations between the Holy See and the Czech and Slovak Federative Republic.

What is this idea? It seems that the entire importance of this present historic act is summed up in the specific title which was used at the beginning of my address. Most Holy Father. How many times has the Pope been designated such? On the other hand, how many of the people who have addressed the Pope as such have really thought about the meaning of these three words? Often it was only a matter of etiquette, politeness, protocol. . . . Obviously these aspects cannot be lacking when it is a question of an official meeting inaugurating diplomatic relations between two states. However, in the present case, we want to emphasize the true and original meaning of the noun which designates the Head of the Catholic Church. Here and now, the Pope is, indeed, first of all a father welcoming his lost and refound child. I do not need to explain that the Ambassador cannot identify with the person in the Scripture, with the prodigal son returning to the father's open arms, it is rather the people – Czechs and Slovaks together. Like every comparison, mine can only fit the broad outlines of the situation. But, however beautiful and moving a symbol of the rebirth of friendship between the Holy See and our Republic this audience may be, it is only a pale reflection of the scene from St. Luke's Gospel.

The ideal relationship between the Father and the Son exists only within the Blessed Trinity. Here below, in a world darkened by the results of original sin, we can only approach the ideal to a greater or lesser degree, without however ever attaining or grasping it. Besides, history teaches us that even the most just and pious princes had, often at the price of great difficulties, to seek to maintain a delicate balance between the spiritual and secular realms. It would be dangerous and misleading to suppose that in the future there would be no more problems between the Vatican and Czechoslovakia. Nonetheless, I dare to hope that they will not be many, and I firmly believe that we will find solutions which are acceptable to both parties.

The events of the past year can, indeed, presage that all the exchanges of view between the two States can take place in a spirit of friendship. The first one to be mentioned, of course, is the memorable visit by which Your Holiness designed to honor my country during the month of April. However, this event must not be considered the only positive fact to have marked the spiritual climate of my country.

All that seemed impossible just 15 months ago has already become commonplace. My country has its complete number of bishops, the religious orders of monks and nuns exercising their vocation. In total freedom, we witness the publication – with no constraints – of Catholic books and periodicals; Catholic schools are reopening and the theological faculties are reintegrated with their rights within the unions of the universities from which they were ousted some time ago by the communists; the spiritual culture promoted by Christian academies and other associations is gaining ground.

Can the father be content with his spiritual children? Since President Havel told me that from his two meetings with the Pope he has the impression of true father – son meetings, it allowed me to suppose that by and through the person of the Head of our Republic, the fatherly love of John Paul II reaches out to and embraces all of the two nations, Czech and Slovak.

The beginning of the new relations between the Holy See and the Czech and Slovak Federative Republic can also be expressed in the symbol of the relationship of love between a father and child. That holds true even for the dull and ordinary period which will follow the brilliance of these solemn moments; may this symbol enlighten the path which, of necessity, will not always be easy. The problems which totalitarianism accumulated for my country are many and serious. It will probably be difficult to find unanimity in resolving them. However, the goodwill shown by both sides will overcome all the difficulties, this is the wish of those who have sent me, and mine as well.

Unworthy and weak as I am, in all humility and fully aware of the situation, I accept the office of Ambassador in order to participate in this noble task; that of fostering good and friendly relations between the Holy See and the homeland of the Czechs and Slovaks. May Almighty God guide my steps.

Most Holy Father, I have the honor of presenting to you my Letters of Credence.

Papal Response:

Mister Ambassador,

1. Our meeting for the presentation of the Letters by which you are accredited to the Holy See by His Excellency Mr. Vaclav Havel, President of the Czech and Slovak Federative Republic, is an event which I welcome with joy. You are being received at this time when relations between your country and the Apostolic See, which had been interrupted for a long time, are being restored. Your country's return to freedom and democracy has happily permitted the re-establishment of the ancient bonds between the peoples of Bohemia and Slovakia and the center of the Catholic Church.

You have delicately emphasized, Your Excellency, the specific nature of these bonds, given the nature of the mission of the Holy See, which desires to play its role in the international community in complete fidelity to the spirit of the Gospel, in love for people who are open to the transcendent dimension of their destiny.

2. You have mentioned the significance of the pastoral visit which I had the honor to make to your country in April last year. Indeed, the reception which I received in Prague, Velehrad and Bratislava allowed me to appreciate the great fidelity of these peoples to Christianity, their desire to express their faith without obstacles, and to express clearly their belonging to the great community of believers. Rest assured that in my heart's memory the recollection of that visit to your homeland is ever alive, and with great emotion I recall the meetings, the moments of intense communication which I had with the bishops, the priests and religious, the Catholic faithful and the entire population.

3. Now the Czech and Slovak Federative Republic is undertaking the renewal and strengthening of its institutions; it is working for the improvement in the standard of living of its citizens. Catholics are resolved to do their part in the immense task which must be directed to the common good. In that which concerns her own religious mission, the Church wants to have the room that she needs to offer the people who count on her the service which it is in her vocation to fulfill. She does not ask for privileges, she wants to develop freely her activities, convinced that her place in society is not only based on an inheritance from the past, but also on an inspiration that is still alive in the hearts of our contemporaries.

Thus a trusting dialogue between the Church communities and the government authorities will allow the resolution of the problems which remain after the difficulties which have marked recent decades. Well-integrated into society, these communities need to have adequate means for their mission. In this regard, it is desirable that we may soon see the resolution of Church property. It is not only a question of the Church's institutions receiving their legitimate patrimony, it is a question of their being able to develop their own life, to place themselves at the service of others, particularly through educational and charitable activity.

4. In relations with the States, the Holy See seeks in all circumstances to support the good of the person, the person in all his or her dimensions, the person who is free to lead his or her life according to the principles dictated by conscience and faith. Therefore, in the concert of human rights which the contemporary world is striving to recognize and defend, religious freedom has a position at the forefront. In the name of this basic freedom, the Church respects the convictions of persons who do not share her faith and expects equal respect for them for the various aspects of her activity, including their public manifestation. It is thus that the Church asks to be able to give her members a spiritual and moral formation consistent with their faith, to train her clergy and designate her bishops, to organize religious education among children and young people in collaboration with their families, to find expression in the mass media and to have the publications which she deems useful.

I have no doubt, Mister Ambassador, that the government which you represent here is ready to grant the Church the concrete conditions for the free exercise of her mission in the various fields which I just mentioned. I was grateful to hear you give the assurance that, on both parts, goodwill will be able to resolve whatever difficulties may still exist.

5. As a pilgrim to Velehrad on April 22, I had the joy of recalling in that great place

the work done on behalf of the Slav people by the two great apostles: Cyril and Methodius. They are beacons for the Church. On the European continent of which, together with St. Benedict, they are the patrons, we want to follow their example to be of service to the whole of society. I was pleased to be able to announce there, at the tomb of St. Methodius, the convocation of an important assembly of bishops whose task it will be to give new impetus to the Church's mission in Europe, to her contribution to fraternity and solidarity among the millions of men and women who aspire to develop today the Christian values long rooted in their soul.

Your homeland has a choice place at the center of this continent. I am sure that it will have a significant part to play in the construction of a community of nations which must protect the dignity and well-being of all its members and work for peace in the whole world.

6. Mister Ambassador, this audience is taking place just a few days before Christmas. At this time my best wishes for your fellow citizens and their leaders are even more ardent. I ask you to assure His Excellency Mr. Vaclav Havel and the government authorities, as well as all your fellow citizens, of the most amicable sentiments which Peter's Successor has for them.

In all that concerns you, Mister Ambassador, with all my heart I wish you success in your mission and I assure you that you will always find an understanding welcome here. My collaborators are all disposed to listen to you and to facilitate your task.

With fervor I invoke for your country the intercession of the great saints who have marked its history, and I implore God's blessing for its happiness and prosperity.

November 28, 1992
(*OR*, December 9, 1992, p. 12)

Papal Response to H.E. Gopal P. Sharma, Ambassador to the Kingdom of Nepal:

Mr. Ambassador,

I am pleased to accept the Letters of Credence appointing you Ambassador Extraordinary and Plenipotentiary of the Kingdom of Nepal to the Holy See. It is almost 10 years since Nepal and the Holy See agreed to the exchange of representatives, and shortly afterwards I met here in the Vatican His Majesty King Birendra Bir Bikram Shah Dev. Since that time the international order has undergone momentous changes which have had a profound impact not only on the conduct of diplomacy but on the very destinies of whole nations and peoples. In welcoming you to the Vatican today, I express my hope that in this altered world climate – with so many opportunities for advancing the cause of justice and solidarity – your service as your country's Ambassador will help to foster relations between Nepal and the Holy See so that, through mutual understanding, no chance to strengthen peace will be lost.

The establishment of a Catholic community in Nepal is quite recent, and it is small in numbers. Nevertheless, from the very beginning its members have sought to serve the nation by works of solidarity and development, especially in the fields of education and social assistance. In building up the society of which they form an integral part and to which they are lovingly devoted, the Catholics in your country seek to work in harmony and cooperation with the followers of all religious traditions and with all people of good will.

Your affirmation that political and economic choices must always be made in the light of the principle that man has both a spiritual and a material dimension clearly reflects the age-old traditions and values of the people of your country. Shaped over the centuries by a venerable wisdom about the meaning of man's existence and his relationship to the divine, Nepalese culture bespeaks an attentiveness to man's transcendent destiny. As you have stated, without a concern for man's spiritual good, efforts at development are counter-productive. On this point the Catholic Church has expressed herself in affirming the subordination of *having* to *being*; "to 'have' objects and goods does not in itself perfect the human subject, unless it contributes to the maturing and enrichment of the subject's 'being,' that is to say unless it contributes to the realization of the human vocation as such" (Encyclical Letter *Sollicitudo Rei Socialis*, no. 28). Technological advances which are not based upon sound ethical principles or which are not ordered to man's true happiness in fact worsen his condition, a point to which the history of this century gives eloquent testimony in all too many cases.

In relations with States and in the international forum the Holy See seeks to be a persevering voice in support of an integral vision of the human person. In accordance with its specific competence, the Holy See desires to foster all that unites individuals and societies and all that works for their greater good. It promotes effective cooperation among those dedicated to building a world marked by justice and peace. As a partner in the search for the full development of peoples, the Holy See feels particularly obliged to speak out clearly in defense of the whole range of human rights, especially the right to religious liberty. This right is a fundamental requirement of the dignity of every person and in effect it is the cornerstone of the entire structure of human rights. Even when circumstances cause the civil authority to extend special legal recognition to one particular religious body, the State has a duty to ensure that for all citizens, and also for resident foreigners, the right to freedom of conscience is legally recognized and effectively protected (cf. *Message for the 1988 World Day of Peace*, n. 1). As a recognition of the inviolability of man's conscience, respect for religious freedom must be considered an irreplaceable factor of individual and social good and an essential element for peaceful human coexistence.

Mr. Ambassador, I am grateful for the warm greetings you have brought from your Sovereign, and I ask you kindly to convey to him and to Her Majesty the Queen my personal best wishes. I also ask you to convey my greetings to the Prime Minister. I assure you that you will receive the full cooperation of the Holy See in your efforts to discharge successfully your responsibilities. I pray to Almighty God for the prosperity and well-being of the people of Nepal.

May 7, 1993
(*OR*, May 19, 1993, p. 10)

H.E. Edward Tsu-yu Wu, Ambassador of China:

Your Holiness,

It is an honor beyond words for me to come to Vatican City to present to Your Holiness the Letters of Credence by which His Excellency President Lee Teng-hui accredits me as Ambassador Extraordinary and Plenipotentiary of the Republic of China to the Holy See. At the same time, I present to Your Holiness the Letter of Recall for the completion of my distinguished predecessor, Ambassador Hoang Sieou-je.

In all humility, I am fully aware of the importance of my mission, and of my unworthiness of it. As a diplomat representing my country, I cannot conceive of a mission that would bring me greater honor, for I stand as a humble instrument in helping to bring closer together the greatest spiritual force of humanity and an Asian people whose roots reach back to remote antiquity.

Personally, I find this mission particularly providential, for, 46 years ago, my late father, John C.H. Wu, traveled a similar road to this "mountain of myrrh and hill of frankincense" and stood before His Holiness Pope Pius XII, in what my father called his "diplomacy of love." Thus this occasion is, for me, truly a divine wish fulfilled, for the thrill and honor I feel this day is no less than that of my father.

The Holy See has over long decades stood steadfast in her friendship toward the Republic of China. This sincere and warm message of love, peace and support has always been with us; Your Holiness, for, as a civilization established over many centuries on the foundations of Confucianism, we too share with the Roman Catholic Church the implicit belief that it is spirit and right, not matter and might, that ultimately matter in both persons and nations.

Your Holiness, as emissary of the Republic of China, I am here not only to represent my country, but to serve as a disciple at the foot of Christ, to be always mindful that the ongoing humanization process and the fulfillment of Confucianism in China and among the Chinese are linked irrevocably with an ever increasing understanding of the Gospel message and, finally, that we all need one another for mutual fulfillment.

Today I come to the Holy See in the same spirit of openness as that of Matteo Ricci and his Jesuits sojourning with great expectations in China in the 16th and 17th centuries. These men of God were also great Sinologists who dedicated their lives to the understanding of Chinese culture through the illumination of their faith; moreover, they served to conjugate the spirit of Jesus and the moral dictates of the Chinese sages into the minds of the common people of the world, leaving a most valuable legacy.

In a similar fashion, I feel that as an emissary learning from her sacred springs, part of my mission will be to help update and to renew the spirit of Catholicism in my country so that our basically humanistic tradition will, perhaps, be able to find its true meaning in the very bosom of the Holy Spirit itself.

When I was at home recently, I met with a good many local and foreign missionary priests and sisters as well as Catholic lay people. Their continuous enthusiasm for the work and future of the Church clearly indicates the ever growing vitality and spiritual maturity of the Catholic Church in my country and the unsung labor of the religious in general. They all wish to show their affection and love to Your Holiness through their daily prayers.

I have deemed myself as a lay apostle since my wife, Elizabeth, and I were joined in holy matrimony on the holy ground of Saint Peter's Basilica on April 30, 1947, the day of the 400th anniversary of Saint Catherine of Siena. It was on that particular occasion that I committed myself to becoming an apostle-diplomat. Since then, I have been on a 44–year diplomatic journey covering six continents. Wherever there were Papal Nuncios or important religious events, I have always been an enthusiastic participant. Ever since then, I have believed that the ecumenical endeavors of the Church will bring the highest possible benefits to mankind in our search for human dignity and world peace.

The Holy See has repeatedly sent out messages to every corner of the world to promote justice and peace, ceaselessly emphasizing that peace can only be achieved on the basis of love. During Your Holiness' apostolic visits to foreign lands, great multitudes, irrespective of religious or ethnic differences, have been brought together to share the paternal love of Your Holiness. Being an essentially peace-loving people, the Chinese naturally cherish the lofty ideals of the Roman Catholic Church and find a resounding echo of these ideals deep in their hearts. Your Holiness has done much to help us confirm that traditional Chinese philosophy of life which teaches that "all men are brothers."

The whole world is undergoing a time of intense change, and my country is no exception. At the present time, the Republic of China is in the midst of a far-reaching reconstruction based on her own democratic ideals of "liberty, democracy and spiritual and material prosperity." We are certain that before long a lasting harmony based on the above principles will be realized and that these principles will serve as fundamental guidelines for a new, united and vigorous China.

Finally, I wish to assure Your Holiness, that I shall, with profound humbleness, joy and hope, and in the spirit of the respective "little flowers" of Saints Francis and Therese, gratefully embark upon this solemn mission, my own "diplomacy of love." Assisted by the grace of God, I will do my utmost to strengthen the good relations between the Holy See and my country. I will venture in my path with the support of moral simplicity and the nourishment of mysticism. The star of the new Catechism will illuminate my way toward a new era of renaissance and great success. I am confident that the benevolence of Your Holiness will certainly encourage and help me in the accomplishment of my high mission.

In the atmosphere of warmest cordiality, H.E. Lee Teng-hui, President of the Republic of China, being himself an ardent Christian and the promoter of religious and moral renewal in our country, has charged me to convey to Your Holiness the best of good wishes for a long and prosperous reign.

May Our Lady of Czestochowa, the Queen of Poland, protect Your Holiness and give us strength to promote world peace and understanding among the peoples of good will.

Papal Response:

Mr. Ambassador,

I am pleased to welcome you today to the Vatican as the newly appointed

Ambassador Extraordinary and Plenipotentiary of the Republic of China. In accepting your Letters of Credence, I thank you for the greetings and good wishes which you have conveyed on behalf of His Excellency President Lee Teng-hui, and I ask you kindly to assure him of my goodwill and of my prayers for his well-being and the happiness of all his fellow-citizens. I am happy for you personally, that you find special satisfaction in following the footsteps of your own father who at one time was his country's representative to my predecessor Pope Pius XII.

The memory of your father takes us back to a very difficult period of your people's history and to the moment when the Holy See's diplomatic representative was obliged to leave a continental China. After a brief interlude in Hong Kong, the Holy See's diplomatic mission was welcomed in Taiwan, and a relationship was established, the deepest meaning of which is to be found in the Holy See's desire to continue to maintain close and friendly relations with the great and noble Chinese family. The Church deeply appreciates the respect for freedom of religion which the Republic of China has upheld and fostered from the beginning in relation to all its citizens, and she is grateful that as a result she has been able to fulfill her spiritual and humanitarian mission without interference or discrimination, at the service of individuals and of the country as a whole.

As the Republic of China developed into a complex and highly productive society, the Catholic community too extended its efforts in the fields of education, health care and other related social services. In pursuing her spiritual goals, the Church is always ready to cooperate in as many ways as possible in assuring the common good. As the Second Vatican Council teaches, the Church and the political community serve the personal and social vocations of the same human beings, and "this service can be more effectively rendered for the good of all, if each works better for wholesome mutual cooperation" (*Gaudium et Spes*, no. 76). The possible areas of cooperation extend as far as the needs of the members of the human family itself.

At the beginning of the year, in greeting the representatives of over 140 countries having diplomatic relations with the Holy See, I spoke of two sorts of evil which still hold the human family in their grip and condemn millions of human beings to an existence which harms and jeopardizes their very dignity as men and women, *war and poverty*. Despite the monumental changes which have come about on the international level in the last five years, armed conflict, with its trail of death and destruction, has not disappeared from the world's horizon. Indeed, new and terrible instances of bloody conflict and threats of violent strife are before the eyes of everyone. The Holy See cannot but hope that the leaders of nations will do everything possible to meet this challenge and definitively *"win the war" of peace* by establishing effective and just structures of harmonious coexistence and cooperation.

And what of poverty? Hundreds of millions of human beings are imprisoned in situations of material and moral poverty which constitute a serious attack on the value of life and strike at the heart of the peaceful development of society. To be poor is to suffer some form of exclusion from the banquet of life. There are countless ways in which this happens: through hunger, illness, homelessness, unemployment, illiteracy, to mention only a few. In my Message for the World Day of Peace this year, I emphasized the threat to peace and social stability posed by poverty. The situation is all the more tragic insofar as the world does not possess the technological and organizational capabilities to change this situation and to improve conditions of life.

The question therefore which stands before the international community and before the public authorities, especially in the developed world, is not one of resources alone. It is a question of human solidarity, a question of the vision which underlies political policies and programs at every level. It is *ultimately a question of moral responsibility*.

Through its presence in the international community, the Holy See seeks to keep before public opinion the ethical and moral dimensions of public life: the demands of justice, the dignity of the individual, the inviolability of human rights, the nature of the family as the fundamental cell of society, the universal destination of the world's goods, the duties of States and other corporate bodies to serve the integral well-being of people. In this regard I wish to recall what I said at the meeting with the Diplomatic Corps to which I have already referred: "The Catholic Church, present in every nation of the earth, and the Holy See, a member of the international community, in no way wish to impose judgments or precepts, but merely to give the witness of their concept of man and history, which they know comes from a divine Revelation. Society cannot afford to forgo this original contribution without becoming the poorer for it and without violating the freedom of thought and expression of a large part of its citizens" (*Speech to Diplomatic Corps*, January 16. 1993, no. 7).

It is here, Mr. Ambassador, that your reference to the achievements of traditional Chinese philosophy and culture is particularly appropriate. The encounter between the Chinese humanism and Catholicism has given rise to a very profound and fruitful exchange, not least in the life and work of Matteo Ricci whom you mentioned, but in a continuing way in the Catholic community in your own country and elsewhere. It is my earnest hope that this cultural and moral dialogue will advance at the deepest level, at the level of the vital questions facing all individuals and societies: the meaning of life and the path which leads to fulfilling that meaning. The Church intends to be a loyal partner in such a dialogue, with no pretence or privilege or exclusiveness, aiming only at the truth and acting only out of genuine love for the human family.

Mr. Ambassador, your mission as representative of your country to the Holy See will reflect the special nature of the diplomacy involved, not questions of power or commercial interest, but the promotion of man's unique dignity and vocation, and the fostering of justice and peace in international relations. I assure you of the cooperation of the various departments of the Holy See in the exercise of your lofty duties, I pray that you will be happy here, and that you and your family will have many reasons for joy and satisfaction. Upon you and your fellow citizens I invoke an abundance of divine blessings.

March 10, 1994 (A)
(*OR*, March 23, 1994, p. 4)

Papal Response to H.E. Bruno Bottai, Ambassador of Italy:

Mr. Ambassador,

In accepting the Letters of Credence with which you are inaugurating your mission as Ambassador Extraordinary and Plenipotentiary of the Italian Republic to the Holy See, I address my cordial wishes to the Head of State, Mr. Oscar Luigi Scalfaro, as well as to the entire people of Italy, whose sentiments of loyalty and sincere devotion you have so eloquently interpreted.

Constant attention to and pre-eminent pastoral concern for the universal Church and the religious needs of peoples do not prevent me from devoting equal consideration to the destiny and to the human and spiritual problems of Italy, "which from the beginning of my Pontificate has shown me such great goodwill, . . . that I feel able to speak of Italy as my second homeland" (Letter to the Italian Episcopate, January 6, 1994; *L'Osservatore Romano* English edition, January 19. 1994, p. 5).

For a considerable number of years now, after bitter tensions and painful interruptions, relations between the Holy See and Italy have found a fortunate and vital balance in the Lateran Pacts, confirmed by the Revision Agreement in 1984, whose 10th anniversary occurs this year. The time that has passed since this event makes it possible to declare that the greatest significance of the Agreement is precisely the "reciprocal collaboration for the promotion of man and the good of the county" to which in Art. I the State and the Church are solemnly and sincerely bound.

As is known, some important aspects of the implementation phase of the Agreement have yet to be completed, such as safeguarding the great heritage of the Church's cultural property in Italy. Its preservation and appreciation are intended for the good of the individual as a whole, as well as for the civil and cultural development of society. No less can one observe how this "healthy co-operation" (*Gaudium et Spes*, no. 76) has been positively employed in various sectors precisely by virtue of the common, though distinct, purpose of the Church and the political community in serving mankind.

Aware that all legal regulations, even those of conventional origin, are not made to halt the ceaseless development of human society but to guide it and accompany it in the march of history toward objectives and goals that are identified from time to time, it is easy to imagine that this dedication to the human cause can and must be broadened to include other areas, even if these are not directly addressed by the above-mentioned Agreements.

I would like to refer to the just and legitimate expectations – recalled over the past few days – entertained by the Italian ecclesial community with respect to the future of Catholic schools, which serve all civil society, especially its weakest and most alienated members. The search for satisfactory and balanced solutions in this regard would, on the one hand, recognize the value of a necessary dimension of the Church's evangelizing mission, and on the other, would permit the implementation of a freer and fuller contribution by Christian families to the construction and defense of the nation's unique cultural, moral and social heritage. It must be constantly kept in mind that "man's horizons are not bounded only by the temporal order; living on the level of human history he preserves the integrity of his eternal destiny" (*Gaudium et Spes*, no. 76).

Italy has much to offer Europe

Mr. Ambassador, in your address you remembered the Holy See's enduring effort to encourage peace, and with courteous and appreciative words you stressed how the Successor of Peter continues to raise his voice in favor of overcoming new and old antagonisms, painful and inhuman wounds, exasperated nationalisms and bloody conflicts like those destroying Bosnia, convinced that the Church's evangelizing mission in also a commitment to the proclamation and promotion of human dignity and the rights of peoples.

I thank you for your words: the urgency of this mission is actually confirmed if one looks at the "altered geopolitical map of Europe . . . in constant evolution" that predicts "great challenges and new scenarios for the years ahead . . . " (Letter to the Italian Episcopate, no. 2). Indeed, if the recent disturbances in Central and Eastern Europe have shown the absurdity of the claims of atheistic and totalitarian regimes to uproot man's faith and his freedom and have enabled entire nations to reappropriate their own history, they have also caused serious tensions, and divisions to emerge. To be healed, the help of the whole European continent is needed.

In this context, I renew my conviction that Italy as a nation has "a great deal to offer Europe as a whole" (ibid., no. 4) in fostering unity and solidarity throughout the continent, a unity made more fruitful by the light and power of the Gospel.

A contribution to be measured, of course, in practical and concrete initiatives to promote co-operation and integration between the East and the West of Europe; but, even before that, it is destined to be put at the service of all, in defense of the "religious and cultural heritage linked to Rome by the Apostles Peter and Paul"; a heritage, which, as is known, some recent orientations of European institutions risk seriously jeopardizing, reducing it to a purely economic and secular dimension (cf. ibid., no. 4).

I am referring to some instances which – as I recalled in my recent "Letter to Families" – appear more directly to threaten the basic rights of the family, "seminarium rei publicae," as it was already considered in ancient Rome, itself the "natural society based on marriage" (art. 29 of the *Italian Constitution*).

I cannot but hope that remembering its incomparable moral and civil heritage and aware of the extent to which the family can foster serene social coexistence, the Italian nation may always prove to be the jealous custodian of the dignity and rights of this basic institution of natural law. In the present, somewhat unfavorable social and cultural context, the family urgently needs to be supported by an organic policy that is able to satisfy its various economic, juridical and social needs, and is committed to safeguarding the sacredness of the life from conception to its natural decline.

Mr. Ambassador, in my recent message to the Italian Episcopate, prompted only by the love that I feel for the Italian nation, I was able to reflect on the delicate moment of history that the whole country is experiencing, and I expressed my hope that Italy will be able to overcome it successfully, strengthening its own spiritual and cultural identity in harmony and solidarity. In renewing these wishes, I am now pleased to assure you of the commitment with which both the Italian Bishops and all the members of the ecclesial community share in the human and civil events of the beloved Italian nation. In particular, then, Catholic citizens will not fail to continue to make their constructive contribution in the forefront of generous dedication to serving the common good.

Mr. Ambassador, the matters I have just now sketched allow a glimpse of the paths on which further, worthwhile collaboration between the Holy See and Italy will be able to proceed on behalf of peace among the peoples and of the strenuous defense of the basic rights of the human person. I likewise trust that with God's help, this harmony of objectives may be reinforced by successful results, also through the activities that you are preparing to undertake.

As I assure you of my high esteem, I offer my most fervent wishes for the success of your mission and impart my Apostolic Blessing to you with all my heart, Mr. Ambassador, gladly extending it to your co-workers, to their respective families and to all the beloved Italian people.

December 19, 1994 (B)
(*OR*, January 4, 1995, p. 9)

Papal Response to H.E. Julio C.T. Ayala, Ambassador of Colombia:

Mr. Ambassador,

I am very pleased today to receive the Letters of Credence you have presented to me after being appointed Ambassador Extraordinary and Plenipotentiary of the Republic of Colombia to the Holy See. As I offer you a cordial welcome, I would also like to express my gratitude to you for your courteous words which confirm the noble sentiments of closeness and loyalty to the Chair of Peter, present in the hearts of many citizens of the Colombian nation. I am likewise particularly grateful to you for the respectful greetings you bring me from Dr. Ernesto Samper Pizano, President of the Republic, to whom I return my very best wishes and the assurance of my prayers for the prosperity and spiritual well-being of all the children of this beloved country.

Your presence here on this solemn occasion vividly reminds me of the unforgettable celebrations at which I had the joy to preside during my Pastoral Visit in 1986. On that memorable occasion, I was able to observe how the principles and values which emanate from the Gospel have penetrated Colombia's history and culture, for the great and noble-hearted Colombians have always shown openness to the Church's mission.

Peace, as Your Excellency has said, is your people's great aspiration at this time when social coexistence is sometimes disrupted by an almost endemic violence and by the drug trade, which is relentlessly claiming so many lives. The Government which you represent has shown its intention to encourage an *alternative model of development*. For this reason, it will be necessary to make the various national policies coincide with ethical principles; moreover, development is not only the result of planning and economic policy, but also the fruit of the will and the joint effort to serve the common good. These conditions, indispensable if this objective is to be reached, are based on an education that fosters respect for the life and dignity of the human person, just as certain political directives assure social coexistence, the right to work and above all, promote justice and peace, values postulated in the Preamble to the new Colombian Constitution. In this way, citizens can be asked to make their own the indisputable values such as truth, freedom, mutual understanding and solidarity.

In this regard, I am pleased to recall that this aspiration reaches its fulfillment when God is placed at the center of life and human history and when culture deriving from this is rooted in the "moral sense, which is in turn rooted and fulfilled in the religious sense" (*Veritatis Splendor*, no. 98).

A comprehensive view of man leads to reaffirming the irreplaceable role which must be played by *the family*, whose deep identity must be safeguarded and accepted as a "firmly grounded social reality" and "in a way entirely its own, a *sovereign society* . . ." (*Letters to Families*, no. 17). In fact, the family unit should be at the service of a fully human life and should be the basis of social harmony. This year, which the Church has celebrated as the Year of the Family, I have recalled that "no human society can run the risk of permissiveness in fundamental issues regarding the nature of marriage and the family! Such moral permissiveness cannot fail to damage the authentic requirements of peace and communion among people. It is thus quite understandable why the Church vigorously defends the identity of the family and encourages responsible individuals and institutions, especially political leaders and international organizations, not to yield to the temptation of a superficial and false modernity" (ibid., no. 17).

In this sense, the Church fulfills her mission in the areas which belong to her, enlightening with spiritual and moral principles the environments which contribute to the common good. By preaching the Word of God and by her teaching in the social context, she is willing to continue to collaborate with the various public institutions, so that your nation's citizens may find satisfactory responses to their needs of the present time.

To achieve this mutual collaboration, a Concordat was negotiated between the Holy See and your country. I have been concerned to observe that there has been widespread criticism of the value of the agreed norms, but your Government's determination, shared by the Holy See, to find a satisfactory solution to the problems which have emerged in this context, especially over the past few years, has always given cause for hope. There is no doubt the desirability of having a legal framework that defines the exercise of religious freedom, a right of individuals, which "must also be accorded to men when they act in community" (*Dignitatis Humanae*, no. 4). In addition, the State and the Church are thus offered a means to collaborate for the common good.

The Church neither seeks nor demands privileges. She only asks that the necessary conditions which ensure individuals their natural rights be recognized, so that she may fulfill her role and enable individuals and peoples to exercise the inalienable right to freedom, especially religious freedom, and to seek the truth, in accordance with the dictates of each one's conscience. Each State for its part, must set a high ethical standard as a reference to guide its policy both for the genuine development of the national community and in international relations. This is why the Holy See deems it mutually beneficial to reinforce and to regulate its relations with States.

Mr. Ambassador, your presence and your words demonstrate the respect for and appreciation of the Church's specific mission in this nation which, amidst the many complex challenges, teaches and works under the wise and prudent guidance of her Pastors, so that the moral values and Christian concept of life may be an inspiration to all those who in one way or another, are doing their utmost to safeguard the dignity and cause of man, who is "the primary and fundamental way for the Church" (*Redemptor Hominis*, no. 14).

At the time you are entering the high office which has been assigned to you, I would like to offer you my best wishes for the happy and successful outcome of your mission to this Apostolic See which desires to preserve and strengthen its good relations with Colombia. As I ask you to convey to the President of the Republic, your Government, the authorities and the beloved Colombian people, my sentiments and hopes, I assure you of my prayers to the Almighty that through the intercession of Our Lady of Chiquinquira, his gifts may always accompany you and your distinguished family, your colleagues, and the Government leaders and citizens of your noble country, which I remember with special affection.

February 19, 1996
(*OR*, March 6, 1996, p. 4)

Papal Response to H.E. A. d'Oliveira Pinto da Franca, Ambassador of Portugal:

Mr. Ambassador,

As I receive the Letters accrediting you as Ambassador Extraordinary and Plenipotentiary of Portugal to the Holy See, I welcome you with great pleasure and offer you my best wishes for the fruitful and successful outcome of your mission.

On this occasion, I offer a grateful and deferential greeting to the President of the Republic, Dr. Mario Soares, for appointing Your Excellency and for his kind greetings which you convey at this time of the "changing of the guard" in this high post. It coincides with his retirement from government service, during which on several occasions I was the object of his attention and for which I am grateful. I pray to God to bless him and his family with complete happiness. I remember that during my second visit to Portugal he kindly accompanied me to the Shrine of Fatima. I went there with the desire once again to show my filial gratitude to Our Lady, for the motherly care with which she watches over men's destiny and progress.

I was also accompanied by the beloved Portuguese people, with the expressive eloquence of their faith and trust in the Virgin Mary. Your Excellency wished to recall their past and present, marked by sentiments of loyal unity and sincere devotion to the Successor of Peter, through his respectful address. Thank you! At this time, may I address a fraternal greeting to all the Catholic faithful in Portugal, as well as to their dedicated Pastors.

Your Excellency, I see that in assuming your new duties, you are inspired by the idea of serving the "age-old and fruitful relations" which exist between Portugal and the Holy See, guided by the love of peace and justice which directs your country's international activity. It is not necessary for me to tell you that in this you can rely on my co-workers' full understanding and support.

Indeed, all those who work sincerely for the integral development of human society will find in the Catholic Church a co-worker who professes not only real respect for the dignity of each one of the world's nations and for their cultural wealth but who even more so never tires of recalling, for their own good, that the different cultures can and must complement each other within the unity of the great human family.

I am grateful to you, Mr. Ambassador, for the importance you gave in your address to the Catholic Church's constant commitment to furthering peace and understanding everywhere, defending constructive dialogue between the interested parties as the only way to overcome differences and conflicts. To promote dialogue and solidarity between individuals and peoples is a duty of all nations and one of the most urgent moral needs of our time. By its own presence in the international community, the Holy See seeks to encourage and support this dialogue, especially with regard to the spiritual and ethical values which are the essential basis of a just society and of a true and lasting peace.

These are the principles which your country shares. They have served in various situations of which the most recent concerns East Timor, whose inhabitants "are still waiting for proposals capable of allowing the realization of their legitimate aspirations to see their special cultural and religious identity recognized" (*Address to the*

Diplomatic Corps, January 13, 1996, no. 5; *L'Osservatore Romano* English edition, January 17, 1996, p. 2). I implore all those who have at heart or who are involved in the Timor problem, to do [their] part to facilitate and support the dialogue which has been started. I am convinced that Portugal will be able to invest the best – I am quoting – of its "capacity for dialogue and respect for the identity of others, possible only with the strength of a sound humility," which its history has demanded and taught. I appeal to the courage of the friends and servants of peace!

Lastly, Mr. Ambassador, I would like to mention the emotion you feel at arriving in Rome on the threshold of the Great Jubilee of the Year 2000, which must be – as I hope and pray insistently – an event of grace and salvation for the Church and for the world. It will demand from both and from others, that they seriously "[meet] the challenge of secularism," in order to broach "the vast subject of the crisis of civilization, which has become apparent especially in the West, which is highly developed from the standpoint of technology but is interiorly impoverished by its tendency to forget God or to keep him at a distance" (Apostolic Letter *Tertio Millennio Adveniente*, no. 52). Portuguese society, I am certain, in its different classes and members, and in fidelity to its history and the example of its ancestors, will know how to accept this challenge, with courage and freedom from preconceptions deriving from a non-religious and amoral vision of the person and the human community.

As I bring this meeting to a close, I repeat my cordial wishes that your lofty mission which begins today may be crowned with success. I entrust your person, your loved ones, your co-workers and all Portuguese society to Almighty God, invoking upon everyone an abundance of heavenly favors through the intercession of Our Lady of the Immaculate Conception, who, 350 years ago, was chosen by Portugal to be served and honored as patroness and queen in the Shrine of Vila Vicosa, through the voice of its highest civil authority and with the explicit adherence of the nation's representatives. May God bless and protect Portugal!

March 1, 1997
(*OR*, March 12, 1997, p. 4)

Papal Response to H.E. Pjeter Pepa, Ambassador of the Republic of Albania:

Mr. Ambassador,

1. I am pleased to welcome you at a special audience for the presentation of your Letters of Credence. In addressing a cordial greeting to you, I ask kindly to convey my sentiments of respectful esteem to the President of the Albanian Republic, to whom I offer my most heartfelt wishes for fruitful service to the welfare of the Albanian people.

As I take pleasure in receiving the Letters accrediting you as Ambassador Extraordinary and Plenipotentiary to the Holy See, I also express my wish, Mr. Ambassador, that you will fulfill the lofty mission entrusted to you with the same spirit expressed in your noble words and will reap the satisfaction Providence promises to those who work generously for the common good.

2. Meeting you, Mr. Ambassador, reminds me of April 25 four years ago, when I had the joy of making a Pastoral Visit to Albania. Although it was quite short, this was one of the most intense and significant of my Apostolic Visits because of the tragic events your homeland had previously experienced. Indeed, only a few years ago a papal visit would have been absolutely unthinkable. Images and impressions of it remain clearly in my mind and heart. Naturally, I remember in particular the Catholic community of Albania, for which I had the joy of ordaining the first four new Pastors in the cathedral of Shkodre, after long years of oppression and communist dictatorship. I likewise remember the entire population and especially my last great meeting with the Albanian people in Skanderbeg Square in Tirane.

Mr. Ambassador, through your kind offices I would like to assure the beloved Albanian nation and its political leaders that the Holy See and the Catholic Church intend to show with renewed commitment their effective closeness and prompt solidarity, so that the progress of the country's young democracy can advance quickly and bring about the expected human and social development.

3. The Church's contribution cannot fail to be connected with her evangelizing mission: that is, sowing the good seed of the Gospel in the furrows of peoples' history, so that by welcoming the vital seed of saving faith, they can produce fruits of justice and peace, freedom and truth. This will certainly encourage the citizens to live together in fraternal love and solidarity. Particularly in Albania, where for a long period a violent, systematic deprivation of religious freedom was practiced, the Church knows she is sent to carry out a new and, so to speak, "refounding" evangelization. Christ, the liberator of man, must be able once again to walk freely in the country's cities and villages, healing all those who are weary and oppressed, and spreading comfort and hope.

Only if the sense of certain basic values, beginning with the inviolable dignity of the person and of human life, is reinforced and recognized, will it be possible to establish democratic coexistence on firm and lasting foundations (cf. *Message to All the*

People of Albania, Tirane, April 25, 1993, no. 4; *L'Osservatore Romano* English edition, May 5, 1993, p. 4).

As I could see during the above-mentioned Pastoral Visit to Albania, "recognition of this value centered in the human person will certainly ensure that in the economy the proper balance is maintained between the rationale of efficiency and the priorities of solidarity, and will make political involvement a responsible search for the common good, to be pursued always with full respect for all the ethical and moral demands" (ibid., no. 5: *L'Osservatore Romano* English edition, May 5, 1993, p. 4).

While respecting these principles, one can and must seek a solution to the problems of the present time, initiating a dialogue with all the responsible forces of society who, despite the many difficulties they must overcome, are working to strengthen the democratic system in Albania.

The Catholic Church wishes to make her own contribution to this effort, in a spirit of deep respect and loyal collaboration with the other great religious communities, first of all with Orthodox Christians as well as with Muslims, I renew my hope that believers will feel committed to contributing to the country's moral renewal, constantly witnessing to those relations of mutual esteem and cordial collaboration of which they are rightly proud.

4. Mr. Ambassador, you have courteously wished to offer me the book you have edited, which documents the atrocious persecutions of the communist regime and the heroic witness of so many innocent victims, including many priests. I warmly thank you for this tribute, which I greatly appreciate.

The book gives me the idea of returning to a reflection of great importance not only for Albania, but for every nation. If the tragedy of the dictatorship should be left behind as soon as possible, the memory of the suffering and tyranny of that period should be preserved as a warning for the present and the future, and as an incentive to constant spiritual and moral renewal. At the end of a century in which humanity has experienced aberrant human exploitation and unprecedented violence, the generations facing the third millennium have a right to be helped in forming their own critical judgment about the causes and consequences of such phenomena, to alert them to and enable them to oppose the negative tendencies that unfortunately continue to ensnare man and even the social structure of contemporary society.

The memory of the martyrs is a positive source of courage and hope, because it shows that the forces of faith and love are superior to every kind of wickedness. In the end the victory is theirs. May this vivid memory of the sacrifice of her countless children light the way for the present and future generations of Albania, on whom I invoke the protection of Our Lady of Good Counsel and an abundance of divine blessings.

January 31, 1998
(*OR*, February 11, 1998, pp. 4,9)

H.E. Mark Pellew, Ambassador of Great Britain and Northern Ireland:

Your Holiness,

I have the honor to present the Letters by which Her Majesty The Queen recalls my predecessor, Miss Maureen MacGlashan, and those by which she accredits me as her Ambassador Extraordinary and Plenipotentiary to the Holy See. I have also the honor to convey to Your Holiness greetings from Her Majesty. A warm relationship based on goodwill, understanding and respect exists between the Holy See and the United Kingdom and continues to flourish.

In the United Kingdom, Her Majesty's Government is heartened by the start of substantive negotiations on the future of Northern Ireland. For the first time in three quarters of a century, political representatives of the main parties are sitting at the same table discussing a possible settlement for Northern Ireland. There is real prospect of an agreement on all aspects of this problem which can engage the support of both sides of the community in Northern Ireland and of people throughout the Island of Ireland. The untiring efforts of Church leaders in Northern Ireland have been very much appreciated, as has your own support for the peace process.

A tremendous opportunity for reaching a political settlement which could help bring lasting peace in Northern Ireland now exists. Her Majesty's Government believes that such a settlement is achievable and has pledged to do all in its power to bring it about. But there are no illusions about the difficult task that lies ahead. It will require compromise and a spirit of genuine co-operation from all concerned if there is to be a successful outcome.

Her Majesty's Government is now preparing legislation to incorporate the European Convention on Human Rights into law, so that the people of the United Kingdom will have access to the fundamental rights and freedoms of the Convention through the courts. The Government has committed itself to carrying through an ethical foreign policy founded in respect for human rights which we will work to promote throughout the world. In July, the Government adopted a new set of guidelines for the export of conventional arms. As a major supplier, it carries a particular responsibility to ensure that the arms trade is managed responsibly, so as to avoid the use of arms exports for internal repression or external aggression. The Government also announced that it would work for the introduction of a European Code of conduct setting high common standards to govern arms exports from all EU member States. We have been taking this initiative forward with a view to agreeing the code during the current UK Presidency of the EU.

Her Majesty's Government shares the Holy See's concerns about the terrible suffering caused by anti-personnel landmines. By implementing its commitment to ban these weapons, the Government has demonstrated its determination to address this humanitarian issue. In Ottawa last month, we signed the international convention to ban them and we are urging as many countries as possible to sign the convention to achieve a truly global ban. We are also helping to remove mines already laid and have doubled our funding for this to 10 million pounds sterling over three years.

Her Majesty's Government shares the views expressed in Your Holiness' recent message for the celebration of the World Day of Peace about the heavy burden of external debt for the world's poorest countries. We attach importance to achieving a commitment by the international community to resolve these problems by the end of the century.

Her Majesty's Government is concerned about the situation of refugees and displaced persons around the world. We will continue to work with the UN High Commissioner for Refugees and others to ensure that the 1951 Refugee Convention and other international instruments concerning refugees are respected. We will work to tackle the root causes of political, social and economic instability which can lead to forced population movements.

The UK is committed to working with the international community, under the coordinating framework of the OSCE, to help Albania out of its difficulties. The progress made over recent months toward overcoming last February's events has been remarkable.

We remain deeply concerned by the situation in Kosovo. In the Federal Republic of Yugoslavia, the UK has worked to promote a meaningful dialogue between Serbian officials and leaders of the Kosovo Albanians and to bring about the early implementation of the education agreement to allow Kosovo Albanian students access to State education facilities. We wish to see prosperous and democratic States in the region fully reintegrated into the international community, but this will entail meeting international standards, including in the fields of human rights and of religious and ethnic tolerance.

Her Majesty's Government, like the Holy See, feels a strong commitment to the successful transformation of the countries of Central and Eastern Europe into open, democratic and prosperous societies and, in co-operation with our EU partners, we are continuing to assist these countries to meet their international human rights obligations. We have warmly welcomed the steady progress made in recent years and recognize with admiration the role which Your Holiness has played in this important process. We share too your concern about the new Russian law on freedom of conscience and religious association, and we will be monitoring its implementation closely, in particularly the spirit in which it is implemented both in Moscow and in the regions.

Her Majesty's Government also shares your deep concern over events in the Great Lakes region of Africa. Bilaterally and with our partners in the EU and with the UN, we are working for stability, democracy, respect for human rights and the rule of law. We are seeking a constructive relationship with the Democratic Republic of the Congo, to help the people of that country achieve political stability and economic prosperity. At the same time, we are pressing President Kabila's Government to respect human rights and to co-operate fully with the UN. In Burundi, we are supporting political dialogue, especially in the efforts of regional States and ex-President Nyerere to achieve a peaceful end to the conflict there, as well as supporting peace and reconciliation in Rwanda.

Her Majesty's Government continues to attach importance to a just settlement in the Middle East. The Foreign Secretary's visit in November demonstrated our commitment to the peace process and our determination to do everything possible to maintain it. The new Government has reaffirmed our long-held position on Jerusalem: that we believe its status has yet to be determined but that we wish to see access for all to worship at their holy places. We continue to call for the Israeli authorities to prevent settlement activity in East Jerusalem and the West Bank. My Government applauds the tireless efforts of Your Holiness to work for a comprehensive peace throughout the Middle East. We share your concern for the suffering of the civilian population in Iraq which has been alleviated in part by the introduction of Security Council Resolutions 986 and 1111. But there can be no question of relaxing sanctions until Iraq complies with all relevant Resolutions.

Her Majesty's Government also shares Your Holiness' concern about the terrible violence in Algeria and we call on those responsible to stop the killings. We support the democratization process in Algeria and we believe that solutions to this conflict must come from the Algerians themselves.

We remain concerned about the human rights situation in East Timor and we fully support all efforts made with the aim of creating a just, comprehensive and internationally acceptable settlement to the problem.

Her Majesty's Government has followed with interest and admiration the progress of Your Holiness' recent visit to Cuba. We share your wish to see the development in Cuba of greater respect for human rights and fundamental freedoms, and we believe that your visit will bring hope and sustenance to many within Cuba and in the wider Cuban community. We congratulate Your Holiness on the success of this historic visit.

Papal Response:

Mr. Ambassador,

I am pleased to extend a cordial welcome to you as you present the Letters of Credence whereby Her Majesty Queen Elizabeth II has appointed you her Ambassador Extraordinary and Plenipotentiary to the Holy See. I am grateful for the greetings which you bring from Her Majesty and I ask you to convey to her the assurance of my prayers and good wishes.

You mention your Government's concern for the promotion of a foreign policy founded on respect for human rights. The celebration of the 50th anniversary of the promulgation of the Universal Declaration of Human Rights is an appropriate occasion for world leaders to renew their commitment to defending the fundamental rights of the human person. The preamble of that document declares that the "recognition of the inherent dignity and of the equal and inalienable rights of all members of the human family is the foundation of freedom, justice and peace in the world." The Declaration emphasizes that the same rights belong to every individual and to all peoples. In my recent *Message for the World Day of Peace*, I drew attention to a tendency in some quarters to weaken the universal and indivisible character of human rights. It is therefore vital that the international community should feel duty bound to ensure that the same basic social, economic and cultural rights are available to all.

The commitment to defend and protect human rights is closely linked with the Church's mission in the modern world, convinced as she is that the promotion of peace, justice and solidarity is a truly practical and effective witness to the Gospel message regarding the sacred character of human life. Hence the Holy See insists firmly on every individual's fundamental right to life as well as the right to live in a united family, to develop one's intelligence and freedom in seeking and knowing the truth, the right to share in the work which makes use of the earth's resources, and the right to derive from that work the means to support oneself and one's dependents (cf. *Centesimus Annus*, no. 47).

Among these basic rights, religious freedom, "understood as the right to live in the truth of one's faith and in conformity with one's transcendent dignity as a person" (*Centesimus Annus*, no. 47), is an essential requirement of the dignity of every person and a cornerstone of the structure of human rights. Religious freedom includes the freedom to practice one's faith within an organized religious community. Everyone must be allowed to do so free of coercion (cf. *Dignitatis Humanae*, no. 1), and therefore the State, which cannot claim authority, direct or indirect, over a person's religious convictions, should find the way to ensure that the rights of all individuals and communities are equally guaranteed, while safeguarding public order. It is important that Governments work together to guarantee that the fundamental right to religious freedom is everywhere respected, and I am heartened by your own Government's concerns in this regard.

As experience shows, efforts to promote peace among peoples can succeed only if there is a willingness to engage in a dialogue which respects the rights of all the parties concerned and without recourse to means contrary to the very nature of the negotiating process. This dialogue is admittedly difficult, and patience, goodwill and genuine openness are required in order to bring it to fruition. In this regard, I cannot but encourage the present dialogue between the various parties in Northern Ireland, in the hope that the desire for reconciliation and trust will prevail, in spite of the enormous difficulties involved and recurring moments of crisis.

In my recent speech to the Diplomatic Corps, I referred to the various trials which afflict the peoples of the Great Lakes region of Africa: "Armed conflict, displacement of persons, the tragedy of refugees, deficient health conditions, a defective administration of justice" (*Speech to the Diplomatic Corps*, January 10. 1998, no. 4). While the leaders of the countries in this region have the primary responsibility to find solutions to these problems, Governments such as your own can help in no small way to achieve a cessation of hostilities and ensure that the basic principles of justice are observed. The Holy See and the various Catholic aid organizations are already engaged in joint efforts with various international organizations to improve the quality of human life not only in that part of Africa but throughout the world. This too is an area in which there is ample room for co-operation between us.

In effect, the promotion of world peace calls for a commitment on the part of the international community to the integral development of all peoples and nations. In this regard the Holy See subscribes to appeals coming from many quarters for world leaders to take steps to reduce the heavy burden of external debt which hinders the social, political and economic progress of poorer countries (cf. *Message for the World Day of Peace* 1998, no. 4). I welcome your Government's resolve to find a solution to this problem before the end of the century.

A particular difficulty with regard to development is posed by the arms trade. Some poorer countries are tempted to exhaust much needed resources on the acquisition of military technology, instead of using them to guarantee a better standard of living for their citizens. Nations which produce and export arms have a serious moral responsibility to ensure that this trade does not further increase the threat to peace within countries and among nations. It is to be hoped that the European Union's deliberations on establishing a code of conduct to regulate the export of arms will go some way toward diminishing the temptation for developing countries to waste their resources in this way.

In this regard, public opinion has welcomed the signing in Ottawa of the international convention banning anti-personnel land-mines, which have been a major obstacle to the peaceful reconstruction of war-torn regions throughout the world. I share your hope that this convention will eventually be signed by all members of the international community, and I commend your Government's decision to allocate funds for the removal of these devices. There is a need for continued international cooperation to ensure that the dangers and threats to development posed by such weapons are permanently removed.

Your Excellency, in mentioning only a few of the important issues which you have raised, I have sought to indicate how the Church's concern for peace is based essentially on her spiritual mission to serve the human person, created in God's image and likeness and called to eternal life. As you undertake your duties, I am confident that your mission will serve to strengthen the friendly relations existing between the United Kingdom and the Holy See. I assure you of the co-operation and assistance of the various departments of the Roman Curia, and I invoke God's blessings upon you and upon all those whom you represent.

May 20, 1999
(*OR*, May 26, 1999, p. 4)

Papal Response to H.E. Nina Kovalska, Ambassador of Ukraine:

Your Excellency,

It gives me great pleasure to welcome you to the Vatican and to accept the Letters of Credence by which you are appointed Ambassador Extraordinary and Plenipotentiary of Ukraine. It is a fitting occasion for us to reaffirm the friendship and cooperation which exist between your country and the Holy See, bonds which go back in history 1,000 years to the Baptism of Kievan Rus' and which have taken on new form and vigor since the advent of your nation's independence. I see your presence here today as a sign of our mutual desire to consolidate the diplomatic relations established between Ukraine and the Holy See in 1992. I am grateful for the greetings which you have conveyed on behalf of His Excellency President Leonid Kuchma, whose visits to the Vatican I vividly remember and to whom I express my good wishes. I renew the assurance of my prayers for the peace and prosperity of your country.

The countries of Eastern Europe, including your own, are undergoing a period of rapid and profound transformation in the social, economic and political spheres. While such changes are not without great difficulty and cost, they are essentially positive changes, moving as they do in the direction of respect for the liberty and self-determination of peoples. After decades of being closed in a world order established on imposed decisions and ideological barriers, nations which lacked a voice of their own in the international community are now asserting their sovereignty and pursuing their destiny as equal partners on the world stage. The present moment therefore is one of extreme importance in the life of these peoples, and of grave responsibilities for their leaders.

With the effort and dedication of so many of your fellow citizens, Ukraine is making great strides along the path of progress toward a more prosperous, just and democratic society. Your Excellency has indicated your country's intention to achieve a "complete reintegration into the European space which rests on Christian values." In striving for this goal you are rediscovering the strength of the spiritual and cultural roots which lie at the very heart of your nation's identity and your people's journey through history. The challenge is to grow in the noblest traditions of the past while being open to all the demands of the consciousness maturing among the world's peoples of the universal nature of human dignity and human rights.

In spite of the hard lessons of this violent century, Europe is unfortunately once again the theatre of the oppression of man by man and of the daily thunder of weapons of death and destruction. In the name of distorted ideals of cultural and ethnic distinction, the fundamental and real value of the inviolable dignity of every human being is being utterly denied. Beyond the rhetoric in which such conflicts are generally presented, it should be clear that the atrocities occurring every day on European soil in the Balkans are not the result of peoples' genuinely held aspirations; they have instead been fueled by unspoken motives representing particular interests and very definite forms of the thirst for power.

It must be the concern of everyone to ensure that dialogue replaces conflict. Dialogue and negotiation would signify the triumph of reason, while the continuance of ethnic conflicts and power struggles in any part of the world are a defeat of reason and a sign of the failure of solidarity and human partnership. We must hope that Europe will manage to find in its rich millenary heritage the truths and incentives it needs to restore the rule of reason and law.

Ukrainian Christians, both Orthodox and Catholic, are reviving the institutions and public expressions of their faith. In the Gospel and the traditions of their Churches they are finding inspiration and strength for the enormous tasks before them as responsible citizens of their newly independent country. It must be the conviction of all Ukrainian believers that mutual understanding and cooperation, not prejudice or rivalry, are what their faith requires of them. Difficulties between Christians must be resolved not just at the level of justice and equity, but at the much deeper level of *koinonia* before God and in Jesus Christ. I repeat a thought which I expressed to the Latin-rite Ukrainian Bishops on the occasion of their *ad limina* visit in March of this year: "If respect for each other's identity is required by justice, it is even more a demand of love, which is the supreme law for the Christian." As Your Excellency has rightly pointed out, the fast-approaching celebration of a new Christian millennium is a wonderful opportunity for all Christians to grow in peace, tolerance and respect for one another and for all people. I earnestly hope that a wise and positive unfolding of democracy and freedom in your country, coupled with a renewal of religious conviction and moral commitment, will bring about an era of flourishing development, and that Ukraine's presence and actions in the family of nations will contribute to that better and more peaceful world which people everywhere long for. May the already warm relations between Ukraine and the Holy See lead to increased understanding and cooperation in matters of common concern.

Your Excellency, I offer you my best wishes as you begin your mission, and assure you of the readiness of the offices of the Holy See to assist you in your work. Upon you and your fellow citizens I cordially invoke the abundant blessings of Almighty God.

October 19, 2000
(*OR*, November 1, 2000, pp. 4, 6)

Papal Response to H.E. W. Hans-Theodor Wallau, Ambassador of the Federal Republic of Germany:

Mr. Ambassador,

1. Please accept my sincere thanks for your very friendly words on the occasion of the presentation of your Letters of Credence as the new Ambassador Extraordinary and Plenipotentiary of the Federal Republic of Germany to the Holy See. I cordially welcome you as you take office and I congratulate you on this noble and important task. At the same time, I ask you to convey my greetings to the Federal President and my best wishes for his health. You are beginning your service as the Great Jubilee of the Year 2000 draws to a close. The motto, "Jesus Christ is the same yesterday, today and forever" has put the human person again in the light which lets his value as the image and likeness of God shine in full splendor.

2. Calling attention to the message about the inalienable value of every human being is particularly urgent at the end of the 20th century, especially since the last hundred years, soaked in blood and tears, will go down in history for their wars and conflicts as well. But in recent weeks your compatriots, the citizens of friendly neighboring States and countless people in Europe and throughout the world were also able to commemorate the happy events which over 10 years ago had so carefully and, at the same time, so resolutely begun your country's reunification process that it could finally arrive at the memorable event on October 3, 1990: Germany – a united homeland. The Berlin Wall had fallen. The Brandenburg Gate, which has been closed for decades and symbolized division, was opened and once again represented what it had before: a sign of unity. The Constitution's demand that the unity of Germany be realized in free self-determination was thus fulfilled. We can rightly say: the Brandenburg Gate has become the gate of unity and freedom.

Through the gentle revolution, which had opened the way to freedom without bloodshed, great hopes were raised for over 10 years. The saying about scenes of prosperity, which had long been dismissed as utopian, has proved to be accurate – even if delayed – in not a few areas of the new German states. But unemployment and new poverty are the other side of the coin, which, seen from the obverse, shows the economic upturn and outward prosperity, the vast array of goods for sale and the strengthening of the infrastructure. Above all, overcoming the spiritual aimlessness and inner emptiness caused by decades of communist indoctrination is a task that cannot be dealt with quickly and requires every effort.

Many people have bravely accepted the challenges of the past 10 years and made their contribution, so that what is outwardly reunited may inwardly grow closer and closer. They see this as a school of solidarity, in which one can learn to support in word and deed those who want to put their lives on solid ground. I express my sincere appreciation to your country's government leaders and to all who, at various levels and in the different sectors of society, foster the inner unification of the once artificially separated parts of Germany and the welfare of its citizens. By joining forces it has been possible to deal peacefully with a difficult phase of German history. Barricades, barbed wire and orders to shoot, which once painfully separated families from one another, have given way to connecting bridges, unrestricted streets and open doors.

3. I am delighted that the heavy commitment to German unity has not obscured the vision of European unification. On the contrary, the reunification of your homeland even became an incentive for the leaders of State and society to broaden their view beyond Germany to Europe, to which the fall of the Iron Curtain has given a whole new horizon. With deep respect I realize that the Federal Republic of Germany is a respected international authority and a sought-after partner. Germany has accepted increasing responsibility and plays a crucial role in the European unification process. It is in a position to carry out its task effectively, since decades of experience show that the State's democratic institutions are solid and the overwhelming majority of citizens support them. I would like to take this occasion to express to you, the ambassador of a country which is certainly one the "pillars" of the European house, my hope that it will succeed, within the framework of the negotiations about expanded membership, in bringing the East and the West of the old continent closer together, those two lungs without which Europe cannot breathe.

Through their preservation and mutual enlightenment, the variety of Eastern and Western traditions will enrich Europe's culture, as well as provide the foundation for the longed-for spiritual renewal. Perhaps, then, we should speak less of the "Eastern expansion" than of the "Europeanizing" of the whole continent. What became German's motto after the collapse of the Wall can also serve as a rule for European unification: What belongs together should grow together.

These thoughts are not prompted by boldness or reverie, but by a vision based on hopeful realism. Precisely my three Pastoral Visits to Germany, a treasury of European civilization, have led me to an important realization: European art and culture, history and the present moment were and are still so greatly molded by Christianity that a dechristianized or atheistic Europe is really impossible. At the same time, I am convinced that Germany and Europe have a future only if they know about their origins.

4. Particularly since your esteemed country remains aware of its own history in a kind of ongoing, collective examination of conscience and is attentively working on the "purification of its memory," it is especially sensitive to injustice and the disregard of human rights. Indeed, it can be increasingly observed in many modern democracies that a spontaneous propensity to violence precisely among young people is combined with a politically desired and organized ideology, which could weigh permanently on domestic peace. General appeals and pleas to learn from history are not enough to overcome the widespread intellectual and spiritual vacuum. What is called for instead is an attentive and sensitive culture of spiritual values among the younger generation, as well as a concrete work of reconciliation which not only offsets the past, but will help in the future to break down mutual prejudices and thus enable Germany to be a solid pillar of support for the common European home.

I realize that this plan sets high standards. For a Western European island of affluence must become more and more an all-European area of freedom, justice and peace. Material sacrifices will be unavoidable for the more affluent countries, if the tremendous drop in prosperity within Europe is gradually to decline. Moreover, spiritual help is needed to support the further building of democratic structures and a political culture in accordance with the conditions of a State governed by law. In these efforts the Catholic Church offers her selfless help to all in her many religious and social institutions. She presents Catholic social teaching as a guide for this development, in which the focus is on care and responsibility for man: "We are not dealing here with man in the 'abstract,' but with the real, 'concrete,' 'historical' man," whom the Church cannot abandon (Encyclical Letter *Centesimus Annus*, no. 53).

5. In this connection, I return to an issue that is very close to my heart and prompts me to raise my voice precisely at this historical moment, which is marked by rapid, tremendous scientific advances. Since man is at the point of deciphering the complex blueprint of human genetics, what is called for now is to direct the course of science to a culture of life and love. Man may not do everything he can do. For "in our present social context, marked by a dramatic struggle between the 'culture of life' and the 'culture of death,' there is need to develop a deep critical sense, capable of discerning true values and authentic needs . . . All together, we must build a new culture of life: new, because it will be able to confront and solve today's unprecedented problems affecting human life; new, because it will be adopted with deeper and more dynamic conviction by all Christians" (Encyclical Letter *Evangelium Vitae*, no. 95).

6. Thus there are two key points which I would like to consider more closely. The newness of the problem lies first of all in the context of freedom, in whose name many people think that you may do whatever you want. But freedom does not mean doing whatever you like. Whoever turns freedom into license has dealt it a deathblow. Freedom requires commitment. Whoever is really free knows that his understanding and behavior are bound to the truth. The first and greatest truth about man is that he is not self-made, but is God's creation. Just as man did not give himself life, so can no one claim the right – even on supposedly humanitarian grounds – to take his own life or someone else's.

This fundamental truth compels me tirelessly to recall the inviolable value of every human being, from the moment of his conception until natural death. I am pleased that the Constitution of the Federal Republic of Germany rests on the same foundation. It is inspired with the "awareness of its responsibility before God and men" (*Preamble*), and before making any other statement it recognizes: "The value of the human person is inviolable. It is the obligation of all State authority to respect and protect it" (art. 1). Precisely when the value of the human person is at stake, the Church would like to stand by the State's side. For pluralistic societies do not expect a value-free State.

That is why the Church makes an offer to the State that she understands as a service to man: he should be enabled to learn and to live a true freedom worthy of human beings. This is also why the Church is present in so many State institutions such as schools, universities, hospitals and barracks. I am pleased to learn that the Church's outstretched hand has also been taken by the new federal states, which was expressed in the Concordat agreements that the Holy See has been able to conclude in the years since the turning-point with the states of Saxony, Thuringia, Mecklenburg-West, Pomerania and Saxony-Anhalt. A framework was thus created for the Church to intensify her pastoral work for human beings in an area where talk of God had been stifled for decades.

7. Ecumenism, which you yourself spoke of, is another key point to be mentioned in relation to the newness of our time. Just as Germany is the country where the Reformation began, so there are also hopeful signs for the future. I am pleased to recall the solemn signing of the Joint Declaration by representatives of the Catholic Church and the Lutheran World Federation, which took place almost a year ago in Augsburg. I see it as a "milestone on the difficult path to re-establishing full unity among Christians" and reaffirm that the document represents a sound basis for further theological research in the ecumenical field and for addressing the remaining problems with a better founded hope of resolving them in the future (*Angelus*, October 31, 1999).

While I never tire of thanking the Lord of history that we have achieved this intermediate goal, at the same time I consider it advisable to give direction to the ecumenical journey toward full unity, a direction which is more timely than ever precisely in view of the culture of life. Perhaps at times there has been so much concentration on ecumenism in doctrine and worship that the strength has been lacking for ecumenism in political parties and parliaments, in the social and cultural sphere. This includes a shared commitment to the kingdom of God which goes beyond the realm of the pulpit and altar and includes everything – individuals, society, the whole world – in order to permeate politics, the economy and culture. Precisely the newness of the problems, which affect man in his personal dignity, cries out for the common witness of all who call themselves Christians.

This ecumenism of witness for the sake of an authentic culture of life is a service that Christians owe to their contemporaries. In addition, there are other issues such as the preservation of creation, the defense of Sunday and the sacredness of marriage as "an institution confirmed by the divine law even in the eyes of society" (Pastoral Constitution *Gaudium et Spes*, no. 48) and the protection of the family as the foundation of society (ibid., no. 52). For in the eyes of a world in which people live more and more as if God did not exist, "cooperation among Christians [must] become a form of common Christian witness" (Encyclical Letter *Ut Unum Sint*, no. 40). Above all, when it is a question of human life and death, there can be no compromise for Christians, but only the compass of the truth which God himself has revealed about man.

8. I cannot conclude my reflection without expressing my confidence that the friendly relations between the Federal Republic of Germany and the Holy See, which you rightly stressed in your address, will grow even more fruitful. The close reciprocal relationship between the Church and State, which both sides view with sensitive responsibility and from proven experience, and regard as enriching, constitutes a reliable premise for this. Mr. Ambassador, as I cordially wish you a good start to your new post in Rome, I gladly impart the blessing of Almighty God to you, to your esteemed colleagues at the embassy and especially to your dear family.

September 13, 2001
(*OR*, September 19, 2001, pp. 1–2)

H.E. R. James Nicholson, Ambassador to the United States:

Your Holiness:

It is an immense honor to present to you my credentials as Ambassador Extraordinary and Plenipotentiary of the United States of America.

I am very grateful to President Bush for the opportunity to represent him and my country to the Holy See. It is a gratifying responsibility and the highlight of my public service.

Shortly before leaving the United States, President Bush told me how profoundly moved he was by his recent visit with you at Castel Gandolfo and he also asked me to give you his warmest greetings.

President Bush has reinvigorated the giving spirit of my country through his Faith-Based Initiatives and his model of compassion for those among us who are less fortunate. The goal of his leadership is to leave no one behind. His concern for his fellow man is deep and sincere, Holy Father.

Having grown up in a family of seven children in a house without plumbing or electricity and frequently without enough food to eat, I have experienced the blessing of generosity that comes from neighbors and relatives. It helped my family to survive and stay together. Generosity is a trait of my country.

As I recall, Your Holiness offered wise counsel to one of my predecessors, Ambassador Wilson, when he, as the first U.S. Ambassador to the Holy See, presented his credentials to you in 1984. At that time you said that the renewed collaboration between the United States and the Holy See should mean: "exerting common efforts to defend dignity and the rights of the human person – every human person, every man, woman and child on this Earth."

We are working well together out of mutual respect, and with common goals, and I am confident we will succeed, by the grace of God, in our determined endeavors to obtain peace, justice, freedom, including religious freedom, economic opportunity and democracy for all mankind.

I feel blessed to participate in this collaboration between my country and the Holy See, which will soon enter its third decade, and which has been of significant spiritual and material benefit to the world. Still much more remains to be done. As you said to President Bush, Holy Father, we are in need of a "revolution of opportunity." My country, and I personally, have thrived on the gifts of freedom and opportunity. We stand committed, like the Holy See, to bring both freedom and opportunity to those, who in your words, "seem cut off from them."

The United States also looks forward to working closely with the Holy See on intercommunal reconciliation, especially in Africa and the Balkans, to ending the trafficking of human beings, to stemming the scourge of AIDS, and to bringing peace and prosperity to the Holy Land.

Your Holiness, on behalf of President Bush, I wish to stress our desire for close cooperation in these endeavors, and, in so doing, fulfilling what certainly must be God's will, which is to help our fellow man achieve a life of peace and dignity, with the freedom to worship as he chooses.

Your Holiness, thank you for allowing me to present to you my letter of credence.

Papal Response:

Mr. Ambassador,

I am pleased to accept the Letters of Credence appointing you Ambassador Extraordinary and Plenipotentiary of the United States of America to the Holy See. You are beginning your mission at a moment of immense tragedy for your country. At this time of national mourning for the victims of the terrorist attacks on Washington and New York, I wish to assure you personally of my profound participation in the grief of the American people and of my heartfelt prayers for the President and the civil authorities, for all involved in the rescue operations and in helping the survivors, and in a special way for the victims and their families. I pray that this inhuman act will awaken in the hearts of all the world's peoples a firm resolve to reject the ways of violence, to combat everything that sows hatred and division within the human family and to work for the dawn of a new era of international cooperation inspired by the highest ideals of solidarity, justice and peace.

Esteem for the founding principles of the republic

In my recent meeting with President Bush, I emphasized my deep esteem for the rich patrimony of human, religious and moral values which have historically shaped the American character. I expressed the conviction that America's continued deep moral leadership in the world depends on her fidelity to her founding principles. Underlying your nation's commitment to freedom, self-determination and equal opportunity are universal truths inherited from its religious roots. From these spring respect for the sanctity of life and the dignity of each human person made in the image and likeness of the Creator; shared responsibility for the common good; concern for the education of young people and for the future of society; and the need for wise stewardship of the natural resources so freely bestowed by a bounteous God. In facing the challenges of the future, America is called to cherish and live out the deepest values of her national heritage: solidarity and cooperation between peoples; respect for human rights; the justice that is the indispensable condition for authentic freedom and lasting peace.

Revolution of freedom must mean a revolution of opportunity

In the century now opening before us, humanity has the opportunity to make great strides against some of its traditional enemies: poverty, disease, violence. As I said at the United Nations in 1995, it is within our grasp to see that a century of tears, the 20th century, is followed in the 21st century by a "springtime of the human spirit." The possibilities before the human family are immense, although they are not always apparent in a world in which too many of our brothers and sisters are suffering from hunger, malnutrition and the lack of access to medical care and to education, or are burdened by unjust government, armed conflict, forced displacement and new forms of human bondage. In seizing the available opportunities, both vision and generosity are necessary, especially on the part of those who have been blessed with freedom, wealth and an abundance of resources. The urgent ethical issues raised by the division between those who benefit from the globalization of the world economy and those who are excluded from those benefits call for new and creative responses on the part of the whole international community. Here I would emphasize again what I said in my recent meeting with President Bush, that the revolution of freedom in the world must be completed by a "revolution of opportunity" which will enable all the members of the human family to enjoy a dignified existence and to share in the benefits of a truly global development.

Peace process in the Holy Land

In this context, I cannot but mention, among so many disturbing situations throughout the world, the tragic violence which continues to affect the Middle East and which seriously jeopardizes the peace process begun in Madrid. Thanks also to the commitment of the United States, that process had given rise to hope in the hearts of all those who look to the Holy Land as a unique place of encounter and prayer between peoples. I am certain that your country will not hesitate to promote a realistic dialogue which will enable the parties involved to achieve security, justice and peace, in full respect for human rights and international law.

Democracy to survive must have moral vision and resolve

Mr. Ambassador, the vision and the moral strength which America is being challenged to exercise at the beginning of a new century and in a rapidly changing world call for an acknowledgment of the spiritual roots of the crisis which the Western democracies are experiencing, a crisis characterized by the advance of a materialistic, utilitarian and ultimately dehumanized world view which is tragically detached from the moral foundations of Western civilization. In order to survive and prosper, democracy and its accompanying economic and political structures must be directed by a vision whose core is the God-given dignity and inalienable rights of every human being, from the moment of conception until natural death. When some lives, including those of the unborn, are subjected to the personal choices of others, no other value or right will long be guaranteed, and society will inevitably be governed by special interests and convenience. Freedom cannot be sustained in a cultural climate that measures human dignity in strictly utilitarian terms. Never has it been more urgent to re-invigorate the moral vision and resolve essential to maintaining a just and free society.

Spiritual and moral education of young people

In this context my thoughts turn to America's young people, the hope of the nation. In my Pastoral Visits to the United States, and above all in my visit to Denver in 1993 for the celebration of World Youth Day, I was able personally to witness the reserves of generosity and good will present in the youth of your country. Young people are surely your nation's greatest treasure. That is why they urgently need an all-around education which will enable them to reject cynicism and selfishness and to grow into their full stature as informed, wise and morally responsible members of the community. At the beginning of a new Millennium, young people must be given every opportunity to take up their role as "craftsmen of a new humanity, where brothers and sisters – members all of the same family – are able at last to live in peace" (*Message for the 2001 World Day of Peace*, no. 22).

Mr. Ambassador, as you begin your mission as your country's representative to the Holy See, I reiterate my hope that in facing the challenges of the present and future the American people will draw upon the deep spiritual and moral resources which have inspired and guided the nation's growth, and which remain the surest pledge of its greatness. I am confident that America's Catholic community, which has historically played a crucial role in the education of a responsible citizenry and in the relief of the poor, the sick and the needy, will be actively present in the process of discerning the shape of your country's future course. Upon you and your family and all the American people I cordially invoke God's blessings of joy and peace.

April 10, 2002
(*OR*, April 24, 2002, p. 4)

H.E. D. Tanaskovic, Ambassador of the Federal Republic of Yugoslavia:

Your Holiness,

I am imbued with the feelings of high honor and responsibility. There are many reasons for this.

As Your Holiness is well aware, in the last decade or so, the people living within the borders of the former Yugoslav federation went through trials and existential damage. Your Holiness has appealed for reason, peace and dialogue, but, unfortunately, as in other parts of the world, blind selfishness, hatred and war have prevailed. Although it cannot be said that the region has reached a final and lasting stability, recently the foundations for it have been laid, as well as legal and institutional frameworks, due to the dedication of all the subjects in the area and with the help of the international community. However, what is left are serious consequences of the tragic events: hundreds of thousands of refugees and displaced families, ruins, crippled economies, poverty . . . and, what is hardest to heal, many wounded souls. The Federal Republic of Yugoslavia is painfully aware of all this. Without a rapid material and moral recovery, without giving a realistic hope to the desperate ones and without a full integration of South-eastern Europe into a new political, economic and cultural structure of the Old Continent, to which the Balkans was the cradle, we cannot look to the future with reliable optimism. And it is not only the future of the Balkans that is in question, but also the future of the whole unified Europe.

Your Holiness,

The Federal Republic of Yugoslavia, in which deep-rooted political changes occurred, is dedicated, while building its own society and State on a legal and democratic basis, to consistently, constructively and sincerely contribute to the turning of a new page in the life of South-eastern Europe. In this task, Yugoslavia needs the understanding and support of all those in international relations, who in their hearts have the ideals of dialogue, peace, happiness, and well-being for the people and nations, regardless of the differences and different fates that separated them in the past and, unfortunately, still continue to do so. Your indefatigable and self-sacrificing striving by personal example for bringing people and nations to a tolerant and open dialogue, for the purpose of finding out the truth that will bring salvation to us all, as well as for guiding the actions of the Roman Catholic Church in that direction, assure us that with the principles by which they are guided in international relations and the goals that they aspire to, there is a high possibility of agreement between the Federal Republic of Yugoslavia and the Holy See. Because of that I am confident that practical bilateral cooperation between the two countries will continue in the spirit of full trust, mutual understanding and friendship.

Citizens of the Federal Republic of Yugoslavia cannot forget the lack of understanding and the injustices that in the last decade they have often been subjected to, but because of that, with even more gratitude they remember those who, like Your Holiness, were consistent in their solidarity with the victims and who knew how to voice their disagreement with the injustices that were done to the innocent. You pointed out the harmfulness and the unjustifiability of economic sanctions, you condemned the use of force in international relations and warned against its counterproductive nature, you were against the exclusion of Yugoslavia from international organizations, and the people of Belgrade will never forget that under the bombs, for the whole duration of the air strikes, in 1999, their fellow townsman was the Apostolic Nuncio.

Like the Holy See, the Federal Republic of Yugoslavia also believes in the perspective of a unified Europe that "breathes with both lungs," so that economic globalization may become an opportunity for all, in the affirmation of the principles of solidarity and the rule of law in international relations, with the avoidance of the use of double standards, in giving advantage to dialogue and the elimination of violence, and especially of all forms of terrorism.

Papal Response:

Mr. Ambassador,

1. It is with pleasure that I welcome you to the Vatican at the beginning of your mission as Ambassador Extraordinary and Plenipotentiary of the Federal Republic of Yugoslavia to the Holy See. In accepting your Letters of Credence, I thank you for your gracious words, and I ask you to convey to the President, Dr. Vojislav Kostunica, my heartfelt best wishes and the assurance of my prayers for the good of the nation at this important and complex time in history.

Reconciliation within Yugoslavia itself

2. The conflict which occurred in your country left in its wake, as you say, "material and moral damage," with an entire society in need of rebuilding. This is a long and difficult process which, I am pleased to note, is already under way in Serbia and Montenegro; but great determination and patience on the part of the people and continuing solidarity from beyond your borders are required if this process is to come to full term.

In the first place, there is *a need for reconciliation within Yugoslavia itself*, so that all may work together, with respect for one another's differences, to rebuild society and the common good. This is never easy, and it is made still more difficult in the case of Yugoslavia because of the instability and conflicts which followed the collapse of the former regime based on atheistic materialism.

As the process of reconciliation and, in a real sense, of authentic peace-making goes forward, there is a need to put aside ethnic and nationalistic introversion, and to further build a nation whose democratic institutions, while sustaining unity, ensure that all its peoples, especially the minorities, are active and equal participants in the political and economic life of their communities.

Dialogue, solidarity and forgiveness to resolve cultural antagonisms

3. Looking further afield, it is important to pursue *the process of reconciliation within the Balkan region as a whole*, and to reject definitively any resort to violence as a way of settling disputes. Your own country has known better than most through its history that violence begets more violence, and that *dialogue alone can break that death-*

dealing spiral. The ethnic and religious differences in the region are real, and many of the antagonisms have deep historical roots, which at times make the prospect of true and lasting peace seem remote.

In my Message for the 2001 World Day of Peace, I noted that "in the past, cultural differences have often been a source of misunderstanding between peoples and the cause of conflicts and wars" (no. 8); yet I went on to insist that "dialogue between cultures [is] a privileged means for building the civilization of love" and that this dialogue "is based upon the recognition that there are values which are common to all cultures because they are rooted in the nature of this person" (ibid., no. 16). Among these universal values, I named *solidarity, peace, life and education*, and for the peoples of Yugoslavia these are the beacons lighting the path into the future. I would also echo my Message for the 2002 World Day of Peace, which stresses *forgiveness as an overarching value*, for there is no peace without justice, and there is no justice without forgiveness; and there will only be true healing for those many "wounded souls" whom you have mentioned if there is forgiveness and reconciliation.

The need to build bridges extends beyond the Balkan region to *the whole of Europe*. The continent's efforts to build a new kind of unity require, as you have observed, "full integration of South-eastern Europe into a new political, economic and cultural structure." *Europe needs the Balkan nations, and they need Europe*. This is a fact which recent antagonisms may have obscured, but upon which history and culture insist.

Church seeks full development of all peoples and solidarity with those in need
4. The Catholic Church, faithful to the spiritual and ethical principles of her universal mission, seeks to promote not some narrow ideological or national interest but *the full development of all peoples, with particular attention to and solidarity with those most in need*. That is why, with her ethos of communion and long experience of negotiating differences, the Church is deeply committed, through her religious and cultural action, to cooperate with Yugoslavia as it develops a mature and forward looking democracy based on respect for the dignity, freedom and rights of every human person.

It is important for all to recognize that in a situation such as the one you face, *religion is not the root of the problem, but an essential part of its solution*. At the recent Day of Prayer for Peace in Assisi, I stressed that "religions are at the service of peace" and that it is their duty "to foster in the people of our time a renewed sense of the urgency of building peace" (*Address*, January 24, 2002, no. 3). That is why I am pleased that religious education has been re-introduced in Serbian schools, for it provides a special opportunity to teach the young those universal values which are rooted in the nature of the person and ultimately in God. In this way citizens are trained in a genuine humanism and culture of peace. Religious education also *opens the young to transcendence* in a way that would make any relapse into the soul-destroying world of atheistic materialism more difficult.

Offices of the Holy See are ready to cooperate
5. Mr. Ambassador, as you enter the community of diplomats accredited to the Holy See, I assure you of the ready collaboration of the various Offices of the Roman Curia. May your mission serve to strengthen the bond of friendship and cooperation between

your Government and the Holy See; and may that bond contribute richly to the well-being of your nation at this decisive time. Upon Your Excellency and the beloved peoples of the Federal Republic of Yugoslavia I invoke the abundant blessings of Almighty God.

May 15, 2003
(*OR*, May 21, 2003, pp. 3,10)

Papal Response to H.E. Dr. John J. Herron, Ambassador of Australia:

Your Excellency,

It is a pleasure for me to extend a cordial welcome to you today as I accept the Letters of Credence by which you are appointed Ambassador Extraordinary and Plenipotentiary of Australia to the Holy See. Though some years ago now, my Pastoral Visits to your country remain clearly etched in my mind. I especially recall the beatification of Mary MacKillop, that loyal daughter of the Church who, for Australians in particular, has become a model of Christian discipleship. I thank you for the greetings which you bear from the Government and the people of Australia. Please convey to them my sincere best wishes and assure them of my prayers for the peace and well-being of the nation.

The common ideals and human values with which both the Holy See and Australia seek to confront the problems facing humanity today must continue to find resonance even in societies marked by strong individualism and increasing secularism. In this regard, the Holy See's diplomatic mission seeks to present a vision of hope to an increasingly divided world. The Church's commitment to this aim, seen in her defense of the dignity of human life and the promotion of human rights, social justice and solidarity, arises out of the recognition of the common origin of all people and points to their common destiny. In this perspective the transcendent dimension of life works to counter tendencies toward social fragmentation and isolation so sadly prevalent in many societies today.

Solidarity with developing nations is a well known and laudable trait of your people. Involvement of Australians in peace-keeping missions, their generous assistance with aid projects and more recently their support of the newly independent nation of East Timor, all speak well of their desire to contribute to the international security and stability necessary for authentic social and economic advancement. Drawing on the strength of Australia's many years of sound diplomacy, her emerging role as a leader in the Asia-Pacific region gives your nation the opportunity to become an increasingly important agent of peace for those countries seeking a maturity in international solidarity. This has been particularly noted in the wake of acts of terrorism which tragically shatter the hopes for world peace.

Involvement of Australians in peace-keeping missions

Acts of solidarity are more than just unilateral humanitarian acts of good intent. True humanitarianism recognizes and expresses God's universal plan for humanity. It is only in accord with this vision of worldwide solidarity that the complex challenges of justice, freedom of peoples and the peace of humanity can be effectively addressed (cf. *Familiaris Consortio*, no. 48). At the heart of this vision is the belief that all men and women receive their essential and common dignity from God and the capacity to transcend every social order so as to move toward truth and goodness (cf. *Centesimus Annus*, no. 38). It is in this light that your dialogues and partnerships with those countries north of your continent, which do not share a Christian heritage, will find their proper and stable foundation. Similarly, it is only within this perspective of the essential unity of mankind that the trying difficulties associated with the reception of refugees and with the lingering question of Aboriginal land rights will find compassionate and truly humanitarian solutions.

Uphold the sacredness of marriage and family life

Your Excellency has observed that tolerance is a further trait of the people of Australia. Indeed this characteristic has endeared many to your land and is reflected in the integration of the multiple ethnic communities now found there. The respect due to all persons does not, however, find its origin simply in the fact of differences between peoples. From the understanding of the true nature of life as gift stems the requirement that men and women must respect the natural and moral structure with which they have been endowed by God (cf. *Centesimus Annus*, no. 38). While political emphasis on human subjectivity has certainly focused on individual rights, it is sometimes the case that tendencies of "political correctness" seem to neglect that "men and women are called to direct their steps toward a truth which transcends them" (*Fides et Ratio*, no. 5). Sundered from that truth, which is the only guarantee of freedom and happiness, individuals are at the mercy of caprice and undifferentiated pluralism, slowly losing the capacity to lift their gaze to the heights of the meaning of human life.

In Australia, as in many other countries, the struggle to interpret choices of lifestyle in relation to God's plan for humanity is manifested in the pressures facing marriage and family life. The sacredness of marriage must be upheld by both religious and civic bodies. Secular and pragmatic distortions of the reality of marriage can never overshadow the splendour of a life-long covenant based on generous self-giving and unconditional love. This splendid vision of marriage and stable family life offers to society as a whole a foundation upon which the aspirations of a nation can be anchored.

Respond generously to serious problems of modern society

For her part the Catholic Church in Australia will continue to provide support for family life, through which the future of humanity passes (cf. *Familiaris Consortio*, no. 86). She is already heavily involved in the spiritual and intellectual formation of the young, especially through her schools. Additionally, her social apostolate extends to those facing some of the serious problems of modern society – alcohol, drugs, behavioral addiction – and I am confident that the Church will continue to respond generously to new social challenges as they arise.

Your Excellency, I know that your mission will serve to strengthen further the bonds of friendship which already exist between Australia and the Holy See. As you take up your new responsibilities I assure you that the various offices of the Roman Curia are ready to assist you in the fulfillment of your duties. Upon you, your family and fellow citizens, I cordially invoke the abundant blessings of Almighty God.

Chapter III
The Pope and the United Nations
The Culture of Peace as Collective Moral Responsibility

Article 1 of the United Nations Charter defines the primary purposes of the organization. The UN's is a mandate "to maintain international peace and security and to that end: to take effective collective measures for the prevention and removal of threats to peace . . . and to bring by peaceful means . . . adjustment or settlement of international disputes." The UN also focuses upon cooperative efforts to achieve progress in economic, cultural, and social matters. And while most readers are probably familiar with the General Assembly (governing mechanism), Secretariat (executive section), and Security Council (chief security component), they should not overlook the many other facets of the UN structure. These include, to name but a few: the International Court of Justice, Trusteeship Council, the UN Environment Program, UN Institute for Disarmament Research, Commission on Human Rights, International Labor Organization, World Health Organization, and the UN offices at Geneva, Vienna, and Nairobi. The very existence of the United Nations is testament to the fact that when States dedicate themselves on behalf of the culture of peace, that culture becomes permanent and visible.

In October 1965, Pope Paul VI became the first pontiff to personally address the UN General Assembly. During the years of his papacy (1963–1978), Pope Paul met frequently with UN officials and delegations, always supporting the ideals of the UN's founding Charter (1945) and the tenets of its Universal Declaration of Human Rights (1948). Pope John Paul II furthered the Holy See's attentiveness to the plethora of UN undertakings. What follows are the texts of the Pope's speeches to the UN General Assembly on October 2, 1979, and on October 5, 1995. They constitute a virtual primer of his philosophy about the UN's capacity to influence the contours of the culture of peace. Additionally, the chapter's inclusion of the Pope's remarks to UNESCO, to the XXVI Session of the Conference of the FAO and to the UN Secretary General and Administrative Committee on Coordination, convey how the pontiff correlates the work of the many UN agencies and entities with the overall goals of the United Nations. The Pope's involvement with UN diplomats and representatives permits us to deduce that the culture of peace:

(21) . . . strives "to do away with the very possibility of provoking war" (General Assembly, 1979, para. 16).

The entirety of the Pope's 1979 Address may be understood as a delineation of ways in which war can be prevented. Pope John Paul contends that the UN and its numerous institutions are able to discover the "roots of hatred, destructiveness and contempt – the roots of everything that produces the temptation to war, not so much in the hearts of the nations as in the inner determination of the systems that decide the history of whole societies" (idem). Therefore, where the UN would have the culture of peace reject the culture of war, the UN must analyze how tensions still assault the inalienability of human rights (para. 18), how human dignity becomes impaired (para. 19), how "the world of material values" often competes with "that of spiritual values" (para. 21), and how faulty economic premises retaliate against community (para. 22–23).

(22) . . . *accepts risk as a corollary of commitment to peace.*

On the fiftieth anniversary of the United Nations (1995), Pope John Paul asked UN delegates, "Inspired by the example of all those who have taken the risk of freedom, can we not recommit ourselves also to taking the risk of solidarity – and thus the risk of peace?" (no.15). Risk. It implies that the diplomacy of the culture of peace admits of a very reduced comfort zone. There are neither convenient nor ingratiating nor definitive nor automatic ingredients of prolonged peace. Instead, there is the risk of having to "learn to conquer fear" (no. 16), the risk of embracing "the weakest and the suffering" (no. 17), the risk of awakening to the "soul of the civilization of love" (no. 18).

(23) . . . *proposes that education should integrate man, not alienate him.*

Representatives of UNESCO met with the Pope on June 2, 1980. The twenty-three articles of his speech are significant in that they outline why the Pope perceives humanity to be inextricably bound to culture. The Pope insists that "man cannot do without culture," since it "is a specific way of man's 'existing' and 'being' . . . determining the inter-human and social character of human existence" (no. 16). According to Pope John Paul, the essential role of culture is to educate. And education consists, the Pope states, "in enabling man to become more man, to 'be' more and not just to 'have' more" (no. 11).

The task in a culture of peace is both to moderate and to regulate all that would debase man's nature. But humanity must remain alert lest education result in alienation. Such will inevitably transpire when education accentuates too little of what man "is" and too much of what he "can take advantage of in the field of . . . possession." What this yields is a loss of subjectivity, so much so that the vacuum becomes filled by multiple political, social and economic "manipulations" (no. 13). Education is meant to defeat estrangement, not to escalate it.

(24) . . . *perpetuates awareness that the resources of the earth are predictably finite.*

The Pope annually meets delegates to the conference of the UN's Food and Agricultural Organization. On the fortieth anniversary of the inauguration of FAO headquarters in Rome, he delivered the address cited in Chapter III. On this occasion (November 14, 1991), he expressed his "anxiety for the plight of the world's hungry" (para. 2). His argument shows that within the culture of peace there must be pervasive mindfulness of what is demanded for fidelity to humanity's stewardship of creation. That stewardship requires at least five elements: knowledge that the planet's natural resources must not be taken for granted, that those resources must be replenished whenever possible, that their utilization must be cooperatively organized, that over-exploitation must cease (para. 4), and that training centers should be established to ensure the proper "sharing of know-how and skill" (para. 5). The biblical injunction to "subdue the earth" (Gen 1:28) is the exact opposite of allowing for a devastation or depletion of the earth.

(25) . . . *regards trends toward globalization as potentially beneficial for the whole of mankind.*

Political science authors carefully distinguish between globalism (efforts to spread a country's interests everywhere) and globalization. The latter is generally portrayed as a byproduct of economics. The world is seen as a market and where money, ideas, and goods freely move in the direction of their customers. However, not every country is equally enthusiastic about becoming actively engaged in this capitalist enterprise (e.g. Cuba, North Korea). But is a restricted view of globalization the only viable understanding of it? Pope John Paul advocates a broader conceptualization. Speaking to Kofi Annan, UN Secretary General, and to the UN's Administrative Committee on Coordination (April 7, 2000), the Pope noted how the United Nations seeks to remind States that the "global dimension" of their interdependence "requires new ways of thinking and new types of cooperation" (no. 1b). And while there may be "socio-economic causes of humanitarian crises," globalization also means that cooperating States become sponsor of a more positive and widespread development on various levels beyond economics and technology. The culture of peace is not an alliance for special interests (globalism); rather, it is a "convergence of the varied interests and needs – regional and particular – of the world at large" (no. 3a).

October 2, 1979
(http://www.newadvent.org/docs/jp02u1.htm)

Address to the General Assembly

Mr. President:

I DESIRE TO EXPRESS MY GRATITUDE to the General Assembly of the United Nations, which I am permitted today to participate in and to address. My thanks go in the first place to the Secretary General of the United Nations organization, Dr. Kurt Waldheim. Last autumn, soon after my election to the Chair of St. Peter, he invited me to make this visit, and he renewed his invitation in the course of our meeting in Rome last May. From the first moment I felt greatly honored and deeply obliged. And today, before this distinguished assembly, I also thank you, Mr. President, who have so kindly welcomed me and invited me to speak.

The formal reason for my intervention today is, without any question, the special bond of cooperation that links the Apostolic See with the United Nations organization, as is shown by the presence of the Holy See's permanent observer to this organization. The existence of this bond, which is held in high esteem by the Holy See, rests on the sovereignty with which the Apostolic See has been endowed for many centuries. The territorial extent of that sovereignty is limited to the small state of Vatican City, but the sovereignty itself is warranted by the need of the papacy to exercise its mission in full freedom and to be able to deal with any interlocutor, whether a government or an international organization, without dependence on other sovereignties. Of course the nature and aims of the spiritual mission of the Apostolic See and the Church make their participation in the tasks and activities of the United Nations very different from that of the States, which are communities in the political and temporal sense.

Besides attaching great importance to its collaboration with the United Nations organization, the Apostolic See has always since the foundation of your organization, expressed its esteem and its agreement with the historic significance of this supreme forum for the international life of humanity today. It also never ceases to support your organization's functions and initiatives, which are aimed at peaceful coexistence and collaboration between nations. There are many proofs of this. In the more than 30 years of the existence of the United Nations, it has received much attention in papal messages and encyclicals, in documents of the Catholic episcopate and likewise in the Second Vatican Council. Pope John XXIII and Pope Paul VI looked with confidence on your important institution as an eloquent and promising sign of our times. He who is now addressing you has, since the first months of his pontificate, several times expressed the same confidence and conviction as his predecessors.

This confidence and conviction on the part of the Apostolic See are the result, as I have said, not of merely political reasons but of the religious and moral character of the mission of the Roman Catholic Church. As a universal community embracing faithful belonging to almost all countries and continents, nations, peoples, races, languages and cultures, the Church is deeply interested in the existence and activity of the organization whose very name tells us that it unites and associates nations and states. It unites and associates, it does not divide and oppose. It seeks out the ways for understanding and peaceful collaboration, and endeavors with the means at its disposal and the methods in its power to exclude war, division and mutual destruction within the great family of humanity today.

This is the real reason, the essential reason, for my presence among you, and I wish to thank this distinguished assembly for giving consideration to this reason, which can make my presence among you in some way useful. It is certainly a highly significant fact that among you in the representatives of the States, whose *raison d'être* is the sovereignty of powers linked with territory and people, there is also today the representative of the Apostolic See and the Catholic Church. This Church is the Church of Jesus Christ who declared before the tribunal of the Roman judge, Pilate, that he was a king, but with a kingdom not of this world (cf. Jn 18:36–37). When he was then asked about the reason for the existence of his kingdom among men, he explained: "For this I was born, and for this I have come into the world, to bear witness to the truth" (Jn. 18:37). Here, before the representatives of the States, I wish not only to thank you but also to offer my special congratulations, since the invitation extended to the Pope to speak in your assembly shows that the United Nations accepts and respects the religious and moral dimension of those human problems that it is her duty to bring to the world. The questions that concern your functions and receive your attention – as is indicated by the vast organic complex of institutions and activities that are part of or collaborate with the United Nations, especially in the fields of culture, health, food, labor and the peaceful uses of nuclear energy – certainly make it essential for us to meet in the name of man in his wholeness, in all the fullness and manifold riches of his spiritual and material existence, as I have stated in my encyclical *Redemptor Hominis,* the first of my pontificate.

Now, availing myself of the solemn occasion of my meeting with the representatives of the nations of the earth, I wish above all to send my greetings to all the men and women living on this planet. To every man and every woman, without any exception whatever, every human being living on earth is a member of a civil society, of a nation, many of them represented here. Each one of you, distinguished ladies and gentlemen, represents a particular state, system and political structure, but what you represent above all are individual human beings; you are all representatives of men and women, of practically all the people of the world, individual men and women, communities and peoples who are living the present phase of their own history and who are also part of the history of humanity as a whole, each of them a subject endowed with dignity as a human person with his or her own culture, experiences and aspirations, tensions and sufferings, and legitimate expectations. This relationship is what provides the reason for all political activity, whether national or international, for in the final analysis this activity comes from man, is exercised by man and is for man. And if political activity is cut off from this fundamental relationship and finality, if it becomes in a way its own end, it loses much of its reason to exist. Even more, it can also give rise to a specific alienation; it can become extraneous to man; it can come to contradict humanity itself. In reality, what justifies the existence of any political activity is service to man, concerned and responsible attention to the essential problems and duties of his earthly existence in its social dimension and significance, on which also the good of each person depends.

I ask you, Ladies and Gentlemen, to excuse me for speaking of questions that are certainly self-evident for you. But it does not seem pointless to speak of them, since the most frequent pitfall for human activities is the possibility of losing sight, while performing them, of the clearest truths, the most elementary principles.

I would like to express the wish that, in view of its universal character, the United Nations will never cease to be the forum, the high tribune, from which all man's problems are appraised in truth and justice. It was in the name of this inspiration, it was through this historic stimulus, that on June 26, 1945, toward the end of the terrible World War II, the Charter of the United Nations was signed and on the following October 24, your organization began its life. Soon after, on December 10, 1948, came its fundamental document, the Universal Declaration of Human Rights, the rights of the human being as a concrete individual and of the human being in his universal value. This document is a milestone on the long and difficult path of the human race. The progress of humanity must be measured not only by the progress of science and technology, which shows man's uniqueness with regard to nature, but also and chiefly by the primacy given to spiritual values and by the progress of moral life. In this field is manifested the full dominion of reason, through truth, in the behavior of the individual and of society, and also the control of reason over nature; and thus human conscience quietly triumphs, as was expressed in the ancient saying, "Genus humanum arte et ratione vivit."

It was when technology was being directed in its one-sided progress toward goals of war, hegemony and conquest, so that man might kill man and nation destroy nation by depriving it of its liberty and the right to exist – and I still have before my mind the image of World War II in Europe, which began 40 years ago on September 1, 1939, with the invasion of Poland and ended on May 9, 1945 – it was precisely then that the United Nations arose. And three years later the document appeared which, as I have said, must be considered a real milestone on the path of the moral progress of humanity – the Universal Declaration of Human Rights. The governments and states of the world have understood that, if they are not to attack and destroy each other, they must unite. The real way, the fundamental way to this is through each human being, through the definition and recognition of and respect for the inalienable rights of individuals and of the communities of peoples.

Today, 40 years after the outbreak of World War II, I wish to recall the whole of the experiences by individuals and nations that were sustained by a generation that is largely still alive. I had occasion not long ago to reflect again on some of those experiences, in one of the places that are most distressing and overflowing with contempt for man and his fundamental rights – the extermination camp of Oswiecim (Auschwitz), which I visited during my pilgrimage to Poland last June. This infamous place is unfortunately only one of the many scattered over the continent of Europe. But the memory of even one should be a warning sign on the path of humanity today, in order that every kind of concentration camp anywhere on earth may once and for all be done away with. And everything that recalls those horrible experiences should also disappear forever from the lives of nations and states, everything that is a continuation of those experiences under different forms, namely the various kinds of torture and oppression, either physical or moral, carried out under any system, in any land; this phenomenon is all the more distressing if it occurs under the pretext of internal security or the need to preserve an apparent peace.

You will forgive me, Ladies and Gentlemen, for evoking this memory. But I would be untrue to the history of this century, I would be dishonest with regard to the great cause of man, which we all wish to serve, if I should keep silent, I who come from the country on whose living body Oswiecim was at one time constructed. But my purpose in invoking this memory is above all to show what painful experiences and sufferings by millions of people gave rise to the Universal Declaration of Human Rights, which has been placed as the basic inspiration and cornerstone of the United Nations organization. This declaration was paid for by millions of our brothers and sisters at the cost of their suffering and sacrifice, brought about by the brutalization that darkened and made insensitive the human consciences of their oppressors and of those who carried out a real genocide. This price cannot have been paid in vain! The Universal Declaration of Human Rights – with its train of many declarations and conventions on highly important aspects of human rights, in favor of children, of women, of equality between races, and especially the two international covenants on economic, social and cultural rights and on civil and political rights – must remain the basic value in the United Nations with which the consciences of its members must be confronted and from which they must draw continual inspiration. If the truths and principles contained in this document were to be forgotten or ignored and were thus to lose the genuine self evidence that distinguished them at the time they were brought painfully to birth, then the noble purpose of the United Nations could be faced with the threat of a new destruction. This is what would happen if the simple yet powerful eloquence of the Universal Declaration of Human Rights were decisively subjugated by what is wrongly called political interest, but often really means no more than one-sided gain and advantage to the detriment of others, or a thirst for power regardless of the needs of others – everything which by its nature is opposed to the spirit of the declaration. Political interest understood in this sense, if you will pardon me, Ladies and Gentlemen, dishonors the noble and difficult mission of your service for the good of your countries and of all humanity.

Fourteen years ago my great predecessor Pope Paul VI spoke from this podium. He spoke memorable words, which I desire to repeat today: "No more war, war never again! Never one against the other," or even "one above the other," but always, on every occasion, "with each other."

Paul VI was a tireless servant of the cause of peace. I wish to follow him with all my strength and continue his service. The Catholic Church in every place on earth proclaims a message of peace, prays for peace, educates for peace. This purpose is also shared by the representatives and followers of other churches and communities and of other religions of the world, and they have pledged themselves to it. In union with efforts by all people of good will, this work is certainly bearing fruit. Nevertheless we are continually troubled by the armed conflicts that break out from time to time. How grateful we are to the Lord when a direct intervention succeeds in avoiding such a conflict, as in the case of the tension that last year threatened Argentina and Chile.

It is my fervent hope that a solution also to the Middle East crises may draw nearer. While being prepared to recognize the value of any concrete step or attempt made to settle the conflict, I want to recall that it would have no value if it did not truly represent the first stone of a general overall peace in the area, a peace that, being necessarily based on equitable recognition of the rights of all, cannot fail to include the consideration and just settlement of the Palestinian question. Connected with this question is that of the tranquility, independence and territorial integrity of Lebanon within the formula that has made it an example of peaceful and mutually fruitful coexistence between distinct communities, a formula that I hope will, in the common interest, be maintained, with the adjustments required by the developments of the situation. I also hope for a special statute that, under international guarantees – as my predecessor Paul VI indicated – would respect the particular nature of Jerusalem, a heritage sacred to the veneration of millions of believers of the three great monotheistic religions, Judaism, Christianity and Islam.

We are troubled also by reports of the development of weaponry exceeding in quality and size the means of war and destruction ever known before. In this field also we applaud the decisions and agreements aimed at reducing the arms race. Nevertheless, the life of humanity today is seriously endangered by the threat of destruction and by the risk arising even from accepting certain tranquilizing reports. And the resistance to actual concrete proposals of real disarmament, such as those called for by this assembly in a special session last year, shows that together with the will for peace that all profess and that most desire there is also in existence – perhaps in latent or conditional form but nonetheless real – the contrary and the negation of this will. The continual preparations for war demonstrated by the production of ever more numerous, powerful and sophisticated weapons in various countries show that there is a desire to be ready for war, and being ready means being able to start it; it also means taking the risk that sometime, somewhere, somehow, someone can set in motion the terrible mechanism of general destruction.

It is therefore necessary to make a continuing and even more energetic effort to do away with the very possibility of provoking war, and to make such catastrophes impossible by influencing the attitudes and convictions, the very intentions and aspirations of governments and peoples. This duty, kept constantly in mind by the United Nations and each of its institutions, must also be a duty for every society, every regime, every government. This task is certainly served by initiatives aimed at international cooperation for the fostering of development. As Paul VI said at the end of his encyclical *Populorum Progressio*, "If the new name for peace is development, who would not wish to labor for it with all his powers?" However, this task must also be served by constant reflection and activity aimed at discovering the very roots of hatred, destructiveness and contempt – the roots of everything that produces the temptation to war, not so much in the hearts of the nations as in the inner determination of the systems that decide the history of whole societies. In this titanic labor of building up the peaceful future of our planet the United Nations has undoubtedly a key function and guiding role, for which it must refer to the just ideals contained in the Universal Declaration of Human Rights. For this declaration has struck a real blow against the many deep roots of war, since the spirit of war, in its basic primordial meaning, springs up and grows to maturity where the inalienable rights of man are violated.

This is a new and deeply relevant vision of the cause of peace, one that goes deeper and is more radical. It is a vision that sees the genesis, and in a sense the substance, of war in the more complex forms emanating from injustice viewed in all its various aspects; this injustice first attacks human rights and thereby destroys the organic unity of the social order and it then affects the whole system of international relations. Within the Church's doctrine, the encyclical *Pacem in Terris* by John XXIII provides in synthetic form a view of this matter that is very close to the ideological foundation of the United Nations. This must therefore form the basis to which one must loyally and perseveringly adhere in order to establish true peace on earth.

By applying this criterion we must diligently examine which principal tensions in connection with the inalienable rights of man can weaken the construction of this peace which we all desire so ardently and which is the essential goal of the efforts of the United Nations. It is not easy, but it must be done. Anyone who undertakes it must take up a totally objective position and be guided by sincerity, readiness to acknowledge one's prejudices and mistakes and readiness even to renounce one's own particular interests, including any of these interests. It is by sacrificing these interests for the sake of peace that we serve them best. After all, in whose political interest can it ever be to have another war?

Every analysis must necessarily start from the premise that – although each person lives in a particular concrete social and historical context – every human being is endowed with a dignity that must never be lessened, impaired or destroyed but must instead be respected and safeguarded. if peace is really to be built up.

In a movement that one hopes will be progressive and continuous, the Universal Declaration of Human Rights and the other international and national juridical instruments are endeavoring to create general awareness of the dignity of the human being, and to define at least some of the inalienable rights of man. Permit me to enumerate some of the most important human rights that are universally recognized: the right to life, liberty and security of person; the right to food, clothing, housing, sufficient health care, rest and leisure; the right to freedom of expression, education and culture; the right to manifest one's religion either individually or in community, in public or in private; the right to choose a state of life, to found a family and to enjoy all conditions necessary for family life; the right to property and work, to adequate working conditions and a just wage; the right of assembly and association; the right to freedom of movement, to internal and external migration; the right to nationality and residence; the right to political participation and the right to participate in the free choice of the political system of the people to which one belongs. All these human rights taken together are in keeping with the substance of the dignity of the human being, understood in his entirety, not as reduced to one dimension only. These rights concern the satisfaction of man's essential needs, the exercise of his freedoms and his relationships with others; but always and everywhere they concern man, they concern man's full human dimension.

Man lives at the same time both in the world of material values and in that of spiritual values. For the individual living and hoping man, his needs, freedoms and relationships with others never concern one sphere of values alone, but belong to both. Material and spiritual realities may be viewed separately in order to understand better that in the concrete human being they are inseparable, and to see that any threat to human rights, whether in the field of material realities or in that of spiritual realities, is equally dangerous for peace, since in every instance it concerns man in his entirety. Permit me, distinguished Ladies and Gentlemen, to recall a constant rule of the history of humanity, a rule that is implicitly contained in all that I have already stated with regard to integral development and human rights. The rule is based on the relationship between spiritual values and material or economic values. In this relationship, it is the spiritual values that are preeminent, both on account of the nature of these values and also for reasons concerning the good of man. The pre-eminence of the values of the spirit defines the proper sense of earthly material goods and the way to use them. This pre-eminence is therefore at the basis of a just peace. It is also a contributing factor to ensuring that material development, technical development and the development of civilization are at the service of what constitutes man. This means enabling man to have full access to truth, to moral development, and to the complete possibility of enjoying the goods of culture which he has inherited, and of increasing them by his own creativity. It is easy to see that material goods do not have unlimited capacity for satisfying the needs of man: They are not in themselves easily distributed and, in the relationship between those who possess and enjoy them and those who are without them, they give rise to tension, dissension and division that will often even turn into open conflict. Spiritual goods, on the other hand, are open to unlimited enjoyment by many at the same time, without diminution of the goods themselves. Indeed, the more people share in such goods, the more they are enjoyed and drawn upon, the more then do those goods show their indestructible and immortal worth. This truth is confirmed, for example, by the works of creativity – I mean by the works of thought, poetry, music, and the figurative arts, fruits of man's spirit.

A critical analysis of our modern civilization shows that in the last hundred years it has contributed as never before to the development of material goods, but that it has also given rise, both in theory and still more in practice, to a series of attitudes in which sensitivity to the spiritual dimension of human existence is diminished to a greater or lesser extent, as a result of certain premises which reduce the meaning of human life chiefly to the many different material and economic factors – I mean to the demands of production, the market, consumption, the accumulation of riches or of the growing bureaucracy with which an attempt is made to regulate these very processes. Is this not the result of having subordinated man to one single conception and sphere of values?

What is the link between these reflections and the cause of peace and war? Since, as I have already stated, material goods by their very nature provoke conditionings and divisions, the struggle to obtain these goods becomes inevitable in the history of humanity. If we cultivate this one-sided subordination of man to material goods alone, we shall be incapable of overcoming this state of need. We shall be able to attenuate it and avoid it in particular cases, but we shall not succeed in eliminating it systematically and radically, unless we emphasize more and pay greater honor, before everyone's eyes, in the sight of every society, to the second dimension of the goods of man: the dimension that does not divide people but puts them into communication with each other, associates them and unites them.

I consider that the famous opening words of the Charter of the United Nations, in which the peoples of the United Nations, determined to save succeeding generations from the scourge of war, solemnly reaffirmed "faith in fundamental human rights, in the dignity and worth of the human person, in the equal rights of men and women and of nations large and small," are meant to stress this dimension.

Indeed, the fight against incipient wars cannot be carried out on a merely superficial level, by treating the symptoms. It must be done in a radical way, by attacking the causes. The reason I have called attention to the dimension constituted by spiritual realities is my concern for the cause of peace, peace which is built up by men and women uniting around what is most fully and profoundly human, around what raises them above the world about them and determines their indestructible grandeur – indestructible in spite of the death to which everyone on earth is subject. I would like to add that the Catholic Church, and I think I can say, the whole of Christianity sees in this very domain its own particular task. The Second Vatican Council helped to establish what the Christian faith has in common with the various non-Christian religions in this aspiration. The Church is therefore grateful to all who show respect and good will with regard to this mission of hers and do not impede it or make it difficult. An analysis of the history of mankind, especially at its recent stage, shows how important is the duty of revealing more fully the range of the goods that are linked with the spiritual dimension of human existence. It shows how important this task is for building peace and how serious is any threat to human rights. Any violation of them, even in a peace situation, is a form of warfare against humanity.

It seems that in the modern world there are two main threats. Both concern human rights in the field of international relations and human rights within the individual states or societies.

The first of these systematic threats against human rights is linked in an overall sense with the distribution of material goods. This distribution is frequently unjust both within individual societies and on the planet as a whole. Everyone knows that these goods are given to man not only as nature's bounty; they are enjoyed by him chiefly as the fruit of his many activities, ranging from the simplest manual and physical labor to the most complicated forms of industrial production and highly qualified and specialized research and study. Various forms of inequality in the possession of material goods, and in the enjoyment of them, can often be explained by different historical and cultural causes and circumstances. But, while these circumstances can diminish the moral responsibility of people today, they do not prevent the situations of inequality from being marked by injustice and social injury.

People must become aware that economic tensions within countries and in the relationship between states and even between entire continents contain within themselves substantial elements that restrict or violate human rights. Such elements are the exploitation of labor and many other abuses that affect the dignity of the human person. It follows that the fundamental criterion for comparing social, economic and political systems is not, and cannot be, the criterion of hegemony and imperialism; it can be, and indeed it must be, the humanistic criterion, namely the measure in which each system is really capable of reducing, restraining and eliminating as far as possible the various forms of exploitation of man and of ensuring for him through work, not only the just distribution of the indispensable material goods, but also a participation, in keeping with his dignity, in the whole process of production and in the social life that grows up around that process. Let us not forget that, although man depends on the resources of the material world for his life, he cannot be their slave, but he must be their master. The words of the book of Genesis, "Fill the earth and subdue it" (Gn 1:28), are in a sense a primary and essential directive in the field of economy and of labor policy.

Humanity as a whole, and the individual nations, have certainly made remarkable progress in this field during the last hundred years. But it is a field in which there is never any lack of systematic threats and violations of human rights. Disturbing factors are frequently present in the form of the frightful disparities between excessively rich individuals and groups on the one hand, and on the other hand the majority made up of the poor or indeed of the destitute, who lack food and opportunities for work and education and are in great numbers condemned to hunger and disease. And concern is also caused at times by the radical separation of work from property, by man's indifference to the production enterprise to which he is linked only by a work obligation, without feeling that he is working for a good that will be his or for himself. It is no secret that the abyss separating the minority of the excessively rich from the multitude of the destitute is a very grave symptom in the life of any society. This must also be said with even greater insistence with regard to the abyss separating countries and regions of the earth. Surely the only way to overcome this serious disparity between areas of satiety and areas of hunger and depression is through coordinated cooperation by all countries. This requires above all else a unity inspired by an authentic perspective of peace. Everything will depend on whether these differences and contrasts in the sphere of the possession of goods will be systematically reduced through truly effective means, on whether the belts of hunger, malnutrition, destitution, underdevelopment, disease and illiteracy will disappear from the economic map of the earth, and on whether peaceful cooperation will avoid imposing conditions of exploitation and economic or political dependence, which would only be a form of neocolonialism.

I would now like to draw attention to a second systematic threat to man in his inalienable rights in the modern world, a threat which constitutes no less a danger than the first to the cause of peace I refer to the various forms of injustice in the field of the spirit.

Man can indeed be wounded in his inner relationship with truth, in his conscience, in his most personal belief, in his view of the world, in his religious faith, and in the sphere of what are known as civil liberties. Decisive for these last is equality of rights without discrimination on grounds of origin, race, sex, nationality, religion, political convictions and the like. Equality of rights means the exclusion of the various forms of privilege for some and discrimination against others, whether they are people born in the same country or people from different backgrounds of history, nationality, race and ideology. For centuries the thrust of civilization has been in one direction: that of giving the life of individual political societies a form in which there can be fully safeguarded the objective rights of the spirit, of human conscience and of human creativity, including man's relationship with God. Yet in spite of this we still see in this field recurring threats and violations, often with no possibility of appealing to a higher authority or of obtaining an effective remedy.

Besides the acceptance of legal formulas safeguarding the principle of the freedom of the human spirit, such as freedom of thought and expression, religious freedom and freedom of conscience, structures of social life often exist in which the practical exercise of these freedoms condemns man, in fact if not formally, to become a second class or third class citizen, to see compromised his chances of social advancement, his professional career or his access to certain posts of responsibility, and to lose even the possibility of educating his children freely. It is a question of the highest importance that in internal social life, as well as in international life, all human beings in every nation and country should be able to enjoy effectively their full rights under any political regime or system.

Only the safeguarding of this real completeness of rights for every human being without discrimination can ensure peace at its very roots.

With regard to religious freedom, which I as Pope am bound to have particularly at heart, precisely with a view to safeguarding peace, I would like to repeat here, as a contribution to respect for man's spiritual dimension, some principles contained in the Second Vatican Council's declaration *Dignitatis Humanae*. "In accordance with their dignity, all human beings, because they are persons, that is, beings endowed with reason and free will and therefore bearing personal responsibility, are both impelled by their nature and bound by a moral obligation to seek the truth, especially religious truth. They are also bound to adhere to the truth once they come to know it and to direct their whole lives in accordance with its demands."

"The practice of religion of its very nature consists primarily of those voluntary and free internal acts by which a human being directly sets his course toward God. No merely human power can either command or prohibit acts of this kind. But man's social nature itself requires that he give external expression to his internal acts of religion, that he communicate with others in religious matters and that he profess his religion in community" (*Dignitatis Humanae*).

These words touch the very substance of the question. They also show how even the confrontation between the religious view of the world and the agnostic or even atheistic view, which is one of the signs of the times of the present age, could preserve honest and respectful human dimensions without violating the essential rights of conscience of any man or woman living on earth.

Respect for the dignity of the human person would seem to demand that, when the exact tenor of the exercise of religious freedom is being discussed or determined with a view to national laws or international conventions, the institutions that are by their nature at the service of religion should also be brought in. If this participation is omitted, there is a danger of imposing, in so intimate a field of man's life, rules or restrictions that are opposed to his true religious needs.

The United Nations has proclaimed 1979 the Year of the Child. In the presence of the representatives of so many nations of the world gathered here, I wish to express the joy that we all find in children, the springtime of life, the anticipation of the future history of each of our present earthly homelands. No country on earth, no political system can think of its own future otherwise than through the image of these new generations that will receive from their parents the manifold heritage of values, duties and aspirations of the nations to which they belong and of the whole human family. Concern for the child, even before birth, from the first moment of conception and then throughout the years of infancy and youth, is the primary and fundamental test of the relationship of one human being to another.

And so, what better wish can I express for every nation and the whole of mankind, and for all the children of the world than a better future in which respect for human rights will become a complete reality throughout the third millennium, which is drawing near.

But in this perspective we must ask ourselves whether there will continue to accumulate over the heads of this new generation of children the threat of common extermination for which the means are in the hands of the modern states, especially the major world powers. Are the children to receive the arms race from us as a necessary inheritance? How are we to explain this unbridled race?

The ancients said: "Si vis pacem, para bellum." But can our age still really believe that the breathtaking spiral of armaments is at the service of world peace? In alleging the threat of a potential enemy, is it really not rather the intention to keep for oneself a means of threat, in order to get the upper hand with the aid of one's own arsenal of destruction? Here too it is the human dimension of peace that tends to vanish in favor of ever new possible forms of imperialism.

It must be our solemn wish here for our children, for the children of all the nations on earth, that this point will never be reached. And for that reason I do not cease to pray to God each day so that in his mercy he may save us from so terrible a day.

At the close of this address, I wish to express once more before all the high representatives of the states who are present a word of esteem and deep love for all the peoples, all the nations of the earth, for all human communities. Each one has its own history and culture. I hope that they will live and grow in the freedom and truth of their own history. For that is the measure of the common good of each one of them. I hope that each person will live and grow strong with the moral force of the community that forms its members as citizens. I hope that the State authorities, while respecting the just rights of each citizen, will enjoy the confidence of all for the common good. I hope that all the nations, even the smallest, even those that do not yet enjoy full sovereignty, and those that have been forcibly robbed of it, will meet in full equality with the others in the United Nations organization. I hope that the United Nations will ever remain the supreme forum of peace and justice, the authentic seat of freedom of peoples and individuals in their longing for a better future.

October 5, 1995
(http://christusrex.org/www1/pope/UN-speech.html)

Address to the General Assembly

Mr. President,
Ladies and Gentlemen,
1. It is an honor for me to have the opportunity to address this international Assembly and to join the men and women of every country, race, language and culture in celebrating the fiftieth anniversary of the founding of the United Nations Organization. In coming before this distinguished Assembly, I am vividly aware that through you I am in some way addressing the whole family of peoples living on the face of the earth. My words are meant as a sign of the interest and esteem of the Apostolic See and of the Catholic Church for this institution. They echo the voices of all those who see in the United Nations the hope of a better future for human society.

I wish to express my heartfelt gratitude in the first place to the Secretary General, Dr. Boutros Boutros-Ghali, for having warmly encouraged this visit. And I thank you, Mr. President, for your cordial welcome. I greet all of you, the members of this General Assembly: I am grateful for your presence and for your kind attention.

I come before you today with the desire to be able to contribute to that thoughtful meditation on the history and role of this Organization which should accompany and give substance to the anniversary celebrations. The Holy See, in virtue of its specifically spiritual mission, which makes it concerned for the integral good of every human being, has supported the ideals and goals of the United Nations Organization from the very beginning. Although their respective purposes and operative approaches are obviously different, the Church and the United Nations constantly find wide areas of cooperation on the basis of their common concern for the human family. It is this awareness which inspires my thoughts today; they will not dwell on any particular social, political, or economic question; rather, I would like to reflect with you on what the extraordinary changes of the last few years imply, not simply for the present, but for the future of the whole human family.

A common human patrimony
2. Ladies and Gentlemen! On the threshold of a new millennium we are witnessing an extraordinary global acceleration of that quest for freedom which is one of the great dynamics of human history. This phenomenon is not limited to any one part of the world; nor is it the expression of any single culture. Men and women throughout the world, even when threatened by violence, have taken the risk of freedom, asking to be given a place in social, political, and economic life which is commensurate with their dignity as free human beings. This universal longing for freedom is truly one of the distinguishing marks of our time.

During my previous Visit to the United Nations on October 2, 1979, I noted that the quest for freedom in our time has its basis in those universal rights which human beings enjoy by the very fact of their humanity. It was precisely outrages against human dignity which led the United Nations Organization to formulate, barely three years after its establishment, that Universal Declaration of Human Rights which remains one of the highest expressions of the human conscience of our time. In Asia

and Africa, in the Americas, in Oceania and Europe, men and women of conviction
and courage have appealed to this Declaration in support of their claims for a fuller
share in the life of society.

3. It is important for us to grasp what might be called the inner structure of this worldwide movement. It is precisely its global character which offers us its first and fundamental "key" and confirms that there are indeed universal human rights, rooted in the
nature of the person, rights which reflect the objective and inviolable demands of a
universal moral law. These are not abstract points; rather, these rights tell us something
important about the actual life of every individual and of every social group. They also
remind us that we do not live in an irrational or meaningless world. On the contrary,
there is a moral logic which is built into human life and which makes possible dialogue between individuals and peoples. If we want a century of violent coercion to be
succeeded by a century of persuasion, we must find a way to discuss the human future
intelligibly. The universal moral law written on the human heart is precisely that kind
of "grammar" which is needed if the world is to engage this discussion of its future.

In this sense, it is a matter for serious concern that some people today deny the
universality of human rights, just as they deny that there is a human nature shared by
everyone. To be sure, there is no single model for organizing the politics and economics of human freedom; different cultures and different historical experiences give
rise to different institutional forms of public life in a free and responsible society. But
it is one thing to affirm a legitimate pluralism of "forms of freedom," and another to
deny any universality or intelligibility to the nature of man or to the human experience. The latter makes the international politics of persuasion extremely difficult, if
not impossible.

Taking the risk of freedom
4. The moral dynamics of this universal quest for freedom clearly appeared in Central
and Eastern Europe during the non-violent revolutions of 1989. Unfolding in specific
times and places, those historical events nonetheless taught a lesson which goes far
beyond a specific geographical location. For the non-violent revolutions of 1989
demonstrated that the quest for freedom cannot be suppressed. It arises from a recognition of the inestimable dignity and value of the human person, and it cannot fail to
be accompanied by a commitment on behalf of the human person. Modern totalitarianism has been, first and foremost, an assault on the dignity of the person, an assault
which has gone even to the point of denying the inalienable value of the individual's
life. The revolutions of 1989 were made possible by the commitment of brave men and
women inspired by a different, and ultimately more profound and powerful, vision: the
vision of man as a creature of intelligence and free will, immersed in a mystery which
transcends his own being and endowed with the ability to reflect and the ability to
choose – and thus capable of wisdom and virtue. A decisive factor in the success of
those non-violent revolutions was the experience of social solidarity: in the face of
regimes backed by the power of propaganda and terror, that solidarity was the moral
core of the "power of the powerless," a beacon of hope and an enduring reminder that
it is possible for man's historical journey to follow a path which is true to the finest
aspirations of the human spirit.

Viewing those events from this privileged international forum, one cannot fail to grasp the connection between the values which inspired those people's liberation movements and many of the moral commitments inscribed in the United Nations Charter: I am thinking for example of the commitment to "reaffirm faith in fundamental human rights [and] in the dignity and worth of the human person"; and also the commitment "to promote social progress and better standards of life in larger freedom" (Preamble). The fifty-one States which founded this Organization in 1945 truly lit a lamp whose light can scatter the darkness caused by tyranny – a light which can show the way to freedom, peace, and solidarity.

The rights of nations

5. The quest for freedom in the second half of the twentieth century has engaged not only individuals but nations as well. Fifty years after the end of the Second World War, it is important to remember that that war was fought because of violations of the rights of nations. Many of those nations suffered grievously for no other reason than that they were deemed "other." Terrible crimes were committed in the name of lethal doctrines which taught the "inferiority" of some nations and cultures. In a certain sense, the United Nations Organization was born from a conviction that such doctrines were antithetical to peace; and the Charter's commitment to "save future generations from the scourge of war" (Preamble) surely implied a moral commitment to defend every nation and culture from unjust and violent aggression.

Unfortunately, even after the end of the Second World War, the rights of nations continued to be violated. To take but one set of examples, the Baltic States and extensive territories in Ukraine and Belarus were absorbed into the Soviet Union, as had already happened to Armenia, Azerbaijan, and Georgia in the Caucasus. At the same time the so-called "People's Democracies" of Central and Eastern Europe effectively lost their sovereignty and were required to submit to the will dominating the entire bloc. The result of this artificial division of Europe was the "cold war," a situation of international tension in which the threat of a nuclear holocaust hung over humanity. It was only when freedom was restored to the nations of Central and Eastern Europe that the promise of the peace which should have come with the end of the war began to be realized for many of the victims of that conflict.

6. The Universal Declaration of Human Rights, adopted in 1948, spoke eloquently of the rights of persons; but no similar international agreement has yet adequately addressed the rights of nations. This situation must be carefully pondered, for it raises urgent questions about justice and freedom in the world today.

In reality the problem of the full recognition of the rights of peoples and nations has presented itself repeatedly to the conscience of humanity, and has also given rise to considerable ethical and juridical reflection. I am reminded of the debate which took place at the Council of Constance in the fifteenth century, when the representatives of the Academy of Krakow, headed by Pawel Wlodkowic, courageously defended the right of certain European peoples to existence and independence. Still better known is the discussion which went on in that same period at the University of Salamanca with regard to the peoples of the New World. And in our own century, how can I fail to mention the prophetic words of my predecessor, Pope Benedict XV, who in the midst of the First World War reminded everyone that "nations do not die," and invited them "to ponder with serene conscience the rights and the just aspirations of peoples" (*To the Peoples at War and their Leaders*, July 28, 1915)?

7. Today the problem of nationalities forms part of a new world horizon marked by a great "mobility" which has blurred the ethnic and cultural frontiers of the different peoples, as a result of a variety of processes such as migrations, mass-media and the globalization of the economy. And yet, precisely against this horizon of universality we see the powerful re-emergence of a certain ethnic and cultural consciousness, as it were an explosive need for identity and survival, a sort of counterweight to the tendency toward uniformity. This is a phenomenon which must not be underestimated or regarded as a simple left-over of the past. It demands serious interpretation, and a closer examination on the levels of anthropology, ethics and law.

This tension between the particular and the universal can be considered immanent in human beings. By virtue of sharing in the same human nature, people automatically feel that they are members of one great family, as is in fact the case. But as a result of the concrete historical conditioning of this same nature, they are necessarily bound in a more intense way to particular human groups, beginning with the family and going on to the various groups to which they belong and up to the whole of their ethnic and cultural group, which is called, not by accident, a "nation," from the Latin word "nasci": "to be born." This term, enriched with another one, "patria" (fatherland/motherland), evokes the reality of the family. The human condition thus finds itself between these two poles – universality and particularity – with a vital tension between them; an inevitable tension, but singularly fruitful if they are lived in a calm and balanced way.

8. Upon this anthropological foundation there also rest the "rights of nations," which are nothing but "human rights" fostered at the specific level of community life. A study of these rights is certainly not easy, if we consider the difficulty of defining the very concept of "nation," which cannot be identified a priori and necessarily with the State. Such a study must nonetheless be made, if we wish to avoid the errors of the past and ensure a just world order.

A presupposition of a nation's rights is certainly its right to exist: therefore no one – neither a State nor another nation, nor an international organization – is ever justified in asserting that an individual nation is not worthy of existence. This fundamental right to existence does not necessarily call for sovereignty as a state, since various forms of juridical aggregation between different nations are possible, as for example occurs in Federal States, in Confederations or in States characterized by broad regional autonomies. There can be historical circumstances in which aggregations different from single state sovereignty can even prove advisable, but only on condition that this takes place in a climate of true freedom, guaranteed by the exercise of the self-determination of the peoples concerned. Its right to exist naturally implies that every nation also enjoys the right to its own language and culture, through which a people expresses and promotes that which I would call its fundamental spiritual "sovereignty." History shows that in extreme circumstances (such as those which occurred in the land where I was born) it is precisely its culture that enables a nation to survive the loss of political and economic independence. Every nation therefore has also the right to shape its life according to its own traditions, excluding, of course, every abuse of basic human rights and in particular the oppression of minorities. Every nation has the right to build its future by providing an appropriate education for the younger generation.

But while the "rights of the nation" express the vital requirements of "particularity," it is no less important to emphasize the requirements of universality, expressed through a clear awareness of the duties which nations have vis-à-vis other nations and humanity as a whole. Foremost among these duties is certainly that of living in a spirit of peace, respect and solidarity with other nations. Thus the exercise of the rights of nations, balanced by the acknowledgement and the practice of duties, promotes a fruitful "exchange of gifts," which strengthens the unity of all mankind.

Respect for differences
9. During my pastoral pilgrimages to the communities of the Catholic Church over the past seventeen years, I have been able to enter into dialogue with the rich diversity of nations and cultures in every part of the world. Unhappily, the world has yet to learn how to live with diversity, as recent events in the Balkans and Central Africa have painfully reminded us. The fact of "difference," and the reality of "the other," can sometimes be felt as a burden, or even as a threat. Amplified by historic grievances and exacerbated by the manipulations of the unscrupulous, the fear of "difference" can lead to a denial of the very humanity of "the other": with the result that people fall into a cycle of violence in which no one is spared, not even the children. We are all very familiar today with such situations; at this moment my heart and my prayers turn in a special way to the sufferings of the sorely tried peoples of Bosnia-Hercegovina.

From bitter experience, then, we know that the fear of "difference," especially when it expresses itself in a narrow and exclusive nationalism which denies any rights to "the other," can lead to a true nightmare of violence and terror. And yet if we make the effort to look at matters objectively, we can see that, transcending all the differences which distinguish individuals and peoples, there is a fundamental commonality. For different cultures are but different ways of facing the question of the meaning of personal existence. And it is precisely here that we find one source of the respect which is due to every culture and every nation: every culture is an effort to ponder the mystery of the world and in particular of the human person: it is a way of giving expression to the transcendent dimension of human life. The heart of every culture is its approach to the greatest of all mysteries: the mystery of God.

10. Our respect for the culture of others is therefore rooted in our respect for each community's attempt to answer the question of human life. And here we can see how important it is to safeguard the fundamental right to freedom of religion and freedom of conscience, as the cornerstones of the structure of human rights and the foundation of every truly free society. No one is permitted to suppress those rights by using coercive power to impose an answer to the mystery of man.

To cut oneself off from the reality of difference – or, worse, to attempt to stamp out that difference – is to cut oneself off from the possibility of sounding the depths of the mystery of human life. The truth about man is the unchangeable standard by which all cultures are judged; but every culture has something to teach us about one or other dimension of that complex truth. Thus the "difference" which some find so threatening can, through respectful dialogue, become the source of a deeper understanding of the mystery of human existence.

11. In this context, we need to clarify the essential difference between an unhealthy form of nationalism, which teaches contempt for other nations or cultures, and patriotism, which is a proper love of one's country. True patriotism never seeks to advance the well-being of one's own nation at the expense of others. For in the end this would harm one's own nation as well: doing wrong damages both aggressor and victim. Nationalism, particularly in its most radical forms, is thus the antithesis of true patriotism, and today we must ensure that extreme nationalism does not continue to give rise to new forms of the aberrations of totalitarianism. This is a commitment which also holds true, obviously, in cases where religion itself is made the basis of nationalism, as unfortunately happens in certain manifestations of so-called "fundamentalism."

Freedom and moral truth

12. Ladies and Gentlemen! Freedom is the measure of man's dignity and greatness. Living the freedom sought by individuals and peoples is a great challenge to man's spiritual growth and to the moral vitality of nations. The basic question which we must all face today is the responsible use of freedom, in both its personal and social dimensions. Our reflection must turn then to the question of the moral structure of freedom, which is the inner architecture of the culture of freedom.

Freedom is not simply the absence of tyranny or oppression. Nor is freedom a license to do whatever we like. Freedom has an inner "logic" which distinguishes it and ennobles it: freedom is ordered to the truth, and is fulfilled in man's quest for truth and in man's living in the truth. Detached from the truth about the human person, freedom deteriorates into license in the lives of individuals, and, in political life, it becomes the caprice of the most powerful and the arrogance of power. Far from being a limitation upon freedom or a threat to it, reference to the truth about the human person – a truth universally knowable through the moral law written on the hearts of all – is, in fact, the guarantor of freedom's future.

13. In the light of what has been said we understand how utilitarianism, the doctrine which defines morality not in terms of what is good but of what is advantageous, threatens the freedom of individuals and nations and obstructs the building of a true culture of freedom. Utilitarianism often has devastating political consequences, because it inspires an aggressive nationalism on the basis of which the subjugation, for example, of a smaller or weaker nation is claimed to be a good thing solely because it corresponds to the national interest. No less grave are the results of economic utilitarianism, which drives more powerful countries to manipulate and exploit weaker ones.

Nationalistic and economic utilitarianism are sometimes combined, a phenomenon which has too often characterized relations between the "North" and the "South." For the emerging countries, the achievement of political independence has too frequently been accompanied by a situation of de facto economic dependence on other countries; indeed, in some cases, the developing world has suffered a regression, such that some countries lack the means of satisfying the essential needs of their people. Such situations offend the conscience of humanity and pose a formidable moral challenge to the human family. Meeting this challenge will obviously require changes in both developing and developed countries. If developing countries are able to offer sure guarantees of the proper management of resources and of assistance received, as well as respect for human rights, by replacing where necessary unjust, corrupt, or authoritarian forms of government with participatory and democratic ones, will they not in this way unleash the best civil and economic energies of their people? And must not the developed countries, for their part, come to renounce strictly utilitarian approaches and develop new approaches inspired by greater justice and solidarity?

Yes, distinguished Ladies and Gentlemen! The international economic scene needs an ethic of solidarity, if participation, economic growth, and a just distribution of goods are to characterize the future of humanity. The international cooperation called for by the Charter of the United Nations for "solving international problems of an economic, social, cultural, or humanitarian character" (art. 1.3) cannot be conceived exclusively in terms of help and assistance, or even by considering the eventual returns on the resources provided. When millions of people are suffering from a poverty which means hunger, malnutrition, sickness, illiteracy, and degradation, we must not only remind ourselves that no one has a right to exploit another for his own advantage, but also and above all we must recommit ourselves to that solidarity which enables others to live out, in the actual circumstances of their economic and political lives, the creativity which is a distinguishing mark of the human person and the true source of the wealth of nations in today's world.

The United Nations and the future of freedom

14. As we face these enormous challenges, how can we fail to acknowledge the role of the United Nations Organization? Fifty years after its founding, the need for such an Organization is even more obvious, but we also have a better understanding, on the basis of experience, that the effectiveness of this great instrument for harmonizing and coordinating international life depends on the international culture and ethic which it supports and expresses. The United Nations Organization needs to rise more and more above the cold status of an administrative institution and to become a moral center where all the nations of the world feel at home and develop a shared awareness of being, as it were, a "family of nations." The idea of "family" immediately evokes something more than simple functional relations or a mere convergence of interests. The family is by nature a community based on mutual trust, mutual support and sincere respect. In an authentic family the strong do not dominate; instead, the weaker members, because of their very weakness, are all the more welcomed and served.

Raised to the level of the "family of nations," these sentiments ought to be, even before law itself, the very fabric of relations between peoples. The United Nations has the historic, even momentous, task of promoting this qualitative leap in international life, not only by serving as a center of effective mediation for the resolution of conflicts but also by fostering values, attitudes and concrete initiatives of solidarity which prove capable of raising the level of relations between nations from the "organizational" to a more "organic" level, from simple "existence with" others to "existence for" others, in a fruitful exchange of gifts, primarily for the good of the weaker nations but even so, a clear harbinger of greater good for everyone.

15. Only on this condition shall we attain an end not only to "wars of combat" but also to "cold wars." It will ensure not only the legal equality of all peoples but also their active participation in the building of a better future, and not only respect for individual cultural identities, but full esteem for them as a common treasure belonging to the cultural patrimony of mankind. Is this not the ideal held up by the Charter of the United Nations when it sets as the basis of the Organization "the principle of the sovereign equality of all its Members" (art. 2.1), or when it commits it to "develop friendly relations between nations based on respect for the principle of equal rights and of self-determination" (art. 1.2)? This is the high road which must be followed to the end, even if this involves, when necessary, appropriate modifications in the operating model of the United Nations, so as to take into account everything that has happened in this half century, with so many new peoples experiencing freedom and legitimately aspiring to "be" and to "count for" more.

None of this should appear an unattainable utopia. Now is the time for new hope, which calls us to expel the paralyzing burden of cynicism from the future of politics and of human life. The anniversary which we are celebrating invites us to do this by reminding us of the idea of "united nations," an idea which bespeaks mutual trust, security and solidarity. Inspired by the example of all those who have taken the risk of freedom, can we not recommit ourselves also to taking the risk of solidarity – and thus the risk of peace?

Beyond fear: the civilization of love

16. It is one of the great paradoxes of our time that man, who began the period we call "modernity" with a self-confident assertion of his "coming of age" and "autonomy," approaches the end of the twentieth century fearful of himself, fearful of what he might be capable of, fearful for the future. Indeed, the second half of the twentieth century has seen the unprecedented phenomenon of a humanity uncertain about the very likelihood of a future, given the threat of nuclear war. That danger, mercifully, appears to have receded – and everything that might make it return needs to be rejected firmly and universally; all the same, fear for the future and of the future remains.

In order to ensure that the new millennium now approaching will witness a new flourishing of the human spirit, mediated through an authentic culture of freedom, men and women must learn to conquer fear. We must learn not to be afraid, we must rediscover a spirit of hope and a spirit of trust. Hope is not empty optimism springing from a naive confidence that the future will necessarily be better than the past. Hope and trust are the premise of responsible activity and are nurtured in that inner sanctuary of conscience where "man is alone with God" (*Gaudium et Spes*, no. 16) and he thus perceives that he is not alone amid the enigmas of existence, for he is surrounded by the love of the Creator!

Hope and trust: these may seem matters beyond the purview of the United Nations. But they are not. The politics of nations, with which your Organization is principally concerned, can never ignore the transcendent, spiritual dimension of the human experience, and could never ignore it without harming the cause of man and the cause of human freedom. Whatever diminishes man – whatever shortens the horizon of man's aspiration to goodness – harms the cause of freedom. In order to recover our hope and our trust at the end of this century of sorrows, we must regain sight of that transcendent horizon of possibility to which the soul of man aspires.

17. As a Christian, my hope and trust are centered on Jesus Christ, the two thousandth anniversary of whose birth will be celebrated at the coming of the new millennium. We Christians believe that in his Death and Resurrection were fully revealed God's love and his care for all creation. Jesus Christ is for us God made man, and made a part of the history of humanity. Precisely for this reason, Christian hope for the world and its future extends to every human person. Because of the radiant humanity of Christ, nothing genuinely human fails to touch the hearts of Christians. Faith in Christ does not impel us to intolerance. On the contrary, it obliges us to engage others in a respectful dialogue. Love of Christ does not distract us from interest in others, but rather invites us to responsibility for them, to the exclusion of no one and indeed, if anything, with a special concern for the weakest and the suffering. Thus, as we approach the two thousandth anniversary of the birth of Christ, the Church asks only to be able to propose respectfully this message of salvation, and to be able to promote, in charity and service, the solidarity of the entire human family.

Ladies and Gentlemen! I come before you, as did my predecessor Pope Paul VI exactly thirty years ago, not as one who exercises temporal power – these are his words – nor as a religious leader seeking special privileges for his community. I come before you as a witness: a witness to human dignity, a witness to hope, a witness to the conviction that the destiny of all nations lies in the hands of a merciful Providence.

18. We must overcome our fear of the future. But we will not be able to overcome it completely unless we do so together. The "answer" to that fear is neither coercion nor repression, nor the imposition of one social "model" on the entire world. The answer to the fear which darkens human existence at the end of the twentieth century is the common effort to build the civilization of love, founded on the universal values of peace, solidarity, justice, and liberty. And the "soul" of the civilization of love is the culture of freedom: the freedom of individuals and the freedom of nations, lived in self-giving solidarity and responsibility.

We must not be afraid of the future. We must not be afraid of man. It is no accident that we are here. Each and every human person has been created in the "image and likeness" of the One who is the origin of all that is. We have within us the capacities for wisdom and virtue. With these gifts, and with the help of God's grace, we can build in the next century and the next millennium a civilization worthy of the human person, a true culture of freedom. We can and must do so! And in doing so, we shall see that the tears of this century have prepared the ground for a new springtime of the human spirit.

June 2, 1980
(*L'Osservatore Romano*, June 23, 1980, pp. 9–12)

Address to UNESCO

Mr. President of the General Conference,
Mr. President of the Executive Council,
Mr. Director General,
Ladies and Gentlemen,
1. I wish in the first place to express my very cordial thanks for the invitation that Mr. Amadou Mahtar-M'Bow, Director General of the United Nations Educational, Scientific and Cultural Organization, extended to me several times, even at the first of the visits he has done me the honor of paying me. There are many reasons for which I am happy to be able to accept today this invitation, which I highly appreciated immediately.

For the kind words of welcome they have just addressed to me, I thank Mr. Napoleon Leblanc, President of the General Conference, Mr. Chams Eldine El-Wakil, President of the Executive Council, and Mr. Amadou Mahtar-M'Bow, Director General of the Organization. I also wish to greet all those who are gathered here for the 109th session of UNESCO's Executive Council. I cannot conceal my joy at seeing gathered on this occasion so many delegates from nations all over the world, so many eminent personalities, so many authorities, so many illustrious representatives of the world of culture and science.

Through my intervention, I will try to bring my modest stone to the edifice you are constructing with assiduity and perseverance, Ladies and Gentlemen, through your reflections and your resolutions in all the fields that are in the UNESCO's sphere of competence.

2. Allow me to begin by referring to the origins of your Organization. The events that marked the foundation of UNESCO inspire me with joy and gratitude to Divine Providence: the signature of its constitution on November 16, 1945; the coming into force of this constitution and the establishment of the Organization on November 4, 1946; the agreement between UNESCO and the United Nations Organization approved by the General Assembly of the UN in the same year. Your Organization is, in fact, the work of the nations which, after the end of the terrible Second World War, were impelled by what could be called a spontaneous desire for peace, union and reconciliation. These nations looked for the means and the forms of a collaboration capable of establishing this new understanding and of deepening it and ensuring it in a lasting way. So UNESCO came into being, like the United Nations Organization, because the peoples knew that at the basis of the great enterprises intended to serve peace and the progress of humanity over the whole globe, there was the necessity of the union of nations, mutual respect and international cooperation.

3. Prolonging the action, thought and message of my great predecessor Pope Paul VI, I had the honor of speaking before the United Nations General Assembly, in the month of October last, on the invitation of Mr. Kurt Waldheim, Secretary General of the UN. Shortly afterwards, on November 12, 1979, I was invited by Mr. Edouard Saouma,

Director General of the United Nations Food and Agricultural Organization in Rome. On these occasions I had the honor of dealing with all the problems connected with man's peaceful future on earth. In fact, all these problems are closely linked. We are in the presence, so to speak, of a vast system of communicating vessels: the problems of culture, science and education do not arise, in the life of nations and in international relations, independently of the other problems of human existence, such as those of peace and hunger. The problems of culture are conditioned by the other dimensions of human existence, just as the latter, in their turn, condition them.

4. All the same there is – and I stressed it in my address to the UN, referring to the Universal Declaration of Human Rights – one fundamental dimension, which is capable of shaking to their very foundations the systems that structure mankind as a whole and of freeing human existence, individual and collective, from the threats that weigh on it. This fundamental dimension is man, man in his integrality, man who lives at the same time in the sphere of material values. Respect for the inalienable rights of the human person is at the basis of everything (cf. Address to the UN, nos. 7 and 13).

Any threat to human rights, whether in the framework of man's spiritual goods or in that of his material goods, does violence to this fundamental dimension. That is why, in my address to FAO, I emphasized that no man, no country and no system in the world can remain indifferent to the "geography of hunger" and the gigantic threats that will ensue if the whole direction of economic policy, and in particular the hierarchy of investments, do not change in an essential and radical way. That is also why, referring to the origins of your Organization, I stress the necessity of mobilizing all forces which direct the spiritual dimension of human existence, and which bear witness to the primacy of the spiritual in man – and of what corresponds to the dignity of his intelligence, his will and his heart – in order not to succumb again to the monstrous alienation of collective evil, which is always ready to use material powers in the exterminating struggle of men against men, of nations against nations.

5. At the origin of UNESCO, as also at the basis of the Universal Declaration on Human Rights, there are, therefore, these first noble impulses of human conscience, intelligence and will. I appeal to this origin, to this beginning, to these premises and to these first principles. It is in their name that I come today to Paris, to the headquarters of your Organization, with an entreaty: that at the end of a stage of over thirty years of your activities, you will unite even more round these ideals and principles on which the beginning was based. It is in their name also that I shall now take the liberty of proposing to you some really fundamental considerations, for it is only by their light that there shines forth fully the meaning of this institution, which has the name UNESCO, the United Nations Educational, Scientific and Cultural Organization.

6. Genus humanum arte et ratione vivit (cf. St. Thomas, commenting on Aristotle, in *Post. Analyt.*, no. 1). These words of one of the greatest geniuses of Christianity, who was at the same time a fruitful continuer of the thought of antiquity, take us beyond the circle and contemporary meaning of Western culture, whether it is Mediterranean or Atlantic. They have a meaning that applies to humanity as a whole, where the different periods of its culture, meet. The essential meaning of culture consists, according to these words of St. Thomas Aquinas, in the fact that it is a characteristic of

human life as such. Man lives a really human life thanks to culture. Human life is culture in this sense too that, through it, man is distinguished and differentiated from everything that exists elsewhere in the visible world: man cannot do without culture.

Culture is a specific way of man's "existing" and "being." Man always lives according to a culture which is specifically his, and which, in its turn, creates among men a tie which is also specifically theirs, determining the inter-human and social character of human existence. In the unity of culture as the specific way of human existence, there is rooted at the same time the plurality of cultures in the midst of which man lives. In this plurality, man develops without losing, however, the essential contact with the unity of culture as the fundamental and essential dimension of his existence and his being.

7. Man, who, in the visible world, is the only ontic subject of culture, is also its only object and its term. Culture is that through which man, as man, becomes more man, "is" more, has more access to "being." The fundamental distinction between what man is and what he has, between being and having, has its foundation here too. Culture is always in an essential and necessary relationship to what man is, whereas its relationship to what he has, to his "having," is not only secondary, but entirely relative. All man's "having" is important for culture, is a factor creative of culture, only to the extent to which man, through his "having," can at the same time "be" more fully as a man, become more fully a man in all the dimensions of his existence, in everything that characterizes his humanity. The experience of the various eras, without excluding the present one, proves that people think of culture and speak about it in the first place in relation to the nature of man, then only in a secondary and indirect way in relation to the world of his products. That in no way detracts from the fact that we judge the phenomenon of culture on the basis of what man produces, or that we draw from that, at the same time, conclusions about man. Such an approach – a typical way of the "a posteriori" process of knowledge – contains in itself the possibility of going back, in the opposite direction, to ontic-causal dependencies. Man, and only man, is the "protagonist," or "architect" of culture; man, and only man, expresses himself in it and finds his own balance in it.

The complete man the subject of culture
8. All of us present here meet on the ground of culture, the fundamental reality which unites us and which is at the basis of the establishment and purposes of the UNESCO. We thereby meet around man and, in a certain sense, in him, in man. This man, who expresses himself and objectivizes himself in and through culture, is unique, complete and indivisible. He is at once subject and architect of culture. Consequently, he cannot be envisaged solely as the resultant – to give only one example – of the production relations that prevail at a given period. Is this criterion of production relations not at all, then, a key to the understanding of his culture and of the multiple forms of his development? Certainly, this criterion is a key, and even a precious key, but it is not the fundamental, constitutive one. Human cultures reflect, there is no doubt, the various systems of production relations; however, it is not such and such a system that is at the origin of culture, but man, man who lives in the system, who accepts it or tries to change it. A culture without human subjectivity and without human causality is

inconceivable; in the cultural field, man is always the first fact: man is the prime and fundamental fact of culture.

And he is so, always, in his totality; in his spiritual and material subjectivity as a complete whole. If the distinction between spiritual culture and material culture is correct with respect to the character and content of the products in which the culture is manifested, it is necessary to note at the same time that, on the one hand, the works of material culture always show a "spiritualization of matter," a submission of the material element to man's spiritual forces, that is, his intelligence and will – and that, on the other hand, the works of spiritual culture manifest, specifically, a "materialization" of the spirit, an incarnation of what is spiritual. In cultural works, this double characteristic seems to be equally permanent.

Here is, therefore, by way of theoretical conclusion, a sufficient basis to understand culture through the complete man, through the whole reality of his subjectivity. Here is also – in the field of action – a sufficient basis to seek always in culture the complete man, the whole man, in the whole truth of his spiritual and corporeal subjectivity; the basis which is sufficient in order not to superimpose on culture – a truly human system, a splendid synthesis of spirit and body – preconceived divisions and oppositions. In fact, whether it is a question of an absolutization of matter in the structure of the human subject, or, inversely, of an absolutization of the spirit in this same structure, neither expresses the truth about man or serves his culture.

9. I would like to stop here at another essential consideration, a reality of a quite different order. We can approach it by noting the fact that the Holy See is represented at UNESCO by its permanent Observer, whose presence is set in the perspective of the very nature of the Apostolic See. This presence is, even more widely, in harmony with the nature and mission of the Catholic Church and, indirectly, with that of the whole of Christianity. I take the opportunity which is offered to me today to express a deep personal conviction. The presence of the Apostolic See in your Organization – though motivated also by the specific sovereignty of the Holy See – has its justification above all in the organic and constitutive link which exists between religion in general and Christianity in particular, on the one hand, and culture, on the other hand. This relationship extends to the multiple realities which must be defined as concrete expressions of culture in the different periods of history and all over the world. It will certainly not be an exaggeration to state in particular that, through a multitude of facts, the whole of Europe – from the Atlantic to the Urals – bears witness, in the history of each nation as in that of the whole community, to the link between culture and Christianity.

Recalling this, it is not at all my intention to belittle the heritage of other continents, or the specific character and value of this same heritage which is derived from the other sources of religious, humanistic and ethical inspiration. What is more, I wish to pay the deepest and most sincere tribute to all the cultures of the human family as a whole, from the most ancient to the contemporary. It is in thinking of all cultures that I wish to say in a loud voice, here in Paris, at the headquarters of UNESCO, with respect and admiration: "Here is man!." I wish to proclaim my admiration before the creative riches of the human spirit, before its incessant efforts to know and strengthen the identity of man: this man who is always present in all the particular forms of culture.

10. Speaking, on the contrary, of the place of the Church and of the Apostolic See in your Organization, I am thinking not only of all the works of culture in which, in the course of the last two millennia, the man who had accepted Christ and the Gospel expressed himself, or of the institutions of different kinds that came into being from the same inspiration in the fields of education, instruction, charity, social work and in so many others. I am thinking above all, Ladies and Gentlemen, of the fundamental link between the Gospel, that is, the message of Christ and the Church, and man in his very humanity. This link is in fact a creator of culture in its very foundation. To create culture, it is necessary to consider, to its last consequences and entirely, man as a particular and autonomous value, as the subject bearing the transcendency of the person. Man must be affirmed for himself, and not for any other motive or reason; solely for himself! What is more, man must be loved because he is man; love must be claimed for man by reason of the particular dignity he possesses. The whole of the affirmations concerning man belongs to the very substance of Christ's message and of the mission of the Church, in spite of all that critics may have declared about this matter, and all that the different movements opposed to religion in general and to Christianity in particular may have done.

In the course of history, we have already been more than once, and we still are, witnesses of a process of a very significant phenomenon. Where religious institutions have been suppressed, where ideas and works born of religious inspiration, and in particular of Christian inspiration, have been deprived of their citizenship, men find again these same elements outside institutional ways, through confrontation operated, in truth and interior effort, between what constitutes their humanity and what is contained in the Christian message.

Ladies and Gentlemen, you will kindly forgive my making this statement. Proposing it, I did not want to offend anyone at all. I beg you to understand that, in the name of what I am, I could not abstain from giving this testimony. It also bears within it this truth – which cannot be passed over in silence – on culture, if we seek in it everything that is human, the elements in which man expresses himself or through which he wants to be the subject of his existence. And in so speaking, I wanted at the same time to manifest all the more my gratitude for the ties of which my presence today is intended as a particular expression.

11. A certain number of fundamental conclusions can be drawn from all that. In fact, the considerations I have just made show clearly that the primary and essential task of culture in general, and also all culture, is education. Education consists in fact in enabling man to become more man, to "be" more and not just to "have" more and consequently, through everything he "has," everything he "possesses," to "be" man more fully. For this purpose man must be able to "be more" not only "with others," but also "for others." Education is of fundamental importance for the formation of inter-human and social relations. Here too, I touch upon a set of axioms on the basis of what the traditions of Christianity that have sprung from the Gospel meet the educative experience of so many well-disposed and deeply wise men, so numerous in all centuries of history. In our age, too, there is no lack of them, of these men who reveal themselves as great, simply through their humanity which they are able to share with others, in particular with the young. At the same time, the symptoms of crises of all kinds to which there succumb environments and societies which are among those best-off in

other ways, – crises which affect above all young generations – vie with each other in bearing witness that the work of man's education is not carried out only with the help of organized and material means, however excellent they may be. They also show that the most important thing is always man, man and his moral authority which comes from the truth of his principles and from the conformity of his actions with these principles.

12. As the world Organization most competent in all problems of culture, UNESCO cannot neglect this other question which is absolutely fundamental: what can be done in order that man's education may be carried out above all in the family?

What is the state of public morality which will ensure the family, and above all the parents, the moral authority necessary for this purpose? What type of instruction? What forms of legislation sustain this authority or, on the contrary, weaken it or destroy it? The causes of success and failure in the formation of man by his family always lie both within the fundamental creative environment of culture which the family is, and also at a higher level, that of the competence of the State and the organs, on which these causes depend. These problems cannot but cause reflection and solicitude in the forum where the qualified representatives of the State meet.

There is no doubt that the first and fundamental cultural fact is the spiritually mature man, that is, a fully educated man, a man capable of educating himself and educating others. Nor is there any doubt that the first and fundamental dimension of culture is healthy morality: moral culture.

13. Certainly, there are many particular questions in this field, but experience shows that everything is connected, and that these questions are set in systems that plainly depend upon one another. For example, in the process of education as a whole, and of scholastic education in particular, has there not been a unilateral shift toward instruction in the narrow sense of the word? If we consider the proportions assumed by this phenomenon, as well as the systematic increase of instruction which refers solely to what man possesses, is not man himself put more and more in the shade? That leads, then, to a real alienation of education: instead of working in favor of what man must "be," it works solely in favor of what man can take advantage of in the field of "having," of "possession." The further stage of this alienation is to accustom man, by depriving him of his own subjectivity, to being the object of multiple manipulations: ideological or political manipulations which are carried out through public opinion; those that are operated through monopoly or control, through economic forces or political powers, and the media of social communication; finally, the manipulation which consists of teaching life as a specific manipulation of oneself.

The apparent imperatives of our society
These dangers in the field of education seem to threaten above all societies with a more developed technical civilization. These societies are confronted with man's specific crisis which consists of a growing lack of confidence with regard to his own humanity, to the meaning of the fact of being a man, and to the affirmation and joy derived from it, which are a source of creation. Modern civilization tries to impose on man a series of apparent imperatives, which its spokesmen justify by recourse to the principle of development and progress. Thus, for example, instead of respect for life,

"the imperative" of getting rid of life and destroying it; instead of love which is the responsible communion of persons, "the imperative" of the maximum sexual enjoyment apart from any sense of responsibility; instead of the primacy of truth in actions, the "primacy" of behavior that is fashionable, of the subjective, and of immediate success.

In all that there is indirectly expressed a great systematic renunciation of the healthy ambition of being a man. Let us be under no illusions: the system constructed on the basis of these false imperatives, these fundamental renunciations, may determine the future of man and the future of culture.

14. If, in the name of future of culture, it must be proclaimed that man has the right to "be" more, and if for the same reason it is necessary to demand a healthy primacy of the family in the overall work of educating man to real humanity, the law of the Nation must be set along the same line; it, too, must be placed at the basis of culture and education.

The Nation is, in fact, the great community of men who are united by various ties, but above all, precisely by culture. The Nation exists "through" culture and "for" culture, and it is therefore the great educator of men in order that they may "be more" in the community. It is this community which possesses a history that goes beyond the history of the individual and the family. It is also in this community, with respect to which every family educates, that the family begins its work of education with what is the most simple thing, language, thus enabling man who is at the very beginning to learn to speak in order to become a member of the community of his family and of his Nation.

In all that I am now proclaiming, which I will develop still further, my words express a particular experience, a particular testimony in its kind. I am the son of a Nation which has lived the greatest experiences of history, which its neighbors have condemned to death several times, but which has survived and remained itself. It has kept its identity, and it has kept, in spite of partitions and foreign occupations, its national sovereignty, not by relying on the resources of physical power, but solely by relying on its culture. This culture turned out in the circumstances to be more powerful than all other forces.

What I say here concerning the rights of the Nation to the foundation of its culture and its future is not, therefore, the echo of any "nationalism," but it is always a question of a stable element of human experience and of the humanistic perspective of man's development. There exists a fundamental sovereignty of society which is manifested in the culture of the Nation. It is a question of the sovereignty through which, at the same time, man is supremely sovereign. When I express myself in this way, I am also thinking, with deep interior emotion, of the cultures of so many ancient peoples which did not give way when confronted with the civilizations of the invaders: and they still remain for man the source of his "being" as a man in the interior truth of his humanity. I am also thinking with admiration of the cultures of new societies, those that are awakening to life in the community of their own Nations – just as my Nation awakened to life ten centuries ago – and that are struggling to maintain their own identity and their own values against the influences and pressure of models proposed from outside.

15. Addressing you, Ladies and Gentlemen, you who have been meeting in this place for over thirty years now in the name of the primacy of the cultural realities of man, human communities, peoples and Nations, I say to you: with all the means at your disposal, watch over this fundamental sovereignty that every Nation possesses by virtue of its own culture. Cherish it like the apple of your eye for the future of the great human family. Protect it! Do not allow this fundamental sovereignty to become the prey of some political or economic interest. Do not allow it to become a victim of totalitarian and imperialistic systems or hegemonies, for which man counts only as an object of domination and a bait for various interests, and not as a subject: the subject of sovereignty coming from the true culture which belongs to it as its own. Are there not, on the map of Europe and the world, Nations which have a marvelous historic sovereignty derived from their culture, and which are, nevertheless, deprived of their full sovereignty at the same time? Is this not an important point for the future of human culture, important above all in our age, when it is so urgent to eliminate the vestiges of colonialism?

16. This sovereignty which exists and which draws its origin from the specific culture of the Nation and society, from the primacy of the family in the work of education, and finally from the personal dignity of every man, must remain the fundamental criterion of the manner of dealing with the problem, an important one for humanity today, namely, that of the media of social communication (of the information which is bound up with them, and also of what is called "mass culture"). Since these media are "social" media of communication, they cannot be means of domination over others, on the part of agents of political power as well as of financial powers which impose their program and their model. They must become the means – and what an important means! – of expression of this society which uses them, and which also ensures their existence. They must take into account the culture of the Nation and its history. They must respect the responsibility of the family in the field of education. They must take into consideration the good of man, his dignity. They cannot be subjected to the criterion of interest, of the sensational and of immediate success but, taking into account ethical requirements, they must serve the construction of a "more human" life.

17. *Genus humanum arte et ratione vivit.* Fundamentally, it is affirmed that man is himself through truth, and becomes more himself through increasingly perfect knowledge of truth. I would like to pay tribute here, Ladies and Gentlemen, to all the merits of your Organization and at the same time to the commitment and to all the efforts of the States and institutions which you represent, in regard to the popularization of instruction at all grades and all levels, as regards the elimination of illiteracy, which signifies the lack of all instruction, even the most elementary, a lack which is painful not only from the point of view of the elementary culture of individuals and environments, but also from the point of view of socio-economic progress. There are distressing indications of delay in this field, bound up with a distribution of goods that is often radically unequal and unjust; think of the situations in which there exist, alongside a plutocratic oligarchy limited in numbers, multitudes of starving citizens living in want. This delay can be eliminated not by way of bloody struggles for power, but above all, by means of systematic alphabetization through the spread and popularization of instruction. An effort in this direction is necessary if it is then desired to carry

out the necessary changes in the socio-economic field. Man, who "is more," thanks also to what he "has," and to what he "possesses," must know how to possess, that is, to order and administer the means he possesses, for his own good and for the common good. For this purpose, instruction is indispensable.

18. The problem of instruction has always been closely linked with the mission of the Church. In the course of the centuries, she founded schools at all levels; she gave birth to the mediaeval Universities in Europe; in Paris and in Bologna, in Salamanca and in Heidelberg, in Krakow and in Louvain. In our age, too, she offers the same contribution wherever her activity in this field is requested and respected. Allow me to claim in this place for Catholic families the right which belongs to all families to educate their children in schools which correspond to their own view of the world, and in particular the strict right of Christian parents not to see their children subjected, in schools, to programs inspired by atheism. That is, indeed, one of the fundamental rights of man and of the family.

19. The system of education is organically connected with the system of the different orientations given to the way of practicing and popularizing science, a purpose which is served by high-level educational establishments, Universities and also, in view of the present development of specialization and scientific methods, specialized institutes. These are institutions of which it would be difficult to speak without deep emotion. They are the work benches at which man's vocation to knowledge, as well as the constitutive link of humanity with truth as the aim of knowledge, become a daily reality, become, in a sense, the daily bread of so many teachers, venerated leaders of science, and around them, of young researchers dedicated to science and its applications, as also of the multitude of students who frequent these centers of science and knowledge.

We find ourselves here, as it were, at the highest rungs of the ladder which man has been climbing, since the beginning, toward knowledge of the reality of the world around him, and toward knowledge of the mysteries of his humanity. This historical process has reached in our age possibilities previously unknown; it has opened to human intelligence horizons hitherto unsuspected. It would be difficult to go into detail here for, on the way to knowledge the orientations of specializations are as numerous as the development of science is rich.

UNESCO, meeting point of human culture
20. Your organization is a place of meeting, a meeting which embraces, in its widest sense, the whole field, so essential, of human culture. This audience is therefore the very place to greet all men of science, and to pay tribute particularly to those who are present here and who have obtained for their work the highest recognition and the most eminent world distinctions. Allow me, consequently, to express also certain wishes which, I do not doubt, will reach the thought and the hearts of the members of this august assembly.

Just as we are edified in scientific work – edified and made deeply happy – by this march of the disinterested knowledge of truth which the scholar serves with the greatest dedication and sometimes at the risk of his health and even his life, we must be equally concerned by everything that is in contradiction with the principles of disinterestedness and objectivity, everything that would make science an instrument to reach aims that have nothing to do with it. Yes, we must be concerned about everything that proposes and presupposes only these non-scientific aims, demanding of men of science that they should put themselves in their service without permitting them to judge and decide, in all independence of mind, the human and ethical honesty of these purposes, or threatening them with bearing the consequences when they refuse to contribute to them.

Do these non-scientific aims of which I am speaking, this problem that I am raising, need proofs or comments? You know what I am referring to; let it suffice to mention the fact that among those who were brought before the international courts, at the end of the last world war, there were also men of science. Ladies and Gentlemen, I beg you to forgive me these words, but I would not be faithful to the duties of my office if I did not utter them, not in order to return to the past, but to defend the future of science and human culture; even more, to defend the future of man and the world! I think that Socrates, who, in his uncommon integrity, was able to sustain that knowledge is at the same time moral virtue, would have to climb down from his certainty if he could consider the experience of our time.

Direct science to defense of man's life

21. We realize it, Ladies and Gentlemen, the future of man and of the world is threatened, radically threatened, in spite of the intentions, certainly noble ones, of men of learning, men of science. It is threatened because the marvelous results of their researches and their discoveries, especially in the field of the sciences of nature, have been and continue to be exploited – to the detriment of the ethical imperative – for purposes that have nothing to do with the requirements of science, and even for purposes of destruction and death, and that to a degree never known hitherto, causing really unimaginable damage. Whereas science is called to be in the service of man's life, it is too often a fact that it is subjected to purposes that destroy the real dignity of man and of human life. That is the case when scientific research itself is directed toward these purposes or when its results are applied to purposes contrary to the good of mankind. That happens in the field of genetic manipulation and biological experimentations as well as in that of chemical, bacteriological or nuclear armaments.

Two considerations lead me to submit particularly to your reflection the nuclear threat which is weighing upon the world today and which, if not staved off, could lead to the destruction of the fruits of culture, the products of civilization elaborated throughout the centuries by successive generations of men who believed in the primacy of the spirit and who did not spare either their efforts or their fatigue. The first consideration is the following. Geopolitical reasons, economic problems of world dimension, terrible incomprehension, wounded national pride, the decadence of moral values have led our world to a situation of instability, to a frail balance which runs the risk of being destroyed any moment as a result of errors of judgment, information or interpretation.

Another consideration is added to this disquieting perspective. Can we be sure, nowadays, that the upsetting of the balance would not lead to war, and to a war that would not hesitate to have recourse to nuclear arms? Up to now it has been said that nuclear arms have constituted a force of dissuasion which has prevented a major war from breaking out, and it is probably true. But we may wonder at the same time if it will always be so. Nuclear arms, of whatever order of magnitude or of whatever type they may be, are being perfected more and more every year, and they are being added to the arsenal of a growing number of countries. How can we be sure that the use of nuclear arms, even for purposes of national defense or in limited conflicts, will not lead to an inevitable escalation, leading to a destruction that mankind can never envisage or accept? But it is not you, men of science and culture, that I must ask not to close your eyes to what a nuclear war can represent for the whole of humanity (cf. Homily for the World Day of Peace, January 1, 1980).

22. Ladies and Gentlemen, the world will not be able to continue for long along this way. A conviction, which is at the same time a moral imperative, forces itself upon anyone who has become aware of the situation and the stake, and who is also inspired by the elementary sense of responsibilities that are incumbent on everyone: consciences must be mobilized! The efforts of human consciences must be increased in proportion to the tension between good and evil to which men at the end of the twentieth century are subjected. We must convince ourselves of the priority of ethics over technology, of the primacy of the person over things, of the superiority of spirit over matter (cf. *Redemptor Hominis*, no. 16). The cause of man will be served if science forms an alliance with conscience. The man of science will really help humanity if he keeps "the sense of man's transcendence over the world and of God's over man" (Address to the Pontifical Academy of Sciences, November 10, 1979, no. 4).

Thus, seizing the opportunity of my presence at the headquarters of UNESCO today, I, a son of humanity and Bishop of Rome, directly address you, men of science, you who are gathered here, you the highest authorities in all fields of modern science. And through you I address your colleagues and friends of all countries and all continents.

I address you in the name of this terrible threat which weighs over mankind, and, at the same time, in the name of the future and the good of humanity all over the world. I beseech you: let us make every effort to establish and respect the primacy of ethics, in all fields of science. Let us do our utmost particularly to preserve the human family from the horrible prospect of nuclear war!

I tackled this subject before the General Assembly of the United Nations Organization in New York, on October 2 of last year. I am speaking about it today to you. I appeal to your intelligence and your heart, above passions, ideologies and frontiers. I appeal to all those who, through their political or economic power, would be and are often led to impose on scientists the conditions of their work and its orientation. Above all I appeal to every scientist individually and to the whole international scientific community.

All together you are an enormous power: the power of intelligences and consciences! Show yourselves to be more powerful in our modern world! Make up your mind to give proof of the most noble solidarity with mankind: the solidarity founded on the dignity of the human person. Construct peace, beginning with the foundation: respect for all the rights of man, those which are connected with his material and economic dimension as well as those which are connected with the spiritual and interior dimension of his existence in this world. May wisdom inspire you! May love guide you, this love which will suffocate the growing threat of hatred and destruction! Men of science, commit all your moral authority to save mankind from nuclear destruction.

23. Today, I have been given the possibility of realizing one of the deepest desires of my heart. I have been given the possibility of penetrating, here, within the Areopagus which is that of the whole world. I have been given the possibility of saying to all, to you, members of the United Nations Educational, Scientific and Cultural Organization, to you who are working for the good and for the reconciliation of men and peoples through all fields of culture, science and information, to say to you and to cry to you from the inmost depths of my soul: Yes! The future of man depends on culture! Yes! The peace of the world depends on the primacy of the Spirit! Yes! The peaceful future of mankind depends on love!

Your personal contribution, Ladies and Gentlemen, is important, it is vital. It lies in the correct approach to the problems, to the solution of which you dedicate your service.

My final word is the following: Do not stop. Continue. Continue always.

November 14, 1991
(http://www.vatican.va/holy_father/john_paul_ii/speeches/1996/documents/hf_jp-
ii_spe_14111991_xxvi-session-fao-conference_en.html)

Address to the XXVI Session of the Conference of the Food and Agricultural Organization

Mr. Chairman,
Mr. Director-General,
Your Excellencies,
Ladies and Gentlemen,

I am very pleased to meet once again the representatives and experts of the States and Organizations associated in the Food and Agriculture Organization of the United Nations. This Twenty-sixth General Assembly is particularly worthy of note, because it marks the fortieth anniversary of the establishment of the headquarters of FAO in Rome. I offer heartfelt good wishes on this significant occasion. The selection of this city as the center of your activity has helped to foster an especially close level of understanding and collaboration between your Organization and the Holy See. It is encouraging to see the many convergences between the new objectives and methods which the Organization has evolved for itself and the Church's teaching about social development and her call to understand it in the light of the ethical dimension and transcendent destiny of the human person.

Even after four decades of intense efforts by men and women of good will the objectives of FAO continue to have a pressing urgency. Now as much as in the past, there is a need to make the production and distribution of food more efficient, to improve the lot of agricultural workers and thus to contribute to the general expansion of the world economy, in order to eliminate hunger from our world. As one charged with continuing "the teaching and activity of Christ, from whom the sight of a hungry crowd prompted the moving exclamation: 'I feel sorry for all these people; they . . . have nothing to eat' (Mt 15:32)" (Pope Paul VI, Address to Participants of the World Food Conference, November 9, 1974), I take the occasion of this meeting to express once more my anxiety for the plight of the world's hungry. We share a burning concern for them, and so I pray that our meeting will be an opportunity for rededication to their service.

Through long experience and the accumulation of extensive data, FAO's approach has moved beyond broad references to the struggle against hunger and a simple call for its elimination to a recognition of the multiplicity of hunger's causes and the need for a correspondingly sophisticated response. This insight into the complexity of the situation, far from dampening the zeal of the members of FAO, should serve as a spur, to action, since efforts made to remedy problems which have been accurately analyzed stand the best chance of achieving success.

The growing recognition of the many dimensions to be addressed in any attack on hunger and malnutrition has led to the identification of important social and political issues which have a direct impact on the matter. Concern for the health of the environment is one of the issues which has a particular bearing on the concerns of FAO, and its complex ramifications have to be taken into account in any campaign against hunger. In fact, respect for the fields, forests and seas, and their preservation from over-exploitation, form the very foundation of any realistic policy aimed at increasing the world's food supply. The world's natural assets, given by the Creator in trust to all mankind, are the source from which human labor brings forth the harvest upon which we depend. With the aid of scientific expertise, sound practical judgment must point out the path which lies between the extremes of asking too much of our environment and asking too little, either of which would have disastrous consequences for the human family.

Growing awareness of the finite resources of the earth casts into ever sharper relief the need to make available to all who are involved in food production the knowledge and technology required in order to ensure that their efforts will yield the best possible results. The widespread establishment of training-centers and institutions which foster the sharing of know-how and skill is one of the most effective lines of action to be pursued in the struggle against hunger. The development of the specifically human capacity to work increases vastly the otherwise limited potentiality of the earth. Hence, the emphasis must be more and more on the application of productive intelligence. The land and the sea yield their abundance precisely in the measure in which they are worked with wisdom. As I wrote in my Encyclical Letter *Centesimus Annus*: "Today the decisive factor [in production] is increasingly man himself" (no. 32; cf. no. 31). I am happy to note that this truth about man's labor is reflected in your Medium-Term Plan, 1992–97, with its emphasis on the importance of human resources for solving the problem of hunger.

Ladies and Gentlemen, the Holy See is deeply interested in the specific role of FAO as an impetus for socio-economic development. The guiding principle of the Church's teaching on development is expressed in the Second Vatican Council's Pastoral Constitution *Gaudium et Spes*, which states: "In the socio-economic realm too, the dignity and total vocation of the human person must be honored and advanced along with the welfare of society as a whole. For man is the source, center and the purpose of all socio-economic life" (no. 63). Development which is worthy of the human person must aim at advancing people in every aspect of life, the spiritual as well as the material.

Indeed, economic advancement achieves its proper end precisely to the degree that it advances the whole good and destiny of human beings.

One of the implications of this truth is that the clear affirmation of the dignity and worth of those who work to produce our food is an indispensable part of any solution to the problem of hunger. They are special cooperators with the Creator as they obey his command to "subdue the earth" (cf. Gen 1:28). They perform the vital service of providing society with the goods needed for its daily sustenance. The recognition of their dignity is echoed in the call of FAO for rural people to be regarded not as mere means of increasing food production "but as the ultimate users and beneficiaries of the development process" (Medium-Term Plan, p. 75). It is of particular importance in this regard to design programs which will increase the scope for free and responsible action by farmers, fishermen and those who manage forestry resources, and will enable them to take an effective part in formulating the policies which affect them directly.

It is also important to keep in mind that projects aimed at eliminating hunger must be in harmony with the fundamental right of couples to establish and foster a family (cf. *Familiaris Consortio*, no. 42). Any initiative which would seek to increase the world's food supply by an assault upon the sanctity of the family or by interference with parents' right to decide about the number of their children would oppress rather than serve the human race (cf. *Gaudium et Spes*, no. 47; *Familiaris Consortio*, no. 42; *Laborem Exercens*, no. 25). Rather than forbidding the poor to be born, truly effective programs for developing the food supply will ensure that the poor share even now in the material goods which they need in order to support their families, while they receive the training and assistance they require so that eventually they can produce these goods by their own labor (cf. *Centesimus Annus*, no. 28).

The years leading up to this last decade of the Millennium have witnessed monumental shifts in relations between peoples and nations. The great changes which have taken place present FAO with new challenges and new opportunities. The disruption of what had become the customary patterns of production and exchange in many places means that the fight against hunger must be vastly extended. I am confident that your Organization, with its tradition of intergovernmental cooperation, will know how to respond effectively.

The reduction of world tensions, for so long the goal of mankind's hopes and prayers, gives leaders of governments and their peoples a fresh chance to work together to build a society worthy of the human person. The elimination of hunger and its causes must be a fundamental part of this project. One hopes that a particular consequence of the lessening of antagonism in international relations will be a decrease in the amount of money spent on the manufacture and purchase of arms. The resources thus released can then be devoted to development and to food production. I pray that the governments of the world will delicate themselves to this noble task with the same energy as was given to protecting themselves against those whom they once considered their foes.

The tasks before you, Ladies and Gentlemen, will tax your courage, but you can take heart from the nobility of your cause, a nobility which more than justifies the effort and sacrifice involved. You are pledged to ensure the satisfaction of the right to have enough to eat, to have a secure and stable share in the produce of land and sea. Renew your commitment to this struggle! In saying this I lend my voice to all the poor and hungry whom I have met on my Pastoral Visits to so many parts of the world. I pass on to you their appeal; I express to you their gratitude.

I give the assurance of my prayers for the success of your deliberations in establishing your work project for the next two years, and I invoke upon you the peace and strength which comes from Almighty God, who "does not forget the cry of the afflicted" (Ps 9:12).

April 7, 2000
(*OR*, April 12, 2000, p. 4)

Address to the UN Secretary General and Administrative Committee on Coordination

Mr. Secretary General,
Distinguished Guests,
1. It gives me great pleasure to welcome you all on the occasion of the meeting in Rome of the Administrative Committee on Coordination of the United Nations system. Recognizing the work undertaken by your Committee for the good of peoples around the world, I pray that God will give you and all taking part in your meeting the gift of wise discernment in your deliberations. Thank you, Mr Secretary General, for your kind words of presentation, and I am certain that your recent "Millennium Report" will serve as an excellent framework for the Committee's work during these days.

As that report makes clear, the millennium just ended has left in its wake a series of unusual challenges. These challenges are unusual not because they are new – there have always been wars, persecutions, poverty, disasters and epidemics – but because the world's increasing interdependence has given them a global dimension, which requires new ways of thinking and new types of international cooperation if they are to be effectively met. At the dawn of the new millennium, humanity has the means to do this. The United Nations, in fact, and the large family of specialized organizations represented by you are the natural forum for developing such a mentality and strategy of international solidarity.

In the task of formulating this new perspective, the Administrative Committee on Coordination has a fundamental role to play. It brings together the most senior members of the different specialized agencies, under the direction of the Secretary General, for the express purpose of coordinating the various policies and programs. This is why your Committee has concentrated its reflections and efforts on the implications of globalization for development, on the socio-economic causes of humanitarian crises and of the persistent conflicts in Africa and other parts of the world, and on the institutional capacity of the United Nations system to respond to new international challenges.

2. The unbounded expansion of world commerce and the amazing progress in the fields of technology, communications and information exchange are all part of a dynamic process that tends to abolish the distances separating peoples and continents. However, the ability to exercise influence in this new global setting is not the same for all nations, but is more or less tied to a country's economic and technological capacity. The new situation is such that, in many cases, decisions with worldwide consequences are made only by a small, restricted group of nations. Other nations either manage – often with great effort – to bring these decisions into line with what is in the interest of their citizens or – as happens with the weakest countries – they try simply to adjust to these decisions as best they can, sometimes with negative consequences for their people. The majority of the world's nations, therefore, are experiencing a

weakening of the State in its capacity to serve the common good and promote social justice and harmony.

Moreover, the globalization of the economy is leading to a globalization of society and culture. In this context, Non-Governmental Organizations, representing a very broad spectrum of special interests, are becoming ever more important in international life. And perhaps one of the best results of their action so far is the awareness which they are creating of the need to move from an attitude of defense and promotion of particular and competing special interests to a holistic vision of development. A case in point is their increasing success in creating a keener awareness in industrialized countries of their shared responsibility for the problems facing less developed countries. The campaign to reduce or cancel the foreign debt of the poorest nations is another example, though not the only one, of a growing sense of international solidarity.

3. The growth of this new awareness in society presents the United Nations system with a unique opportunity to contribute to the globalization of solidarity by serving as a meeting place for States and civil society and as a convergence of the varied interests and needs – regional and particular – of the world at large. Cooperation between International Agencies and Non-Governmental Organizations will help to ensure that the interests of States – legitimate though they may be – and of the different groups within them, will not be invoked or defended at the expense of the interests or rights of other peoples, especially the less fortunate. Political and economic activity conducted in a spirit of international solidarity can and ought to lead to the voluntary limitation of unilateral advantages so that other countries and peoples may share in the same benefits. In this way the social and economic well-being of everyone is served.

At the dawn of the twenty-first century, the challenge is to build a world in which individuals and peoples fully and unequivocally accept responsibility for their fellow human beings, for all the earth's inhabitants. Your work can do much to empower the multilateral system to bring about such international solidarity. The premise of all this effort is the recognition of the dignity and centrality of every human being as an equal member of the human family and, for believers, as God's equal children. The task then is to ensure the acceptance at every level of society of the logical consequences of our shared human dignity, and to guarantee respect for that dignity in every situation.

4. In this regard, I must express my deep concern when I see that certain groups try to impose on the international community ideological views or patterns of life advocated by small and particular segments of society. This is perhaps most obvious in such fields as the defense of life and the safeguarding of the family. The leaders of Nations must be careful not to overturn what the international community and law have laboriously developed to preserve the dignity of the human person and the cohesion of society. This is a common patrimony which no one has the right to dissipate.

Invoking divine guidance upon every effort and undertaking of your Committee in its mission of coordinating the activities of the United Nations system, I pray that your work will be thoroughly pervaded by a generous and ambitious spirit of global solidarity. God bless you, Mr. Secretary General, and all who are gathered with you at this meeting!

Chapter IV
Special Addresses to the Diplomatic Community
The Culture of Peace as Promotion of Solidarity

The Vatican Information Service states (October 13, 2003) that during the twenty-five years of his papacy, Pope John Paul II has made a staggering 143 pastoral visits within Italy and another 102 foreign apostolic trips. This means that as Pope he has traveled nearly 750,000 miles. And the pace of these trips could hardly be described as leisurely. For example, while spending two days in Turkey (November 1979), he gave 12 speeches. Everywhere it has been the same: three days in Portugal (May 1982) with 22 speeches; 50 speeches during eleven days in Canada (September 1984); 10 speeches while passing a single day in Czechoslovakia (April 1990). And this does not take into consideration the schedule of his countless other activities while abroad or of his presiding at Eucharistic liturgies for throngs of the faithful.

During many of the Pope's foreign travels, his preference is to meet with members of the Diplomatic Corps assigned to the nation being visited. The text of five of these addresses follows. They illustrate how the Pope regards the role of the Diplomatic Corps in fostering the culture of peace. Readers will note how the tenor of these remarks tends to be somewhat more precise than,; for example, his New Year series to international diplomats. What these indicate is that the culture of peace:

(26) . . . *"contribute[s] to the rapprochement of peoples"* (Brasilia – June 30, 1980).

When requested to define diplomacy, Wynn Catlin once answered humorously that it is "the art of saying 'nice doggie' till you can find a rock." He may have thought that diplomats always reserve as a final option that States should smash, bash, and mash when not being otherwise successful in the resolution of their disputes. By contrast, rapprochement is a phase in diplomatic process – a stage of reducing tension between nations formerly hostile to each other. Rapprochement denotes openness to the healing of what might have been mutually inflicted wounds. The search is not for a rock, but for realistic means to buttress States' "mutual esteem and understanding," to encourage "their exchanges," to facilitate "their cultural or economic collaboration" and to mobilize their confidence in peace (para. 3). Pope John Paul, in his remarks to diplomats assembled at the Nunciature in Brasilia, implied that for rapprochement to occur at least three prior conditions ought to arise: world leaders, diplomats among them, must be solidly grounded in their "convictions and principles" (para. 5); States must validate that their domestic security is "deserved," because it enshrines the common good (para. 6); and "power" must refuse to manifest itself as "unjust threats" or as indifference camouflaged as non-interference (para. 7–8).

(27) . . . *verifies that fraternal love is no mere platitude.*

On February 18, 1981, the Pope spoke in Manila to diplomats serving in the Philippines. He was doubtless informed about the situation whereby many of the nation's wealthy elitists flaunted their excess in sight of a majority of the population which was mired in poverty. Each seemed to hold the other in contempt. The Pope probably also knew about the corrupt regime of the unpopular president, Ferdinand Marcos (ousted in 1986). Scholars have categorized his administration as a "kleptocracy" – a government that functions by rampant theft from its own citizenry. The Philippines which the Pope visited appeared to have forgotten that charity and equality are at the heart of Catholic doctrine, just as they are at the heart of ethics in international affairs. Although surrounded by a raging contradiction to his stance on moral integrity, the pontiff boldly bade for the renewal of "a love that is deeply felt and effectively expressed in concrete actions." The Pope asserted that "only love can make peoples really responsive to the call of the needy" (no. 5b). The culture of peace is obviously one in which society's "sources of uneasiness" (no. 4b) number not only the tragedy of misery stared at by plenty, but a subjugation which derives both from militarism and from the charade of failed scruples posing as peace (idem).

(28) . . . *"concretely and sympathetically" values "each other's specific qualities."*
(Japan, February 24, 1981)

Empathy is frequently evident in the realm of diplomacy. The Pope would not have startled his hearers when appealing that they be sympathetic in the assessment of a population's qualities. But the term "concretely" may have evoked a contrary response. Quite possibly, the Pope reasoned that people tend to project their own shortcomings and inadequacies upon their neighbor. Why should diplomats be any more immune to the transference of negative traits and motives than the rest of society? The Pope's word choice (no. 3b) prefaces his counsel that diplomats "view with impartiality" all that pertains to "other peoples." Without a basic and accurate comprehension of the "aspirations, needs and achievements of one's partner in dialogue and collaboration," the prospect of a culture of peace utterly disintegrates.

(29) . . . *speaks the language of destiny, not fate.*

Most dictionaries define fate as implying an inevitable and usually adverse outcome. The same does not hold, however, for destiny. Here the dictionary centers on being foreordained and with a great and noble course or end. Life in the south central African nation of Zambia is likely thought by diplomats to lean heavily in the direction of fate. Amid Africa's problems of discrimination, abysmal poverty, famine, and war, the idea of fate seems apt. But on May 3, 1989, the Pope's message to diplomats in Lusaka rejected that approach. According to Pope John Paul, diplomacy enlivens in nations "the realization of their destiny" (no. 2a). Social evils and economic disaster are not irreversible. They can be altered. Racism can be overcome (no. 3b). International creditor agencies can elect "sensitivity to the real circumstances of indebted nations" (no. 4a). Displaced persons may become welcomed and supported (no. 5a). And the culture of peace may be inspired by Pope Paul VI's certainty that "Development is the new name for peace" (no. 2b).

(30) . . . *refutes the many "forms of modern imperialism."*

The motto of the Queen of Denmark, Margrethe II, begins with the phrase, "The help of God." It so befits the tone of the Pope's address to diplomats gathered on June 7, 1989, in the garden of the Apostolic Nunciature in Copenhagen. The Pope contrasted the philosophy of two very different Danish thinkers. First, he spoke about Søren Kierkegaard and implications of Kierkegaard's concept of existential dread. "In that school, the human spirit was prepared for radical despair" (para. 4). The second was a scientist, Blessed Niels Stensen, "the famous anatomist and the founder of scientific paleontology, geology and crystallography." After Stensen's extensive university studies, he was subsequently ordained to the priesthood and was later consecrated a bishop (para. 5). Unlike Kierkegaard, Stensen's worldview captured the grandeur and beauty imbedded in the whole of reality. It was a worldview that was optimistic, practical and holy, a worldview captivated by "the help of God." The Pope's comparison led him to warn of the effect of today's "modern imperialism" with its "real forms of idolatry" (e.g. "the worship of money, ideology, class or technology" – no. 3, para. 7). This refutation by the culture of peace becomes an affirmation of the universality of humanity's individual and collective spiritual journey.

June 30, 1980
(*L'Osservatore Romano*, July 7, 1980, p. 6)

Brasilia, Brazil

Your Excellencies,
Ladies and Gentlemen,

On the first day spent in the Brazilian capital, I am very happy to meet the Heads and members of the diplomatic missions accredited to the Government of this country. I thank you heartily for having come this evening to this rendezvous with the Pope, who has representatives himself in most of your countries.

Expressing to you, to one and all, my cordial greetings, I am thinking also of the nations whose sons you are and whom you represent in Brazil. It is to all these peoples scattered in the American continent and in the other continents that I express the esteem and the sincere good wishes of the Church. The latter wishes to be catholic, that is universal, open to all human societies, the original blossoming of which she desires, thanks to the development of what is best in their country, their culture and in men themselves.

Your task as diplomats takes its place among the noble means which contribute to the rapprochement of peoples, to their mutual esteem and understanding, to their exchanges, their cultural or economic collaboration, let us say, to peace.

The diplomatic way is a way of wisdom in the sense that it counts on the faculty of men of goodwill to listen to one another, understand one another, find negotiated solutions, and progress together, instead of coming to clashes. Today, more than ever, the problems of peace, security and development are not limited to bilateral relations. It is a complex whole in which each country can make its contribution to the improvement of international relations, not only to avoid conflicts or reduce tensions, but to cope in solidarity with the great problems of the future of mankind which concern us all.

And here it must be hoped that every man, especially the leaders of nations and therefore their representatives, will have convictions and principles capable of promoting the real good of persons and peoples, within the international community. The Holy See wishes to bear witness to it also by making her specific contribution at the level of consciences.

In the framework of this short meeting, I can merely recall these principles of peace at home and peace abroad. It may seem commonplace to stress that each country has the duty of preserving its peace and its security at home. But it should in a certain way "deserve" this peace, by ensuring the common good of everyone and respect of rights. The common good of a society demands that it should be just. Where justice is lacking, the society is threatened from within. That does not mean that the changes necessary to bring about greater justice must be carried out by violence, revolution, bloodshed, for we Christians cannot subscribe to that. But it means that there are social changes, sometimes deep ones, to be realized constantly, gradually, effectively and realistically, through peaceful reforms.

All citizens have a part in this duty, but in particular, of course, those who exercise power, for the latter is in the service of social justice. Power has the right to make its strength felt by those who cultivate a group selfishness, to the detriment of the whole. It should in any case show that it is in the service of men, of every man, in the first place of those who are most in need of support. The Church, on her part, will constantly endeavor to recall concern for the "poor," for those who are underprivileged in some way. In no case can power allow itself to violate the fundamental rights of man, and I do not have to enumerate here those that I have often mentioned, in particular in my address on October 2 of last year before the United Nations.

With regard to other countries, each nation must be recognized as having the right to live in peace and security, on its own soil, without undergoing unjust threats from outside, whether they are of military, economic or ideological character. On this fundamental point men of goodwill, and I venture to say, diplomats in the first place, should be unanimous. But non-interference is not enough; for that would mean only indifference to the fate of peoples whom nature or historical circumstances have treated unfavorably to the extent that today a large number of their children lack the necessary minimum for a worthy human life, whether it be a question of bread, hygiene or education. There is an international solidarity to be promoted. There is a great deal of talk about it, but its implementation is too limited or burdened with conditions that are tantamount to new threats. Peace, here, passes through development in solidarity, and not through the accumulation of the arms of fear, or the upsurge of revolt, as I recalled recently at UNESCO.

It is by confronting ourselves constantly with this world task of peace in justice and development that we will find the words and the acts which, by degrees, will construct a world worthy of human beings, the world that God wishes for men, and the responsibility for which he entrusts to them, enlightening their conscience. It is the trust I have in you, dear diplomats, which has urged me to share this ideal with you. May God inspire you and bless you! May he bless your families! May he bless and protect your countries! May he guide the international community along the ways of peace and brotherhood!

February 18, 1981
(*OR*, March 2, 1981, pp. 1–2)

Manila, Philippines

Your Excellencies,
Ladies and Gentlemen,
1. I have come to this part of the world to meet the Catholic communities of the Philippines and Japan, and to present to both nations the expression of the profound esteem in which the Church holds them. At the same time I am also very pleased to have the opportunity to be with you this evening, since, as diplomats accredited to the Government of this land, you represent peoples not only in Asia but throughout the whole world. Later in my program, I shall address myself directly to the Asian peoples: but I cannot let the present occasion pass without expressing here before you the joy I experience in being able, through you, to greet the peoples and the Governments of your nations, many of whom maintain most cordial relations with the Holy See. I wish to reiterate the deep esteem which the Catholic Church has for the noble cultural and religious traditions of all peoples, and to reaffirm her desire to be of service to all in the common pursuit of peace, justice and human advancement.

2. The Church has no political ambitions. When she offers her own specific contribution to the great permanent tasks of mankind – peace, justice, development and every worthy effort aimed at promoting and defending human dignity – she does so because she is related to her mission. This mission is concerned with the salvation of man: the whole human being, the individual person who fulfills his or her eternal vocation in temporal history, within a complex of communities and societies. When giving attention to individuals' and peoples' needs and aspirations, the Church follows the command of her Founder; she implements the solicitude of Christ for each and every person, especially for the poor and for those who are suffering. Her own contribution to the humanization of society and the world derives from Jesus Christ and his Gospel. Through her social teaching, the Church does not present prefabricated models, nor does she align herself with prevailing and passing practices. Rather, with reference to Jesus Christ she strives to bring about a transformation of hearts and minds so that man can see himself in the full truth of his humanity.

3. The Church's action therefore is not political, or economic, or technical. The Church is not competent in the fields of technology or science, nor does she assert herself through power politics. Her competence, like her mission, is religious and moral in nature; and she must remain within her proper field of competence, lest her action be ineffective or irresponsible. It is the Church's practice therefore to respect the specific area of responsibility of the State, without interfering in the tasks of the politicians and without participating directly in the management of temporal affairs. At the same time the Church encourages her members to assume their full responsibility as citizens of a given nation and to seek together with their fellow human beings the paths and models which can best promote the progress of society. She sees as her specific contribution the strengthening of the spiritual and moral bases of society, and as a service to humanity she assists people in forming their consciences correctly.

4. It is in this sense that I wish my journey through Asia to be a call for peace and for human progress, and an encouragement for all those who are engaged in protecting and promoting the dignity of all human beings. I also hope that my meeting with you this evening will reinforce your own sense of mission in the service of your countries and of the whole human family. For is it not the mission of a diplomat to be a builder of bridges between nations, to be a specialist in dialogue and understanding, to be a defender of the dignity of man, so that the common welfare of all may be promoted? Beyond the fostering of the legitimate interests of your own nation, your mission directs you in a special way to the wider concerns of the whole human family, particularly on this Asian continent. Inspired as you are by the noblest ideals of brotherhood, you will, I am sure, share my concern for peace and progress in this area and you will understand the need to face the deeper causes of the problems that plague nations and peoples. In my recent Encyclical on the Mercy of God I have indicated what I believe to be the "sources of uneasiness." I have cited the fear connected with the prospect of a conflict that, in view of the stockpiling of atomic weapons, could mean the partial self-destruction of humanity. I have drawn attention to what human beings can do to other human beings through the means provided by an ever more sophisticated military technology. But I have also drawn attention to other elements when I wrote, "Man rightly fears falling victim to an oppression that will deprive him of his interior freedom, of the possibility of expressing the truth of which he is convinced, of the faith that he professes, of the ability to obey the voice of conscience that tells him the right path to follow. The technical means at the disposal of modern society conceal within themselves not only the possibility of destruction through military conflict, but also the possibility of a peaceful subjugation of individuals, of environments, of entire societies and of nations, that for one reason or another might prove inconvenient for those who possess the necessary means and are ready to use them without scruple" (no. 11). I have mentioned the tragic problem of the many who suffer from hunger and malnutrition and of the increasing state of inequality between individuals and nations whereby "side by side with those who are wealthy and living in plenty there exist those who are living in want, suffering, misery and often actually dying of hunger" (ibid).

5. But in that same document, I also stated (and I would like to leave this thought with you for your reflection): "The experience of the past and of our own time demonstrates that justice alone is not enough, that it can even lead to the negation and destruction of itself, if that deeper power, which is love, is not allowed to shape human life in its various dimensions" (no. 12).

Yes, dear friends, my message to you this evening concerns this same power of love. A love that is deeply felt and effectively expressed in concrete action, individual as well as collective, is indeed the moving force that enables man to be true to himself. Only love can make peoples really responsive to the call of the needy. And may it be this same force – fraternal love – that impels you to ever higher peaks of service and solidarity. Ladies and Gentlemen, in the lofty diplomatic mission that is yours be assured of my total support.

February 24, 1981
(*OR*, March 9, 1981, pp. 13–14)

Tokyo, Japan

Your Excellencies,
Ladies and Gentlemen,
1. In the course of my pastoral visit to East Asia and to the Catholic communities of the Philippines, Guam and Japan, I am happy and honored to have the opportunity of meeting with the Diplomatic Corps accredited to the Government of Japan in this city of Tokyo.

My visit, as I have already had the occasion to emphasize during this journey, is of a religious nature. I come to bring to the Catholic communities the fraternal support of the Church in Rome and throughout the world. I likewise come to meet the people of a region that has ancient cultures and religions. While being Successor of the Apostle Peter in the See of Rome, I am also heir to the tradition of another Apostle, Paul, who, having received faith in Jesus Christ, traveled tirelessly to the different parts of the then known world to bear witness to what he believed in, and to speak a word of brotherhood, love and hope for all.

Church and State serving humanity
2. Your presence here today shows that you understand my mission and also the activity of the Catholic Church and the Holy See, in the different parts of the world. Because of its mission, which is religious in nature and worldwide in dimension, the Holy See is always eager to promote and to maintain a climate of mutual trust and of dialogue with all the living forces of society, and, therefore, with the authorities who have received from the people the mandate of fostering the common good. The Catholic Church, in fidelity to her evangelical mission, wishes to be at the service of all humanity, of today's society, so often threatened or attacked. For this reason she strives to maintain friendly relations with all civil authorities and also, if they so desire, relations at the diplomatic level. Thus there is established, on the basis of mutual respect and understanding, a partnership of service for the progress of humanity.

Church and State – each in its own sphere, spiritual or temporal, each with its own proper means, without renouncing its own distinctive mission, without confusing its specific task – each one endeavors to carry out this service to humanity in order to promote that justice and that peace to which all humanity aspires.

I desire to pay homage here to the cordial relationship which the Government of Japan maintains with the Holy See, and which is exemplified by the presence of an Ambassador to the Holy See and of a Papal Representative in Tokyo. The latter has a special [place] among the leaders of the Catholic community of this land but, like all of you, he also has the task of promoting a spirit of understanding and cooperation in the international domain.

A school for mutual understanding
3. Ladies and Gentlemen, in the capital of this nation you are bearers of a mission that draws its meaning and inspiration from the ideals of peaceful and fraternal collaboration. You are all deeply conscious of your task. Without any doubt it is an important

one; in many circumstances it is difficult; but it is always rewarding, since at the same time it is a school for mutual understanding and a testing ground for worldwide concerns.

The basis for any fruitful activity in promoting peaceful relations among nations is certainly the capacity for correctly and sympathetically valuing each other's specific qualities. Japan certainly offers a true school for understanding, for Japan is unique in its history, in its culture and in its spiritual values. Through the course of many centuries, Japanese society has constantly honored its own traditions by maintaining a true appreciation of the spiritual. It has expressed those traditions in its temples, in the arts, in literature, in the theatre and in music, at the same time preserving, even in the midst of increasing economic and individual development, its distinctive Japanese characteristics. As diplomats, you are witnesses to and sometimes sharers in the events that mark the history and the life of the Japanese people and especially of its culture, and so you are able to acquire a deeper understanding of the differences that shape the character and the spirit of each nation and people. Indeed, as I said last month in my address to the Diplomatic Corps accredited to the Holy See: "Culture is the life of the spirit; it is the key which gives access to the deepest and most jealously guarded secrets of the life of the peoples; it is the fundamental and unifying expression of their existence" (Address of January 12, 1981, no. 6). Just as it is necessary to be deeply rooted in one's own culture in order to understand the values and the spirit of one's own nation, so also it is necessary to view with impartiality the manifestations of the cultural life of other peoples, in order to understand the aspirations, needs and achievements of one's partner in dialogue and collaboration.

Instruments for good
4. There is a second aspect to the function of the diplomat. You are called to be instruments – even to be on the front line – in building a new order of relations in the world. Precisely because each people is distinguished from others by its cultural inheritance and its achievements, it can offer a unique and irreplaceable contribution to all the others. Without surrendering their own values, nations can work together and build a true international community characterized by shared responsibility for the universal common good. More than ever, the world situation today demands that this common responsibility be taken up in a true universal spirit. Every diplomatic community thus becomes a testing ground for worldwide concerns. In your daily personal contacts with your colleagues, in your official dealings with the host government and its agencies, in endeavoring to know and to understand the local culture, in taking an active part in the life of the community that offers you its hospitality, you will develop those attitudes of respect and appreciation that are so needed in order to build fraternal relations between the nations of the world.

Intercultural relations
5. Many of you have already accumulated a rich experience in intercultural relations and exchange, gained through years of service to your own country in different parts of the world. It is my hope that your mission here in Japan will help you to discover and understand more profoundly beyond the Japanese context, the rich reality of all Asia and of all the Asian peoples. Asia has a special role to play in building up and strengthening the community of nations. So many problems of worldwide dimension

remain to be solved, and Asia must participate in undertakings begun for this purpose. I wish to convey to you my conviction that world problems will not be solved unless each continent and nation plays its rightful role and makes its own specific contribution. The nations of Asia must assume the role that is theirs by reason of their centuries-old cultures, their religious experience, their dynamism and enduring industriousness. The mainland and the archipelagos of Asia are certainly not devoid of problems (and which nation anywhere in the world can claim that it has solved all its people's problems?) but there is no greater challenge for a people than to share of its substance with others while at the same time trying to find the full solutions to its own problems.

Political determination
6. Today, we are at a point in history where it has become economically and technically feasible to relieve the worst aspects of the extreme poverty that afflicts so many of our fellow human beings. The kinds of poverty are many: malnutrition and hunger, illiteracy and lack of basic education, chronic disease and high infant mortality, lack of meaningful employment and lack of proper housing. The obstacles to overcoming these problems are no longer primarily economic or technical, as they were in the past, but are now to be found in the spheres of convictions and institutions.

It is not in fact a lack of political determination – at both national and international levels – that is the main obstacle to the successful elimination of the gravest forms of suffering and need? Is it not an absence of strong personal and collective convictions that prevents the poor from sharing more fully and equitably in their own development? The present economic difficulties which in varying ways and degrees are affecting all nations must not become a pretext for giving in to the temptation to make the poor pay for the solution to the problems of the rich, by permitting a standard of living lower than what a rational definition of human decency would allow. Although there are many compelling reasons for eliminating abject poverty, particularly in the developing world, I do not hesitate to state that the fundamental case against poverty is a moral one. It is the sign of a healthy community – whether it be the family, the nation or the international community itself – to recognize the moral imperative of mutual solidarity, justice and love. The generosity and the sense of fairness already at work in many international undertakings and programs must be further reinforced by an increased awareness of the ethical dimension. The public and governments must become ever more conscious of the fact that nobody may stand idly by as long as human beings are suffering and in need. The Holy See will never cease to raise its voice and to commit full weight of its moral authority to increasing public awareness in this regard.

International peace issue
7. The opportunity will be given to me later in the course of my short stay in Japan to speak about the overriding concern for international peace, and to encourage the international community to increase its efforts in favor of peaceful relations between nations. On the present occasion just let me emphasize that endeavors for peace cannot be separated from the quest for a just society and for the effective development of all nations and peoples. Justice and development go hand in hand with peace. They are

essential parts of a new world order still to be built. They are a path leading to a future of happiness and dignity.

Ladies and Gentlemen, yours is a splendid mission: to be the heralds of universality, the builders of peace among nations, the promoters of a new and just world. May each one of you, with your own governments, as well as international meetings and institutions, be the advocate of less privileged people and nations. The ideal of international brotherhood in which we all so profoundly believe demands this. And by acting in this way you will indeed serve your own country and all humanity well.

May the peace and justice of Almighty God dwell in your hearts always. May his blessing come down upon you, upon your families, upon your nations and upon all your untiring efforts in the service of humanity.

May 3, 1989
(*OR*, May 29, 1989, pp. 10–11)

Lusaka, Zambia

Ladies and Gentlemen,

1. I am very happy to have this occasion to meet the distinguished Heads of Mission and Diplomatic Personnel accredited to the Government of Zambia. Through you I greet each of the nations and people you represent. I also extend greetings to the representatives of International Organizations. You are all working for the well-being and peaceful progress of peoples, conscious of the fact that true peace and development must be based on good will, justice and cooperation in international relations. Yours is a demanding task, and one which requires much dedication and sensitivity. I express my esteem and encouragement for you in your service in this part of Africa.

2. As you realize, my present visit is above all a visit of the Bishop of Rome, the Successor of the Apostle Peter, to the Catholic communities of Zambia, Malawi, Madagascar and La Reunion. At the same time, my visits to different countries allow me to manifest the Holy See's profound solidarity with the peoples of the world as they work for the realization of their destiny. With unfailing respect for the aspirations of all peoples to live their identity in freedom and security, with deep concern for the way in which human dignity and human rights are respected and promoted, the Holy See is present in the international community – not as a political, economic or military power – but as seeking especially to foster a moral and ethical reflection and dialogue on the great questions and problems affecting the lives of the men and women of our time.

The person – in the fullness of human dignity – is the object of the Church's mission and responsibility. The Holy See is convinced that only a higher perspective of moral ideals and of the principles of goodness, truth and justice in human relations can solve the complicated questions affecting the world community. The integral development and well-being of individuals, and of all peoples, must more and more become the objective which public authorities, governments and international organizations pursue, if the world is to overcome the tensions and conflicts which continue to threaten peace. In the words of my predecessor Pope Paul VI: "Development is the new name for peace" (*Populorum Progressio*, no. 87).

3. The Holy See has consistently called for moral and ethical reflection on the grave problems affecting society, problems which require closer cooperation between developed and developing nations, between North and South, East and West. I wish to refer briefly to the subjects of two recent statements: one on racism and the other on the international debt question.

Racism and its expression in systems of social, economic and political discrimination are considered by the Church as clearly contrary to Christian faith and love. Unfortunately, racism's theoretical and practical manifestation continue to exist in the world on a vast scale, in many forms and degrees, even though the system of apartheid is a most obvious and dramatic instance. In combating this moral problem, the Church advocated needed change, but a constructive change brought about by peaceful means.

Discrimination must be overcome, not through fresh violence but through reconciliation. It is my frequent and earnest prayer that Almighty God will inspire all concerned to understand that the basis of a genuine solution to racism in general and apartheid in particular is the conviction of the equal dignity of every human being as a member of the human family and child of God.

4. The problem of international debt is a clear example of the interdependence which characterizes relations between countries and continents. It is a problem which cannot be solved without mutual understanding and agreement between debtor and creditor nations, without sensitivity to the real circumstances of indebted nations on the part of creditor agencies, and without a wise and committed policy of growth on the part of the developing nations themselves. Is it merely a rhetorical question to ask how many infants and children die every day in Africa because resources are now being swallowed up in debt repayment? There is no time now to lament policies of the past or those elements in the international financial and economic picture which have led to the present situation. Now is the time for a new and courageous international solidarity, a solidarity not based on self-interest but inspired and guided by a true concern for human beings.

Recent moves on the part of the developed and creditor countries to lessen the burdens of repayment on the economies of debtor nations are obviously a step in the right direction. Such moves deserve to be encouraged. But much more remains to be done. It is to the ethical and moral values involved that the Church primarily directs her attention. Her appeal is to the conscience and the heart of those who can bring about a just solution to the problem, in respect for the equal dignity of all people. It is her task, in obedience to the Gospel, always and everywhere, to emphasize justice, reconciliation and love. It has become more and more evident that measures of solidarity are imperative so that hope may be restored to many sorely tried peoples. I pray that those in a position to influence events will truly express that solidarity in a new and generous approach to the problems of international debt.

5. In this distinguished gathering, I cannot but make reference to the tragic situation being experienced in Africa and elsewhere by millions of human beings forced to flee their homes and native lands because of famine, war and terrorism. We must heed the sufferings of these brothers and sisters. There are so many men and women offended in their inalienable human dignity, injured in body and mind, condemned to a miserable existence through no fault of their own. As I have so often stated, the plight of millions of refugees to different continents is a festering wound which typifies and reveals the imbalances and conflicts of the modern world (cf. *Sollicitudo Rei Socialis*, no. 24).

I wish to take this opportunity to express appreciation to the Governments of the two countries of continental Africa that I am visiting for what they are doing to offer hospitality to and meet the needs of the many refugees residing in their territories. Zambia is giving an example of openness and solidarity which honors its leaders and its people. Malawi is deeply affected by a large influx of refugees from neighboring Mozambique, and is to be commended for its heroic efforts in caring for them, even to the point of diminishing its own essential resources. I would appeal to you as diplomats to see this tragedy not in political terms but as a deeply human drama to which you draw the attention and seek the assistance of your own peoples and of the organizations you represent. The care of refugees includes not only meeting their immediate needs, but also helping them preserve their social, cultural and religious identity. For it is precisely this identity which sustains them in their plight and offers them hope for a new and better future.

6. In recent months there have been signs of progress toward peace and reconciliation in Southern Africa. Lusaka itself has been center for both official and unofficial meetings of the parties involved in conflicts. Specifically, the world looks with expectation and hope to the steps being taken to implement the New York Accords leading to the independence of Namibia and the withdrawal of foreign forces from Angola. It is important that these processes should be promoted and further strengthened through the support of the international community.

Here again we see proof of the interdependence of the world's nations. To all those who hear my voice, I make an appeal that Namibia, the latest country in Africa to become independent, be fully accepted into the family of nations, that it be sustained in its independence and given every assistance on the road to economic, social and political autonomy.

International solidarity calls for the abandonment of policies which are selfish or inspired by interests that are too partisan. True statesmanship implies a realistic and worldwide view of the paths that the human family is taking in its search for a better and more dignified existence. Essential to humanity's progress is the conviction that differences and tension should be resolved not by force or the threat of force, but through sincere and peaceful methods. In this the diplomatic community has a most immediate role to play.

7. Dear friends: for those who believe in divine Providence and God's loving plan for the human family, the hope of peace and progress becomes an ardent prayer, rising from the depths of our hearts, where we feel ourselves bound to every other human being in brotherhood and solidarity.

> The Lord bless you and keep you:
> The Lord make his face to shine upon you,
> and be gracious to you:
> The Lord set his gaze upon you, and give you peace (Num 6:24–26).

May God bless each one of you and your families. May he pour out his gifts upon the countries and peoples you represent. May he love and protect the people of Zambia, our gracious hosts and friends.

June 7, 1989
(*OR*, June 19, 1989)

Copenhagen, Denmark

Ladies and Gentlemen,

1. Both at the Vatican and on my journeys to the Church in various parts of the world, I have frequent opportunities to meet members of the diplomatic community. Today, I have the great pleasure of meeting you, the distinguished Heads of Mission and diplomatic personnel accredited to Her Majesty the Queen of Denmark. I greet you all and thank you for your presence here. Through you I pay tribute to the nations and peoples you represent. In your service to your respective countries and to the world community I see a direct contribution to the realization of the ardent hope that burns in human hearts everywhere, the hope that an ever more peaceful and humane world will result from the transformations taking place in peoples and in the relations between the forces that shape our history.

I wish to speak to you this morning as a friend in our common humanity, as one concerned for the genuine well-being and advancement of the human family, and as a disciple of Jesus Christ whose Church I have been called to serve in a ministry of unity and faith.

2. In preparing for this visit to Denmark, I have been strongly reminded of two Danish thinkers. As a former professor of ethics in my own country, I have long been familiar with the writings of one of them: Søren Kierkegaard. Kierkegaard was deeply absorbed by a sense of the limited and finite nature of existence, and by a consequent sense of dread – a sense of foreboding which he understood as something not merely psychological but essentially metaphysical, and therefore inevitably present in all of human experience. For Kierkegaard, this anguish was the fundamental category defining the relationship of the individual to the world. For him, the whole of existence is permeated by the possibility of not being. Hence everything is somehow, at the same time, nothing. "What I am" wrote Kierkegaard, "is nothing" (*Intimate Diary*).

Kierkegaard's escape from this negativity was through his Christian faith and his obedience to God. In a certain sense he went against the intellectual climate of his time by drawing attention back to the individual and the individual's personal relationship to God. Some later philosophers were much affected by Kierkegaard's concept of existential dread. Of these, some found no way out but to extol the orientation toward death and nothingness inherent in being "situated" in the world. In that school, the human spirit was prepared for radical despair and a denial of meaning and freedom in life.

The other Danish scholar who comes to mind was the seventeenth century scientist Niels Stenson, the famous anatomist and the founder of scientific paleontology, geology and crystallography. As I had occasion to point out at last year's beatification ceremony for this outstanding son of Denmark, his life followed a double course: he was a keen observer of the human body and of inanimate nature, and at the same time he was a deeply believing Christian who placed himself at the service of God's will in a humble yet forthright and fearless way. His pursuit of scientific knowledge led him to attend the Universities at Amsterdam, Leyden, Paris and Florence. His journey of faith led him to a profound experience of conversion, to ordination as a priest, to becoming a bishop and a missionary. His personal holiness was so notable that the Church holds him up as an example to the faithful and as an intercessor for them before God.

3. The memory of these two Danish intellectuals and believers provokes reflections which may be far removed from our daily and immediate concerns, but which never-theless form the undercurrent of all thought and decision, and therefore determine as it were the very sense of our daily struggles, both personal and collective. These reflections are related to the meaning of life with obvious limitations, its sufferings and its mysterious outcome which is death. They concern the place of religion in his-tory, culture and society, and the perennial question about the relationship between faith and reason. On the practical plane, they concern the pressing need for collabo-ration between men and women of religion, science, culture, politics and economics in facing the great problems of the world: the preservation of the planet and its resources, peace between nations and groups, justice in society, and a prompt and effective response to the tragic situation of poverty, sickness and hunger affecting mil-lions of human beings.

Our own century has experienced such terrible wars and political tensions, such offenses against life and freedom, such seemingly intractable sources of suffering – including the present-day tragedies of the international drug trade and the increasing spread of AIDS – that some people may hesitate to express too much hope or to be over optimistic about the future. Yet many will agree that the world is living through a moment of extraordinary awakening. The old problems remain, and new ones arise; but there is also a growing awareness of an opportunity being offered to give birth to a new and better era; a time to involve one another in frank and truthful collaboration in order to meet the great challenges facing humanity at the end of the twentieth cen-tury. The opportunity I speak of is not something clearly definable. It is more like the confluence of many complex global developments in the fields of science and tech-nology, in the economic world, in a growing political maturity of peoples and in the formation of public opinion. Perhaps it is right to say that we are experiencing is a change, however slow and fragile, in the direction of the world's concerns, and an increasing, if sometimes grudging, willingness to accept the implications of a plane-tary interdependence from which no one can truly escape.

I speak of these things to you, distinguished members of the Diplomatic Corps, because of your personal and professional capability of evoking an appropriate response to the challenges which have appeared on the horizon of humanity's progress. Mine is an invitation to you, and to all men and women with responsibility for the public life of nations, to do everything possible to encourage this moral awak-ening and to further the peaceful processes which seek to implement freedom, respect for human dignity and human rights throughout the world. In this you and your Governments and peoples will have the full encouragement of the Catholic Church.

The Church has little or no technical advice to give, nor an economic or political program to promote. Her mission is eminently spiritual and humanitarian. She seeks to be faithful to Jesus Christ, her divine founder, who declared: "My kingdom is not of this world" (Jn 18:36), but who, at the same time, was moved to compassion at the sight of the sufferings of the multitudes (cf. Mt 9:36). The Church exists to proclaim the dominion of God, the loving Father, over creation and over man, and seeks to educate people's consciences to accept responsibility for themselves and for the world, for human relationships and for the common destiny of the human family. Specifically, the Church teaches a doctrine of creation and redemption which places the individual at the center of her worldview and activity. Her temporal objective is the full development of individuals. She stimulates and appeals to personal responsibility. She encourages and calls upon society to defend and promote the inalienable worth and rights of the person, and to safeguard these values through legislation and social policies. She wishes to pursue these goals in cooperation with all who serve the common good.

From the beginning of my own pontificate I have endeavored to give voice to a preoccupation which is already present in biblical accounts of man's efforts to build a world without reference to God. Today this preoccupation assumes an immediacy all its own, by reason of the immensely magnified potential for good or evil which man has fashioned. The danger is that "while man's dominion over the world of things is making enormous advances, he may lose the essential threads of his dominion and in various ways let his humanity be subjected to the world and become himself something subject to manipulation" (*Redemptor Hominis*, no. 16).

As man increasingly takes charge of his world, the fundamental question remains ever the same: "whether in the context of this progress man, as man, is becoming truly better, that is to say, more mature spiritually, more aware of the dignity of his humanity, more responsible, more open to others, especially the most needy and the weakest" (ibid., no. 15).

The basic questions therefore are those related to truth and meaning, to moral good and evil. These are perennial questions, since each generation, and indeed each individual, is called upon to respond to them in the ever changing circumstances of life. The unbalanced development taking place at present and posing the greatest threat to the stability of the world – where the rising material standards of some are in stark contrast with the deepening poverty and misery of others – is not the result of blind and uncontrollable forces, but of decisions made by individuals and groups. I am fully convinced, and have so written in my 1987 Encyclical on the Church's Social Concern, that certain forms of modern "imperialism" which appear to be inspired by economics or politics, are in fact real forms of idolatry: the worship of money, ideology, class or technology. The true nature of the inequalities which plague our world is that of moral evil. To acknowledge this is important, for, "to diagnose the evil in this way is to identify precisely, on the level of human conduct, the path to be followed in order to overcome it" (*Sollicitudo Rei Socialis*, no. 37).

Ladies and Gentlemen: these are the thoughts that I wish to leave with you, trusting that you share my concern for the direction in which humanity is going at the end of the Second Christian Millennium. The path forward is the path of a profound solidarity, which is not a feeling of vague compassion or shallow distress at the misfortunes of others, but a firm and persevering determination to commit oneself to the common good (ibid., no. 38). Such a commitment to solidarity befits your status as diplomats at the service of peace and progress. My plea to you therefore is that we may work together to build an era of effective worldwide solidarity in openness to the moral dimensions implicit in every human endeavor.

May Almighty God be with you in your work. May his blessings be upon you and your families and upon the countries which you serve. Thank you.

January 1, 1993
(*OR*, January 6, 1993)

St. Peter's Basilica, Rome

On the occasion of Mass for the World Day of Prayer for Peace

1. "He was named Jesus" (Lk 2:21). Today is the eighth day since the birth of the Son of Mary that night at Bethlehem. Today "he was named" Jesus, "the name given him by the angel before he was conceived in the womb" of his mother (Lk 2:21).

"God sent his Son, born of a woman" (Gal 4:4). The eternal Father wanted his only-begotten Son to be given this very name Jesus, which means "God saves." It is a name that was in use in Israel, and many before him bore it. However, only the Redeemer was given this name by the eternal Father, and on the day of his circumcision, Mary and Joseph were the humble executors of his will. The heavenly Father wanted his Son – the Son who is consubstantial with him, God from God – as a man, as the Son of man, to bear the name of Jesus.

Such a name was meant to signify for all times the mission fulfilled by him in "the fullness of time" (cf. Gal 4:4). God sent his Son into the world so "that the world might be saved through him" (Jn 3:17). The name of Jesus has a universal character, that is, it expresses God's saving will regarding the world, all humanity. "God wills everyone to be saved and to come to knowledge of the truth" (1 Tm 2:14).

2. To save – means to liberate from evil, and Jesus commanded us to pray to the Father for this, "Deliver us from evil." Thus he united our prayer to his mission in the world, a mission which already marks the time of his birth at Bethlehem: "Natus est nobis Salvator mundi."

To save! To liberate from evil, to overcome evil – but what this really means is to make room for good. When a person has eliminated evil, a vacuum should not remain, evil recedes and vanishes in the presence of good.

The Son of God's coming into the world means that God wants to uproot definitively the evil that is in humanity, introducing people into the divine dimension of good. In fact, this is what the Apostle teaches us in the Letter to the Galatians: "God sent his Son, born of a woman, born under the law, to ransom those under the law, so that we might receive adoption. So you are no longer a slave but a child" (Gal 4: 4–7). A child, a person, that is, in whom the power of the Spirit can cry out to the Father, "Abba, Father!" (Gal 4:6). In fact, the Holy Spirit has been sent as the Spirit of the Son.

Those who become God's adoptive children in his only-begotten Son at the same time become heirs: as heirs they share in the imperishable Good which is God himself.

All this truth [is] contained in the name of "Jesus." Jesus, the Savior.

3. According to Jesus' own words, divine adoption is linked with the spread of peace. "Blessed are the peacemakers, for they shall be called children of God" (Mt 5:9). Today, the first day of the new year, we want to profess and proclaim that Jesus is our Peace. Jesus, whose name means "God saves." The good of peace is included in his saving mission. Christ himself, whom the Old Testament prophet called the Prince of Peace, brings about reconciliation between God and humanity. This reconciliation is the first dimension of peace. In it all peace which the children of God are called to

spread in the world and among people begins and has its roots, thus they become participants, or rather co-artisans of the messianic salvation proclaimed by the name of Jesus and brought into the world by peace: peace in its every dimension is a good that is included in salvation. It is an essential aspect of God's salvific plan offered to humanity in Christ his Son. That is why he wanted the Redeemer's name to be "Jesus."

4. "Peace to those on whom his favor rests" (Lk 2:14). "Peace on earth to people of good will." The message that night at Bethlehem speaks of a close link between peace on earth and the Savior's mission.

Could it be otherwise? To save means to deliver from evil and does not the antithesis of peace show all the signs of being evil? Our century, the 20th century, unfortunately brought that to light in a singular way through the terrible experiences of the two world wars, and through so many other conflicts which, although not termed "world" wars, were still "wars," with all that such a dramatic reality implies.

During the course of the 1980s, when the threat of nuclear war was very real, Christians and representatives of the world's other religions gathered at Assisi to cry out – in a single place – "deliver us from this evil," "grant us peace." Is it possible to believe that such a confident prayer was not heard by him who is the God of peace?

Today the horror of nuclear destruction seems to be more remote from humanity, but the good of peace has not been consolidated everywhere. This can be seen by recent events taking place outside Europe and even in it. Unfortunately, on our continent, too, in particular in the Balkans, the spread of evil of destructive war and violence has not subsided. Can Europe remain aloof from such situations and not feel challenged by them?

Christ's disciples and those who confess his name – his Church – cannot refrain from thinking and acting in the spirit of the eight Beatitudes: "Blessed are the peacemakers." For this very reason all the Episcopal Conferences of Europe, together with the Bishop of Rome, have proclaimed this first of January as a Day of Prayer for Peace in Europe, in particular in the Balkans. Therefore, as we did in 1986, we shall go once again on pilgrimage to Assisi.

5. Europe! Europe! "The Lord look upon you kindly and give you peace!" (Num 6:26).

Thus we exclaim in the name of Jesus, in the name, that is, of him who is the Savior of the world, of man, of all people: of the nations and countries and continents. He, Jesus, does not have at his disposal all the means that the states and the mighty ones of the world can use. His power is in the poverty of that night at Bethlehem, and then on the cross on Golgotha. However, his is a power that penetrates more deeply. In fact, it alone can uproot from the depths of the human being hatred, the first enemy of peace. It alone is capable of turning those who make war and destruction into builders of peace, whom it is possible to call God's children.

6. Mary! Today the Church mediates on the mystery of your motherhood. You are the "memory" of all God's mighty deeds. You know the ways by which the Son, the Word, one in being with the Father, came into the world. Christ, the Savior of the world! He, our Peace.

Mary, Mother of Peace, intercede for us with him. Intercede for us! Amen.

Chapter V
Conclusion

By way of conclusion, I recall an incident in which Napoleon was once asked his opinion about diplomats. He replied that they were simply "police in grand costume." That was probably a fairly reliable summary for his era, indeed for the style of his own governance. Because the diplomacy of the late eighteenth and early Nineteenth centuries was regularly embellished by drama and intrigue, by secrecy and deception. Few practitioners could subscribe to anything which resembled "clean hands." But diplomacy seems to have shifted in the path of its orbit. Such eminent scholars of diplomatic history and theory as Sir Harold Nicolson, Edward Satow, Geoff R. Berridge, and Chester A. Crocker, depict modern diplomacy in a much more favorable light. Despite the normalcy of recurring debate; for example, over career versus appointed Ambassadors, or concerns about whether a diplomat's main loyalty is to a Head of State or to the State Department, secular diplomacy today provides an invaluable resource of persons who are distinguished and generous in the record of their civic dedication.

Papal diplomacy has also evolved. Diplomats as "noble ecclesiastics," reminiscent of the aristocratic lineage of those clerics who were once groomed for a diplomatic "career," have been replaced by Nuncios who are expected to reflect the pastoral solicitude of the Holy See and its adherence to an outlook compliant with the Gospels. The transition is to a vocation of service. The more adventuresome of readers may wish to refer to canons 362–367 of the 1983 *Code of Canon Law*. In many respects said canons legislate what amounts to a change in mentality, a change which stems from the documents of Vatican II (e.g. *Gaudium et Spes*, nos. 1–3, *Lumen Gentium*, no. 23) and from Pope Paul VI's Motu Proprio of 1969, *Sollicitudo Omnium Ecclesiarum*.

Chapters I to IV of this text propose thirty characteristics of the culture of peace which are suggested by the diplomatic discourse of Pope John Paul II throughout twenty-five years of his pontificate. The intent is to illustrate that the humanism which is evident elsewhere in current secular diplomacy, together with the ministry of service which is prominent in papal diplomacy, combine in the approach of the Pope toward secular diplomats who are either assigned to the Holy See or who are otherwise in direct contact with him. The Pope's philosophy of the culture of peace challenges diplomats to work diligently "to make room for good" (Homily, January 6, 1993, no. 2b). The nature of that "good" is able to transform the very foundations of the world. For the culture of peace is synonymous with mankind's total liberation. It is a liberation from all that besets the dignity of each person. It is liberation for all that promises to perfect the human community. And, ultimately, it is a liberation which [for] yearns union with "the imperishable Good. . . . God Himself" (idem., no. 2d).

Appendix
Pope John Paul II: A Theory of International Diplomacy
Bernard J. O'Connor

Reprinted from *Foundation Theology 2002* (Bristol, Ind.: Cloverdale, 2003).

Eric Clark, commenting upon the Vatican's presence within the sphere of international diplomacy, remarks that when Letters of Credence are presented by new ambassadors to the Holy See, "speeches are made in the normal way, and are devoid of any controversial points." Clark cites the 1970 example of a British diplomat who used the occasion with Pope Paul VI to outline his government's general policy. In reply, the Pope urged an attitude of ongoing cooperation between Britain and the Catholic Church. He also conveyed that a united Europe would prove "a source of strength and stability for the world." And the Pope concluded with an expression of greetings to Queen Elizabeth II.[1]

By 2002, the Vatican has formalized diplomatic relations with 172 states, and participates in over 30 intergovernmental organizations (e.g., World Food Program) and 10 regional intergovernmental bodies (e.g., Arab League, Cairo).[2] Accreditation of ambassadors continues to consist of reciprocal speeches. But those delivered by Pope John Paul II since his election in 1978 are anything but an exercise in superficial pleasantry. The pontiff is candid and specific in his remarks, and does not hesitate to state his concern, his disappointment, and his desire to challenge nations to behave in accord with what befits human dignity and aspirations for world peace. Pope John Paul has also continued a practice begun by Pope Paul VI of personally addressing the United Nations. Moreover, as with several of his modern predecessors, the Pope annually assembles the corps of diplomats assigned to the Vatican, usually around the commencement of the New Year. Again, his remarks summarize how he perceives that the international community has either made progress or has failed to do so in terms of such issues as the advance of economic collaboration, armaments reduction, religious toleration, and the embrace of human rights.

I. Objective
To date, scant scholarly attempt has been made to analyze Pope John Paul's political philosophy. Instead, academic focus tends to center upon his contribution to the dethronement of communism, notably in Eastern Europe. It is commonly held, for example, that U.S. President Ronald Reagan credits the Pope as being crucial to the 1989 collapse of the Berlin Wall. This essay recognizes that Pope John Paul's political activity derives from a systematic, coherent, and consistent philosophical framework. It is possible to uncover in the record of the Pope's thought his response to questions of profound academic significance. One such question involves the role of international diplomacy. In an era when many are rather ambivalent toward traditional or Track I diplomacy, and more inclined to prefer a non-governmental or Track II diplomatic approach, Pope John Paul II maintains that conventional diplomats remain capa-

ble of actually influencing the outlook of their respective countries. It is diplomats who, for example, encourage their countries' political leaders to interpret national interests as best furthered by an agenda which embodies global interests. This essay identifies an overview of major elements which comprise the Pope's concept of international diplomacy's nature and role. While by no means an exhaustive treatment, it is a study which may demonstrate that the pontiff's view represents a persuasive synthesis of historical insight, political analysis, and theological reflection.

II. Methodology

Pope John Paul II's message to the United Nations General Assembly on October 5, 1995, serves as starting point for this discussion of his vision for international diplomacy. It was in this setting that he advocated the idea that not only individuals and groups are the subject of rights, but that nations should also be regarded by the international community as a legitimate holder of natural rights. And he elaborated upon the logic underlying that position, together with an implicit assertion that UN delegates were empowered to actualize its content and implications. The elements of diplomacy which emerge from that UN speech are not an isolated phenomenon. In his New Year addresses to the diplomatic corps between 1996 and 2002, the Pope reinforced essential themes and dynamics apparent in his prior text. The present study intends to examine those seven speeches in comparison with the thirty-eight paragraphs delivered on the occasion of the fiftieth anniversary of the United Nations.

III. International diplomacy: constitutive elements

(A) Diplomacy: witness to the universal longing for freedom
UN representatives are reminded that they "are witnessing an extraordinary global acceleration of [a] quest for freedom." But that witness does not mean an option to interpret freedom in exclusively subjective categories. Delegates are confronted by freedom's objective character. Freedom, because it is the finale to a "quest," is the culmination of a rational and deliberate process, one that is deeply embedded in the contours of human history. The Pope insisted that freedom transcends every inclination to confine it by geographic or cultural boundaries. It belongs no more to one area than to one group. Freedom is characterized by authentic universality.

The idea of "quest" denotes an external manifestation, admittedly global in scope and perceptible in features. What, however, motivates such a quest? According to Pope John Paul, the outer quest corresponds to an inner quest, an inner longing that is similarly universal. And that longing "has its basis in those universal rights which human beings enjoy by the very fact of their humanity." It is for that reason, the Pope said, that people are willing to take "the risk of freedom," even in the face of violence. What they ask is that "commensurate with their dignity as free human beings," they may "be given a place in social, political and economic life." UN delegates ensure a diplomacy dedicated to the safeguarding of human dignity, especially from all forms of outrage which may assail it.[3]

On January 10, 1998, Pope John Paul reminded the diplomatic corps that "man is unfortunately capable of betraying his humanity" and his freedom. However, freedom is not a barrier to progressive enlightenment when that enlightenment acknowledges those institutions, organizations, and belief systems which may so serve human sojourners that they "can always find again the sources of life and order which the Creator has inscribed in the most intimate part of [man's] being." Freedom, according to the Pope, is both ontological and anthropological. Freedom belongs to the order of created being, an order for which man is designed to participate. Because man is fashioned for freedom, the act of appeal to the very ground of "life and order" means, in reality, that man consents to actualize what is his own intrinsic nature.

It is a free nature which allows individuals and their social groupings to enter into solidarity without loss of their identity and integrity. The Pope cited the example of Africa. "Africans ought not to rely on outside assistance for everything." Africans are endowed with the human resource capacity "to meet the challenges of our time and to manage societies in an appropriate way." It would be erroneous to deduce that freedom thus described as the byproduct of a patronizing benevolence. Quite the opposite. Freedom for Africans in this instance – and by extension to all others – means alignment with the fact of a potential which is inherently oriented toward positive evolution and development.[4]

(B) Diplomacy: engaged in the responsible use of freedom – a moral truth
A purpose of diplomacy is to recognize the practical consequences of a determination to live on behalf of freedom. That life, the Pope urged the UN, necessitates a response which pertains to the dimensions of "the spiritual growth [of humanity] and to the moral vitality of nations." Freedom possesses a distinct moral structure. Diplomats must be aware that freedom is neither unbridled license nor the mere absence of oppression. The Pope stated that freedom has its own proper inner "logic." "Freedom is ordered to the truth." And just as freedom has been depicted as a quest originating in an interior longing, the fulfillment of that quest is not realized solely when freedom is attained, but when that freedom is attached to "truth about the human person." Truth comprehends that the aforementioned license signals a deterioration of individuals' lives. Applied to political life, freedom removed from truth "becomes the caprice of the most powerful and the arrogance of power." Knowledge of truth concerning the human person, Pope John Paul said, is "universally knowable." In other words, truth is not an idea or an ideal; it is not defined by the shifting sands of relativism; nor is it the prerogative of intellectual elitism. Truth is part of the fabric of the omni-pervasive natural, moral law. Hence, connecting truth to freedom does not limit the latter or threaten it in any manner. Rather, that connect becomes the "guarantor of freedom's future."

Repeatedly, the Pope links the cause of "the integral development of the human person" to the need for a return to insistence upon the moral foundation of political action. Otherwise, what passes for agreement or consensus amounts simply to façade. The Pope, in his 1997 New Year message to diplomats, observed that there is a profusion of "written conventions [and] forums for self-expression." Quite obviously, unresolved problems on the international scene illustrate that such are not a reliable or efficient solution. The deficiency consists of the absence of "a moral law and the courage to abide by it." Again, in 1998, the Pope cautioned diplomats that the community of nations "cannot escape the duty of fidelity to the unwritten law of the human conscience." He cited a passage (no. 46) from his encyclical letter, *Centesimus Annus*. The tenor is strongly reminiscent of his words to the 1995 UN General Assembly. "If there exists no ultimate truth which guides and directs political action, then ideas and convictions can be easily exploited for the benefit of the powerful."[5] Freedom deprived of truth risks slippage into demagoguery.

(C) Diplomacy: called to endorse the rights of nations

The United Nations' Charter, the Pope said, is testament to the organization's commitment to "defend every nation and culture from unjust and violent aggression." Certainly, World War II yielded staggering violations of the rights of nations, often stemming from "lethal doctrines" which argued "the inferiority of some nations and cultures." By contrast, history is replete with examples of attempts to resolve the dilemma of the "full recognition of the rights of peoples and nations." The Pope recalled three major instances when that debate thoroughly sided with "the rights and just aspirations of peoples." He referred to the fifteenth century's Council of Constance ("right of certain European peoples to existence and independence"), the same era's University of Salamanca ("peoples of the New World"), and Pope Benedict XV's 1915 plea to World War I antagonists ("nations do not die").

Pope John Paul noted that, despite increased mobility among populations, and despite the flourish of mass-media and globalized economies – all trends toward universality – there is counterbalance in the evidence of an "explosive need for identity and survival." The particular and the universal are not disposed to the annihilation of each other. Instead, basic anthropological considerations reinforce that the rights of nations "are . . . human rights fostered at the specific level of community life." Also, it is vital to realize that the concept of "nation" "cannot be identified a priori and necessarily with the State." Consequently, there is a right for nations to exist which is not identical with sovereignty as a state. No state or nation can deem another individual nation to be unworthy of existence. And, due to a people's free exercise of their self-determination, that people, that nation, is entitled "to its own language and culture." These suggest a "spiritual sovereignty." It is that variety of sovereignty which justifies a claims of a "right to shape its life according to its own legitimate traditions," and of "right to build its future" through the education of "younger generations." Such traits reflect the particularity of the rights of nations. But there are abiding requirements of universality as well. Foremost among them is to strive to live "in a spirit of peace, respect and solidarity with other nations."

The example of East Timor was mentioned by the Pope in his 1996 New Year address. This population was said to be "still waiting for proposals capable of allowing the realization of their legitimate aspirations to see their spiritual, cultural and religious identity recognized." It is significant that Pope John Paul acknowledged before the assembled diplomats that East Timor awaits a process by which the international community will respond to formal proposals, a process which implies a willingness to collaborate with that community, and a process which seeks *de facto* and *de iure* recognition as a state. The Pope asserted that East Timor's aspirations of validity as a state are legitimate. That population, then, acts in accord with the "rights of nations" rationale. It should be noted that in 1999 the UN presided over elections in East Timor, whereby the residents voted for independence. The Indonesian occupation of this former Portuguese colony was concluding. After a transitional administration of East Timor by the UN, statehood became a reality in 2002.

Also in his 1996 remarks, the Pope referenced no. 14 of his UN address. He repeated his insistence that "not just States but Nations" are entitled to have their rights both defined and ratified. Those same rights presume "the importance of corresponding duties." What the Pope calls the "family of nations" involves far more "than simple functional relations or a mere convergence of interests." There must be a genuine condition of "mutual trust, mutual support and sincere respect." The "family of nations" image was invoked by the Pope in subsequent speeches to diplomats, notably on January 11, 1999. Here he spoke of the expanding movement toward a European "community with a common destiny." The Pope believes it vital to emphasize that member countries should not be thought of as being subsumed into such an entity. Instead, each country's sense of their own irreplaceable history must allow them to be "able to reconcile their history with the same common project," and always with the aim of achieving the overall "common good."[6]

(D) Diplomacy: pivotal to the resolution of conflicts
Pope John Paul reminded UN delegates that their organization truly serves "as a center of effective mediation for the resolution of conflicts." Such a mission enhances the quality of international life, not simply by providing a reliable mechanism for dispute settlement, but "by fostering values, attitudes and concrete initiatives of solidarity." As a result, relations between nations may acquire more of an "organic" character and not merely an "organizational" one. The hope is that "existence with others" may translate as "existence for others." But the Pope remains steadfastly committed to his conviction that non-violent conflict resolution and management are indispensable to the welfare and destiny of humanity. It is a theme which constantly echoes throughout his speeches to successive diplomatic gatherings. The 1999 New Year message was unequivocal in its declaration that "war is always destructive of our humanity and that peace is undoubtedly the pre-condition for human rights."

"Effective mediation" may well have been an aspect of what the Pope had in mind when, in 1996, he implored the international community to offer "juridical and diplomatic instruments" on behalf of "the sensitive issue of the City of Jerusalem." According to the Pope, the conduct of negotiation is basic to any hope for a "just and adequate solution" to this dilemma. And he went on to commend the "strenuous work of courageous negotiators" as they labor throughout the world's numerous trouble-laden locations.

One such application of that negotiation endeavor is the divisiveness and deprivation of property taking place in Cyprus. Should negotiations be intensified, a "successful conclusion" is at least possible. The Pope regrets that "dialogue and negotiation" are rejected, however, by Southern Sudan. But he is able to credit "patient negotiations" as being critical to preparations for the 1997 return of Hong Kong to the sovereignty of mainland China. It is those negotiations which accentuate key issues of "respect for differences," for fundamental human rights, and for an embrace of the rule of law. Similarly, it is the "negotiating table" which may yield a remedy for the region of the African Great Lakes. The regional organizations of Africa, for instance, are compelled to probe why international indifference is often the reaction to the area's humanitarian tragedies. An increase in political activity must offset such dangers as "the carving up of territories or the displacement of populations." Otherwise, the results may defy control. "The security of a country or region cannot be founded on the accumulation of risks."[7]

Diplomatic negotiations presume that importance is attributed to dialogue. All forms of dispute settlement, mediation among them, are "effective" only inasmuch as they generate an ongoing willingness to dialogue. The term "dialogue" is a constant in Pope John Paul's diplomatic discourse. For example, in 1998 he sought to "encourage the resumption of dialogue" between opposition parties in Northern Ireland. And he requested that those voices in Algeria "who believe in dialogue and fraternity" might be "finally heard." Similarly, he pledged that the Holy See will "continue to dialogue" as regards the Middle East peace process. The Pope thus wishes to further the principles of the 1991 Madrid Conference and "the guidelines of the 1993 Oslo meeting." It is diplomatic dialogue, he contends, which may rescue "peace and . . . heal the wounds of injustice."

Dialogue undertaken on behalf of China is again mentioned in the Pope's speech of 1999. Also on that occasion he talked of the capacity of dialogue to defuse hostilities in the Balkans. "Only honest dialogue," notably in the instances of the Middle East, Algeria, and Cyprus, can dissolve political deadlock and spare people from being wedged "indefinitely between war and peace." In his 2000 speech to the diplomatic corps, "calm dialogue between cultures and religions" was numbered as a "precise commitment to international solidarity." And dialogue as the core of multilateral diplomacy was praised for instituting conversation between the two Koreas, and between "the government and armed groups in Colombia."

The UN designated 2001 as the International Year of Dialogue between Civilizations. The Pope specifically acknowledged the event by stating that dialogue illustrates how "distrust, conflict and the vestiges of past crises can always be overcome through good will." Negotiators are said to be among those responsible for sustaining that good will. By 2002, the Pope extolled that "direct dialogue" has begun between Cypriot leaders and also between the disputants in Sri Lanka. And he expressed satisfaction that delegations from the two Chinas now participate in the World Trade Organization.[8]

(E) Diplomacy: commitment to transformation by persuasion
Intelligible discussion about humanity's future is possible, Pope John Paul advised the UN. In fact, it is the urgency and necessity of that discussion which may enable "a century of violent coercion to be succeeded by a century of persuasion." However, it is vital to insist that the viability of "the international politics of persuasion" is impeded, perhaps obliterated, by any diplomatic stance which amounts to a denial of "intelligibility (as) to the nature of man or to the human experience." Diplomats are obligated to reflect upon such realities as the excruciating legacy of modern totalitarianism, and that in contrast to what motivated the "revolutions of 1989." Diplomats must comprehend that these latter occurrences verify that political persuasion in the service of human betterment stems from acceptance of an indispensable philosophical premise. That premise may be summarized: "the vision of man [is] as a creature of intelligence and free will, immersed in a mystery which transcends his own being and endowed with the ability to reflect and the ability to choose – and thus capable of wisdom and virtue." What has been presented previously in this essay relevant to freedom, human rights, moral truth, negotiation, etc., rests upon the seriousness of a belief that humanity's condition can only be improved when his perennial and essential nature is measured against the challenge posed by unprecedented technologies, scientific

advances, and political strategies. Diplomats are expected to enact in their aggregate of proposals, plans, discourse and interventions, provision for the constancy, and universality entailed in being human.

The primacy of personhood is frequently accentuated in the papal New Year messages to diplomats. The Pope, in 1997, quoted a "Founding Father" of post-war Europe, Jean Monnet. "We do not make coalitions of States, we unite people." The politics of persuasion must be attuned to the centrality of the human factor when directing its energies toward the institutional and organizational factor. And it is that same centrality of the notion of personhood which best reinforces diplomatic resolve to rally "political determination" in such a way as to "strike at the causes of the disorders which too often disfigure the human person." Pope John Paul referred specifically to diplomatic initiatives undertaken to eliminate the victimization of children, together with "the battle against organized crime," drug smuggling, and "efforts to oppose every form of contemptible trafficking in human lives." The Pope appealed that "the leaders of societies" must become persuaded – and must persuade – that persons are never reducible to their productivity. Basic to Christian doctrine is the teaching that each and every individual person is "created in the image of God, able to love as Jesus did." And, while science embodies much that is admirable, humanity should be mindful of the temptation to exaggerate the merit of science by attributing to it a capability of making us the sole "masters of nature and of history." It is that image of science which may foster the illusion that people are "objects to be manipulated," inhabiting "a self-enclosed world" characterized by "an attitude of self-sufficiency, domination, power and pride."[9]

(F) Diplomacy: mission to promote a "culture of peace"
Pope John Paul informed UN delegates that the end of the Cold War era contained among its implications that Central and Eastern Europe could then anticipate "that the promise of peace" should come to pass. For many victims of that period of international tension, peace surfaced with the restoration of the sovereignty of former "People's Democracies." But peace is never so facile or automatic. The "risk of peace" is multi-faceted and relentless in its demands to cancel preoccupation with agendas of isolated self-interest.

Attaining "a climate of peace" means, for instance in Bosnia-Herzegovina, that diverse ethnicities must discover that the benefits of their seeking "harmony" are unsurpassed. The Pope's 1996 address outlined difficulties which surround prospects for an "enduring peace." The peace process involves diplomats in a struggle to achieve certain conditions. These include: "the free flow of peoples and ideas; the unhindered return of refugees to their homes; . . . truly democratic elections; and . . . sustained material and moral reconstruction." But one should not be pessimistic about "the work of building and consolidating peace," either in this region or elsewhere. Because when "indifference or selfishness" is admitted, horrendous "unforeseeable consequences" may be averted. In 1999, diplomats were told, again with regards to normalization in the Balkans, that "the culture of peace" faces "persistent dissension." Still, the international community should not despair of the value of diplomatic endeavors. It was diplomacy which concluded an agreement (October 26, 1998) between Ecuador and Peru. The guarantor countries consented "to accept a compromise and to resolve their differences in a peaceful way." Theirs is a "peace brought by . . . treaties" and according to which violence is explicitly renounced. The preservation of that peace, the Pope stated, is aided by the Catholic faith which is common to many of the countries' citizens. Diplomats may see in this religious dimension not a peripheral or incidental corollary to the stable peace but a resource to procure "reconciliation through prayer and action."

Peace incorporates practical exigencies. African countries, for example, "should all assist one another in the analysis and evaluation of political options." Said diplomacy may lead to formal agreement "not to take part in arms trafficking" and to reject discriminatory sanctions. Issues pertinent to territorial disputes, economic contentions and human rights may be submitted to peace-making teams and tribunals, through the operation of which "equitable and peaceful solutions" may arise. The Pope added that where armed conflict and disruption prevail, peace-keeping forces may be called upon as a final resort. These forces, however, ought to be "composed of African soldiers." The "law of retaliation," the Pope said on January 10, 2002, fails to qualify as a "path . . . to peace." This is among the reasons why he requested diplomats to forward a series of his several "reflections" to their respective governments. These include: the elimination of poverty (through, for example, a program of debt reduction), disarmament (as through "the reduction of arms sales to poor countries"), and efforts to demonstrate respect for human rights (especially for those most vulnerable – children, women and refugees). Diplomatic engagement for the cause of peace ought to espouse such a range of priorities.[10]

(G) Diplomacy: engenders adherence to the norms of law
Several times in his 1995 UN speech, Pope John Paul reminded delegates of their relationship to law. For example, this is implicit when he spoke of the 1948 Universal Declaration of Human Rights as well as the absence of the "rights of nations" theme in its passages. The Pope requested that representatives consider the question of justice which that lacuna raises. Justice is regularly associated with and manifested in the realm of law. Law is counted with ethics and anthropology as a vehicle for the "serious interpretation, and . . . closer examination" of such problematics as when ethnic and cultural consciousness becomes a "counterweight" to trends toward global uniformity. The Pope insisted that the goal of "equality of all peoples" is qualified. That equality is predicated by the adjective "legal"; a legal equality which presumes international recognition that the world is composed of a "family of nations."

In his 1996 diplomatic message, the Pope directly commented upon a principle of international law, the concept of reciprocity. Reciprocity is contrary to "despotic nationalistic ideologies." Its authentic meaning is that people willingly accept the identity of their "neighbor." "Each nation must be prepared to share its human, spiritual and material resources in order to help those whose needs are greater than the needs of its own members." Sadly, some nations not only refuse to encourage an attitude of "welcome"; they actively discriminate. For example, they behave punitively toward those who practice a religious faith. The pontiff deemed this to be "an intolerable and unjustifiable violation . . . of all the norms of current international law." Diplomats must strive to uphold what law requires.

The "rule of law" is valid for the community of nations without exception. And, as a juridic system, the common good is always both its foundation and ultimate end. The Pope's 1997 message to diplomats strongly emphasized that "international law itself is founded on values." Moral principles, for example, human dignity or "guaranteeing the rights of nations," are antecedent to the express juridic norms which comprise the rule of law. This explains why the intellectual precursors of *ius gentium* may be traced to philosophers and theologians, particularly between the fifteenth and sixteenth centuries. They understood that the function of law rests upon a moral imperative, granting to each person what justice decrees as owed to them. The Pope also noted that the thrust of contemporary international law is less in the direction of "a mere law between States," and more in the direction of human rights. Examples include "the international right of health care or the right to humanitarian aid." Moreover, he applauded "attempts to form an international criminal justice system." This step is said to be evidence of "real progress in the moral conscience of the nations." By extension, diplomats should be mindful of that conscience in their official deliberations and activities. Part of this task is to attest that fundamental morality – because it is an articulation of what is "right and good" – has "a preparatory role in the making of international law" itself. When this role is secured, the Pope stated in 1999, human rights will be recognized as the connective between "all juridic norms." International law may therefore escape disintegration into a law of fluctuating consensus or of "the law of the stronger." Again, in 2000, Pope John Paul appealed for diplomats to so influence political will that international relations can become "increasingly imbued with and shaped by the rule of law." Because sovereign states are de facto unequal, existing legal instruments need to be rigorously applied in the interests of "stability . . . and cooperation between peoples."

Diplomacy, according to the Pope's remarks on January 13, 2001, has an actual "capacity to bring about the rule of order [and] equality." Recourse to law is an element of that capacity. The juridic "instruments of diplomacy" are also an element, an example being the peace agreement signed (December 2000) in Algiers between Ethiopia and Eritrea. But, it is apparent, the Pope stated, that the principles of international legality are jeopardized and must be revived. They are weakened, for example, wherever territory is acquired by force, where the self-determination of peoples is violated and where contempt is leveled against UN resolutions or the Geneva conventions.[11]

(H) Diplomacy: respecter of religious conscience

UN delegates were instructed by Pope John Paul that their mission involves the safeguard of the "fundamental right to freedom of religion and freedom of conscience." The Pope maintains that these rights jointly constitute "the cornerstones of the structure of human rights and the foundation of every truly free society." Obviously alluding to political authority, the Pope said that no one is entitled to suppress these rights "by using coercive power to impose an answer to the mystery of man." Pope John Paul's appeal for religious freedom is inherently ecumenical. For example, he did not solicit preferred status for Christianity in general or for Catholicism in particular. And what is further suggested is that just as coercive power is inappropriate for secular leaders and institutions, it is as inappropriate for religious leaders and institutions. Neither sphere may "impose" its ideology, its theology, its worldview. Freedom of religion clearly means a freedom for all religion and religions. And it even allows for freedom from religion. Conscience dictates whether and how that freedom will be actualized.

In section (G) above, there is mention of Pope John Paul's 1996 criticism of those nations which campaign for the extinction of religious practice within their borders. That same address expanded upon the notion of what transpires with religious oppression. Persecuting countries suffer a loss of credibility before the international order, and simultaneously invite a threat to their own internal life. The Pope reasons that "a persecuted believer will find it difficult to have confidence in a State which presumes to regulate his conscience." In his 1997 remarks the Pope decried that religious intolerance instigated the brutal murder of seven Trappist monks in Algeria and of Oran's Bishop Pierre Cheverie. The pontiff returned to his ecumenical rationale. "All people together, Jews, Christians and Muslims, Israelis and Arabs, believers and non-believers, must create and reinforce peace." Hence, in 1998, the Pope stressed that the evolving movement toward European union must not overlook "the spiritual families . . . especially of Christianity" which have so greatly contributed to the continent's civilization. Far from diminishing, their influence today seems more decisive. The combination of social problems and social inequalities begs them to "proclaim the tenderness of God and the call to fraternity."

Political leaders, including those to whom diplomats are directly accountable, are administrators of the *res publica*. That is to say, their choices and implementation programs "guide whole societies either toward life or toward death." Thus, in 2000, the Pope encouraged all believers to assume "their duty to take an active part in the public life of the societies to which they belong." Reasonably, the worth of political activism at both the leadership and grassroots levels can only be fruitful if believers are "granted a place in public life." The Pope argued (2001) that because "religious experience is part of human experience," it is fallacy to want to relegate religion to the private sphere or to exhibit reluctance about referring to humanity's religious aspect. These latter are prejudicial against religious liberty. Pope John Paul, exactly aware of post-September 11th prejudice and suspicion against Muslims, invited Christians, in his 2002 address, to reach out openly to the "followers of authentic Islam, a religion of peace and love of neighbor."

Diplomats should be especially receptive to the positive impact which religion exerts upon world opinion, and upon the refinement of world disposition on behalf of security and solidarity. And it is diplomats who should be mindful of and grateful for the Holy See's status of sovereignty. For it is this status which permits the Holy See to impartially and vigorously "defend the dignity, the rights and the transcendent dimension of the human person."[12]

(I) Diplomacy: discernment of cautionary counsel
The Pope, when speaking to the UN, did not conceal his adamancy against the philosophical theory of utilitarianism. He offered several reasons to explain why this position warrants dismissal. (a) This is a doctrine which "defines morality not in terms of what is good but of what is advantageous." (b) Utilitarianism undermines "the freedom of individuals and nations." (c) It inspires an aggressive nationalism, "justifying the subjugation of a smaller or weaker nation." (d) And it prompts "more powerful countries to manipulate and exploit weaker ones." (e) Such utilitarianism probably facilitates the inequalities of the North-South rift, so familiar to political economists.

Pope John Paul's assessment of utilitarianism implied a related issue which is apropos to diplomacy. Doubtless, the Pope desired that UN representatives attend to his words for something beyond their general interest value. He would logically expect that they reflect upon his critique aside from the session in which it was delivered. And the duty of diplomats then becomes to either uphold his stance or to modify his position or to disregard it entirely. It would be woefully inadequate for the Pope's audience to have heard his words, while failing to have listened to them. Regardless of how diplomats opt to respond to his view, they are certainly obligated to attempt to discern the quality of the counsel by which he cautions. However, the Pope seems never to demand that diplomats automatically conform to his appraisal of utilitarian theory or any other, but that their intellectual integrity be such that they are willing to objectively scrutinize content. This is an area where a rush-to-judgment may be amount to a conclusion that diplomatic praxis manages to thrive upon disregard for theoretical debate and challenge. If that outlook is potentially valid, there is conspicuous need for its defendants to step forward to plead its cause.

Diplomats must judiciously apply their reason and discernment, not only to papal perspective on political and economic philosophy, but to recommendations and interpretations of fact which the Pope presents with as staunch a resolve. A few of many examples from his New Year addresses come to mind. In 1996, Pope John Paul described Liberia and Somalia as "still governed by the law of violence and of special interests." That is despite international assistance. Meanwhile, normalization in Angola is thwarted because of "political antagonisms and social disintegration." As for Africa, its political leaders are warned about their failure to commit themselves to "national democratic dialogue." Continuing, the Pope pointed to the necessity of their "strict" administration of "public funds and external credits." African governments should not imagine that they are entitled to help when their political credibility is dubious. If Africa refuses to heed, the continent "will ever remain on the margin of the community of nations."[13] Diplomats are left to ponder. Are Liberia and Somalia really so ruled? Does the Pope reliably portray Angolan governance? Is Africa's overall political leadership as precarious and decrepit as the Pope depicts? And is Africa's future so bleak if it embarks upon a path at variance with Pope John Paul's warning? Should diplomats deduce that the Pope's political characterization is accurate, then their overt and concrete support for his position should follow directly from their realization of intellectual congruity.

(J). Diplomacy: herald of an optimism salutary of humanity's future

Pope John Paul's UN address contains two very brief final paragraphs. They are condensed, possibly brief because they stand as the threshold of a future which is yet to be written. The Pope acknowledged that humanity approaches tomorrow with a degree of fear. That fear is no mirage. Nor is its existence hypothetical. The fear is actual. But by the Pope's insistence that "we must overcome our fear of the future," he implied that a prolongation of this same fear is not inevitable. It is a fear which we are able to overcome. Collectively, humanity contains an "answer" which is a definitive antidote to that fear. Putting aside coercion, repression, and such like, the answer consists of a "common effort to build the civilization of love." Lest critics scoff that love is tenuous and intangible, the Pope stated that the enterprise is constructed upon an array of universally accepted value: "peace, solidarity, justice and liberty." These are known. These are prized. And these engage us as our international interactions unfold with constancy and "soul." That "soul" is "lived in self-giving solidarity and responsibility." It invites us "not [to] be afraid of the future" and "not [to] be afraid of man." Indeed, humanity is cleansed of that fear when recalling this century's "tears." Those tears have not been shed in vain. For they "have prepared the ground for a new spring-time of the human spirit."

Despite what seems to be ample justification for pessimism and cynicism when we survey the contemporary global scene, diplomats must decline to concur. Service to their representative countries and to the international community means that they are equipped to counter-balance the negative swirl. Their own diligence and dedica-tion, their own perseverance and determination, prove that humanity can and will be salvaged. In Christian parlance, man is not merely salvageable; man is redeemable and even perfectible. The very prospect of human solidarity is fecund, it parents a mature and solid optimism, before which fear and its progeny can be seen to dissipate.

The phrase "fear of a future," strongly reminiscent of no. 18 of the Pope's 1995 UN text, is stated in his New Year address of 2002. Such fear is linked to diverse inter-national dilemmas. Among them is reference to terrorism and to "the abhorrent attacks of last 11 September." The Pope described terrorist acts as "barbarous aggres-sion." But he also spoke about the importance of the need to search for the "most effective means of eradicating terrorism." This is not a statement which presupposes terrorism's ultimate triumph. Rather, what is presumed is that "means" do exist for the eradication of terrorism, that "effective" means are identifiable among lesser con-tenders and that terrorism definitely can be eradicated. Additionally, the community of nations faces questions to which we are able to respond. These are questions about "legitimate defense," about the causation behind terrorist antics, and about measures to promote that kind of "healing" which "overcomes fear" and decreases violence.[14] Diplomats might note that terrorism, however extensive and excessive, is anything but absolute. Diplomacy should proceed as the accompaniment to an ascending hope.

IV. Conclusion: an idealism of wishful thinking?
Readers familiar with the formal theories posited by international relations scholar-ship are likely to conclude that what has been stated in this essay concerning Pope John Paul's view of diplomacy may be assigned to the general category of Idealism, also called Liberalism. Shades of Neoliberal Institutionalism are also evident. For example, author Karen Mingst presents Liberalism as holding that the innate goodness of human nature "makes societal progress possible." When humanity engages in unac-ceptable behaviors, one may look for signs of deficient or corrupt institutions or faulty political leadership. Liberals assert that war is not inevitable, since interstate cooper-ation may remove its threat. Recall the discussion about the Pope's advice and warn-ing to the African nations. Recall also his petition that the international community recognize its being a "family of nations." In these examples, as elsewhere throughout the preceding sections, Liberalism's tenets are unmistakable. Likewise, the Pope's addresses to diplomats reflect Neoliberal Institutionalists' devotion to the notion that institutions actually promote security and preserve a framework for future interac-tions. The Pope's remarks about the rule of law, about the primacy of international law and about the laudatory value of the UN's activities certainly suggest a Neoliberal Institutionalist mindset.

The Realist school of international relations, largely derived from Hans Morgenthau (dec. 1980), would probably argue that the Pope has underestimated the force of national interest which is reflected in the "largely objective and rational" approach of states as they "struggle for power." Here, Roskin's and Berry's analysis of Morgenthau and his Realism is significant. "At bottom, the great realist was a great moralist."[15] Scholars' assertions and objections abound. However, not even Morgenthau could successfully banish morality from Realist school precincts. Idealism's moral claims need not hurry to exit the theoreticians' stage. Other "schools" (i.e. Marxism), which also aspire to refute Idealist/Liberal thought, are no more convincing when it comes to their rebuttal.

Pope John Paul's vision for international diplomacy should not be dismissed as some species of pious Catholic fantasy. Quite the contrary. The Pope presents what might be called a Realist Idealism – a sense of what humanity can accomplish – and one that exists in terms of a kind of Idealist Realism, where national interest is achieved by mutual interest, and power is attained when the sources and resources of power are distributed widely.

Notes

1. Clark, Eric. *Diplomat: The World of International Diplomacy.* New York: Taplinger Publishing Co., 1973, 236–237.

2. "Bilateral and Multilateral Relations of the Holy See," in http:/ /www.vatican.va/ roman_curia/secretariat_state/documents/rc_seg-st_20010123_holy-see-relations_en.html

3. The text of the Pope's 1995 *Address to the United Nations General Assembly* may be found at:http://www.vatican.va/holy_father/john_paul_ii/speeches/1995/october/documents/hf_jp-ii_spe_05101995_address-to-uno_en.html. These thoughts on freedom as intrinsic to a common human patrimony are discussed in no. 2.

4. See nos. 4 and 5 of the Pope's speech to the diplomatic corps for January 10, 1998. The text for this and for speeches cited subsequently may be found on the Vatican web site. Search: http://www.vatican.va/holy_father/john_paul_ii /speeches/index.htm. The New Year addresses to the diplomatic corps are indicated clearly, as are the Pope's speeches to IGOs, NGOs and for ambassadorial accreditation.

5. See 1995 UN address, no. 12. See also the 1997 address to the diplomatic corps, no. 4, and the 1998 New Year message, no. 5.

6. Nn. 5–8 of the Pope's 1995 UN speech treat the theme of the rights of nations. No. 5 of the 1996 address to the diplomatic corps refers to East Timor's "legitimate aspirations." Discussion about eventual statehood and the UN's role in the steps toward independence is offered by Joshua S. Goldstein in his *International Relations* (New York: Longman, 2003, 275–276). The rights of nations theme is expanded in no. 8 of the 1996 papal address, as well as in that of January 11, 1999, no. 2.

7. Mediation is referred to in no. 14 of the UN text. Peace as a precondition for human rights is cited in no. 3 of the 1999 diplomatic corps address. Diplomatic negotiations concerning Jerusalem are noted in the 1996 address, no. 2. Cyprus

as a context for negotiations is mentioned in no. 4. Southern Sudan's refusal to permit negotiation is indicated in no. 6. The matter of Hong Kong is treated in no. 2 of the address for 1997. The Great Lakes region of Africa is the subject of no. 3.

8. See Northern Ireland as referenced in no. 2 of the diplomatic corps address for January 10, 1998. No. 4 speaks of dialogue concerning both Algeria and the Middle East peace process. The necessity of dialogue relative to China, the Balkans, Algeria, Cyprus and the Middle East, is discussed in no. 2 and no. 3 of the 1999 message. nos. 5–6 of the address for January 10, 2000, deals with dialogue and solidarity, as well as with the examples of the Koreas and Colombia. Dialogue as an indicator of an antidote to distrust, etc., is identified in no. 4 of the address for January 13, 2001. Rapprochement as a result of dialogue is noted in no. 2 of the message for January 10, 2002.

9. See 1995 UN address, nos. 3–4, for emphasis on the "politics of persuasion" and the "vision of man." The Monnet citation is found in the 1997 diplomatic message, no. 3. The 1998 text, in no. 3, contains focus upon social disorders and attempts by international leaders to eradicate the same. That for 2001, nos. 6–7, speaks of the issues of productivity and contemporary science.

10. In the Pope's UN text, no. 5 and 16 speak about peace. His diplomatic addresses also discuss this theme. See: 1996 (no. 3), 1998 (no. 4), 1999 (nos. 2–3), and 2002 (no. 6).

11. Paragraphs applicable to law are found in nos. 6, 7, 14, and 15 of the 1995 UN message. Law is also topical in the Pope's diplomatic addresses: 1996 (no. 8), 1997 (no. 4), 1999 (no. 4), 2000 (no. 6), 2001 (nos. 1–3), and 2002 (no. 6).

12. Freedom of religion is dealt with in no. 10 of the UN address. Religious freedom is also discussed in the New Year messages: 1996 (no. 9), 1997 (no. 3), 1999 (no. 2), 2000 (no. 7), 2001 (no. 7), and 2002 (no. 5). There are numerous examples which demonstrate that the Holy See acts according to its legal sovereignty. See no. 2 of 1996 message (official recognition of the Representative of the Palestinian People), no. 3 (the Church and the demilitarization process), and no. 7 (ban of nuclear testing). See also no. 2 of 1997 message (disarmament treaty), together with no. 3 of 1998 (ban of antipersonnel mines), no. 4 ("pitiless embargo" against Iraq), and no. 5 (associated with World Trade Organization).

13. The Pope's anti-utilitarianism views are stated in his UN 1995 address, no. 13. Examples of the Pope's interpretation of political fact and its purported consequences are found in no. 6 of his 1996 New Year address.

14. Fear of the future and its implications are discussed in no. 18, the final section of the Pope's 1995 UN text. "Fear of a future" is stated in no. 1 of the diplomatic address for January 10, 2002, while terrorism is treated in no. 3 and in no. 5 of the same papal speech.

15. See Karen Mingst's synthesis of Liberalism/Neoliberal Institutionalism in her, *Essentials of International Relations* (New York: W.W. Norton. 1999, 66–70). Compare with M.G. Roskin and N.D. Berry's appraisal of Morgenthau's Realism in their *IR: The New World Order of International Relations* (Upper Saddle River, N.J.: Prentice Hall, 2002, 31).

Index